ALSO BY TONY KORNHEISER

The Baby Chase

✳ PUMPING IRONY ✳

PUMPING IRONY

Working Out
the Angst of
a Lifetime

TONY KORNHEISER

TIMES ⒯ BOOKS

RANDOM HOUSE

All rights reserved under International and Pan-American Copyright
Conventions. Published in the United States by Times Books, a division of
Random House, Inc., New York, and simultaneously in Canada by Random
House of Canada, Limited, Toronto.

All of the articles that appear in this work were originally published in *The
Washington Post*. Additionally, some articles also appeared in the author's
syndicated column.

Library of Congress Cataloging-in-Publication Data
Kornheiser, Tony.
    Pumping irony: working out the angst of a lifetime / Tony Kornheiser.
      p.   cm.
    ISBN 0-8129-2474-6 (hardcover)
    I. Title.
PN4874.K67P86 1995
814'.54—dc20   95-21256

Manufactured in the United States of America
9 8 7 6 5 4 3 2
FIRST EDITION

For Karril,

Elizabeth,

and Michael

CONTENTS

THE LONG-AWAITED INTRODUCTION

Originally, the title for this book was *Dave Barry Is Dead*. I thought that would help me sell books to two important book-buying constituencies:

1. The millions of people who like murder mysteries;

2. The millions of people who buy books just because Dave Barry's name is on the cover.

However, it was pointed out to me by Dave's best friend that Dave might not like being called "dead" in print, and might therefore refuse to give me a favorable blurb.

So I changed the title to *THE BEST OF DAVE BARRY* . . . —which would be in capital letters splashed across the cover, and then, in really small type at the bottom of the page— . . . *is better than anything in this tepid collection by Tony Kornheiser.*

This had the advantage of accuracy. But it was still a cheap, obvious attempt to pander to Dave Barry fans and cash in on his name. Dave liked both the title and the impulse, but thought his publishers might not. He asked where I got the idea, and I told him—(take note how I'm subtly insinuating a true friendship with DAVE BARRY, hoping to make you think that since I'm his buddy, I'm probably as funny as he is, and you ought to buy this book)—about the album that was released when the Beatles were at their height, called *Best of the Beatles*. Millions of people bought it, thinking it was an album of Beatles tunes; in reality it was an album of horrid songs by Pete Best, who was the Beatles' first drummer and got dumped for Ringo Starr.

Anyway, I had to come up with another title. I sat around with a legal pad and scratched out titles by the hundreds. I started with long ones, the kind Lewis Grizzard used. The one I liked best was *Unlike Dave Barry, Lewis Grizzard Really Is Dead and Probably Can't Sue, and He Sold Tons of Books, So Maybe This Will Work for Me*. It has the advantage of getting BOTH *Dave Barry* and *Lewis Grizzard* in the title.

From there I went into my standard refuge, old rock 'n' roll lyrics that were meaningful at the time. I offered *Come and Beat Your Crazy Head Against the Sky*, *She Wouldn't Have a Willy or a Sam* and, of course, *Do The Freddy*. These were all met with blank stares.

Then I got caught up in a gerund thing—and I'm sure I don't have to tell erudite people like you, educated but cheap people who stand around reading books in bookstores instead of buying them, what a gerund is. I think we all know what a gerund is, don't we? That resulted in titles like *Bicycling Toward Antarctica*, *Shish-ke-bobbing John*, and *The Bridges of East Brunswick, N.J.*, which doesn't contain any gerunds, but always struck me as a good title for a book. Nobody liked them either.

Then I tried titles that would appear self-effacing and at the same time suggest humor, like (a) *I Suppose You Think That's Funny, Mister*, (b) *If You Like These, I'll Write More*, and (c) *Read Two of These, and Call Me in the Morning*. But I was fearful reviewers might be cruel and say:

a. No, as a matter of fact, I don't think it's funny.

b. Please don't bother.

c. Thanks just the same, but I'd rather vomit all night.

Now, to fill out the required thousand words of this introduction—and could someone please tell me why I have to write my own introduction, and why the publisher won't spring for someone funny like P. J. O'Rourke, Roy Blount, Jr., or DAVE BARRY to write this?—here are some other titles I suggested.

Filtering the River. (Rejected as idiotic.)

The Mirth Canal. (Rejected as tasteless and idiotic.)

Panhandling at the Petting Zoo. (Rejected as inscrutable and idiotic.)

My last try was *No One's Using Lew Alcindor Anymore*, and not a single person I showed that to, including my own personal self, had even the slightest idea what I was trying to say.

Ultimately it became clear to everyone that I wasn't going to come up with a good title. I could have told them from the beginning that I wasn't very creative. I barely wrote any of the columns in this collection. You will notice that an inordinate number of my columns seemed to be filled with lines supplied by several recurring characters: My Smart Friend Martha, Mr. Henry (America's Best-Loved Feature Writer), My Friend Nancy, Man About Town Chip Muldoon, and My Friend Gino. You probably assume that this is a classic literary trick to give my columns breadth by using different personae and voices that are really alter egos for myself. You would be wrong. These are pseudonyms of real live persons, colleagues of mine who are far funnier than I am. Roughly 92 percent of everything I write is stolen from them. I would put their real names here and finally give them the credit they so richly deserve, but, hey, then I might have to share royalties.

Anyway, the title we finally settled on was *Pumping Irony*, which was written by Vicky the Layout Person. We chose this because it seems to most accurately describe my *oeuvre*, which relies on the subtle juxtaposition of incompatible frames of reference in a manner reminiscent of Benchley and Thurber and my fabulous close personal friend and intimate, MISTER DAVE BARRY, and because it sucked a little less than the others.

Thank you.

Tony Kornheiser
Washington, D.C.

NURTURING A MESS

✳

Pumping Irony

Since my body began to sag under the weight of all my midlife crises, I have joined a gym.

I have a personal trainer. His name is Tom. I hate him because he is my age, and looks twenty years younger. He is, as we say, ripped. You could hang draperies from his pecs. Even the bags under his eyes have definition.

Tom is very excited about training me. To fitness trainers, I am what a lump of clay is to a sculptor. Actually, I am more like what a lump of sugar-cured ham is to a schnauzer. Trainers want to strip me to the bone.

They measured my body fat the other day. I am human Häagen-Dazs. I could charge six bits for a lick of my elbow.

"I'm glad you're doing this," Tom told me on my first visit to the gym. "What made you decide to start working out?"

"I'm getting older, and I don't want to be buried in a piano case," I said.

He asked me if I'd ever lifted weight, and I told him I was pretty sure I could get 205 pounds off the ground. Then I jumped in the air.

But seriously, folks . . .

Before we began training, Tom preached to me about the

benefits of water; he told me to drink at least one hundred ounces of water each day, that it had many, many therapeutic benefits. I've been drinking lots of water for a week now, and it has taught me the important therapeutic principle that when you consume large volumes of water, it makes you pee like a cow.

Tom thought I ought to start on my upper body; I told him that within the last few years it had moved to my lower body. So he stood me in front of a mirror and handed me some ridiculously light weights—three pounds apiece—and told me to lift them slowly. There I am lifting these baby Day-glo dumbbells that look like a starter set for Arnold Schwarzenegger's daughter's Barbie dolls, and the guy next to me, who just happens to be Rene Knott, the likable sportscaster on Channel 7, who is built like a condominium, is lifting a two-hundred-pound dumbbell with each hand. Standing side by side we looked like a "Far Side" cartoon.

Caption: "At that moment, Anthony finally understood he would never realize his dream of wrestling as The Human Threshing Machine."

I can't tell you how odd it felt for me to walk around using all the different exercise equipment. When I was young, a gym was someplace where fat, middle-aged men went to escape from their wives. They took steam and they played cards; nobody actually exercised. There was only one exercise then—you went to the garage, picked up a barbell, and lifted it over your head. Gradually you raised the weight until Vinny came over. Vinny spent all his time in metal shop, making bullets; he was on the fast track to Attica. Vinny put three hundred pounds on the bar, bent down, grunted like a garbage truck downshifting on an ice floe, and lifted the bar over his head. Case closed. Nobody ever suggested to Vinny that he ought to try low-impact aerobics.

I looked around at all these young men with their broad

shoulders and big chests, and I thought to myself—why do they all want to look like Mae West?

At that point Tom began his pep talk. He told me I wasn't in nearly as bad a shape as I thought, and that I had to start thinking positively. He said I had displayed great motor skills in my last exercise. "I wouldn't have started most people on something so advanced," Tom told me. I recalled that all I had done was move a small weight by lifting up my leg; I was quite sure a Border collie could have done it.

"How long until I get big muscles like you?" I asked.

"It's not about big muscles, it's about lifestyle," Tom said evasively. "Goals are fine, but this is a never-ending journey."

I don't want it to be never-ending. I'm looking for a finish line.

Hey, I'm looking for a punch line.

My problem is that I'm old already. I'm formed. I'm fat and bald and I have rolls on my stomach like a shar-pei. I'm never gonna have great deltoids; what do I know from deltoids, anyway? I thought deltoids were little airplanes. I'll tell you what a pathetic girlie-man I am: Tom had me doing exercises without weights—just pantomime exercises, and I'd start using weights in them later—and *they* hurt! My heart was beating like a rabbit's, and all I'd done was Kabuki theater.

So what's the best-case scenario for me? Say I do this for five years—bulking up on water, working on my endorphins, eating the kinds of food you see lying at the bottom of the monkey house—what's it gonna get me? I'll look like somebody stapled Charles Kuralt's head onto Joe Piscopo's body. What am I gonna do, quit the newspaper and become a furniture mover?

Not that I have any chance of getting muscles anyway, if my experience on the treadmill is any indication. Tom wanted me to get a "cardio" (that's workoutese for cardiovascular, just as "glutes" is shorthand for "Help! I glued my tuchus to the NordicTrack''), so I got on the treadmill and began walking at a comfortable pace for me, something like one mile every three weeks.

Directly in front of me was an aerobics class, and I hope it doesn't sound sexist of me to suggest that there were some total stacked hardbody babes in that class, and, as I say, they were working out directly in front of me. And I, uh, kind of got animated, and began walking faster than I should have. And not looking where I was going, I walked right up the treadmill, hit the retaining bar and fell over the side! What kind of motor skill is that? I've got to be the only person in the gym who needs a spotter on a treadmill.

I was discouraged by my klutziness, so Tom has encouraged me to exercise with a female partner. "It can be a very intimate experience," he promised.

Fine. I'm game. To preserve my dignity, though, it will have to be someone at my fitness level.

I've got a call in to Estelle Getty.

A Promising Thought

Of the many differences between men and women when it comes to making New Year's resolutions, the most striking difference is:

Men don't mean any of them.

Not a single word. Consider the issue of family finance in recessionary times.

A woman will resolve, "I'm going to keep to a stricter budget this year."

A man will resolve, "I'm going to earn six hundred million dollars this year."

Or say a couple feel something important is lacking in their lives.

The woman: "I resolve to attend church regularly."

The man: "I resolve to become pope . . . by Friday."

Do you notice a pattern here? Women try to be honest with themselves. This is because women view life as a novel, something by Proust maybe, with shadings and subtleties, elaborate character development, Byzantine subplots, all leading to a satisfying denouement based on emotional and spiritual growth.

Men see life as a daily series of three-panel cartoons: Situation. Resolution. Exit line. Thanks, you've been a great audience, see ya tomorrow. This makes for short attention spans, shocking inattention to detail, and unrealistic goal setting—particularly if it involves the use of power tools.

Woman: "I resolve to be kinder to my children."

Man: "I resolve to build my children a three-story treehouse with flush toilets . . . by Friday."

What a great idea! Any kid would want one of those. However, here are the steps this resolution takes in real—not cartoon—life:

a. The man buys the wood.

b. He goes to store the wood in the garage.

c. He can't open the garage because the door is blocked by the tiles he bought for the swimming pool he was going to build last year. And by now his back hurts from schlepping all this damn wood.

d. He gives the kids money and tells them to go to the mall.

Women make smaller, more reasoned resolutions. They actually write them down. They puzzle over them and try desperately to adhere to them—at least through the middle of January. Invariably women make resolutions about their weight. All women think they weigh too much, even the ones who look like they can use a vacuum hose as a sleeping bag. My friend Nancy makes the same resolution every year, "to lose a few pounds just so I can get into a bathing suit." Not to look like Ellen Barkin. To lose *a few pounds*.

Here's the man's take on that: "I resolve to exercise two hours a day for the rest of my life so I can look like Steven Seagal."

There are two reasons why a man would make this resolution:

1. To bag some babe.

2. See Reason No. 1.

Of course the resolution is thoroughly preposterous, since no man alive has any notion of time beyond next Tuesday, and may as well be committing to eating a weasel in Macy's window as to doing anything for two hours a day *for the rest of his life*.

But apropos of that resolution, I'd like to share with you, verbatim, a conversation I just made up:

Sonny: You really think you can look like Steven Seagal just by exercising? You couldn't look like Steven Seagal with plastic surgery and a hair weave.

Tom: I'm definitely joining a health club.

Sonny: Do you have any idea how silly you'd feel in a health club, with all those young kids around? They've got bodies you see in those Calvin Klein ads. They'll take one look at you and start laughing. You're a schlub, Tommy, you got back hair. You'll walk in the door, and they'll start dialing 911.

Tom: Maybe I could start jogging.

Sonny: For what? So you can drop dead on the side of the road, and they'll haul you away like road kill?

Tom: I've got to do something healthy.

Sonny: Start dating a nurse.

Personally, I don't make New Year's resolutions anymore. I can't afford the lumber.

Adipose Complex

Ready or not, the pool season is upon us. Oh sure, the water feels great on a suffocatingly hot summer day. The problem is, you have to wear a bathing suit. Like most of you, I don't look good in a bathing suit. I look like a cantaloupe with back hair.

It's not that I weigh so much more than I did when I was younger—well, okay, maybe a few pounds more, thirty-five pounds isn't so much, is it? You'd hardly notice it on, say, an adult rhinoceros. But it all seemed to settle in one place: my front. I take off my shirt and sit down on a lounge chair, and I look like a shar-pei. My kids bring their friends around and say, "We can tell how old our daddy is by counting the rings on his stomach." Most people get tan lines where their bathing suits end. I have permanent pale creases on what used to be my chest. It looks like I take sun through a venetian blind.

I try not to let it show, especially around the women. If I'm standing when a woman passes by, I suck in my stomach and hold my breath. But it's a problem if she stops to chat, because after holding in my stomach like that for a long while, when I finally speak, my voice sounds like I've swallowed helium.

I love the guys who wear the tight, skimpy bathing suits—

the ones that look like a Ped attached to a rubber band. The last thing in the world I want is something revealing. If I hauled the waistband of my suit up any higher, I'd be wearing my jock over my Adam's apple.

There are different types of people at a swimming pool. There are the psycho lappers, who blow by like Flipper on bennies; the paddlers, who regularly get in the lappers' lanes and come away with punctured spleens; the divers, who preen on the board and then hit the water with the grace of a penguin dropped from a cropduster; and people who don't swim, they stand. I'm a stander. In my pool there's me and all the women who've just come from the beauty parlor. I'm easy to recognize. I'm the one with the stretch marks.

Each winter I tell myself I ought to get in better shape for the opening of pool season to avoid this anxiety. Apparently I am not alone. My friend Nancy is dreading her Hawaiian vacation, because she'll have to spend ten straight days in a bathing suit. "If you could just swim in black tights and culottes," she sighed. "My husband, bless his heart, wants me to buy a two-piece. I told him I was way past the age of doing that." I asked her, what's the age when a woman can't buy a two-piece anymore? "The age of reason," she told me.

What's the point of dieting, anyway? (Incidentally, my idea of dieting is to use small utensils. I once ate a porterhouse steak with a cocktail fork. If you think that was tough, try having a bowl of wonton soup with a coke spoon.) A report this week in *JAMA, the Journal of the American Medical Association* said that if we reduced our dietary fat intake to meet federal recommendations, the average life expectancy would increase by three to four months. That's an awful lot of dry, disgusting rice cakes for three measly months. (My dietitian used to tell me I was eating rice cakes the wrong way, because I slathered cream cheese over them. "You're supposed to eat them plain," he insisted. "*Gandhi* wouldn't eat these plain," I said.) The kicker is: These three extra months come *at the end of your life*! They call that living? You've got no teeth. You've got no hair. You're impotent. You get wheeled around, and left sitting in the sun like a duck. And you're getting three *more* months. I don't want three more minutes at the end. I want the three months tacked on to my junior year in college, when I can do something useful with them, like driving naked.

By the way, the *JAMA* study said that in a best-case scenario, with all Americans reducing their fat intake to the proper level, we'll get "about 60 million years of additional life."

Talk about idiotic statistics that no one can relate to. It's like saying how old George Burns is in dog years. Who cares?

Talk to me in terms I can understand. Don't give me aggregate life spans of everyone who starts eating low-cholesterol, low-sugar, low-salt, no-taste foods, such as I-Can't-Believe-It's-Not-Cauliflower. Talk to me about what it does for me at my pool, now, when I need it.

You want to make a deal on life span? I'll trade you three months to get rid of this back hair and this ear hair that has come upon me in midlife like the very blanket of death. I'm becoming *furry*! I feel like one morning I'm going to wake up and start eating my meals from a dish on the floor.

Of course, by then I'll be 2,309 years old in dog years.

God only knows how much I'll weigh in dog pounds.

Bookshelf to Heaven?

Just when you thought you'd run out of fabulously appropriate surprise fortieth-birthday gifts, along comes Keith Tibbetts of Windsor, Massachusetts, with a mail-order showstopper: a personalized multipurpose coffin that doubles as a bookcase and wine rack. That's right, it's the Life Coffin, which is sure to become a family conversation piece—especially if your family is the Addams Family.

"My, what an interesting, uh, *coffin* you have in the middle of your living room. Sort of a postmodern Transylvanian decor, isn't it? Where'd you do your furniture shopping, Gawler's Funeral Home?"

These are coffins that can be ordered with adjustable shelves for your books and personal mementos, and a twelve-bottle wine rack—so you can not only age your wine, you can take it with you. (The worst-case scenario is that you die, and your wife says, "I've really grown fond of that wine rack," and she buries you in a Glad Bag instead.)

Tibbetts, a forty-year-old woodworker, writes in his brochure, "Death is an inevitable part of our life. Buying a coffin now can help begin a process of education and acceptance. By seeing your coffin every day, you will be reminded of the preciousness of your physical life. . . . And when all is said and done, you can rest peacefully, knowing that you're enclosed in a coffin to which you have added personal meaning." (Previously, I hadn't thought about having a personal relationship with my coffin. It's not that I don't respect my coffin. I just don't spend much time dwelling on it—sort of the way I feel about Jonas Salk.)

This is an old idea that's been resurrected, so to speak. In ancient Egypt, for example, the pharaohs used to be buried with their household goods and some of their favorite things—bad news for the pharaoh's dog and the upstairs maid. Tibbetts began building his Life Coffins more than a year ago. Thus far he has sold eighteen of them (at $350 and up), mainly to older people. "Younger people think they're invincible," Tibbetts sighed. Most buyers order the shelves. The coffin comes with a hook on the back to hang the lid. It has been suggested to Tibbetts that he attach legs to the lid, so it can be used as a card table—presumably on the theory that while death eventually comes to us all, in the meantime, how about a game of bridge?—but as yet no one has specifically requested that. A person might even sleep in his Life Coffin; since most people die in bed anyway, this would help streamline arrangements at an awkward time for the family.

Tibbetts's work has led to interesting, if brief, conversations. "Sometimes at parties," Tibbetts explained, "people who don't know me will ask me what I'm working on these days. And I say, 'I make coffins that people use as a bookcase until they die.' Usually, there's about five seconds of silence after that." Coffins clearly don't make for the smoothest conversation. But they haven't always foreshadowed gloom and doom; in *Moby Dick* it's an empty coffin bobbing in the seas that carries Ishmael away from the *Pequod* and to life. Still, it's hard to imagine a coffin not, shall we say, altering the mood.

"Your teeth are like pearls."

"Oh, Roger."

"Let me put on this Johnny Mathis album."

"That's an interesting record cabinet, Roger."

"Thanks. It's my coffin."

"I, uh, have to be back at the convent by nine."

You have to admit though that having a coffin in your house, and throwing a big party while you lie in it, appeals to the universal fantasy of being present at your own wake and hearing what your friends say about you:

"He looks so natural."

"He should. He's not dead yet."

I might buy a Life Coffin, but there are certain creature comforts that I'd want: It doesn't come with a liner. I have to have a liner. Something soft, and in a soothing color. I'd consult a mortician for what my best color is, though I suppose that might change after awhile. I'd want the ice maker, definitely, and temperature controls I could turn on with the Clapper, because my hands will be in that position. A tanning lamp; most dead people I've seen look absolutely awful. A subscription to the Sunday *Times*, for the death notices, to see who's moving into the neighborhood. (Just to confound those insufferable archaeologists who find a toenail clipping in a peat bog and reconstruct it into the Cro-Magnon man, I'd put in a picture of me and a dinosaur, captioned "Me and Mom, at left.") What else would I put in? Hmmm. A periscope, certainly. A cordless phone, because you never know, right? Maybe Houdini *could* have spoken from the great beyond if he'd only had the technology. By the same token, I ought to have a fax, too; someone might want me to bring something back. Above all I want double-hinged doors, in case a tragic mistake has been made.

The truth of the matter is that if I could have anything I wanted in my own coffin, it would be anything but me.

A Garden of Versus

I was working on a column of monumental intellectual significance, likening the ascension of multiculturalism to the postindustrial decline of structuralism in the visual arts, when suddenly my friend Gino walked in and said:

"Okay, boxing match: Mike Tyson versus Ivan Lendl."

He paused theatrically, the way George C. Scott might.

". . . But Lendl *gets to use his tennis racket.*"

I regarded him as if he were a penguin.

"Fourteen seconds, including the referee's count," I said. "Tyson gets a small welt on his shoulder. Lendl is on the canvas, twitching and drooling."

A chastened silence. "Okay, okay. Tyson versus Yogi Berra. But Yogi has a chain saw."

Hmmm.

This new wrinkle required me to step outside my office and into the *Post*'s main newsroom, a cavernous, gravely serious place where journalistic giants were hunched at their desks, laboring over matters of global import.

I made a general announcement: "Tyson versus Berra, but Yogi has a chain saw."

It was like ringing Pavlov's bell. Every man within earshot stopped what he was doing.

"Tyson, within two."

"Berra, the ref stops it on cuts."

"Does Yogi get to fire that sucker up *before* the bell, or does he have to fiddle with it while Tyson's rushing across at him?"

"Toro or Black & Decker?"

The most astonishing part of this debate is that it was conducted deadpan, in utmost seriousness. Men are accustomed to pointless cerebrations involving hypothetical performances by athletes in handicapped mismatches.

"Tyson versus Joe Theismann, but Joe has a can of Mace."

"Babe Ruth versus Michael Jordan . . . playing squash."

"Tyson versus Navratilova, but Martina has a Rottweiler."

"Tyson versus David Brinkley."

"David Brinkley?"

"Yes, but Tyson is blindfolded."

"Is Brinkley wearing aftershave?"

"Why?"

"Because if he's got on aftershave, then Tyson lays back against the ropes and *smells* Brinkley coming at him. Brinkley throws a jab, Tyson gets the scent, fires out a combination. Referee counts to ten. Less than a minute."

"No aftershave."

"Okay then, the smell of fear. Same thing. Thirty seconds max."

Can you imagine women doing this? Of course not. Women are not idiots.

Take the average weekend. Your average woman will go to the dry cleaner. She'll putter around in the garden. She'll go grocery shopping, making sure to buy meals that are not only nutritionally balanced but contain the requisite amounts of fiber and "good" cholesterol. She'll take the children to a handicrafts

fair as a method of instilling a respect for the dignity of indigenous peoples worldwide. She'll finish writing her novel.

This is how your average man spends his weekend: burping
in front of the TV, watching anything with a half-time.

I am convinced that men become obsessed with athletics as
a way to avoid having to deal with anything else. If you are talking about sports, you do not have to develop relationships with
other people beyond the ability to discuss sports. For example,
this is what I know personally about my editor, a man with
whom I spend at least ten harrowing hours a week:

1. He likes the Yankees.

2. He is willing to endlessly debate whether Wilt Chamber-
lain could beat Sandy Koufax in the hundred-yard backstroke.

3. He has a wife. I think.

Men's conversations are vastly different from women's. An
example: A woman is at home, and her phone rings. It's her
cousin's first wife's former au pair. They talk for more than an
hour about relatives, about kids, about schools, about death,
about the high price of housing, about the most intimate details
of their personal lives. The women get off the telephone feeling
like they've become closer than ever. Now, the same thing happens to a man. The phone rings. It's his brother! He says, "Hey,
how ya doing? Look, I got the ballgame on. Hey, as long as I got
you on the phone, lemme ask you. Seriously, who do you think's
a better bowler—Lou Gehrig or Chris Evert?"

Except for sports, men have no attention span. A woman
can watch a TV show and tell you everything that happened,
everything. You'll ask, "Look, I missed *L.A. Law* this week—
what happened?" A woman will start at the top and go word for
word through the show, even adding stuff that she thinks was
implied by the characters' glances. It will take a man about thirty
seconds to realize that he's in for fifty-nine more minutes of this
stuff, and he'll say impatiently, "Look, did anybody die? Because if nobody died, I'd like to watch the O's." (If you reverse

this scenario, and ask a man to recap an entire *season* of *L.A. Law*, all he will tell you is who got naked.)

I think the world would be a lot better off if women engaged in the same kind of stupid hypothetical arguments as men—even if they're not about sports, as long as they're some idiotic comparison. Involving, say, *relationships*. Someday I want to walk in here and hear women say:

"Okay, Meryl Streep and Bruce Willis."

"Get outta here. She could cut her IQ in half and still pound him into dust. Streep and Bill Hurt."

"Too much woman. Hurt goes crying to Mama in two days. Streep and Alec Baldwin."

"Streep as a Dane or an Australian?"

"Forget Meryl Streep. Geena Davis, and she's driving cross-country, and she gets to run over one person and get away with it. Who?"

"Okay, okay, John McLaughlin."

This Stinks

Smells made the news this week. A team of "fragrance scientists" reported that a sniff of peppermint appears to enhance concentration and attentiveness.

Excuse me . . . fragrance scientists?

This is how we're meeting the challenge of the new world order?

"Hi, I'm Billy. I'm in the sixth grade, and I want to be a scientist, so I can develop a rocket ship to take us to the distant reaches of space."

"I'm Molly. I want to be a scientist and help develop a cure for cancer."

"I'm D'Artagnan. I'm going to become a fragrance scientist, and devote myself to making the world safe for honeysuckle."

My smart friend Martha says this whole thing falls under the heading of "aroma therapy," which she claims has been going on for three thousand years. The title of my next book, *I'm Always the Last to Know*, explains why I've never heard of it. (Cher's an actress? You're kidding me. Since when?)

Last year Martha underwent aroma therapy in London. An aroma therapist put some basil oil on her face. Martha thought she'd been dipped in pesto sauce. "I bought different aromatic oils to pour into my bath. They're supposed to relax you. Sage was the best; I felt like I was dead and rotting in a shallow grave. The problem was, my face began to break out. All the stress left my body, but it showed up on the part that wasn't underwater."

My editor here at *The Washington Post*, whom I will call Nancy (she calls me Ramon), remembered doing something similar in the '60s. She took baths in almond-scented oil and got out smelling like marzipan. "Bees followed me everywhere I went. No men, just bees."

All this fragrance research has a commercial application: to manipulate you in the workplace. It's well known that automobile dealers spray the inside of a new car with "new car smell" and try to get you into the front seat, thinking the smell will entice you into buying the car. Some years ago, Bob Howsam, then the president of the Cincinnati Reds baseball team, tried aroma therapy to lure new customers into his ballpark. Howsam was convinced folks couldn't resist the smell of a bakery; whenever they'd pass one, they'd go inside. Howsam got a scientist to reproduce "bakery smell" and lathered Riverfront Stadium with it. Unfortunately, it didn't attract new customers—and many of the old ones who had come to the ballpark quickly left to buy crullers.

You're nobody without your own personalized perfume these days. Liz Taylor has one. Joan Collins has one. Mikhail Baryshnikov just got one; I'm guessing it smells like mare's sweat. This preoccupation with smells reminds me of the old *New Yorker* cartoon with the two dogs, and one says, "Isn't it a cruel irony that we have the greatest sense of smell in the world . . . and dog breath?"

So this is where we're headed, into the brave new world of dollars and scents. Supermarkets are already gearing up. When you're in the detergent aisle, you'll smell dirty socks. The lottery will offer a scratch-n-sniff ticket that smells like new money.

Personally, I want to spray everything in my house so it smells like Annette Bening.

Office productivity might be enhanced by peppermint, but it would plummet if you misted in the scent of musk. No work would get done. All you'd hear would be the sounds of sighing, followed by office doors slamming shut; the first question at a board meeting would be, "J.P., instead of new desks, why don't we order sofas?"

The truth is, the nose is the organ of the '90s. And here's the nightmare: You're sitting at your desk, and you notice nobody is coming near you. So you ask, "Hey, what am I, chopped liver?" And you might well be.

Making No Concessions

Man About Town Chip Muldoon phoned the other day with another amazing tale of life in the big city. It seems he was enjoying a leisurely meal—he'd gotten through the relish tray, the cheese board, and an order of clams casino and was about to start on his prime ribs—when much to his chagrin an intense flash of light hit him squarely in the eye, startling him so, he dribbled au jus all over his new Perry Ellis shirt.

"Sir, what's that you're eating?"

It was the movie gourmet police!

"Uh, nothing," Muldoon stammered, trying to hide his plate.

"Smells like roast beef," one policeman said.

"A bit overcooked at that," observed his partner.

Hmmm, Muldoon thought, what've we got here, Lt. Columbo and Julia Child?

"Sir, did you purchase that food at our concession stand?"

"I'm afraid not," Muldoon conceded. "I wanted your popcorn. But to buy the smallest bag—I believe you call it the Whole Earth size—I'd have needed a home equity loan."

"You'll have to come with us."

"But Joe hasn't gotten to the volcano yet."

Man About Town Chip Muldoon's plea fell on deaf ears. He was evicted from the movie. This was his second offense. A week ago he was caught with a drumstick from Popeye's hanging out of his mouth, and tried unsuccessfully to argue it wasn't a leg of chicken at all, but a traditional Ecuadoran folklore thermometer.

"My photo's up in every K-B, Odeon, and AMC theater in town. I can't watch a first-run movie without submitting to a strip search," Muldoon moaned.

The Film Food Feud is escalating.

Coming attraction: nacho-sniffing dogs.

Movie theaters may have the right to toss patrons for bringing in unauthorized food, but none of this brinkmanship would have happened if theaters weren't greedy. The colossal gall of Cineplex Odeon to sell its cheapest bag of popcorn for $2.45! And what's with these giant boxes of candy? People used to go to the movies because the stars were bigger than life—not the boxes of candy.

Moviegoers now routinely stop in at 7-Eleven before going into the theater, which is incredible considering 7-Eleven's prices. But people like their malted-milk balls by the ounce, not the metric ton. Don't you love movie flacks telling us they sell nine-pound bags of M&Ms because "we want to give the customer the best value possible." Does this mean we'll be able to buy bulk toilet paper and do-it-yourself furniture in the lobby of the Avalon Theater? That would alleviate your stress at having to choose between *Pretty Woman* and Shoppers Food Warehouse.

Of course people smuggle in food. Most women carry it inside their handbags to avoid detection. My sister smuggled halves of a salami sandwich in the shoulders of her Liz Claiborne T-shirt, where the pads normally fit. "Where did you buy that shirt," I asked, after catching a whiff of her the next day, "the Carnegie Deli?"

My editor devised a brilliant ruse: Some time ago she bought popcorn at the Wisconsin Odeon *and saved the bag.* Now she microwaves popcorn at home, packs it into the Odeon bag and smuggles it inside a big purse. "Open the purses of half the women who go to movies," she says, "you'll find enough food to keep Mitch Snyder in high cotton."

People like to eat at movies—except *The Cook, the Thief, His Wife & Her Lover.* Going to a movie is strenuous enough without making food a crime.

When was the last time you went to a kids' movie? That's a real treat. By 5 P.M. on a weekend, either the aisles are so sticky from spilled soda that it feels like you're walking on flypaper, or so slippery you take one step and slide all the way down to the screen. They don't need a vacuum between shows, they need a Zamboni.

And how about the people who like to talk through an entire movie? Really, *the entire movie.* It's unbelievable. Continuous conversation, like they're in their living room, which is annoying enough, but it gets worse—at critical junctures they start shouting at the screen.

"Don't go through that door, fool."

"No! No! He's in there. He'll slash your lips off."

"Don't you see him? DON'T YOU SEE HIM?"

Boot goofballs like these from the movies. Leave the eaters in peace. The flacks have to stop peddling their phony baloney about "the odor" of hot food bothering the customers. You can't stand within five blocks of any theater without gagging at the overpowering aroma of buttered popcorn, so who's kidding whom?

Face it, the notion of the movie theater as chapel is history. The genie is out of the bottle. This whole Film Food Feud is a consequence of home movie rentals. Through the magic of the VCR, we've learned it's easy to watch a movie and eat a good meal at the same time. Jujubes won't cut it anymore, and nobody is going to pay black-market prices for popcorn. Theaters are going to have to offer menus, and not simply yuppie grazing items such as blue corn chips and Evian. Man About Town Chip Muldoon is predicting Domino's delivering pizzas to the K-B Fine Arts, and promising he'll be there in person when the first Ridgewells catering truck pulls up at the Avalon.

Perpetual Parenthood

My friend Dan, who is my age—
which is to say, much too old to be comparison shopping for
Huggies and Pampers—just had a baby. This is Dan's second
wife and second family. He'd had two babies previously, during
the Nixon administration, so it has been a while between spit-
ups.

Courtney is two months old, and not yet sleeping through
the night. And so the other night, Dan found himself with a
warm bottle in his hand at 4 A.M. as new fathers often do. "I was
rocking her," he said, "and she was almost asleep, and I thought
if I sang to her, that might do it. Then I realized the only song I
know is 'Thunder Road.' "

Anyway, men being pigs, I asked Dan why he was doing the
4 A.M. feeding.

The first time around, in the Nixon administration, Dan's
wife handled the 4 A.M. This was the standard arrangement in
those last-gasp days of the single-income household, when men
were the providers and women were the nurturers. It worked
passably well for five thousand years, until the invention of the
summer home.

Now everyone works and everyone feeds.

Dan and Meg have arrived at a *changer* and *feeder* system. The changer is the preferable role, as you hand off to the feeder, having amused the baby while the bottle was being prepared. As most men would, Dan has tried everything to become the permanent changer, a sort of designated hitter of parenting. He has offered lame reasons, such as "She drinks better with you," and inspired reasons, such as "She's so beautiful and looks so much like you, that I weep when I feed her, and the salt from my tears will get in her mouth and cause colic." Needless to say, nothing has worked, which is what you get, I say, for marrying a Harvard woman.

All this talk about babies got me thinking about lies we tell ourselves about being parents—like how we'd never give our children pacifiers. Pacifiers, yeeccchh! Not only do they look awful, but they'll push the kid's teeth out of line. And they only work for a few minutes, if you've got the Gerber baby. The rest of us are trying to Black & Decker the pacifier into Junior's mouth. "So he'll get braces, okay?"

And you swore you'd never smack your kid, right? Oh God, no, hit a child! Never. I'll reason with mine. I'll never resort to force. Which is fine, until you paint yourself into this corner:

"Okay, Billy, time for bed."

"Billy, bedtime."

"Now's the time, Bill. Go to bed."

"I'm not going to ask you again, William."

"Look, Billy, you either go to bed now or I'm gonna crack you."

Whoops! Did I say that? Did I actually put myself in the put-up or shut-up position with a four-year-old? Gaaaackkk! (This is why it's always better to use this last line: "Billy, if you don't go to bed right now, I'll kill the dog.")

Having had to smack the kid to save face, you now spend the next half-hour cozying up to him trying to convince him you aren't the monster you seemed when you gave him a *zetz*. "Can

I make it up to you, son? Would ice cream help? C'mon, let's go get some ice cream. Tell you what, let's go to Paris and get some ice cream. We'll go to Paris, we'll get some ice cream. Your mom said you were annoying her, and I asked, 'What do you want me to do about it?' And she said something that sounded like 'Spank him.' I thought it was spank. It could have been spahn-kee, a cold-water fish they serve in Stockholm. Anyway, it hurt me more than it hurt you."

And is there anything quite as terrifying as having to discipline your kid in a public place? Which is, naturally, the only place they'll drop straight to the floor and begin howling, straight out of the last scene in *Carrie*. It does no good to say to the people who have gathered around, "I didn't even touch him. Honest." My advice is to head for the frozen foods and pretend it's somebody else's kid. Eventually, he'll either calm down or join the army.

Scenes like this are why, when I take my children shopping, I only go to stores I don't care if I ever go back to again. Like a discount food warehouse. Who cares what your kids do there? You'll never see any of these shoppers again unless it's at a police lineup. The floor there, busted melons everywhere. It looks like Beirut after a thunderstorm. And above the din, this is what you hear clear as a bell, the words you've come to say so often, though you swore you never would: "Because I said so."

Dining at Chez Tray

Ladies and gentlemen, I propose a toast to American ingenuity: Let us raise our Styrofoam cups and celebrate the fortieth anniversary of the TV dinner!

Now, in honor of Swanson, which sent the press release that made this column possible, let's chew and eat our plastic foam cups.

Which actually taste better than Salisbury steak.

(The allegedly edible Salisbury steak can be described as something that, if you stared at it, you'd realize looks like something your dog found in the backyard.)

"Ooooh, Salisbury steak," Mr. Henry, America's most beloved feature writer, said recoiling. "What was that shine on top of the Salisbury steak? That sort of oil slick?"

Ah, the memories.

That crust around the edge of the mashed potatoes that left a pasty rim of white clinging to the aluminum tray and gave you an uneasy feeling that something had gone wrong in the test kitchen; the tray itself, the way the taste of metal got into everything, particularly the gravy, and made you feel you were munching on a ball of tinfoil; that little scream your fork made as it cut through the soggy turkey and scraped along the bottom of the tray. My teeth hurt just thinking about it.

TV dinners proved this about Americans: We'll eat *anything* as long as it's easy to prepare.

The TV dinner was born in the post–World War II convenience boom, when for the first time American homes were casually being stocked with washers, dryers, and other modern appliances, like that little blue thing they hung inside the gas station toilet bowl. The fact that somebody came up with a prepackaged dinner to be eaten specifically in front of a TV acknowledged the TV as the only worthwhile thing in the house—including your parents.

You can tell I grew up on TV dinners, because to this day every time I see a piece of fried chicken, I think of *Sea Hunt.*

The TV dinner was supposed to be great for the family, because:

1. It would give Mom more free time.
2. It would bring everyone in the family together for dinner.

Well, it did give Mom more free time, which she used to read Betty Friedan, and she figured out what a lousy deal she'd been getting all these years, so she left and took an apartment in the city and left us with a pile of fetid aluminum trays; a hell of a lot of good that did us. Now Mom is an arbitrageur and she hasn't been home in three months. She occasionally leaves a note: "Won't be home for dinner. Stick something in the microwave."

And it did bring the family closer together, because in those days nobody had more than one TV, and the screen was twelve inches wide. And we gathered like little rodents, with our TV dinners perched on those wobbly folding tables with the ridiculous dwarf legs and the tops that were either maps of the states or vaguely Polynesian landscapes, with butterflies and grass. And we watched shows such as *Father Knows Best*—which wouldn't get produced now because (a) there were no single parents in it, no dysfunctional parents, no divorced or dead parents, and no loudmouthed kids turning their backs on their parents and saying, "Kiss my butt," and (b) nobody thinks Father knows *anything* anymore. So it brought the family together, but because the family was watching TV nobody said a word—not even "pass the potatoes," since each TV dinner came with its own portion of potatoes, approximately the size of a pat of butter and with the texture of tile grout.

The early TV dinners weren't that convenient, actually; they took about fifty minutes to cook. Technically, a man could cook them, but when dads came home from work in those days, they often started drinking heavily. A dad could get pretty soused in fifty minutes. By the time the dinner was ready, he'd forgotten all about it. If the timer's alarm bell was real loud, he might think he was back in Anzio, and dive behind the couch.

I remember cooking TV dinners (which I preferred over pot pies, where you needed a chain saw to get through the Paleolithic crust, only to discover there was no actual chicken in there) and not eating them because they took so long to make that by the time they were done I'd already eaten fourteen bags of potato chips. It was a shame, too, because I'd done so much preparation: You had to fork-stab the main course and make a tent of the tinfoil over the potatoes, and with twenty minutes to go, peel the foil back from the apple crumb—you could get second-degree burns doing that.

Sadly, the original concept of the TV dinner is unworkable today. You can't gather the family together around the TV anymore, because everyone has his own TV. Anyway, no family eats together nowadays under any circumstances. The parents are out of town: The dad is in the woods beating his chest and eating pine cones, and the mom is at a commodity-trading seminar. The teenage daughter is a vegetarian and hasn't spoken to her parents since joining People for the Ethical Treatment of Animals and splashing deer urine on the leather sofa. And the teen-age son stays in his room and watches endless repeats of Salt-n-Pepa videos and listens to *Tony Bennett Unplugged.* The last thing intelligible he said was: "Pass the remote." You fear he couldn't tell the difference between *Sea Hunt* and C-SPAN.

I miss the old days.

I miss having my metal tray table collapse twice each meal and having to pick corn from my mohair sweater.

I almost miss Salisbury steak.

What a Way to Get Ahead

We begin today by quoting a wire story that would be a testament to good old American ingenuity—if it hadn't happened in Tokyo: "To gain the minimum height requirement to be a sumo wrestler, a Japanese teenager had six inches of silicone implanted under his scalp. Takeji Harada, sixteen, who had failed six previous eligibility tests, finally made the grade in June—thanks to the huge bulge on his head, which added about six inches to his height."

Hmmm.

Lesser journalists than I might be tempted to poke fun at a story such as this, failing to give due consideration to unfamiliar cultural imperatives. After all, this story originates in a society that remains largely mysterious to most Westerners, and we must resist the urge to draw unfair and insensitive conclusions. Still, the story does raise several intriguing scientific questions. Such as:

1. What will he wrestle as, "The Magnificent Beldar"?

2. What a putz.

Anyway, it's not that I don't feel sympathy for Mr. Harada. I do—though I must admit that if I had the opportunity to add a few strategic inches to one of my body parts, my head wouldn't be my first option. *Note to copy editors: Please delete previous joke so I am not fired. Thank you.* The sumo story notes that Mr. Harada's presurgery height was only five feet two inches, and that is hardly his fault—although I'm wondering what kind of high school guidance counselors they have in Japan; shouldn't somebody have said to him, "Sumo? Jockey!"

But why would there be a height requirement for becoming a sumo wrestler anyway? Please don't tell me there is a deep concern for the health of the wrestlers, because we are talking about men who are literally as fat as cows. They weigh 550 pounds. Their cholesterol count is probably higher than the Nikkei average. If you lined up four 550-pound guys, and three were five eight and one was five two, do you honestly think anybody would point at the five-two guy and say, "Will you get a load of *that* tub of lard!" So I feel bad that Mr. Harada was discriminated against because of his height.

On the other hand, having six inches of silicone implanted under your scalp is a hilarious act of desperation. The boy can't really believe this operation has made him *taller*. All that has happened is that some doctor—and where'd he go to medical school, Kuala *Lump*ur? Hahahaha—turned his head into a speed bump! It's sort of like some kid with a D average and 430 combined on his college boards trying to get into Harvard by wearing an Einstein mask.

What's the attraction of being a sumo anyway? As a sports expert, I can attest to the fact that sumo wrestlers are basically hugely fat men with enormous, jiggly bodies. They tie their hair into buns, and they wear diapers. Their job consists of consuming disgusting quantities of rich foods and competing in maybe two matches a year, matches lasting, at most, four seconds each, and entailing no risk of injury beyond being belly-bounced rudely on one's behind—in return for which they receive gargantuan sums of money, are worshiped as gods incarnate, and must fight off phalanxes of lithe ninety-five-pound vixens who want to have acrobatic sex with them constantly.

I mean, who would want *that*?

Okay, so young Mr. Harada was definitely motivated. But even if he had his heart set on getting these implants to become a sumo—"The Silicone Sumo" does have a ring to it—wouldn't it have been smarter to take the injections in the feet, not the head? If he adds six inches to each foot, he's pretty much living with built-in platform heels, like John Travolta in *Saturday Night Fever*. Worse comes to worst, if the sumo thing falls through, he can put on a Qiana shirt and get a job as the world's fattest disco dancer. Now, with this conehead, all he can be is a coatrack.

Finally, in the interests of science, and with basic human concern for Mr. Harada, I asked my research team to telephone an expert in the uses of silicone, who revealed many valuable and frightening things. First, silicone injected directly under the skin tends to "migrate," which is to say it kind of redistributes itself all over the body, sometimes in vaguely unnerving and embarrassing manners. Let us just say that one day you can have a large and inviting bosom, and the next day you could have a smaller bosom and, say, a tail. So Mr. Harada might soon find himself too short once again to be a sumo wrestler, but, for example, perfectly designed as a unicorn, or a bean bag chair.

On the positive side, my expert mentioned that among its many uses, silicone is a key ingredient of Simethicone, a drug that reduces one's output of flatulence. I don't know how this might affect Mr. Harada, but considering his girth and diet, surely it can't be bad.

Taking the Fourth

I hate America.

I begin this way because that is how many readers are going to interpret this anyway, so why not just give them something solid to kvetch about?

Actually, though, I love America. It's the Fourth of July I hate.

Note to letter writers: Yes, this MUST mean I hate America. Have at me. Thank you.

Here's my take on the Fourth: It's about bug bites, bad food, and blowing yourself up. You have to spend the whole day outside in this miserable, steamy summer heat surrounded by people with striated fat rolls that look like Hostess Ho-Hos and armpit stains that resemble the puddles one might find under a '66 Corvair after a front-end collision. You start drinking *way* too early because (1) you're horrified by the sight of these people—who are ordinarily barred from all public places, including Wal-Mart—and (2) it's the only way to lighten the load of the stupid cooler you're lugging around. So by noon you are in desperate need of a bathroom, and the line for the Porta-John stretches to Tegucigalpa, and as you stand there, *shvitzing* like a poodle, you think to yourself: How has it come to this, that I'm the only one without a tattoo?

And then it is two o'clock, and you're sick of the Frisbees, and you're beyond sunburned and into charred—people are looking at your face, which is the color of a prized beefsteak tomato, and asking sympathetically, "Ooooh, doesn't that hurt?" And after awhile you start saying things like, "Well, it would hurt but fortunately my leprosy has deadened all my nerve endings," and then you sneeze on them. And you cannot look at any more of that hideous yellow potato salad that reminds you of the John Lennon line: "yellow-matter custard dripping from a dead dog's eye." And it occurs to you there are STILL SEVEN MORE HOURS UNTIL THE FIREWORKS!

You're stuck in this shimmering heat, being pecked at by mosquitoes the size of onions. Your kids are yapping, but at least you can bop them upside the head. It's the other people's kids' yapping that's driving you nuts. There aren't enough Handi Wipes in creation to get the watermelon juice off your face and hands. It's gridlock; you can't move because every inch of grass is covered with blankets. There's a tuba band warming up, and it's just what you want to hear—the 237th rendition of "The Stars and Stripes Forever and Ever and Ever." It's like being trapped in a really bad Chevy Chase movie. AND THERE ARE STILL SEVEN MORE HOURS UNTIL THE FIREWORKS! No wonder more postal workers become disgruntled on July 5 than on any other day.

Now let's just once tell the truth about the fireworks.

They aren't any good.

The problem with fireworks is that fireworks technology has not appreciably changed since they were invented six thousand years ago to impress the emperor of China, who wore the skins of dead opossums on his behind, and a jingly hat that looked like Santa Claus's underpants. My point is that, back then, people were far more primitive and easy to please. Now fireworks are passé. Rent any Arnold Schwarzenegger movie and you'll see a man's face disintegrate and melt into a snake, and live chickens fly out his eyeballs. So what's something that goes *boom* compared with that? If the guy setting off the fireworks doesn't blow himself up right in front of your eyes like Tommy Lee Jones, or transmogrify into a dinosaur or a griffin and carry away a baby in his teeth, what's the big deal? This is someone's idea of a good time—staring at a few exploding pinwheels like a dodo, then having the soot settle on you like you're standing at a bus stop under Mount St. Helens?

To try to appeal to more demanding tastes, fireworks makers have moved away from displays that merely explode into clusters of colors and have begun producing gimmicky effects that look like something familiar. Remember during the Gulf War celebration when the fireworks formed all those purple hearts and yellow ribbons? Well, things have gotten a little out of hand since then.

"Oooh, honey, look, it's . . . a, a bagel!"

"Ooooh, a Pez dispenser!"

"Ooooh, health care reform!"

The other thing I hate about fireworks is that they begin around a week before the Fourth, suddenly startling you in the middle of dinner, and the dog gets scared and throws up, and the kids crawl under your bed. It's like living in Beirut—only the bread is fresher. This occurs because people start buying fireworks weeks before the Fourth, as soon as those ghastly wooden fireworks kiosks go up. Every June they spring up, like toadstools. You'll be walking along an elegant tree-lined boulevard, past a Christian Science reading room, with the Washington Monument gracefully towering in the horizon, and suddenly you come upon something that looks like an outhouse from the Ozarks, manned by two people in bib overalls ready to sell your kids more rockets than Kim Il Sung.

Anyway, why do we need to celebrate our independence

from England? England is about the only country in the world that still talks to us without Jimmy Carter going over there first.

We built this holiday in praise of the Revolutionary War, which is definitely not politically correct anymore. Celebrating our independence from another country implies that we consider ourselves better than those people. The sensitive American of the '90s wouldn't want to be independent of the British, he'd want to share our cultural diversity with them. If Patrick Henry made a speech today, he wouldn't say, "Give me liberty or give me death!" He'd say, "Give me liberty . . . or if that offends you in any way, I'll accept a modest cost-of-living increase."

As far as holidays go, I rank the Fourth of July *waaay* down there. In fact, I don't like any of the commonly recognized holidays—too commercial. My three favorite holidays are:

1. The first day every spring when the ice-cream man shows up, because he brings joy to all the little children of the neighborhood (and, uh, also because the ice-cream man's appearance generally coincides with the first day women resume wearing halter tops).

2. The day every autumn when you set the clocks back (it is the only time in life one can actually gain time, outside of prison).

3. July 3, which is National Columnists' Day, where no matter how stinko our copy is, you are obliged to read it all the way to the end, and praise us—and you are not even allowed to object to cheap halter-top jokes.

One Man's
Edible Complex

I took my kids to the pool the other day and caught a glimpse of myself in the lifeguard's mirrored sunglasses. (A babe, I might add, so I was actually trying to suck in my stomach; if I had sucked any harder, I'd have inhaled the whole pool.) It was appalling. I was so bald, so fat, so white, I looked like the underside of Free Willy.

Why do middle-aged men get so sloppy? We stand around, exposing our big bellies, and from the side we look like an avalanche.

I think it stems from the way men eat.

Men eat foods that come in slabs.

Slabs and mounds. A slab between two mounds, often yellowish mounds—either by design or age.

This eliminates everything green, everything that swims, and everything that might keep you alive past midnight Wednesday.

It's easy to buy food for a man: Just buy something with a large bone in it that he can wrestle with, and gnaw on, then walk away from with barbecue sauce and flecks of char stuck on his cheek.

Women are not like this.

Women do not enjoy making a display of themselves when they eat.

Women dread it when a man says, "You wanna go for ribs?" (which men always want, because it comes in a slab).

That's the last thing women want—to spend all evening sucking sauce off their fingers and picking corn from their teeth.

Women are like cats. They like to eat from a bowl. They'll eat a little bit, then leave the rest for later.

Men are like dogs. They eat everything in front of them.

Men do not even taste their food. Their task is simply to finish it as quickly as possible.

"Hey, Eddie, what was that thing you just ate, that thing that looked like a piece of fried stuff?"

"I don't know. It was brown, right?"

It is a waste of time for a waiter to recite any of the day's specials to a table full of men. (If it was a waitress, the men would not have listened to anything she said, because men don't ever actually listen to women—they simply wait for a woman to get through talking; then a man understands it is his turn to speak.) Whenever the waiter gets to the last special, say, "fresh sea bass, lightly battered and sautéed in a balsamic vinaigrette, with cilantro and basil, and a bouquet of garden vegetables almondine," a man, realizing he has run out of choices, will say, "Good. Gimme that, and put some nacho cheese on top, okay? And fries."

When men are finished with their food, they pause for a second or so—making a big show of how they are pausing, so you'll understand they are trying to act polite—then they go around the table and eat the food off the plates of the women and children.

"You done with that?" a man will ask impatiently, which reminds me of a joke I cannot tell here, about what Jeffrey said to Lorena.

Women know how this game is played. Women deliberately

leave 20 percent of their food so that men can finish it. Women get their revenge, though, by mixing their foods together.

Men hate this. God, how they hate mixed foods! ("Look, don't put the peas so they are touching the potatoes, okay?")

If a man designed fine china, it would all look like TV dinner trays, with separate compartments for every item in the meal. Men eat one thing at a time.

Every man has a different order, but all men eat purposefully and sequentially. Women eat randomly. (Much the way they shop. They can end up buying *anything*! A man goes in for shirts, this is his task, shirts; he buys his shirts, he leaves.) Women like to mix things. They order premixed things, such as risotto, then mix in more things. They commingle; they create. You look at a woman's plate, it looks like an artist has painted it. You look at a man's plate, it looks like Rin Tin Tin has licked it.

Watch how differently men and women eat at a cocktail party. A woman will "plate-hop." She will circle once. She will take something from this tray, and something from that tray, and a couple of things from the table in the center of the room, and she will put all these things on a small plate and nibble at them for the rest of the party. A man will go straight to the swinging doors and camp there, a toothpick in hand, picking off whatever comes out on a tray, like he's defoliating the jungle. He will put nothing on a plate—he isn't even holding a plate—he will stand there, sniping away. Get him a shovel.

Women know this. And still, women care about how they look eating in front of men.

"Women don't eat at all on the first date," my friend Annie told me. "We don't want a guy to think we're pigs. We order something light, something we can pick at; psychologically we're trying to show him that we're picky with food, and we're picky with men—also, we don't want to give him the impression that if he stays with us, he'll wake up one day twenty years down the road and see he's married to Bossy the Cow. A woman never orders spinach on a first date, because it sticks to your teeth, and it's always there when you smile; never garlic or onion; never spaghetti, even if you like spaghetti, because you don't want to eat anything that might hang out your mouth. Never order dessert either, don't even take a bite when he orders two."

"Aren't you hungry?" I asked.

"*Starving!*" Annie said. "The moment he drops you off, you head straight for the Häagen-Dazs and sit there in a housecoat, stuffing yourself just like . . ."

A man.

The Sexual Life
of the Sponge

Once again we visit the war between the sexes. Today's topic is: residential hygiene.

The other night my friend Walt was hosting a poker game. Walt is no longer married, a condition that becomes apparent when you smell the sponge in his kitchen sink—which you can probably do right now, from where you are sitting. Men are not hung up on sponges. Men will buy a new sponge only after the previous one disintegrates into little wads and falls down the drain. (I can say proudly that I have had to change sponges just twice since 1989.)

Walt also does not go to extreme lengths to tidy up for company. Walt did what most men do to prepare for other men coming over: not a damn thing. He left the small piles of dust in the corners, the rotten fruit on the countertop, the caked-on Prego sauce on the floor, and the newspapers on the kitchen and dining-room tables.

"You saving these for any particular purpose?" I asked Walt.

"I got a lot of reading to catch up on," he said.

"I guess so," I said, holding up a paper with the headline REAGAN FIRES AIR TRAFFIC CONTROLLERS.

Men can do disagreeable stuff if they want to. They will slice a fish from head to tail and scoop out the guts with their bare hands. They would eat a bowl of maggots if they thought it would get them tickets to the Super Bowl. (Some schlemiel in Buffalo, N.Y., actually did this, in a radio promotion. He didn't win. The winner had jumped into a vat of horse poop.) But men will not take the hairball out of the bathroom sink.

The other day, after getting in touch with my feminine side, I went on a cleaning binge. I bought an aerosol can of bathroom cleaner and sprayed it all over. I made the fatal error of spraying it on the mirror. When I went to wipe it off, it left a cloudy film you couldn't get off with a sandblaster. The mirror is now ruined, and I don't consider this my fault. I was doing a good deed by cleaning the bathroom, and I bought something specifically labeled a bathroom cleaner. There should have been a note attached that said: "Tony, Do Not Buy This Product. *You Are Too Stupid to Use It.*"

Take towels. A man will use the same bath towel forever. He figures: I take a shower. My body is then clean. I wipe off my clean body with a towel, then drop it on the floor. Therefore, the towel remains hygienically pure for infinity.

I asked my friend Richie: When do you change towels?

"When the old one has a big hole," he said.

He then called me back to add this: "I forgot about the dog. I'll change the towel if I use it to dry off the dog a few times. I'll let the kids use it a few times after that—but not me."

It's pretty much the same with sheets. A guy will sleep on the same sheet for, oh, six to eight months—or until he becomes concerned that the color has changed in the middle. Then he can turn it over and get four more months out of it. Oh sure, lying down on a new, crisp, cool sheet is a delightful feeling. But you can get that same feeling by just opening the window.

Men are always fascinated when they go to their mother's

house and see thirty-two sheets in the linen closet. What can she be thinking? Who's coming over, the Dallas Cowboys? The most anybody needs is two sheets: one on the bed, and one to replace it. Man About Town Chip Muldoon has narrowed it down even further: "It only takes a couple of hours to wash and dry a sheet," he says. "So I do it in the afternoon, when I'm not using my bed. If I get tired, I nap on the couch."

Towels, sheets . . . dishes. If there were no women in the world, one thing that I am certain of—aside from the fact that there would be no reason for anyone to ever take a shower—is that the fine china industry would not exist. All plates, bowls, serving trays, and even punch bowls would be made out of cardboard. This is because men don't wash. Men throw out and buy new. Cost is not a problem. Men would simply factor into their budget $260 a week for "paper products."

A woman I know complains that her husband never picks up his socks. "He drops them all over the house," she says. "Why can't he pick them up and put them in the hamper?"

The answer is simple: He is making a pile. This is high art, for the male gender. Men love to make piles. (However, men don't sort, nor do they fold.) This starts in early childhood when boy children go into the backyard and make a big pile of dirt— half of which they eat—and girl children respond by making a face and saying, "Eeewwwww!"

Piles are part of the male birthright. It's a hunting-and-gathering response—an instinct, like channel surfing to find naked women. In my room I have piles of clothes on the chair, the bed, and the top of the cedar chest. I haven't worn some of these clothes in years. It's possible they aren't even *my* clothes—they may have come with the house. But being a creature of habit like most men, I can't imagine my room without them. So when I go to sleep I gently move the pile from the bed onto the chair. Or when I want to sit on the chair, I gently move that pile of clothes to the bed. In this way, I suppose, I could be called a nurturer.

Noting how much time I have spent through the years moving the piles, a woman once asked me why I simply don't put the clothes in my drawers.

How naïve. Then where would I put all my paper plates?

THIS IS
THE MODERN
WORLD

✴

Call Me, Ishmael

Once upon a time the telephone was your friend. It connected you with the world at large and filled your life with happy, carefree sounds of friendship.

It was a wondrous machine. It was made of the same dense, black material as a bowling ball. The receiver weighed as much as an unabridged thesaurus; if you dropped it on your foot, you were in traction for a month. It sat on its own special table, because if you put it on the wall, the wall would collapse. It was simple and direct: It rang, you answered.

Now your phone looks like Lieutenant Uhura's instrument panel, in tasteful pastels. You're filled with dread each time it rings—like hearing a knock at your front door. Nobody in his right mind opens his door. Who comes to your house anymore? Either a Bible study group or an ax murderer. Everybody else phones.

It could be the office wanting you to do more work. (Can you ever remember, even once, when they called to give you less work?) It could be your child's school telling you little Stevie has green phlegm, and he's hocking it into the water fountain, and the girls are shrieking, and you must come and get him *now*! It could be another infernal computerized recording, offering you credit cards, or vacation homes, or an organic banana that cures manic-depressiveness.

All calls are bad. So you stop answering. You have Caller ID to identify who's calling, and reject them. You have Call Block to preempt certain callers from ever getting through. You have an answering machine so you can sit there and screen calls. The more sophisticated your phone service, the less you have to talk to people. The ultimate goal in the '90s is no conversations, only messages. I know a guy who has an answering machine on his car phone! Now, you know that guy is ducking your call, because a car phone isn't activated unless someone's in the car. Why won't he take your call? He's too busy talking to a jack-in-the-box at a drive-thru?

I am a misanthrope. I do not want Call Waiting. I do not want a phone in my car. I do not want Call Forwarding. Send me a postcard. (I want Call Far-Forwarding, so I can send your calls to Yugoslavia, and you pay the charges.) I do not want Call Trace. I'm not bucking for a Junior G-Man badge.

Mine is the only house in America that does not have an answering machine. I just take the phone off the hook, and you get a busy signal. Why should I let robbers know I'm not home? Don't you love the people who have a message on their machine that says "I can't come to the phone right now . . ." as though this inspired bit of caginess is going to hoodwink a burglar. "Duh, Spike, we better not hit the Kornheiser home. He's there, but he can't come to the phone. He's probably in the bathroom."

(Oh, you don't think robbers call first? You think they just take a chance and show up? You think you're smart enough to have all these high-tech sensors on the windows and the shoot-on-sight armed response, and they're so dumb they come in with a crowbar, like in *Home Alone*? Grow up. If I did have a machine, I'd record a message that said: "I'll be back in five minutes. I'm picking up a mail-order AK-47 at the post office. Why don't you come over and wait for me? Don't worry about the Doberman. I'm pretty sure I fed him this morning.")

I hate answering machines. Everybody's either a comedian or a disc jockey. "This is John. I'm not here right now. But my friend Jimmy Cagney is, and he'd like to speak to you. You dirty rat, Looie, you killed my brudder. And whoa! Look who just walked into the room. It's Jimmy Stewart. Wu-wu-wu-wuhhh, well, John's not here right now, but if you leave a mu-mu-mu-muuuhhh, message, he'll get back to you." Then you hear this moronic music, often the theme from *The Flintstones*, which goes on for fifteen minutes. By the time it's your turn to speak, the call has already cost you $2,000. This is clever? This putz doing imitations really thinks he's clever?

I don't have Call Waiting, either. Maybe I'm old-fashioned, but if I want to have every third word interrupted by clicking, I'll dial Jimmy Cricket. So now they have Silent Call Waiting. All you hear is dead air. I don't believe there is such a thing as Silent Call Waiting. I believe the person you're talking to just goes off and makes a slice of toast. I think they have Toast Waiting. And when they come back they always say, "Look, I've got to take this other call." No problem. Have a nice lunch.

Now there's Repeat Call to redial the last number you called if it's busy—in almost the same amount of time it would take you to actually do it yourself. I don't need Repeat Call. I might like Petite Call, for short conversations. Or Conceit Call, for recorded messages about how fabulous I am. Or even Discreet Call, for how fabulous we might be together.

They have Select Forward so you can choose which calls will be forwarded. My select forward is Charles Barkley. (Taking calls is much easier than making calls. To call people from a public phone with a credit card you have to dial a thirty-nine-digit code to make contact with the appropriate operator. Then you punch in the number you want and the number of your credit card. That's twenty-four more numbers. You have to be Rain Man to use a pay phone.)

There is also Priority Call, which lets you pick up six telephone numbers that will "ring in a special way." What do they mean, special? Like, if it was somebody really fat, would the phone moo? I want the ring to sound like another five hundred bucks being flushed down the toilet, so I'll know it's my deadbeat brother Stanley calling.

The most intriguing new offering is Call Block, which lets you stonewall six numbers completely. They never get through. I don't know where the calls go, and I don't care. Let them all go to Larry King.

I want callers to hear, "Tony Kornheiser requests that you suck wind."

Here's the ones I block:

My editor. No way am I coming in to rewrite this column.

Anyone to whom I ever said, "Please call if you're in town."

My cousin Marsha's husband Wally, the forensic taxidermist.

Sally Jessy Raphaël. Because I've had it with those glasses.

King Hussein.

ChemLawn.

And, of course, Cliff Robertson, Candice Bergen, and James Earl Jones. Don't call me, I'll call you.

Sorry, I Don't Do Windows

I finally did it. I went out and bought a home computer. It's absolutely *fabulous*. You won't believe all the things it can do. It can do budgets and banking. It can make maps. It can do my taxes. It can play CDs. It can speak Creole. It can make malteds.

Unfortunately, I can't use it.

I've had it for a month. I can plug it in. I can turn it on. After that I'm lost. I sit there staring at a blank screen, waiting for it to do something magical on its own, like it's the Oracle at Delphi. The only thing I can do on that screen is Windex it.

Here is what the screen says:

C:>

That's it. That's as far as I've gotten. The colon, I sense, is telling me I am expected to do something.

So I type in: Help.

Now the screen reads C:> Hepl.

Oop. I am not good at this. I get nervous and make mistakes. So I correct my spelling, and hit Enter.

The computer answers: Bad file name.

So I type in something else.

Now the screen reads: C:> Please, Please, Please Help.

The computer answers: Bad file name. Abort?

I want to abort. God, I want to abort. I want to abort this whole mission. I am unworthy. I am a squashed skunk on the information superhighway.

It's a funny story how I got the computer. As you know, I type columns for a living. I've been doing it for twenty-five years. A few weeks ago my typewriter broke, and I went out to buy another one. The last one I bought, an Olivetti Lettera 32, cost about $80, so factoring in inflation, I figured a new Olivetti would be about $110—which it would have been if anyone in the world made typewriters anymore. Asking for a typewriter at an office products store is like going into a Rite-Aid and asking the pharmacist for leeches. They look at you like you are a virus.

Which is how I came to spend $2,500 on the world's most expensive typewriter.

The computer came with an instruction book the thickness of *Roget's Thesaurus*, only with smaller printing. I started to read it, and stopped after about ten minutes. I felt like Fabio leafing through Kierkegaard.

So I called the store and said I was computer-illiterate. They said I could buy a video that would take me through the steps of the computer's operations—and I'd do that, except I don't know how to use my VCR.

As you may have guessed, I am technophobic. I still don't own a portable phone. I don't have direct deposit. I cut up my ATM card because I was afraid that if I ever used it, it would somehow transfer all my money to a butcher shop in Paraguay. I'm sure that if I had been alive when the wheel was invented, I'd be the last yutz dragging a caribou carcass with a rope.

My children come in, and they start playing around with the computer fearlessly, the way people my age used to play with a hula hoop. They create files effortlessly; they vary typefaces and colors; they play games against the computer. (I thought a hard drive was when you had to clear 180 yards of water off the tee.)

I watch my eleven-year-old daughter fly around the Windows program, and it occurs to me that the way I look at her, in utter amazement, must be the way my parents looked the first time they saw Mr. Pitagorsky's brand-new Philco television set. Good Lord, Rhoda, how did Garry Moore squeeze himself into that little box?

I'd like to be part of the swinging computer crowd. I'd like to have an "address" on the Internet where I would have a swell sign-on like anthonikorn@boomshakkalakkalakka. I'd like to be able to share in the joke when the punch line is, "So I downloaded, see, and it runs an uplink and comes up star bat dot CMD!" I know funny, and that's funny.

But I am hopeless.

(And I'm not the only one. Recently my smart friend Martha could not get her computer to work. She'd turn the machine on and the screen would fill with small, fuzzy shapes, like a Jackson Pollock painting that had been thrown in the toilet. When the repairman came over and removed the top of the computer—which they refer to as "opening the pizza box"—he found, to Martha's horror, so much matted cat hair that it looked like a muskrat was lodged in there.)

At *The Washington Post*, I am famous for my ineptitude at the computer. The newspaper has a giant computer system that everyone in the building, including the janitorial staff, has mastered except for me. I have learned how to sign on and type stories. I don't know how to sign off because I never absolutely had to learn, since the computer signs you off automatically after ten minutes or so of no typing. This is fine, except this means that for ten minutes or so after I have already gone home, my computer is sitting there in my office, signed on as Tony Kornheiser. This means anyone can come in and send E-mail messages to anyone else in the *Post*, and the messages will appear to have come from me.

I know this must happen because periodically I get return

messages from people whom I have not, to my knowledge, communicated with. They go like this one, from the Lord High Assistant Managing Executive Publisher:

"Tony: My behind would be even larger than you seem to think it is, but fortunately I get to exercise it frequently by punting fat, aging, bald, not-so-funny-anymore columnists out the door."

The Hard Cell

When I purchased my cellular telephone, I thought I was getting a great deal. But as soon as I swaggered out of the store with my $70 telephone, I learned that (a) only a complete imbecile would pay *anything* for a cellular phone, since some places let you have them for literally *one cent* because (b) the true cost of a cellular phone has nothing to do with the actual cost of the phone, but is what you pay each month to make and receive calls, which is $4,000 per minute.

Giving me a cell phone is like giving a kangaroo a food processor. The kangaroo might push the buttons, and something mechanical might happen within the big bowl part—but the kangaroo probably wouldn't make a good remoulade sauce.

I am not good at this sort of stuff. I recently ordered voice mail from the phone company for my home phone. For pennies a month, they turn your phone into an answering machine! So after a few days I picked up the telephone in my kitchen and heard a stuttering *beep-beep-beep-beep* sound before my customary dial tone kicked in. I called the phone company and told them my phone was broken.

They told me the choppy sound was the voice mail indicator that I had a message. I expressed surprise.

"How did you think you would be informed you had a message?" the phone company lady asked me.

"Well, my phone at work has a message light, so I figured my phone at home would light up too," I said.

At this point, the phone company lady got very quiet. Extremely slowly, as though talking to a very small and not very bright child, she asked: "Do you see a bulb anywhere on your home phone that could light up?"

"Well, ah," I stammered, "I thought maybe my hall light would flicker or something."

(I should tell you about the message I recorded for the voice mail. The phone company lady patiently walked me through the steps to get me to the point where I could record a message. But I hadn't planned on what I would say, so when it was my actual turn to speak, I wasn't prepared. And this is exactly what you hear when you call my house: "Uh, I, uh, I've, you know, sort of been dragged kicking and screaming into the technological age, so, uh, well, leave a message and see what happens. Is that okay? Did I do that right? Hello?")

Anyway, my first problem with my new cellular phone was trying to figure out which part you talk into. There's no mouthpiece, no familiar grillwork. Below the last row of numbers, there's a tiny slot, no bigger than an eighth of an inch; you couldn't fit a cat's toenail clipping in it. This, I assume, is where you talk. Or maybe I bought the model where you can only listen; you call people and hear them say, "Hello. Hello. Who is this? Is anybody there?" Then they hang up—which is okay, on account of the aforementioned cost of using the phone.

A lot of people tell you they're buying a cell phone for safety. My friend Jeff said he wants to get one so that in case he's carjacked, he can call 911. Like the robber is going to let you make a phone call. This is a carjacking, not *Barney Miller*. (You may be safer not using a car phone at all. Sometimes when my friend Nancy drives to work in the morning, she has one hand holding the phone, one hand holding a cup of coffee, and then she realizes: My God, I'm driving with my knees!)

The truth is, I have no need for a cell phone. I didn't want one for safety. I wanted it so I could look cool. You know how when you see some guy waiting in line at a restaurant and yakking on a cell phone, and you say to yourself, "What a putz!" Well, I want to be that guy. I want the maitre d' to come over and tell me my table's ready, and then as all the seated diners look at me, I sashay by, and I'm holding my cell phone to my ear, laughing like I'm talking to Bob Hope! I want my neighbors to see me standing out on my stoop on a Sunday morning, wearing a Pierre Cardin bathrobe, walking in tiny circles, talking to my agent! Of course what I'd mostly be saying is: "Is it better now? Can you hear me now?" Because on most cell phones you can't hear a word anybody's saying. It's like trying to talk to Boutros Boutros-Rodham-Ghali in the Holland Tunnel.

But that is beside the point. The fact is, I finally have a cell phone!

"How long have you had it?" my friend Gino asked me.

"Two days," I said.

"And how many calls have you made?" he asked.

"It depends on what you mean by calls," I responded, warily. "Do you mean, where I dial a number, and someone answers, and says 'Hello,' and I say something back?"

"Yes, that would be one call."

"Well, by that strict definition—none," I admitted. "But that is because the calls are so expensive."

Gino looked at me. "No it isn't," he said. "It is because you don't know how to make a call. Prove to me you can use your cell phone."

I tried calling the phone on my desk. I punched in the numbers, then hit *send* and waited for the phone to ring. It didn't.

The display on my cell phone informed me my desk phone was "busy." The only thing it was busy doing was making me look like a doofus.

I tried something easier, 411. Nothing.

So, finally, Gino says, "Look, see if your phone is working. Dial your cell phone from your office phone."

"I, ah, don't know my number," I said.

It was hard to hear what he said next, on account of the guffaws and chortles and spittled snorts and gasps, but basically he urged me to call information for the number.

"I can't," I said. "It's unlisted."

Regrettably, everything in this column is absolutely true. Even:

Anthony is an idiot.

The High-Tech Slow Burn

Same-day dry cleaning; twenty-minute workouts; one-hour photos; instant karma. So much in modern life is designed to help us cut corners and save time. I thought about this the other day after waiting ten-deep on line at a McDonald's to get a grinning salesperson who not only screwed up my order twice ("No, not a Big Mac, a Quarter Pounder with cheese; not a vanilla shake, chocolate; if I asked for fries, would you bring me an apple pie?"), but after finally getting it right, happily told me the Quarter Pounders were gone, and I'd have to wait for a new batch. I've often wondered if it wouldn't be better to go to a fast-food place and simply ask, "What do you have that's ready right now?" But it'd probably be the fish filet that's been sitting under the warming light since Memorial Day. There's no such thing as fast food. But if you've been to any of these places, you already know that.

Isn't it ironic that we spend half our lives waiting for things that are supposed to make our lives quicker and easier?

Raise your hand if you've burned half a tank of gas at a bank drive-thru.

Or frittered away an hour on a supermarket express line,

behind people with more than twelve items who say things like, "Will you accept a personal check from a bank in Burma?"

Or stood in the freezing cold at an automatic teller machine waiting your turn, then punched in your code—approximately as long as the first chapter in *The Great Gatsby*—only to be told they're out of cash, come back tomorrow.

Greetings from the Age of Technology.

Take a seat, we'll be with you when we're damned good and ready.

This is all prologue to a story about buying a computer that will underline how the more things change for the better, the more they get worse. After lunch the other day, I went with a friend to buy this basic computer. We walked west on M Street. I remember being across from House of Salad, and in front of Business Land, and thinking: What happened, were we just teleported to Planet of the Morons?

Anyway, she finds the store. She goes in, and immediately spots the one she wants. She tells the salesman she also needs some paper and a cable to plug the computer into a printer. She takes out her checkbook to pay the bill.

All this takes one minute.

The salesman sits down at his computer—a hot-shot deal with multicolor type and fancy graphics—to compose the receipt.

This, as they say in the airline game, is where we start circling.

"I need your address," he says.

He types it into his computer, along with his name, the cashier's name (why would you need the cashier's name?), the date, my friend's name, an invoice number, and an account number. The ability to store all kinds of information has led to an insatiable pursuit of all kinds of information—mostly worthless. The food, as we say at the dinner table, is beginning to get cold.

He types in mysterious codes and slashes, romancing the

computer like this is a deliberate process. Our biological clocks are racing.

Eventually, eight full lines appear on screen. Five of these lines describe options she hasn't bought. I suppose they're noted for archaeological purposes.

She looks at the screen and says, "I thought the computer was $729."

"It is," he says.

"Then why does it say $829?"

He looks at the screen where it says $829. "Did I do that?" he asks.

In order to change the bill he has to go back up through all eight lines of type one at a time. (Does the term *glacial thawing* mean anything to you?) By the time he reaches the top, he's apparently forgotten why he's there, because he announces triumphantly, "That will be $884."

"It can't be," my friend says, nonplussed.

Oops. Again, up we go through the eight lines.

All told, the paperwork took twenty-eight minutes.

"You know," I say, "in the old days, before the computer came along to make your life easier, a salesman could have used a pen and written up a receipt and had you out the door in, oh, maybe as long as two minutes."

"The guy wasn't exactly Einstein at the keyboard," she says.

"Yeah, but you weren't exactly shopping at NASA," I say.

Now my seven-year-old wants a computer, and I can appreciate that it would be a good learning tool. But first I want her to learn to write with a pencil in case she ever has to take a phone message when her computer is on the fritz. Whenever people rely too much on computers, they assume machines are right and people are wrong—and burdensome. The more you depend on a computer, the easier it gets to forget how, as they say, to interface with other people.

"You're so low-tech," I'm told. (I don't have Call Waiting.)

"Yes, but so high-anxiety."

Next year in New York, high school students will be allowed to use calculators on their statewide mathematics exams. I took those exams. I had to do the math by myself. As a result, I can check the accuracy of a lunch check without having to locate a supplementary light source for my solar calculator. What's next? If I take the Spanish final, am I allowed to bring in Charo?

JUST PLANE SCARED

*

On a Wing and a Prayer
and 35,000 Feet of Air

I wanted to go to Norway for the Olympics. Plain and simple. How else was I going to get there, walk?

So I enrolled in USAir's fearful flyer course. At the least, I figured, I'd get a column piece out of it. At best, I'd get to Norway. (Can you imagine, wanting to solve your fear of flying so you could get to Norway in the *winter*? That's like wanting to get over bronchitis so you could take a job working in a coal mine.)

I'm not actually afraid of flying. I'm uncomfortable flying.

I'm *afraid* of crashing.

My fear is quite simple and specific: I believe the plane will break apart in mid-air, and we will all tumble to our deaths in an unspeakable blazing inferno. Other than that, I'm fine.

That fear has been so overwhelming that I have done everything I could to remain earthbound. I won't bore you with a complete recitation of how many times I maneuvered to avoid getting on a plane. But in 1991 I not only started the Bandwagon, but I actually rode the damn thing three full days and 1,500 miles to the Super Bowl in Minneapolis, and then took a twenty-six-hour train trip back to Washington without a shower so I smelled like a goat, and had the standard phoney-baloney fallback line: You never really see the country until you do it on a train. Don't get me wrong, I really do love trains, but I love ice cream, too, and I don't sleep inside a Good Humor truck.

More than 30 million Americans share this fear of flying—though some not as graphically, I suppose. And fifty of them were at National Airport with me taking this course.

You know us. We're the ones who ask, "If flying's so safe, why do they call the building a *terminal?*"

Fear of flying ranks eighth, by the way, on a list of common fears, behind death and ahead of dogs—though I imagine you could go for the quiniella if you were afraid of being bitten to death at 35,000 feet.

I admit I had some trepidation walking into the first class. I thought perhaps I'd be the only one who was really crazy about flying. But I was cheered when we went around the room introducing ourselves and explaining our fears, and the first person the instructor called on said, "I have this fear that the pilot will have a heart attack, and the copilot will panic, because he won't know whether to help the pilot or continue flying the plane." And I thought *I* was crazy.

Surprisingly, almost all the people there were veteran flyers who'd become paralyzed by their fears. Whether they suffered from claustrophobia or a fear of heights or discomfort in giving up control of their lives to a pilot, they were all there for the same reason: They wanted fuller lives. Many had passed up trips. Some had quit jobs because they couldn't get on airplanes. One woman who recently had gotten engaged said pleadingly, "I want to go on my honeymoon."

"You have a disease," Carol Stauffer, the instructor, told us kindly. "The relaxation tape you'll listen to daily and the book you'll read are the medicine."

She laid out the course, the five three-hour sessions culminating in the "graduation" flight—during which, I was certain, the plane would break apart. She said we would get champagne after the flight . . . so, if by some miracle we survived the flight, we could get drunk and kill ourselves on the drive home.

Carol was a social worker, which explains her persistent optimism. She kept talking about the "fun" we'd have. As proof, she introduced a graduate from a recent class, a Mr. Norman Braverman. I muttered: Norman, you're a braver man than I.

As we went around the room elucidating our fears, people recalled episodes of horrifying turbulence that swore them off air travel—like a thunderstorm that bucked the plane so wildly, the flight attendants held hands and prayed. One man said he dwelled morbidly on plane crashes; he read the news accounts and memorized the names of the dead. A woman said she could not fly without drinking, and because her job required her to fly two or three times a week, she was worried she was becoming an alcoholic. Another woman said she cries throughout the flight: "I listen to all the noises the plane makes. When they aren't deafening I feel the engines are being turned off," she said. A man said he panics when people begin to walk around the cabin, because he thinks they will tilt the plane and cause it to turn over in the sky.

When it came my turn, I said, "Boy, am I glad I don't have to fly with you guys. Your fears are so irrational. My fear, on the other hand, makes all the sense in the world: I believe that a giant is going to come along and cut the strings that hold the airplane up."

Frank Petee, a retired pilot, taught the course with Carol Stauffer. He wore his captain's uniform to class, which I found reassuring—though I admit it's a little like Red Auerbach wearing a whistle.

Frank had flown for more than forty years, and offered himself as proof of how safe airplanes are. On an average day, he said, twenty thousand jet planes take off and land, and 99.99 percent of these maneuvers are normal and routine. "You were in much more danger the last time you stepped out of your bathroom shower than you will ever be in an airplane," he told us . . . prompting a woman to ask: "Is it the same if you take baths?"

But statistics are cold comfort if you're up in the air and you're afraid, as is the claim that "the media blows accidents out of proportion." When 288 people fall from the sky, it's simply not the same as a Mazda rolling over the curb into a cappuccino bar.

Still, Frank did his best to calm us. And in my case it helped to know that turbulence will not cause a plane's wings to fall off; that I should think of turbulence in the same vein as driving a car over a bumpy country road; that even if its engines go out, an airplane can glide for miles and find a place to land; and that because of sophisticated onboard computers, a pilot doesn't even have to see out the window to land the plane. "We can make an approach without seeing," Frank said. Which is not to say that I'd necessarily feel relieved to look into the cockpit and see Ray Charles flying the plane.

Afterward I felt slightly foolish that I had been so afraid of turbulence for so long. One of the men in the class who knew my fear sidled up to me and said, "I told you your fear was silly; planes don't break apart. Once they're up in the air, nothing goes wrong. My fear is much more reasonable. It's about take-off."

"What about takeoff?" I asked.

"That we'll fly into a flock of birds and crash."

Like so many pilots, Frank has that reassuring Chuck Yeager voice that Tom Wolfe wrote about in *The Right Stuff*. When Frank told us not to worry, that everything would be all right in the airplane, we all wanted to trust him. For a while I almost forgot what a group of loons we were. Until the question-and-answer period, when one of the men asked, "You said that airlines would try to accommodate special requests by passengers. What if I liked to fly in a certain seat? Could I do that?"

"Certainly," Frank replied. "The airlines will be happy to give you the row you want, window or aisle."

"I mean the color seat I want. Bold colors make me hyper," the man said.

Oh.

Frank was very positive about maintenance. He said airline maintenance was very good. I'd never given airline maintenance a second thought; I mean, I was taking this course to become a better passenger, not a baggage handler. But it gave me a whole new area to be neurotic about. (What about that plane in Hawaii where the top peeled off? *"Look, honey, we're in a convertible."* How was the maintenance on that baby, huh?)

We had a slide show on maintenance. One slide showed the oxygen masks being released—which we greeted with nervous laughter. Somebody asked: What causes the oxygen masks to come down? Frank said they rarely do come down: "Maybe if a window broke, but I haven't heard of a window breaking in many, many years." Wow, a window breaking! I never thought of that. Something else to add to the worry list.

Part of the mental training of the course was to take control of your own thoughts; they told us we were the gatekeepers of our thoughts, we could associate pleasant thoughts with flying if we wanted to. Toward that end we went outside to examine a plane up close, the theory being we would see how sturdy it really was. But up close the rust and the scruffiness unnerved me. So many bolts. What if just one or two fell out over the Atlantic? I tried to follow Carol's advice and banish the bad thoughts and substitute a pleasant one. But all I could think of was: fiery descent into shark-infested water.

As always, Frank said not to worry. Smiling, he told me, "Go ahead and kick the tires. Bang on the wings." So I banged on the fuselage, and the woman sitting in a window seat by the wing felt the plane move, and it scared the color out of her face. I waved at her sheepishly. I tried to banish the thought that the plane seemed flimsy by chanting the most comforting words I knew of when it came to strong, clunky, reliable transportation: "Volvo station wagon."

Halfway through the course, some of us started flying; one of the women went to New York and back, played the relaxation tape on the plane with her, relying on it throughout the flights, and crowed, "It worked, really, it worked. I thought I was going to fall asleep on the flight!" Now you might say: New York is a short flight, a piece of cake. (Though we would say nothing is a piece of cake when you're up in the air.) But one of the men flew to Germany and back. And not only was his return flight turbulent, but the plane was delayed three hours because of a bomb scare! "I was amazed that I didn't panic," he told us. "All the way across I was thinking—Gee, I'm normally petrified. And yet I'm completely calm." We listened raptly to their testimony, like witnesses at a religious revival. That night, when I went home, I played the relaxation tape twice, and kissed it for good luck.

My turning point was the class when two pilots and three flight attendants came and talked to us. These were people who actually flew the plane. Walt had flown weather reconnaissance in the navy; he'd been in worse weather than I could even imagine. So I felt I could trust him when he said that weather will bounce you around, but it won't break the plane. Listening to Frank was comforting, but he was a retired pilot. Joe and Walt were active—they were going up every day. They were my age, maybe even a bit younger. They had small children. They had *volunteered* to fly us on our graduation night! "They love flying, and they want you to love it, too," Frank explained. Looking into their faces, I asked myself: Why would they do this if it weren't safe?

I can't tell you how reassuring it was to talk with people who flew for a living, who did it out of routine, who put a casual face on it. The flight attendants spoke jovially about their work, telling us they call the preflight recitation of the safety procedures "the singing and dancing." Obviously, all of us in a fearful flyer course feel that safety is the A–No. 1 priority, but humor goes a long way in a classroom like that—like when someone asked Walt, "How do you know when to come over the intercom and talk to the passengers?" And Walt deadpanned, "The rule is: Never interrupt the movie." One man, confessing the fears of us all, asked Bonnie, one of the flight attendants, "Is it all right to tell the flight attendants you're a fearful flyer? Will they look after you?" Bonnie sensed his apprehension and smiled. "And give you free liquor, yes."

Much of what was said I wrote down, because I knew I'd eventually do this story. But one thing Joe said I'd have remembered even without my notes: "An airplane is designed and built to fly. It *likes* to fly."

That night, with Joe and Walt at the controls, we taxied. They told us what they were doing each step of the way. They identified each sound. They showed us the spoilers, and how the wing flaps move. They put the engines in reverse thrust so we could become familiar with that sound. They took us down the runway at full throttle briefly—we were light, and if we'd stayed at that speed for just a few more seconds we'd have been airborne.

I sat on an aisle over the wing, silently mouthing, "Go, go, go."

I didn't want another week to think about it. I wanted to fly already.

Carol said we could bring somebody with us on the graduation flight.

But:

1. Don't bring a fearful flyer.

2. Don't bring a small child.

3. Don't bring a first-time flyer.

4. Don't bring anyone who thinks your fear is silly and this flight is no big deal.

That disqualified everyone but Michelle Pfeiffer. I left a message with her agent, but she never returned it. So I went alone.

As always, we met in the classroom and listened to the relaxation tape as a group. In her last-minute instructions, Carol told us, "Boeing built you right into the airplane. You're part of it. Whatever that airplane does, you do it too. Lean with it, not against it. If there are bumps, don't stiffen up, ride with them." It was such a good speech I thought it would be silly to point out that we were flying a McDonnell Douglas plane.

I actually wasn't supposed to be on this flight. I'd said all along I had a previously scheduled engagement. But at the last minute I decided to bag that and take the flight. I was proud of my desire to fly, though I reminded myself that Amelia Earhart probably felt the same way.

I was nervous driving to the airport, because this time was different. This was not a drill, not a simulation—this time we were going up. Fortunately the weather was spectacular: clear, mild, calm. There shouldn't be any turbulence at all. That helped me relax. And because I wasn't expected, when I showed up the rest of the class applauded, which made me feel great. So by the time we boarded the plane, I felt strangely confident.

Briefly, I asked myself: What the hell are you doing? How can you take a flight you don't *have* to take? Are you out of your mind? Quick, run out the door. Everyone will understand. Heck, they'll probably follow you.

But I was committed now.

I saw Carol and Frank on the plane. On the way in I'd said hello to Joe and Walt in the cockpit. All the folks I'd seen in the class for almost two months were in their seats. It felt like family.

We did the tape one more time.

Then the engines started. And we taxied onto the runway, and we went full throttle. And as I said a silent prayer and closed my eyes, we were up—smooth as satin.

There was some applause at liftoff, though not from me; I thought that was premature, considering the fact that we were in a floating metal tube, and if the engines fell off, we were Spam in a can.

I think it goes without saying that no matter how relaxed I may have felt relative to other times in a plane, I was still not relaxed; I still had the nervous system of Don Knotts in a cyclotron. But I wanted to try to feel calm. Carol and Frank had exhorted us not to sit frozen solid in our seats, but to stretch our muscles and alleviate the tension. So I got up and walked straight for the cockpit. We were still in the climbout. I was walking UPHILL! I must have been out of my mind.

Throughout the flight I chatted like a magpie. I went up and down the aisle asking people how they were doing; I felt like a wine steward. I was never entirely comfortable, particularly the one or two times the plane hit a slight bump in that ocean of air. But I was better than ever before. I never reached for my trusty Valium. I never thought the giant would cut the strings.

We stayed airborne almost forty-five minutes, going south to Richmond, then turning north toward the eastern shore of Maryland, and coming back into National. It was such a perfectly clear night that standing in the cockpit—and we were encouraged to do that—you could see forever. Oddly, when you're in the cockpit, you have almost no sensation of moving. It really does feel as if the plane is being held up by strings.

There were tears in my eyes when we landed (and this time I heartily joined in the applause), I was relieved and grateful and proud; I drank the champagne delightedly. They gave us diplomas, and we all felt we'd earned them.

I won't say I was cured, though. I still felt terrified to get on a plane. Most of my fears were still there. The difference was that now I had a method to help me better cope with them. I had the relaxation tape. I had a positive experience to fall back on. I had a support group I could call anytime; in fact, I've called Frank for reassurance before a number of flights. I had the knowledge I could get on a plane.

A few months later I flew to Norway. And back.

The planes I was on were designed and built to fly. They liked to fly.

And nobody cut the strings.

The Zoom and a Boom

Do you remember where you were at ten o'clock last Tuesday morning? It might help if I give you a hint: sonic boom. (What do you mean, give you another hint? That's it: sonic boom. Look, this isn't an essay question. Tuesday morning at ten was when the SR-71 Blackbird spy plane broke the sound barrier over the Washington area. You didn't hear it? You didn't feel it? What, I'm doing *Tommy* here? There was a sonic boom. Was it as good for you as it was for me?)

I was throwing out the garbage when the noise shook the sky. Instinctively, I narrowed the choices:

1. Nuclear attack—in which case I was toast;

2. Mathematically remarkable coincidence: a flock of birds with heartburn;

3. Sonic boom.

I did what any D.C. resident would do under the circumstances: I telephoned District Cable Vision to find out how many days service would be interrupted this time. I'm still on hold.

Do you know how fast this plane was going? Do you know? Do you know? Do you know? (Yo, Wernher, check it out!) Average speed: 2,112 miles an hour. That's so fast, Tattoo only has time to say, "Look, boss, de . . ." before it's gone.

(The *what?* The miles per gallon? Who cares? Hey, buddy, this isn't a van pool. We're not going for environmentally correct, we're going for zoom.)

The average commercial airliner goes coast-to-coast in four hours, fifty minutes. This baby went coast-to-coast in sixty-eight minutes! (Johnny Carson said, "It broke the old record of sixty-nine minutes set by a Domino's Pizza truck.") Sixty-eight freaking minutes! L.A. to D.C. One hour, eight. Ballgame. You can spend one hour, eight sitting on the runway at National just waiting for your plane to take off.

En route, the Blackbird flew from St. Louis to Cincinnati in eight minutes. Granted, that may not be a favorite route of yours. But if you have to take it, this thing gets you there in eight minutes. You can't fax anything that fast. You're *actually there* before your secretary can get an open WATS line. It's Star Trek. Scotty beamed you up!

As you know, they're mothballing the Blackbirds. Putting them in museums. (To show you how old I am, I thought U2 was a spy plane.)

There they go, swinging low, bye-bye, blackbird.

That's nuts. It ought to be: Blackbird, buy! Buy!

Air Force and industry sources say these planes are good for twenty more years. They shouldn't be in museums. People should be allowed to purchase them. Slap a coat of fresh paint on them—maybe those Braniff flying colors from the solvent days—and let's rock 'n' roll. If you've got an evening, we'll give you the world.

"Honey, get a sitter. We're having dinner in Kabul."

It's an airplane for people with money to spend, but no time to waste.

Air Yuppie.

It will be the first airline with no ticket counters. You can only purchase through catalogs.

Imagine what the conversation would sound like on an airplane filled with yuppies. All those whiny, self-indulgent laments:

"Isn't the food in the Caribbean just awful?"

"That's why we're driving a Jaguar; the seats in the BMW were too rigid, too *achtung!*"

"Dockers? They were last year."

"Can you believe the markup on the vineyard-designated Pouilly Fuisse? It's a well-focused, exuberant wine, but excessively fruity by my taste."

"We used to have a Norwegian au pair. You'll be pleased. But there's nothing quite like an English nanny. We wouldn't trade ours for the world."

"The bench-press muscles are too bulky. I want the Nordic-Track muscles."

Okay, back to the plane. It flies at eighty thousand feet. "It's a real smooth ride up there," the pilot, Lt. Col. Raymond Yeilding, reported.

It gets to eighty thousand feet in about six seconds. You spend the first five or so with your eyes closed wondering how Big Daddy Don Garlits got into the cockpit. Then it flattens out and you know you're at eighty thousand feet, because you look up and your eyebrows are pasted to the ceiling.

Because of the quickness of the trip, the flight attendants serve the meal right away. (All Air Yuppie flight attendants—male and female—graduate from the Al Neuharth Sky Girl Academy. In case of emergency, they chew gum and shriek.) Unfortunately, the speed of the aircraft requires a slight alteration in the style of service. The G-force pins the flight attendants to the back wall for the entire flight, so they load a cart with food, then let it loose down the aisle at about 1,300 miles an hour. We're talking FAST food. You grab what you can. Window seat? Best of luck, babe. Hope you're on a diet.

Bathrooms? Don't ask. It's a short flight. Hold it.

There's not enough time to show a full movie. (On the St. Louis–Cincinnati run, there's not even enough time to put up the screen.) So there's a choice of the titles and credits of a real movie, or the new, unbelievably brief Seven-Minute Evelyn Wood/CNN Headline News Half Hour.

Before you know it, you're there.

Then it's the most fun of all: baggage claim. Coast to coast in sixty-eight minutes, and it still takes four hours to get your bags.

Winging It

Welcome to USAir, where "everything we do begins with you."

Except maybe landings. Which begin with Jane.

Jane Zweber is the off-duty flight attendant who sat in the captain's seat while USAir Flight 528 from Tampa was landing in Philadelphia. (How'd she get a great seat like that? Oh, so this is what they mean by airline deregulation.)

And where was the captain?

A good question. According to USAir, Capt. Jon Swartzentruber was sitting in the jump seat at the rear of the cockpit. I guess he drew the line at pushing the drink cart up and down the aisle. It's so demeaning having to say, "Please pay with one-dollar bills. We're short on change."

Interestingly, not one of the 145 passengers was made aware of this game of musical chairs. Capt. Swartzentruber didn't come on the intercom and announce in those dulcet tones pilots have: "Ladies and gentlemen, this is your captain speaking. We're having a little fun up here. I'm letting a stewardess sit in my seat while I put on an evening gown and prance around like a goat. We'll be landing in Philadelphia within the minute, and don't you worry. Say, how about those honey cashews?"

Now I don't think I have to point out that landing is one of the three most dangerous portions of a flight—the others being (1) taking off and (2) being in the air. What makes landing so dangerous is that a plane traveling at about 650 miles an hour is falling out of the sky and attempting to sit on a patch of concrete a little bit wider than a toaster oven.

I don't know about you, but I don't feel secure about that under the best of circumstances—and even if the copilot is at the stick, I certainly don't want someone who's spent most of her in-flight hours collecting barf bags sitting in the captain's seat, while the captain is in the back anticipating all the laughs he's gonna get telling the boys at the Moose Lodge about this one.

Are you kidding me?

This is like being on the operating table having delicate bypass surgery, and you hear the chief surgeon tell a nurse, "Hey, honey, c'mere and close this guy up for me. It's a snap. Last week Molly from payroll did three nose jobs."

Now we know why the Titanic hit the iceberg. The captain was playing Hide the Grey Poupon with a chambermaid.

USAir (catchy new slogan: "Watch Tiffany Land This Bad Boy!") fired the pilot, the copilot, and the flight attendant, sent every passenger a letter of apology . . . and enclosed a free upgrade to the cockpit for you and Sharon Stone.

I can't believe this actually happened. What were they doing over there, running a game show? "Hi, welcome aboard. I'm Scott, your first officer, and in a moment I'll stick my hand into this drum containing all your names, and I'll pick out our lucky passenger who'll come on up here and *fly this plane!*"

Did you ever see *Airport 1975*?

At the end, the stewardess, Karen Black, was flying the plane. I can still see her crazy cross-eyed grin. It's a nightmare. Doesn't anybody at USAir rent movies?

Until a few years ago they used to let children visit the cockpit during a flight. Now I know why they stopped. The airlines didn't want kids to see that the cockpit was a karaoke lounge. (Speaking of airport movies, remember the hilarious *Airplane!* where Peter Graves played Capt. Oveur? And when young Joey came into the cockpit, the captain asked him: "You ever been in a cockpit before, Joey? You ever seen a grown man naked? Ever hang around the gymnasium? Do you like movies about gladiators? You ever been in a Turkish prison?" I loved that movie. I bring it up because I didn't know it was part of the USAir training film library.)

What is going on in the airline industry today?

First Clinton gets his hair cut on the tarmac at LAX, and stacks up planes from here to eternity. (How many frequent-flier miles do you need to get a *haircut* on a plane? And how many would Hillary need for a leg wax?) Then Delta and American announced they were laying off pilots. Delta and American have seen USAir prove you don't need that many pilots to actually fly the planes—you can use baggage handlers in a pinch.

Just the other day Virgin Atlantic Airways announced it plans to offer its passengers the chance to play video poker, slots, and roulette in flight. Now, maybe it's just a matter of semantics, but I'm not comfortable with the concept of gambling at 35,000 feet. I'm not sure I want to fly an airline that can use a slogan like: "Fly With Us. Maybe You'll Get Lucky." I thought when airlines got slots at the better airports they were talking about routings.

Are the pilots going to have video poker in the cockpit? And are the flight attendants going to ply the pilots with free drinks, like in a real casino? That's all we need, right? We can go USAir, where anybody can fly the plane, or go Virgin Air, where the captain doesn't bother to check velocity because he's already three sheets to the wind.

I don't want to depend on my pilot pulling to an inside

straight as we come into LaGuardia. What happens if he winds up with a pair of fours—are we diverted to Hartford?

I can't see how it's a confidence builder to walk past the cockpit on your way to the lavatory and hear your pilot pleading, "C'mon, seven, baby needs a new pair of shoes."

CARPOOLING TO
EXOTICA

✳

Nudes on Ice

Sure, we can quibble about what's tastefully done here. You might think the Mirage, with its outdoor volcano that blows piña colada–perfumed natural-gas flames into the night sky every fifteen minutes (except during high wind conditions for fear they'll singe several hundred potential customers who stand and gape), is excessive. Or you might think the Excalibur, a forbidding architectural concept that looks like Disneyland leverage-brokered by Howard Johnson's, with its gigantic red, teal, and gold medieval spires and knights jousting on real horses in the dirt-floor showroom, is excessive. Or you might think the Flamingo Hilton, with its façade of about 72,000 neon pink flamingos, each twelve feet high, blinking in syncopation like some sort of thermonuclear chorus line, is excessive. You might even think that Caesars Palace, with its grotesquely inappropriate but anatomically accurate Roman statuary and its helpful staff's lobby directions—like "Go straight to the naked Nubian slave barge, then take a left"—is excessive. As I said, we can quibble.

But surely we can agree on the quintessential Las Vegas revue, by which I mean, of course, the long-running *Nudes on Ice*, which combines the two critical elements of a Las Vegas revue: a room with chairs, and nudes. In a pinch, you can make do without the chairs.

Mapplethorpe? Bad.

2 Live Crew? Bad.

Nudes on Ice? Kowabunga! ("Barbara and I go every time we're in town.")

Nudes on Ice—okay, they're not fully nude, just topless; Vegas has standards, you know—is performed twice nightly at the downtown Union Plaza hotel and casino (downtown Vegas being somewhat less refined than the Strip, which itself is to refined what two tin cans and a string is to C&P) in a red-carpeted, red-curtained, red-tableclothed showroom that seems to be somebody's idea of a great party in 1880.

(Before I elaborate on *Nudes on Ice*, let me relate a personal story. I arrived there in the evening, tired from the travel. And like most people on an East Coast body clock, I awoke quite early the next morning and flipped on the TV to the predawn news. Though groggy, imagine how quickly I snapped to upon hearing the newscaster giggling that "an underground nuclear explosion of more than one hundred kilotons"—which sure sounded like it could pop me out of a toaster—"will be detonated around nine A.M., so if you're on a high floor, you might want to hold on to something solid." I stared at my room key: 2207, plenty high enough, considering a hotel maintenance worker informed me that the tallest building in the whole state of Nevada was 30 stories. Welcome to Las Vegas. Can I get you anything—coffee, tea, space in a fallout shelter? Needless to say, at nine A.M. I was on the ground floor.)

Okay, to *Nudes on Ice*.

So named, as executive producer Paul Szigety recalls, because "we were thinking about what to call the show, and one of the owners said, 'We got nudes and we got ice, let's go with *Nudes on Ice*.'" And you wondered where the next flash of creative genius would come from.

It opens with ten female skaters, four of them bare-bosomed; believe me, in this cold you can tell which four. But if you needed a hint, the bare-bosomed ones were the ones standing on platform steps at the back of the stage. Oh sure, they're wearing skates, and once in a while they actually go on the ice so they can glide to the platform steps at the front side of the stage, but skating is not why they were hired. "Skaters are easy to find, nudes aren't," said Szigety, who confessed he's happy "just as long as the nudes don't fall down."

Two lead skaters are bare-bosomed as well, particularly "the sexsational" Kelly Hagen, who does stylish minor jumps on the small rink, but not too many spins, since turning her back to the audience would diminish the marquee appeal. Hagen used to be an aerialist at Circus Circus, but grew tired of hand burns and became a skater. How did Szigety persuade her to skate topless?

"Money," he explained.

This isn't a complicated town.

Not that breasts are the entire show. There's a weak comedian and two terrific novelties: a kid juggler and a wild, randy gaucho act. But now that Ed Sullivan's dead, where do you go with those routines? You'll notice they didn't name the show *A Comedian, a Juggler, Two Gauchos, and Some Skaters, All Clothed. Nudes on Ice* knows where its bread's buttered.

So you get nudes on ice in a Ziegfeld number, and nudes on ice in a Russian Palace number, and nudes on ice in a Brazilian Carnival number—wearing costumes quite similar to the Russian ones except the nudes are wearing fruit baskets on their heads—and nudes in a *Chorus Line* finale, this time with headdresses that look like the Chrysler Building. I could tell you that after awhile you don't notice the nudes, but who's kidding whom?

Nudes on Ice has been running for two and a half years; Szigety says 500,000 people have seen it. It's hard to say how many nude skaters got their big break through this show, but you wouldn't believe some of the stuff they run on cable these days. It occurred to me that *Nudes on Ice* might really go over the top if a big-name skater like Dorothy Hamill agreed to star, but Szigety shook his head unconvinced. "It all depends," he said, shrugging his shoulders. "How big are her boobs?"

This Was Just
Inviting Trouble

Several years ago I got a phone call from the White House inviting me to a black-tie state dinner for President Roh of South Korea. Of course a real journalist would have turned it down flat. A real journalist wouldn't want anything to do with these rich, stuffed-shirt, self-important dilettantes who haven't gotten their hands dirty since the trust funds kicked in. And I would have said so, too—except what came out of my mouth was "Seven-thirty? Sure. Do you validate parking?"

Now that I've been to the White House, I can assure the American people that the country's in great shape on the china front. You get a different plate with every course.

The invitation said seven-thirty. Some people, I was sure, would arrive fashionably late. Not me. I'm an on-time guy. In fact, I'd guess I'm probably the only guy ever invited to a state dinner who even *buys* on time.

You drive onto the White House grounds and the Marines valet-park your car. You get a claim check that promises they'll return it, unless war is declared during the cocktail hour, and then it turns into a park-and-lock deal. You walk into the East Entrance, and a Marine announces your name over a loudspeaker. "Mr. Kornheiser." This happens to me all the time, but usually it's followed by "party of four. Your table's ready." You pass by the press, who are safely herded behind ropes—where they belong—and they ask you questions. In my case, it was "Why were *you* invited?" I said it was because Sununu needed a ride home.

Up a flight of stairs, down a marble corridor, and into the East Room for cocktails. What's really cool is that you can walk all over the White House and you don't have to get your hand stamped. A Marine escort (a "handsome hunk" is the politically correct description, according to interoffice memos at the Nation's Newspaper) led us to a group of people and made a few polite introductions. Famous people were scattered about, like Dick Cheney, Jim Baker, and Frank Gifford, but the group I was led to included *another lowly reporter*! I felt like Dorfman in *Animal House* when he shows up to rush the WASPy fraternity and Greg Marmalard steers him over to Achmed, Mfoom, and the rest of the dweebs.

Suddenly, Dan Quayle walked in, and much to his horror, I'm sure, I reached out my hand and introduced myself, and began babbling that I wanted him to give me golf tips for a sports column. Marilyn Quayle came over, and I could tell from the Mona Lisa smile she gave me that she wanted to get to know me better—or have me shot.

The band started playing "Hail to the Chief," and in walked the Bushes and the Rohs. I was no more than five feet from them, and I clutched at the prospect of being first in the receiving line, so I faded back into the crowd. I cut ahead of Indy 500 winner Rick Mears—something I'd never do on the road—and introduced myself, commenting that it was hard to recognize him without his Valvoline suit. Eventually, I found myself just a few steps from meeting the president.

The chief of protocol asked me my name. In retrospect, I should have said "Dr. Morris Fishbein." That way, if the Bushman said, "Nice to see you, Morris," I'd have known for sure he didn't know me from a plate of kung pao chicken. But I said, "Tony Kornheiser," and now I'll never know, because the president said, "Great to see you, Tony," like we were old pals. And I said, "Mr. President, your fly is open." Just kidding. Actually, that morning I'd telephoned novelist Dan Jenkins, Bush's favorite writer, to get something witty to say, and Dan told me this joke about the rabbi, the priest, and the Aer Lingus stewardess, which I couldn't repeat, so I said, "Mr. President, I bring regards from Dan Jenkins." (Watch for that scintillating quote in the next edition of *Bartlett's*.) Bush gave me a big smile and said, "We've got to get Dan and his wife up here for one of these." I thought to myself, get *them* up here? Like, what am I, chopped liver?

Bush passed me along to President Roh, who beamed as I said that I'd spent three wonderful weeks in his country during the 1988 Summer Olympics. (I didn't mention the kimchi aftertaste that haunts me still.) I moved left, to Barbara Bush, who smiled warmly and said something that sounded like "Nice to meet you, Mr. Porthauser." Not a steady reader, I guess. Then, I shook Mrs. Roh's hand, repeated my Olympics comments—you go with a winner, you know?—and I was led out the door and toward the State Dining Room.

There were fifteen tables, ten people apiece. I was at Table 15 on the far outside. Another foot to the left and I'd have been in the Potomac. Dick Cheney and party monster Georgette Mosbacher were the star attractions at my table. I managed to get a few words with Cheney, who said he liked my column— "sometimes." Had I been quicker, I'd have said I liked his wars too, "sometimes." I told Georgette that I recognized her from her photo, which is in the "Personalities" column so often I thought she was an advertiser.

I sat between Richard Solomon, assistant secretary of state for East Asian and Pacific affairs, and the charming Natalie

Kohler, whose family owns Kohler Industries, which I later discovered produces every kitchen and bathroom fixture in Western civilization—and if I'd only known that at the time, I'd have hit her up for a toilet seat. My dinner companions were great—they told me which forks to use and everything. I only made one rookie mistake, dropping the peach bombé and raspberry sauce dessert on my shirt. But it's a rental, so who cares?

Dinner was terrific. Lobster in champagne jelly, grilled veal, free wine. I was a little disappointed we didn't get goodie bags. I pocketed a copy of the menu, a book of matches—they're white, with the words THE PRESIDENT'S HOUSE in gold letters—some mints, and a cocktail napkin. I considered glomming some silverware, but then I remembered the metal detectors downstairs.

During dessert the strolling violins appeared. They played "In-a-Gadda-Da-Vida." Oops, there I go kidding again. We left the dining room and ambled back to the cocktail room for the evening's entertainment: selections from *The Phantom of the Opera*. During the singing I sat next to the ever-gorgeous Frank and Kathie Lee Gifford. I asked Kathie Lee if she'd ever want to sing at the White House. She said, "No, too much pressure." TV stars. What do they know about pressure? Try making the eleven-thirty deadline after a night game, that's pressure.

Then it was mix-and-mingle in the hall. People began drifting down the stairs to get their cars. In the corridor leading out I spotted Jaclyn Smith, who was almost wearing a white dress. The rules of etiquette say that being guests at the same dinner constitutes an introduction, and I was hardly going to pass up this chance. I found that Jaclyn and I have a great deal in common—like we both wear shoes. Though hers probably weren't rented.

"You made a fool of yourself, talking to her," my wife said later.

"How?" I asked.

"You had drool coming down the sides of your mouth. You looked like Lassie."

A Marine delivered my Honda, and I said to him. "The president of Korea, huh? If I'd had more sense, I'd have brought a Hyundai."

So here I am, just plain old Tony Porthauser, in my rented tux, with White House chocolate mints melting in my pocket and a vision of George turning to Barbara in the family quarters and saying, "A friend of *mine*? Honey, I thought he was a friend of *yours*."

Is this a great country, or what?

Having a Gray Old Time

Before I made this trip, folks would come up to me and ask, "Why would you go to Norway in the winter?"

So let's get this straight: I did not go to Norway. I went to *north* Norway. This may not be the end of the earth, but believe me, you can see it from here. The other day the mailman told me I'm the next-to-last person on his route. After me, he delivers to Santa.

Every morning at 8:00, I wake up and look outside, and wonder why it looks like night—then I remember that's because the sun doesn't rise until about 9:15. And it never gets real high in the sky, only about eye level. Then it goes down at 4:20, which I like, because it makes for a good, long cocktail hour.

Actually, it doesn't really matter when the sun rises, or how high it gets, because you can't see it. The sky is always gray, and it's always snowing, so you have to take the sun on faith. I'd never been in a place before where it's so gray you can't distinguish between the earth and the sky. There is absolutely no contrast. It is just total gray. It's like looking into a bowl of glue soup. The snow is gray. The sky is gray. The trees are gray. The ground is gray. If Jessica Tandy had come here, she'd have been invisible.

It is also very cold, and by very cold I mean that you can't just see your breath, you can *write* on it.

Some people might think all this cold and gray is depressing.

In my limited experience this is not so. I have already met two delightfully different kinds of Norwegians:

1. Those who are inebriated;
2. Those who have committed suicide.

(Attention people in the Norwegian embassy, who are furious now: That was just a joke. Not everybody is drunk or committing suicide—some are flogging themselves with tree branches or applying for exit visas.)

As you can imagine—particularly those of you who have seen Edvard Munch's famous, and truly upbeat, Norwegian painting "The Scream"—Norwegians are not a howlingly funny people. Here is a typical Norwegian joke: Arne and Snorri are . getting drunk in a bar, and Arne says, "Oof, am I depressed." And Snorri says, "So am I." And Arne says, "Let's kill ourselves with hammers." Ha-ha-ha.

This has been a very hard winter in Norway—not that I have any idea what a mild winter in Norway is . . . I mean, it's not like when there's a mild winter in Norway, all the hotels in Miami Beach are empty. But there has been a pile of snow here, even by Norwegian standards. You can walk out of your third-floor window and hail a cab.

The continuous snow has even depressed the moose population. Thousands of moose are committing suicide by throwing themselves in front of trains. (That is not actually true. What is actually true is that there is so much snow on the mountainsides that the moose are having to come down to flat land to forage for food, and almost seventy of them have been hit on the railroad track by the direct train between Oslo and Lillehammer. I hear they are thinking of renaming the train "The Bullwinkle Special.")

Oof, all this talk about depression has made me depressed.

I am looking out the window at the total grayness, and it occurs to me that the difference between a live Norwegian and a dead Norwegian is that after the mortician gets done, a dead Norwegian probably has a bit more color.

I am so depressed now, I am beyond Norwegian—I am Swedish.

I will cheer myself up by telling you that the McDonald's here in Lillehammer serves McSalmon, yes! Okay, in Norwegian it's *McLaks*, but that's what it means: McSalmon. They even have a McSalmon Value Meal! I believe it comes with capers and a souvenir cup of white wine.

By the way, for those of you who are wondering why I would come here, let me inform you that I am here to cover the Winter Olympics. I am staying in Vormstuen, a section of media housing named after Stanley Eugene Vormstuen, a famous Norwegian herring fisherman who got drunk and killed himself with a grappling hook during a Norwegian winter.

My room is totally white. It has white walls, a white frame bed with white sheets and a white comforter, a white closet, and a white desk. I call the look "contemporary mental asylum."

I must tell you about the shower. It is part of the floor. What I mean by that is that you do not step into the shower—the shower is *actually part of the floor*. The drain is on the floor, a few feet from the toilet. It's all on the same level. You walk to the shower, then pull the curtain all around you. It's like being in a voting booth, only less private.

There is a large squeegee in the shower. I have not yet figured out if you are supposed to use it to squeegee the floor after the shower or squeegee yourself during it. I now think of myself as the Squeegin' Norwegian.

Mini and the Moocher

Last weekend I took my kids to a hotel in New York. After the clerk gave me the room keys, he attempted to press another key into my hand: the key to the minibar. I backed away like John Bobbitt would from a Cuisinart demonstration.

I live in fear of the minibar.

It is a sick seductress. It is the Glenn Close of hotel furniture.

I know I shouldn't open it. I know the prices are outrageous. I know I don't really need a tiny foil bag of nine or ten imported cashews for fourteen dollars; where could they be imported from for fourteen dollars—Phobos, the larger moon of Mars? And I know the Minibar Police will get me. They'll barge into my room at 7 A.M. the next day, carrying a clipboard, and they'll say "Housekeeping, here to check the minibar," and I'll stand there sheepishly as they pounce on the broken plastic seal of the minibar as though it were a vital clue, like that taped-up lock at the Watergate. Then they'll gleefully check off "one bag cashews, $14" on their manifest.

Only a fool would open the minibar. You can *grow* cashews for less. But sometime in the middle of the night every middle-aged man in a hotel room eventually gets up and goes (a) to the bathroom to pee and (b) to the minibar to desperately inspect its contents, which will inevitably include Belgian chocolate dusted with a whitish powder indicating it's been lying there since 1973, and no wonder, because who'd spend twenty-two dollars for a chocolate bar except possibly some idiot like me. (Some of us are weaker than others. My pal Mike Wilbon, the Monster of the Minibar, raids the minibar WHILE HE'S WAITING FOR ROOM SERVICE TO ARRIVE!) So I refuse the minibar key, and go cold turkey—which, by the way, costs $203.50 in the Marriott minibar.

And it's not just myself I fear for. It's my children.

It's every parent's worst nightmare in a hotel with the kids: You'll take a catnap, and you'll awaken and find your kids glassy-eyed on the floor, surrounded by empty bags of the world's most expensive potato chips and macadamia nuts, and empty minia-tures of Chivas Regal and Bailey's Irish Cream—watching, on Spectra Vision, *Toilet Slaves of Bangkok*. Think of the guilt and shame! You close your eyes for twenty minutes, and your kids are drunk and corrupted. Far worse, you're out about ninety bucks.

The minibar simply has to be the world's worst deal for the consumer; it makes 7-Eleven, where they routinely charge forty dollars for a box of Pampers, look like an outlet mall.

Often, a person will check into a hotel for a rate of $79 a day, and when he checks out the next morning the bill is $600, and he recalls only a box of M&Ms, a can of orange juice, a bottle of Heineken, and three phone calls. (Recently, my friend Gino was in Nova Scotia and made two collect calls to Washington. I emphasize, these were *collect calls*. His hotel bill included a $26 surcharge covering a hotel operator's fee, a Canadian Provincial fiber-optic cable assessment, and something he remembers as "depreciation of the queen's machinery.")

I think you ought to be allowed to sample from the minibar at no cost—maybe one cashew, for example—the way you can

sample the porno movies; you can usually watch up to five minutes of something like *Ravenous Bulgarian Stewardesses* without
getting charged, which is why I always travel with a stopwatch—
though I tell people I'm there to cover a track meet.

Gino is forever trying to figure out how to fool the Minibar
Police.

"Like with potato chips," he said. "What if you carefully slit
open the bag so you can't tell it was opened. And after you eat
the chips you replace them with something light but bulky, like
the free shoe-buffing cloth in the bathroom?"

"That could work," I said. "But with liquor, once you break
the seal on the bottles, they'll catch you."

Gino has given that a lot of thought, too.

"The whole key is the plastic doodad on the door of the
minibar," he says. "If that's not broken, they'll never even open
the minibar to see if you took anything. So what you gotta do is
you bring in an acetylene torch, bust into the minibar through
the *bottom*, and empty it out!

"No, wait!" he said, on a roll. "What you do is, buy your
own miniatures at a liquor store for ninety-nine cents a pop, and
substitute them for the ones you drink! They'll never catch
you," Gino said triumphantly.

This diabolically brilliant criminal mind still has not figured
out the teensy logical flaw in his plan: If you bought your own,
why would you drink *theirs*?

Almost as bad as the minibar key problem is the room key
problem. Actually, your room key is no longer a key so much as
a stupid slip of plastic. So, say you are at the National Conven-
tion of Fat Sportswriters Who Drink Too Much, and it is 2 A.M.
and you are ready to go upstairs to bed, and you pull out this
stupid key, and much to your horror you see that it doesn't have
your room number on it; no key does anymore, for security reasons, so if you lose your key, no one can get into your room. But
for some reason possibly related to six frozen Kahlua Kiliman-

jaros, you have momentarily forgotten your room number. So whaddaya do then, pal?

Me, I go to the front desk, and say I'm a guest in the hotel, and hold up my key helplessly and ask, "Could you please tell me which room this key opens?"

And they look at me like I'm Himmler.

So I show them my wallet with my IDs, and ask for my room number.

And they say, "You might have stolen that wallet too, along with the key. How can you prove you're Tony Kornheiser?"

So I tell the blind-date and dog joke from a column I once wrote.

And they say, "Anyone who reads Kornheiser could tell the joke. If you are Kornheiser, you know sports. Who won the 1978 Rose Bowl?"

And I don't know. And since they wouldn't ask me the starting lineup of the 1962 New York Yankees (Richardson, Kubek, Maris, Mantle, Howard, Berra, Pepitone, Boyer, and Terry), I knew I couldn't win here.

So I say, "Look, it's late. Here's a credit card. Why don't you give me another room for the night? And you can keep the key to the minibar."

The Sun Also Riles

Good fortune had me in South Florida last week when a big snowstorm socked the Northeast. True, Washington escaped. But cities farther north weren't so lucky. According to the TV news shows in Miami:

New York got eight feet of snow. All schools will be closed until June.

Philadelphia got fourteen feet of snow. The Rocky statue is ear-deep in snow. It looks like an Easter Island head.

Boston got twenty-one feet. They've dispatched Saint Bernards to find Norm at Cheers.

Forget Pittsburgh. Everybody's dead.

I am exaggerating. Only north Pittsburgh.

The point is that every time it snows up north, the newscasts in Florida go crazy with glee. They *hemorrhage* glee. They need to contract out for glee removal. They devote at least twenty-five of their thirty minutes to the terrible weather elsewhere. They open with two or three of their 450 daily homicides (South Florida being one of the few places in the country where they ask tourists their blood type at the airports) and then immediately go to a live remote of snow in Milwaukee or Syracuse.

Look at that old lady, freezing her *tuchis* off!

Look at that guy, having to abandon his car on the interstate and sliding like a hockey puck, and—whoa!—getting whacked by an eighteen-wheeler!

Ha-ha-ha-ha.

Now stay tuned for our warm, beautiful Miami weather.

The Germans have a word for this. It's *Gerplutzenheimerzet-zenpfunff* or something. It means "glee at another's misfortune."

This is what Miami does about weather.

They trot out their poodle-haired TV newscasters—and because it's politically advantageous to be Hispanic in Miami, the newscasters all have these bizarrely hyphenated names like Caitlin McTavish-Ruiz, or Annamaria Gallucci-Gonzalez, or Fong Li-Feldstein-Fernandez, and you are supposed to believe that they are Latino even though the only Spanish words they know are *Gloria Estefan*—who tell you how bad it is where you came from and aren't you glad you're here. (They also do this odd thing where they show you a map of greater Miami, with thirty-five different communities, all within eight blocks of each other, and they give you *each temperature:* "At the airport it's eighty-one and fair, in Coral Gables it's eighty-one and fair, on U.S. One in Hallandale it's eighty-two and fair, on the Tamiami Trail it's eighty-one and fair . . ." Okay, we get the point. It's better than Toledo.

Of course in the summer they get defensive about the weather. (Dave Barry once wrote about this defensiveness, saying that the weatherman will admit, "Okay, true, it's a hundred and seven in the shade here—but that's balmy when compared to the six hundred forty degrees on the surface of Mercury.")

South Florida weather forecasters make no mention of the facts that:

1. They are living with cockroaches the size of Herve Ville-chaize.

2. It is so hot there that not only do M&Ms melt in your

hand, but you melt into the seat of your car, and when you get out of the car you sound like a seal passing gas.

3. Everyone in the state who is over eighty—which is to say almost everyone in the state—is lined up at three forty-five for dinner, because the early-bird specials start at four, and who wouldn't want to get minestrone, three-bean salad, a piece of veal parmigiana left over from the 1960 Olympics in Rome, and a portion of lime Jell-O for $3.95? (Every bit of food in Florida is cooked soft in case you left your teeth in the glass at the condo.)

4. You're taking your life in your hands every time you get on the roads because the worst drivers in the world are in Miami, their geezer heads barely poking above the steering wheel, going five miles an hour, with their foot locked on the brake pedal, making a screaming hairpin left turn from the extreme right lane.

5. And every European who rents a car winds up on a barbecue skewer. (As I was checking in for my flight to Washington, no fewer than five people—total strangers—told me I was crazy to go back to the snow. Three of them were killed at the curbside check-in.)

No, none of that matters.

Because at least they don't have snow.

This, believe me, is *Gerplutzenheimerzetzenpfunff.*

So is what we do here in D.C. Let's be honest, this is a city that is so boring, so utterly lacking in pizzazz, that a man such as the pale, vaguely frightening Supreme Court justice David Souter, who may well be a vampire, is considered the Most Eligible Bachelor in town. Washington has no style whatsoever. It has people who think they're making an avant-garde fashion statement by loosening their neckties. And so what do we say about New York, a truly vibrant, diverse, sophisticated city? We say, "At least *our* subways are clean."

A friend of mine used to go to Bethany Beach each summer

with her family, and she remembers how her father delighted in looking just a few miles up the Delaware coast at Rehoboth Beach, under a dark, ominous cloud, and gloating, "They're getting it in Rehoboth." That is the very essence of *Gerplutzenheimerzetzenpfunff:* It's not enough that we have sun. *You* have to have rain.

To Live and Cry in L.A.

You can't live here. The people here are too beautiful, and too *built*. It's a petri dish for the gorgeous. How did they all get here? What is there, some sort of gravitational pull that only works on Hard Bodies?

Is it the designer vegetables? I mean, doesn't anybody ever need to see a dermatologist here? Or do they round up the average-looking people and float them out to sea?

Talk about having an out-of-body experience.

If I don't get out of this body and into a size thirty-four waist by sundown, I'm in Idaho.

When I arrived here for the Super Bowl, Man About Town Chip Muldoon, who moved to L.A. a year ago so he could strike it rich without ever having to hear anyone say a three-syllable word, immediately drove me to Venice Beach so I could feel even worse about myself. Suddenly I was surrounded by golden California tans, which made me aware of how cadaverous my own East Coast dead-of-winter skin looks. I feel so pale. I feel paler than Michael Jackson—although, thankfully, I'm not in danger of melting, like he is.

Venice Beach is a promenade composed entirely of T-shirt shops and tarot card readers—the connection apparently being that after a psychic tells you, "You are going to have a life of leisure," you can dress appropriately for it.

It was at Venice Beach where I saw the great new trend that will sweep the East, and I am talking, of course, about the Incredible Wiggling Hand. It is a battery-powered, all-too-lifelike severed hand, sticking out of a plastic garbage bag, that wriggles across the ground. A great gift for preschoolers. Buy your kid one, and maybe he'll grow up to be Freddy Krueger!

Another trend to look out for is self-puncturing. Those of you who thought it couldn't get any worse than nose rings, guess again. Lip rings! Yes, lip rings. Two and three at a shot, right through the kisser. The lip-ring capital of the world is the Melrose section of L.A., where everybody under twenty-five seems to be auditioning for a part in the David Lynch version of *Beverly Hills 90210*. Why not take care of all your puncturing needs by marching down to the local Hertz, finding the warning sign that says DON'T BACK UP—SEVERE TIRE DAMAGE, and simply rolling your face over it?

I'm not going to say *anything* about the nipple rings.

It's like another planet here.

What kind of pick-up line is "Who's your agent?"

You one-up someone in Washington by delaying their bill in committee. You one-up someone in L.A. by having bigger hair.

In Washington, women have three names. In L.A., only one.

In Washington, people are named after distinguished ancestors. In L.A., after shrubbery.

People begin conversations in Washington by asking you where you went to college. In L.A., they ask you what you put in your salad. (One benefit of all the recent rain is that people now have mushrooms growing from their ceilings, so they live in a self-contained salad environment.)

Traffic here is totally impossible. Everybody drives. Nobody moves. Court TV moves faster than the cars on Wilshire Boulevard.

The moment you get into your car, you have to be prepared to stay there between forty-five minutes and forty-five hours. So the intelligent commuter stocks up on good tapes and good food. This is why as you wait at the freeway entrance ramp you see people selling huge bags of groceries. The entrance ramp has become the new stop-and-shop. The current theory is that most of the freeway drive-by shootings are committed by people who have either eaten rotten kiwi fruit or listened to Kenny Rogers.

People go stir crazy in their cars. Up until this week, you could see them constantly yakking into their cellular phones. Now with the cancer scare—what's next, toxic toilet paper?—they're throwing their cellular phones out the window along with the rotten kiwis and working on their personal grooming. In the past two days, Man About Town Chip Muldoon saw a man blow-drying his hair in the car and a woman clipping her toenails *with her right foot on the steering wheel.*

The recession has left a lot of Angelenos out of work, and you can see them standing on the entrance ramps holding up hand-lettered signs offering to work for food—though it strikes me as bizarre to think that, say, a film producer might be cruising the Ventura Freeway looking for an experienced key grip. The offers are indigenous to L.A.: "Will Do the Back-of-the-Cab Scene From *On the Waterfront* for Food," "Give You Arsenio Hall's Home Telephone Number for Food."

L.A. is full of fine restaurants. But don't try to get a dinner reservation between seven-thirty and nine-thirty, unless you're a close personal friend of Jack Nicholson. If Jesus had wanted to eat the Last Supper at Spago's, he'd have had to wait until ten.

L.A. has two kinds of people: somebodies and nobodies. The somebodies are the ones who say, "Well, I was talking to Al, and Al says . . ." And the nobodies are the ones who interrupt to ask, "Al who?" I am a nobody.

The other night a group of us nobodies finally got a table, and my friend Mitch was talking about corruption in the movie business, when a steel-bellied, drop-dead beauty wearing a dress the size of a cocktail napkin walked by, and Mitch said, and I'm quoting now, ". . . and *first* you have to pay off some, uh, some gruh, gruh, gurooomah." I missed the rest of it, because I, too, had become distracted by this woman, and had placed a forkful of creamed spinach in my ear.

You can't live here.

You simply *cannot* live here.

Pardon My French

Je suis scandalisé.

(I am outraged.)

The French are accusing us of spying on them.

Now let's get this straight. We marched in and liberated them from the clutches of Satan. In return, they gave us, like, eels on toast. And now they are accusing us of *spying* on them?

Hey, listen. We should be free to go over there and help ourselves to whatever we want. Not that there's much to take. Truffles? A fungus snuffled out of the ground by pigs?

Anyway, I don't want to get into gratuitous French-bashing. After all, the French have given the world many important people, including Marie Curie and, um, hang on a minute. There's Marie, definitely. She was one important chemistry babe. And . . . Charles de Gaulle! He is famous for signing the "letters of transit" in *Casablanca*. Isn't it funny how we keep coming back to the Nazis?

But I digress.

So anyway the ingrates, I mean the French, want to boot five Americans out of France on the grounds that we have been stealing their technological secrets. Like what, how to make a car that looks like a toaster? Have you driven a Citroën lately? They've actually put in a new option for a "crumb disposer."

Remember Renault's Le Car, which was constantly in Le Repair Shop?

How good can their technology be? It certainly hasn't helped them win any wars. French military technology, now there's an oxymoron. What's the first thing they teach in French war college, how to say "I surrender" in German?

But I digress.

I will say this for the French: They are not pikers. They just spent $20 million building a fabulous state-of-the art yacht for the America's Cup. The keel fell off. You know what that is like, building a boat and the keel falls off? You know how pathetic that is? That is like building a bridge but accidentally making it out of pasta.

It is so typically French to purse their lips and assume that their stuff is so good that we'd want to steal it. We've already got everything good they make. (It was over for the French the day you could buy a Croissanwich at Burger King.)

Bread. Sauce. Wine. Perfume.

Am I leaving anything out?

Certainly not soap.

Please don't tell me about French culture.

The Singing Nun. I rest my case.

I know their movies were good at one time. But like Brigitte Bardot chaining herself to a flock of sheep, they have grown old and tiresome. Every year at Cannes they enter a film that reeks like Limburger and loses to something with Wesley Snipes. The French haven't made a decent movie in years, and of course they blame us for cheapening the art form, which is preposterous considering that they . . . no, I won't even mention Jerry Lewis.

French movies generally feature a young woman running around in her underpants. Sometimes she's in a forest; some-times in a field of day lilies; sometimes she's a stewardess on the

Concorde. All the adults in the movie are smoking Gauloises in that snotty way where they look as if they're pinching a derriere, and fretting about whether the Beaujolais nouveau tastes impish enough. It's quite existential. It's all mood and look. It's called film noir. The literal translation of film noir is: Get me out of this *theater* before I flambé myself until *mort*.

Their language is so prissy sounding that you could be challenging someone to a street corner fight and it would sound like an Elizabeth Barrett Browning sonnet. What other language would have a wine named Pouilly Fuisse? Try bellying up to a bar in Detroit and ordering three fingers of that.

The French will eat anything that's cooked in butter. You could sauté a Chiclet in butter and slap some béarnaise sauce on it, and half of Paris would line up. And they're big on glands. They love glands. If it once was in a body and squirted out goo, they love it.

"*Oooh, what ees thees?*"

"It's the anal gland of a ferret."

"*C'est magnifique.*"

Possibly I am sounding somewhat embittered. You would be embittered, too, if you stormed the beach at Normandy, armed only with an M-16 and a pack of unfiltered Luckies, and a belly full of churning guts . . .

Tony, you were no closer to Normandy than you are to Cyd Charisse's daughter, Myrna, who lives in Istanbul.

Well, true.

How can you condemn an entire noble nation of people so cavalierly?

I'll tell you how. When I was in high school, we had a French exchange student named Chris. (Which he pronounced *Kweeeees*.) He had a goatee that made him look like Maynard G. Krebs. He wore a beret. He couldn't play a single American sport. He threw like a girl. He never participated in guy talk, wherein we all sat around and lied about all the thousands of girls we were boinking. I always had total contempt for Chris. But when I went to my ten-year high school reunion, I got to chatting with the women and discovered that half of them had slept with Chris, including many of the ones who wouldn't sleep with me.

The Gaul of that guy!

Urgent Correction: In the previous discussion I referred to the French in ways some French persons might find offensive, such as saying that the only good thing to come out of France was Marie Curie. This was so wrong and unfair of me that I am plotzing in my embarrassment. It turns out that Marie wasn't French at all, but Polish. I hereby pledge to do my research better in the future.

Why My Vacation Was a Bust

I hereby declare myself a mosquito-free zone. I simply have no more blood to give. After two weeks with the mosquitoes in Portugal, I have less blood than George F. Will.

It's not that I didn't bring mosquito repellent. I slathered it on like mayonnaise on a BLT. I must have been repellent to everyone and everything *but* the Portuguese mosquitoes. They took one whiff of me and brought their families around, like I was the All You Can Eat buffet at Denny's.

Not that the threat from mosquitoes is the scariest thing in Europe—it doesn't come close to the threat from European drivers, who drive fast, crazy, and absolutely everywhere. Oh sure, America has guys who like to go eighty-five on the highway. But would they do it four abreast downhill through an alley? Let me put it another way: The skipper of the Exxon *Valdez* is a better driver than anybody I saw in Lisbon.

To begin with, most city streets in Portugal are no wider than your thumb. Plus, they have cars parked on both sides. You'd swear you couldn't squeeze a tube of toothpaste through there. And here come three cars, barreling down on you like you're the last gas between here and the Red Sea. The cars, incidentally, are itty-bitty tin cans straight out of *The Flintstones*, and somehow they have managed to cram in six people and enough luggage to open up an American Tourister outlet. The visual effect of this is fascinating. You think you've wandered into a Farmer Gray cartoon.

Anyway, with the cars bearing down, your first instinct is to jump as far back on the sidewalk as you can. Unfortunately, this is a difficult maneuver in many European cities, as the sidewalks are already chock full of parked cars. Maybe I just don't travel enough, but it still comes as a shock to me when I walk along the sidewalk and bang into someone's front bumper. It's just something I never expect—like opening up the refrigerator and finding a live muskrat the size of Macedonia eating from a tub of cottage cheese. I don't know why so many cars are parked on the sidewalks in Europe. Maybe the rooftops don't validate.

Checking into a hotel in Lisbon, we couldn't find a parking space on the street, and the concierge had us pull up onto the sidewalk and park directly in front of the hotel lobby, so nobody could go in or out without stepping around our car.

"How long can we leave it here?" I asked, assuming we had ten minutes max to unload.

"Checkout is noon," he said.

Which was great, because it gave me more time at the topless beaches. This was my first time at a topless beach, and I think I behaved properly—other than that one silly little episode with the flash attachment, which I still think the police overreacted to. I mean, it's not like I used the whole roll on that one woman. I was simply trying to take pictures of the ocean from the cliffs with the brand-new $700 telephoto lens I happened to purchase from a man named Juan I'd just met on the street. Could I help it if from where I was standing she was right in my line of sight?

It is hard for me to be politically correct on this one. I'm asking my sisters to cut me a little slack. I mean, look at it from my perspective. (To do that you might want to borrow the dark glasses I also bought from my new best friend, Juan, who, I might add, seemed to be doing a fabulous impulse-buy business.) Where am I gonna see babes like this? They're young, they're healthy, they're doctoral candidates in physics or chemistry, I'm sure, and did I mention they're not wearing any tops? It's hard not to notice. Let me give you an example of what I mean. I was at the beach with my friends Mike and Susie, and as one particularly endowed woman bounced by, Susie happened to comment, "Did you see what a cute thing she's done with her hair?"

And I said, "She has *hair*?"

It was actually safer for me to be on the beach. When I was on the road looking down at the beach, I wasn't paying any attention to where I was walking, and so was in grave danger of either smacking into a series of parked cars on the sidewalk or wandering into the street and being run down by a tourist bus (the second leading cause of death in Portugal, after mosquito attack). I imagined my obituary starting out, "Newspaper columnist Tony Kornheiser was tragically killed yesterday in the Portuguese seaside resort of Lagos. Kornheiser apparently was preoccupied with something on the beach below and inadvertently wandered into the street in front of a tourist bus. Eyewitnesses said Kornheiser died with a sly grin on his face, though his eyes were shielded by cheap dark glasses, recently purchased. Kornheiser's best friend, Mike David, who was walking with him, said, 'What bus? I didn't see any bus. There was a bus? Hey, where's Tony?' "

I grant you I was out of control. I wish I would have been cool like the European men. They sat there like a topless beach was no big deal, like it happens to them all the time. Which, of course, it does.

I need to get to that place, where topless is no big deal. I need to get beyond my immature reaction. I'm told that after repeated exposure one gets used to topless beaches. I owe that to my sisters. Which is why I have bought a thirty-year time-share in a Portuguese condo from my main man Juan.

The Flush Of Victory

LILLEHAMMER, NORWAY: In my unceasing effort to ferret out the real news, and not simply the news *they* want you to read, I have uncovered the following scandal, courtesy of a local newspaper (my favorite newspaper here is the Oslo daily *Dagbladet*, because I just love saying, "Here's the news, *Dagbladet!*"), Anyway, according to the newspaper, the sewer system of Lillehammer is dangerously close to overflowing because of EXCESSIVE FLUSHING OF CONDOMS IN THE OLYMPIC ATHLETES VILLAGE!

There is a picture of the manager of the Lillehammer sewer system kneeling beside what looks to be a huge trough of FLUSHED CONDOMS, and he's holding out a small stick, and draped over the far end are—yechhhh—two FLUSHED CONDOMS, which, for all we know, may have come from Alberto Tomba's personal supply. I might describe the look on the sewer manager's face as "bemused."

The story said, in part: *"Under OL har nemlig kondomtrafik-ken blitt manage ganger fordoblet . . . tette til kloakken i Ol-byen."* The problem in quoting from a Norwegian newspaper is that the words are all in Norwegian. Norwegian is a language that uses more than its reasonable share of the letters *t* and *k*, and sounds like the chunkk-ka-chunkk of ice cubes dropping into your freezer bin. Norwegian is not a good make-out language. This is why you will never hear anybody referred to as "the Norwegian Johnny Mathis."

Upon translation, the key element of the story seems to be that the Olympic athletes are DOING IT LIKE RABBITS! Usually, the Lillehammer sewer system gets its largest influx of FLUSHED CONDOMS at 1 A.M. But since the Olympics began, the flushing goes on TWENTY-FOUR HOURS A DAY!

This does not in any way lead me to the subject of the next part of this column: *turisthyttene*, which are cabins in the woods reserved for cross-country skiers. Norwegians love cross-country skiing. They sold 100,000 tickets, and had a waiting list of 200,000 names, for the fifty-kilometer cross-country, which is an event where grown men with icicles in their beards disappear into the pine woods and don't come out until July. There aren't even *seats* for these events. Norwegians just stand in the cold and wave their Norwegian flags. Curiously, this is the single greatest danger you face at the Olympics—getting your eyes poked out as you walk through the crowded streets passing millions of Norwegian flags that stick out of backpacks just at eye level.

Anyway, Norwegians love to cross-country ski (Dan Jenkins once said the reason the Norwegians win all the cross-country races is because that's how they go to the 7-Eleven), and the government encourages them by offering them these cabins to bunk in. There are three classes of cabins. The top class is like a hotel. You get three meals and full service staff for about $120 a night—and they validate your parka. Har har. That's a ski joke. The second class offers beds, cutlery, and canned food, and operates on the honor system; there is a box for you to leave your money in. The third-class cabins are spartan; there might be a bed, or simply a floor where you'd place your bedroll and sleep.

These cabins are literally open to everyone—they have no locks on the doors.

The idea of providing shelter for people is a noble idea, but it strikes me that the cabins underscore some of the cultural differences between Norway and America. We might spring for $120 for three meals and a nice bed—if there were some Marriott points involved. But that "honor system" stuff, I don't know. Where I grew up, in New York, not only would people not *leave* money in the box after they finished eating the food and sleeping in the beds, they would steal the money, and the food, *and* the box. The place would be a crack house in fifteen seconds. In fact, if people in New York read this and realize these cabins are just lying here for the picking in Norway, they'll take up skiing. Personally, I'd be at a loss if I had to leave money in the box. I've been here three weeks and I still have no idea about Norwegian money. I'm not good in math, so it does me no good to know that it's 7 kroner to the dollar; I can't make the conversion in my head. If my dinner costs 230 kroner—and for you weenies in the accounting department, it's always at least that—I have no idea what that is in American money, and I don't try to figure it out, because by the time I do, I'll have missed the bus. To me, 230 kroner is simply two pretty burgundy bills with a picture of a woman from the 1800s, and a smaller green bill with a man with a beard. There are also purplish bills with a picture of the man who wrote the Norwegian constitution, and a blue bill with the composer Edvard Grieg. I love foreign money because it's so pretty. I'll bet in the new, hip countries you can get flaming orange bills, or bills that are black and teal, like those cool Charlotte Hornets hats!

If a sandwich costs 43 kroner, I don't bother trying to come up with the 43 myself, I simply pour all my coins into my hands, hold my hands out like I am the village idiot, and let the Norwegians pick through the small, thick gold coins with King Olaf and the bigger, thinner coins with King Harold, and the tiny wafer coins with the shield or the dog. I trust the Norwegians will take the right amount and not cheat me. How can you not trust people who don't put locks on their cabins?

GETTING TOWED FROM LIFE'S LITTLE PARKING SPACE

✳

Born to Raise Heck

So I'm at a dinner party the other night, a casual thing among friends, and the host, the thoroughly suburbanized E. (not his real initial) announces he is buying a truck.

Mouths open.

A what?

A truck, E. says.

Everybody looks at E. He's never seemed to be the truck type. He is wearing a cashmere sweater and velour shoes. And if his eyes were any worse, he'd be a bat. Nobody can imagine E. at a truck stop—except as a hostage.

A truck? Like to haul pipe?

No, E. says. A small truck, a four-wheel-drive truck.

Oh, a *yuppie* truck. A cross between a big Jeep and a Lincoln Town Car. All the big-feet corporate lawyers have them. Whaddya gonna do with it, drive over to Sutton Place Gourmet and hang out with the Range Rovers?

"It's just your age," someone tells E., who's fifty-one (not his real age). "You're having a midlife crisis."

He's having a midlife crisis, someone tells E.'s wife, J. (not her real initial).

J. shrugs.

"Cheaper than a mistress," she says.

Not really, someone says. It only gets three miles to the gallon.

"Well," J. says, "cheaper than a divorce."

How you gonna put it in four-wheel drive, someone asks E., when you can't even go to the self-serve pump without bringing a change of clothes?

What are ya, nuts, someone else says. Whaddya need a four-wheel drive for? You live in Bethesda (not E. and J.'s real town).

"It's a recreation vehicle," E. says.

A recreation vehicle? Who talks like this? And where might we be recreating in our vehicle, where might we journey off-road to traverse the ecological frontier?

"Suppose I want to go hunting and fishing," E. says.

Marty and Karen (their real names—I'm not making fun of them, what do they care?) are laughing hysterically. Since when do you hunt and fish? What are you, Natty Bumppo? You get squeamish holding a can of tuna.

"Who's gonna give you a hunting license with *your* eyesight?" Karen wants to know. "At twenty yards you can't tell the difference between a deer and the Suez Canal. You'll end up shooting cows!"

I try to picture E. driving down Route 270 with a cow strapped across the hood, and a cop stops him and says, "What're you going after next, Deadeye, a Perdue Oven Stuffer?"

Does it really come with a gun rack? somebody asks.

No, J. says. "It's a yuppie truck. It comes with a brie knife."

E. starts ticking off the features: Tinted glass. Power windows. Reclining leather seats. Sunroof. CD system.

What's it called? someone asks.

"It's a Blazer Lake Tahoe," E. says.

A Lake Tahoe? They're naming trucks after resorts now? What's next, a Chevy Club Med?

Why did you do this?

"He wants to go to Vermont and see the leaves turn," J. says.

And he can't take a bus?

There are leaves around the corner. You can walk.

"Haven't you ever wanted to go fly-fishing?" E. asks.

We look at him as if he were a penguin.

You don't know anything about fishing, someone says. You'll go to cast, and you'll hook the back of your neck and bleed to death in the stream.

He'll never get to the stream, someone else says. He has no idea how much power these things have. Talk about going off-road, the first time E. turns on the engine, he'll crash through his garage and into his living room. He'll demolish his center-hall Colonial (not his real house).

Or worse, he'll slip a disk just climbing into the cab.

"This isn't you," Marty tells E. "You're not an outdoors guy. You gotta buy waders to go fishing. Whaddya know about waders? You hear 'wader,' you think you're ordering Chinese."

"The truck will be fun," E. says.

Fun? What fun? The part where you break down on the road, and some Bubbas come over, and say, "Pretty far from Connecticut and K, ain't you, Hoss?"

Haven't you ever seen *Deliverance*?

"We'll go skiing," E. says.

"I don't want to go skiing," J. says.

"Come on. We'll take a vacation and go skiing," E. says. "With a truck like this, we can go anywhere."

"I want to go to the Bahamas," J. says.

He's having a midlife crisis, J. is assured.

You're having a midlife crisis, someone says to E. You'll get a tool belt, and a chain saw, and the next time any of us see you, you'll be living in a treehouse.

"Not a chance," J. says. "He's afraid of heights. Just sitting in the front seat of the truck will be enough to kill him."

That was a couple of weeks ago. E. has since bought the truck. It's maroon (not its real color). He has never carried anything in it, because the bed is exposed, and he's afraid to leave the truck unattended. On the first day he drove it to work at the National Security Council (not his real place of employment), where he advises the president on domestic affairs (not his real job), his ignition key was stolen from the garage.

So now, E. rides the bus to work. He keeps his truck at home, paranoid that whoever stole the key will break into his home, remove his wide-screen TV, his overhead-projector VCR, his rowing and Nautilus equipment, and his Dolby Surround audio system—and haul them away in his spanking-new truck.

The moral of this story is: The older you get, the wiser you get (not my real point).

Shut Up, Barbie

Apparently, Barbie has made a boo-boo. One of the 270 catchy statements the new Teen Talk Barbie is programmed to say is: "Math class is tough!" This has drawn the wrath of the National Council of Teachers of Mathematics, which, when you think about it, sounds like one wild, happenin' assembly of monster party dudes with plastic pocket pencil caddies.

The math teachers' position is, Teen Talk Barbie plays into a stereotype that girls are stupid in math.

Now, I don't want to offend women, many of whom are real babes. And I certainly don't want to hurt the feelings of all the girls out there—one of whom is my daughter—but unfortunately, girls are—how shall I put this sensitively—stupid in math. Everyone who's been through junior high school knows this.

I give you this example. My own personal daughter, who is nine and whom I love dearly, is extremely conscientious about her homework. She will spend a full hour telling me about the books she read that day. However, when I ask her how much is eight times nine, she says: "Dad, please, I'm on the phone."

My feeling is that girls aren't good in math because the cold logic of it has no appeal. Girls are more interested in emotion and sensitivity. They are nurturers.

Let's look at a typical math question: "A bus leaves Pittsburgh at 7 P.M., heading for Cleveland, and traveling 50 miles per hour. If Cleveland is 200 miles away, at what time will the bus arrive?"

I posed this problem to my daughter.

Her answer was: "Are there enough seat belts on the bus, Daddy?"

Girls are bad in math, and boys are bad in English. Boys grow up with no concept of words and their relationships to each other. Let me re-create a typical boys' conversation:

Boy No. 1: Me and Freddy, we were, you know, like, uh, going, uh, with the thing, and, you know, like, what's doing?

Boy No. 2: [grunts].

So when it comes to a test of their language skills, and there are no uhs, likes, and you knows, boys have no recognition of this particular language and can't negotiate simple terrain. They are lost on standardized English tests:

"Good" is to "best" as "warm" is to . . .

Boys write in: "elevator."

What interests me is the notion that Barbie shouldn't be saying, "Math class is tough!"

Help me out here. Why should anybody expect Barbie to say anything but "hunh?"? I mean, what are we talking about? Teen Talk Barbie isn't the only new Barbie this year—there is also Totally Hair Barbie. *Totally Hair Barbie!*

There has been a Surfin' Barbie, a Stewardess Barbie, Beach Blanket Barbie, Barbie Goes to the Beauty Shop. And *now* they're worried about what Barbie says?

What were you expecting, Kierkegaard Barbie?

Barbie is a bimbo.

Always was.

Totally Hair Barbie! (As opposed to Klaus Barbie, the Totally Herr Barbie.)

Look at Barbie's proportions. If you extrapolated her out, and made her, say, five feet five, her measurements would be something like 45-13-40. This is someone who's likely to make conversation about nineteenth-century agrarian reform?

My daughter has many Barbies already, and every birthday and holiday she asks for more Barbies and more Barbie accessories. She and her friends sit and play Barbie for hours. They spend days planning Barbie weddings, Barbie kitchen renovations, Barbie orthodontist appointments. My daughter loves Barbie.

I, on the other hand, loathe Barbie. (I loathe Legos, too, especially in a dark room at three in the morning, with no socks on. But that's a different column.) Every father will understand why I loathe Barbie: Because I walk around the house picking up tiny, stupid pieces of junk from the floor, which I throw out—and which turn out to be Barbie's shoes, or Barbie's purse, or Barbie's contraceptive device. Who knew? (By the way, Barbie's shoes are usually spiked high heels, a great role-modeling device for small girls. Who designs these things, Tina Turner?)

Anyway, throwing these stupid little things out gets me in big trouble with my daughter, who doesn't buy the explanation that I mistook Barbie's black spiked heels for half-eaten raisins, of the kind she and her brother routinely deposit between the cushions on the couch, and she starts throwing a terrible tantrum, which ultimately results in my driving her to the Barbie store ("How nice to see you back so soon, Mr. Kornheiser. Did we inadvertently throw away Barbie's cotillion fan?"), where I am relieved of eighty bucks, and that afternoon I see spread before me on the floor a host of impossibly tiny plastic gizmos that, I am informed, is Barbie Has a Totally Awesome Picnic.

So anyhow, what's the big deal if Barbie thinks math class is tough? Math class *is* tough. Until I was twelve, I couldn't count past ten without taking off my socks.

But if the math teachers insist, let's think about what Barbie *should* say to be relevant in the '90s.

"You know, you really ought to get that looked at."

"Hi, my name is Barbie and I'm a codependent." *("Hi, Bar-bieeee.")*

"Ken, I am leaving you for Courtney."

"The coefficient of X is inversely proportional to the lateral vector of pi."

"Lower middle class is tough."

And of course:

"Hey, where are my genitals?"

With Liberty and Justice for Gall

As a patriotic American who is saddened by the erosion of values in our communities, I am determined to do my small part to make this country great again. And so I have decided to build an enormous gazebo in my backyard, and to get you to pay for it.

Perhaps this requires some explanation.

"America, the Beautiful" is more than just a song that inexplicably describes mountains as "purple." America the Beautiful is a national credo. Being beautiful is as American as apple pie used to be before the Matsamuto Electronic & Hydraulics Corp. engineered a leveraged buyout of Granny Butterworth's Pies, Inc.

Have you *seen* America lately? Have you checked out the strip malls, the burger joints, the endless parade of car dealerships, the UA Solarplex Cinema 1-2-3-4-5-6-7-8-9-10-11-12-14, where the neon marquee is larger than Mount Rushmore?

Well, I, for one, in a patriotic fervor, have decided to fight back. And I am going to start with my own backyard. The gazebo. A terrace made out of shale chipped from a quarry in Saskatoon. Tiny Japanese bonsai trees, the ones that look like broccoli stuck in dirt. Chinese lanterns hanging from the roof like lollipops. A tethered llama I shall name Maximilian. No expense will be spared. Nothing is too good for America—except, possibly, Jerry Lewis.

And America will get the bill for this because I am applying for tax-exempt status, on the grounds that I am doing my small part to beautify America.

If this sounds a trifle nervy to you, consider the case of William I. Koch, the multimillionaire who rounded up $68.5 million to build a yacht and win the America's Cup—a race nobody ever heard of until ESPN was invented.

You financed his yacht.

Is this a great country, or what?

Koch, whose personal fortune is estimated at 650 million dollars, received tax-exempt status for the America Foundation, which solicited funds to build his yacht, on the theory that he was contributing to the advancement of America's amateur sports effort.

I can see how giving money to cure disease is tax-deductible. I can see how giving money to a school is tax-deductible.

But a *yacht*?

What are we doing here, making the world safe for Blistex?

Is the future of yachting a key national concern?

How many of you yacht?

How many of you have ever had this conversation?

"Hey, Angie, whaddya wanna do tonight?"

"I dunno, Marty, what do *you* wanna do?"

"I was thinkin' maybe we could put on our white ducks and go down to the yacht club, order a dry martini or two, and trim the mainsail."

"Cool. Lemme call Consuela and tell her to have Bitterman bring around the roadster."

Yachting is the least populist sport this side of polo. And it's even less utilitarian. At least in polo, if you get hungry, you can eat the horse. How do you become a yacht skipper anyway? What's the test, parallel-park the QE2?

(While we're on the subject, if it's pronounced "yot," how come they spell it "yacht"? Does anybody say it's "hacht" outside?)

For about 125 years the America's Cup was merely a tin pot that collected dust in a corner of the New York Yacht Club. Every few years a bunch of filthy-rich American bankers and brokers in silly hats and blue double-breasted crested blazers with gold buttons put a boat in the water and raced against a bunch of similarly rich and similarly dressed foreigners, and then drank champagne until they fell overboard and had to be rescued by their chauffeurs and driven home. The world at large didn't care who won. Hardly anybody knew there was a race. Have you ever seen a yacht race? It is not like, say, the Kentucky Derby. You can't even tell which *direction* they're going.

Then one year we lost the Cup, and suddenly it was Armageddon.

Along came people like Dennis Conner and Bill Koch, wrapping themselves in the American flag, braying about how our national honor was at stake—and won't you please send money?

Tax-deductible.

For a yacht.

Defenders of the America's Cup argue that winning it makes everybody in America feel good—although I suspect Sears shoppers could survive its loss, considering that for 125 years nobody even knew we had it. They praise technological advancements, such as lightweight sails. And I suppose that's great . . . if the next time we go to war, we use a fleet of catamarans.

No, yachting is not a valuable American resource, worth protecting. But something else is: the chutzpah that allows a man to tax-deduct his yacht. What could be more of an inalienable American right than gall?

Maledictory Address

Dear high school graduates:

I agreed to address you today because I am concerned for the safety of our republic. As Woody Allen once wrote: "Mankind is at a crossroads. One path leads to oblivion, the other to total destruction. I pray we have the courage to choose correctly."

Many journalists give commencement speeches. We work cheap. We are also considered to be people in the know, filled with canny observations about politics. I will keep mine brief. I love Ross Perot. I admire a guy who thinks he can be president because he ran a successful business. That's why when I want a really good meal, I go to a furrier.

Let me tell you what I remember about my high school graduation twenty-six years ago. We had a speaker who told us to look around at our fellow classmates—because we were the Leaders of Tomorrow. Someday we would be Running the Country.

I'm about the same age as most of your parents. So I want you kids to look at your parents. Are any of them running the country? Your father falls asleep at the dinner table with his mouth open. Your mother plans her whole life around Last Call at Neiman Marcus.

Your parents are such dweebs. They walk around the house humming songs by Wayne Fontana and the Mindbenders! They embarrass you at every waking moment. My daughter is almost ten. She hasn't spoken to me in three years except to say, "More gravy." When her friends come over, she says I'm the gardener. Tell the truth, kids, you can't believe how totally uncool your parents are!

Do they look to you like the Leaders of Today?

You won't be the Leaders of Tomorrow either. You won't Run the Country.

The kids from the St. George Country Day School will.

You should have been smarter.

Anyway, who knows if there'll be a country to run. I've seen so many changes in my lifetime. There's no Soviet Union anymore, no East Germany, no Iron Curtain. Thirty years ago, John Kennedy made his famous *"Ich bin ein Berliner"* speech. Now what would he say? *"Ich bin ein Bosnia-Herzegowinian"*?

I know that most of you plan to go to college and become communications majors. Everybody wants his own talk show. Take my advice, learn to drive a bus. Somebody's got to take all these communications majors to the unemployment office.

Four years from now you'll be back living at home. I lived at home for a while when I got out of school. I was working nights, getting home at 3 A.M. I'd have a snack and sleep until noon. My dad kept telling me it wasn't a hotel—I couldn't keep leaving my dishes in the sink, waiting for my mom to clean them. Soon, Dad actually started putting my dirty dishes in the bed while I was sleeping. I moved out. It took me years to get even. My dad is 82 years old. When he comes to visit, I hide his Depends.

I think back to high school, and I can honestly say almost nothing I learned is of any use to me now—unless I get on *Jeop-*

ardy! and the category is "William the Conqueror." Other than that, I have a calculator to do my math, a computer to correct my spelling, and an editor to correct my syntax, whatever may be that.

The best course I ever took was driver's education. In New York State when I was growing up, you couldn't get your driver's license until eighteen, unless you passed a driver's ed course in high school—then you could get it at seventeen. The first time I ever got in the car, my instructor had me drive up a narrow street in a busy commercial area and parallel-park. I did it. And he said, "Okay, Tony, get out and let Susan Pfeffer drive." I opened the door, and a truck sheared it right off! Boom, the door was gone! Most of my hair fell out right then. The next time I got in the driver's ed car, a girl named Chelsea Nunez-Katz (not her real name) was behind the wheel. Beautiful girl, a cheerleader. My high school was building a swimming pool at the time. Chelsea had just done her nails, and she didn't want to chip the polish on the steering wheel, so she gripped it with her knees and, needless to say, drove us right into the excavation. We were knee-deep in pool water. Chelsea is the only person ever in New York State to get her license and her water safety instructor's card on the same day.

I go to all my high school reunions. I think of my high school friends as the best ones I ever made. They're the ones who knew you when you were the most insecure jerk in the universe, when you couldn't get a date, when you couldn't pass a test. You'll go to these reunions, and people will come up to you and give you a big hug and say, "Gee, your face cleared up."

In closing, let me quote Dean Vernon Wormer of Faber College, and what he said to a student named Kent Dorfman: "Son, fat, drunk, and stupid is no way to go through life."

Thank you.

Good luck.

And drive carefully. I'm out there, too.

This is excerpted from Anthony I. Kornheiser's speech to the 1992 graduating class at Bullis School. Kornheiser will make the same speech to your school for the standard fee of $16,500. But you must send a limo.

Oat Bran Bites the Dust

Boy oh boy do I feel good this morning. I'm sitting down to breakfast with a big smile on my face.

No more guilt.

And no more oat bran.

Praise the Harvard researchers, and pass the butter.

I need a good breakfast today. I have some heavy lifting to do. I've got to go through my pantry and gather up the boxes of oat bran cereal we've bought in the last few years: Post Oat Flakes, Kellogg's Oatbake, Quaker Oat Squares, Oat Bran O's, Oat Bran Options, Cracklin' Oat Bran, Common Sense Oat Bran, 3 Minute Oats Plus Oat Bran, Oh's, Nutrific Oatmeal Flakes, Mother's Oat Bran, Wholesome and Hearty Oat Bran.

Yep, gonna gather them all up. And dump them down the toidy.

And then I'm gonna get a machete and go after Wilfred Brimley. Because it's the *right thing to do*, you old goat? Because it's the *right thing to do*?

Read *The New England Journal of Medicine*, oat breath.

I hate that guy.

Can we be honest about the taste of oat bran?

It was like chewing on a carpet.

Okay, toasted carpet.

That differentiates it from the health food craze of the 1970s, wheat germ, which tasted like sawdust. I resisted the temptation to pour wheat germ on everything including the dog. Why would you eat something called wheat *germ*? By the same token, how does anyone put a spoonful of Mueslix in his mouth? What an awful-sounding word, *Mueslix*. Did you ever see it? It looks like fish food. In our house we have Count Chocula. Maybe it'll kill you, but you'll die smiling.

Nobody actually liked oat bran muffins, you know. (Sorry, I take that back. Secretariat liked them.) "It was like eating a Brillo pad," my friend Jim said. They were the biggest, driest muffins I've ever seen. The first time I saw one, I thought it was a bowling ball for a midget.

The study group was fed five oat bran muffins a day along with their usual diets. Five oat bran muffins a day for six weeks! They don't even eat that many on *thirtysomething*.

And so another cure for high cholesterol bites the dust. Truthfully, I hadn't heard about cholesterol until a few years ago. Nobody ever told me bacon and eggs was death. Stupid me, I actually liked eating steak. Of course, as soon as I learned cholesterol was lethal I immediately started eating foods low in cholesterol, like soybeans, polyester blends, and the cardboard cartons from IKEA. I was particularly conscious of using products fortified with high fiber. My car runs on a high-fiber unleaded gas. I don't know the octane, but after we fill up it automatically pulls over at rest stops.

(What really confused me was finding out there was good cholesterol and bad cholesterol. I was hoping I could get both at the same place—the Carnegie Deli. Unfortunately my HMO doesn't cover pastrami overdose.)

It's a whole new world since cholesterol. I went to a dinner party a couple of months ago where the hostess served nothing but whole-grain breads and water.

"What happens after we eat, does the governor pardon us?" I asked.

"This will reduce your cholesterol," she assured me.

"And I'll live longer?"

"At least five years," she smiled.

"Which five? I'd like to do nineteen over a few times, but if you're giving me eighty-one through eighty-six, save the bread and slap some pork chops on the grill."

I guess oat bran will fall off the face of the earth now. I can assure you the bloom is already off the husk. Yesterday morning, within hours of the news that oat bran was no better at reducing cholesterol than snake meat, my pal John at Bethesda's Chesapeake Bagel Bakery reported that while business was brisk in rye, onion, and plain, there was hardly a dent in his bin of oat bran bagels.

"They're not moving," he said.

"How do they taste?" I asked.

"I put some molasses in to give them flavor. Otherwise, you know, they'd taste like carpet."

On the same day we learned oat bran was a fraud, the *Washington Times*'s wine columnist wrote that heart attacks could be avoided by drinking two to five glasses of wine daily—not exactly hardship therapy. Then, one day later, we're told that if we drink a lot of coffee, our sex life will improve after sixty. (If I drink twice as much, can it start now?) It's like in *Sleeper*, when Woody Allen wakes up two hundred years from now and finds out that chocolate and red meat are actually *good* for you.

Who knew!

"I ate the oat bran to balance the wine that I assumed was killing me," Jim said. "I was hoping to make it to sixty. Now I don't have to eat any oat bran, and if I drink enough coffee, sixty will be the start of my good years. I'm elated.''

It's pretty much good food news in the '90s so far—except for you folks who bought Quaker Oats stock recently.

Oat farmers are hurting, but they can convert to wheat or barley. Think of this as the first shot in the Grain Equality Movement.

Yuppie bakeries might be hurt briefly, but the next muffin trend should be rolling by in thirty seconds.

The problem would seem to be disposing of the massive oat bran storage. (I mean, really, how many bird feeders do we have?) Remember when we had all that surplus cheese? We gave it away on street corners—that's probably what started the cholesterol crisis.

Nobody's going to queue up for oat bran. It'll end up as an export. You're familiar with the TV commercial where the two older kids push a bowl of cereal at the little kid and say, ''Let's see if Mikey likes it.''

Well, let's see if Romania likes it.

Cigarettes and Virile Chicks

Let's hear it for the public-spirited R. J. Reynolds Tobacco Co. Those same geniuses who tried to foist Uptown on black people are at it again with a cigarette brand called Dakota they're aiming at white girls, ages eighteen to twenty, with no education beyond high school and a longing to marry young and have babies.

The phrasemakers for Reynolds publicly call them "virile females." Their studies say VFs are glued to *Roseanne* and nighttime soaps, tag alongside their boyfriends to tractor pulls, and flock together to cruise shopping malls and bars. We can guess what the phrasemakers for Reynolds call them behind closed doors.

R. J. Reynolds should be kidney-punched for marketing this. Like Uptown, Dakota is an unscrupulous attempt to exploit and eventually kill a vulnerable group. In this particular case the sense of outrage is tied to society's protective instinct toward young girls. Symbolically, introducing a cigarette like this borders on molestation. Anyway, we don't really need another brand of cigarette, do we?

Think of the horror parents will face. Bad enough that your daughter comes home smoking. Total nightmare if she comes home smoking Dakotas, the brand of choice of cheap sluts like Kelly Bundy.

"Loretta, is that a pack of Dakotas in your back pocket?"

"What's it to ya?"

"What happened to your neonatology courses? What happened to your dream of attending the University of Chicago and becoming a doctor?"

"That's for losers. I'm gettin' a factory job."

"And I suppose you'll live in a trailer park too?"

"Yeah. Wanna make somethin' of it?"

"Oh honey, I thought you wanted more out of life."

"I do. Someday I want a one-bedroom brick rambler."

I imagine today's virile female sitting at home, spending forty-five minutes a day with hot rollers, a blow dryer, and a curling iron, reading *Soap Opera Digest* and eating bag food. She hopes the trick to cooking is figuring out the gauges on the microwave. She's a little too loud, wears a little too much lip gloss and eye shadow. You've seen her before, Joan Cusack played her in *Working Girl*. She's probably no less honest and no less industrious than everyone else, but when she looks up she sees a lower ceiling. Those marketing geniuses say she likes classic rock 'n' roll (Steppenwolf is my guess). She has a job—not a career—it's something she has to endure until five each day when she gets off and meets her boyfriend, who thinks as short-term as she does. Sha-la la-la-la-la live for today.

I went to high school with girls like this. We called them "hitter chicks," because they liked to hit people, and I adored them for their wild ways. They got in fights, duking it out in the hallways. The guys were astonished at how savagely they fought. Guys never bit or pulled hair or ripped clothing. First thing hitter chicks did in a fight was rip the other girl's blouse off. That's why so many of the boys crowded around.

Their signature look got me crazy: tight dark skirt, black fish-net stockings, and spiked heels. They all dyed their hair either black or blond, and did it up in a rattail bouffant piled high enough to hide a sharp comb inside that they could use as a weapon. They were very big on chewing gum, often grape gum; they'd pop it so loud, it sounded like an air rifle. (The gum you find stuck under chairs and tables? They stuck it there.) They drove Cougars and Camaros with reclining bucket seats and a glove-compartment door that folded down into a tray to hold two large Cokes from McDonald's.

Hitter chicks smoked Marlboros in the red box. ("Marlboro greens only if they were wearing a wedding dress," my friend Henry points out.) Normally they hung out in twos near an outdoor phone booth or a liquor store. On dates, you didn't have to buy a pint to make sure you had a good time, a hitter chick had that covered. Very hetero, very. I used to fantasize about driving to Palisades Park with one for a weekend, knowing if anything went wrong with the car she could fix it.

I rarely took a class with the hitter chicks. (It was hard to major in both Chaucer and stenography.) Once though, in driver's ed, our paths crossed. Three of us in the same car, all sixteen, me, Arthur, and the beautiful Tina. She was quite glamorous. I wanted to go out with her, but she dated much older guys—mostly with criminal records. I believe one of the boys she was pinned to was recently executed.

Other than to practice backing around a church parking lot with my father, I'd never been behind the wheel. Tina had already been driving for four years. She drove to school every day. She owned her own car. I don't know why she was taking driver's ed—she should have been *giving* it. I'd ask, "Tina, how can you drive when you don't have a license? Aren't you afraid of getting in trouble?" She'd French-inhale her cigarette, and laugh and say, "What are they gonna do about it, give me the electric chair?"

They were building a swimming pool at my school then. One day there was an accident. A student drove a car through the barricades and smack into the pool, leaving it hubcap-deep in water at a forty-five-degree angle like a beached freighter. It goes without saying the driver was Tina. She walked away singing "Walking in the Rain."

After all these years, after NOW and ERA and Title IX, isn't it interesting to see the staying power of hitter chicks? After changes upon changes we are more or less the same. I imagine Tina's oldest is about twenty now, just the age the marketing geniuses are aiming at. I hope she doesn't smoke, but if she does, I hope it won't be Dakotas. No second-generation hitter chick should have to buy self-esteem in a cellophane pack.

So Long, Orlon

Orlon, one of the Four Musketeers of sportswear along with Dacron, Ban-Lon, and rayon, will breathe no more. (Or stretch. Or wipe clean with a damp cloth. Or whatever it is that synthetic fibers do.)

The Du Pont Co., which created Orlon forty years ago, said the other day that it will shut down Orlon production "as soon as possible."

Bubba, acrylics are history.

I'll wait while you get a tissue.

(And while some of you clean out your closets.)

Orlon—chemically, it's polyacrylonitryl, and by the way it is not, repeat not, melt-stable (I could explain this to you, as a Du Pont chemist explained it to me, but what's the point? How many of you are going to MIT anyway?)—is found in many things, all of which escape me at the moment.

"You won't particularly miss it," the Du Pont chemist told me.

And that's the truth. We won't miss it. We wouldn't miss Ban-Lon or Dacron or nylon either. They're made-up fabrics. One day they're a shirt, the next day they're a landfill. They look like something else. They feel like something else. They act like something else. And in no case are they as good as that something else.

We won't miss them.

We don't need them.

We ought to celebrate their passing.

Orlon's gone.

Hooray.

Though sexless and dull in that utilitarian way of fabrics that were designed to act like other fabrics—only cheaper—Orlon was distinguished as the only synthetic blend to give its name to a rock 'n' roll group. We remember the Orlons of "Don't Hang Up" and "South Street." But we'll never remember the Dacrons, the Lycras, or Danny and the Naugahydes.

Alas, poor Orlon, we knew you well. Once you defined our existence. Once you were our future. Once you were the only miracle fabric we had. (Well, okay, we had nylon, too, but it's all in the family, isn't it, nylon, pylon, Longylon) And now, what? No one even remembers your washing instructions.

Wash in Woolite.

"No, that was rayon."

Tumble dry.

"No, that was Acrylan."

Do not bleach.

"No, that was the dog."

As a fiber, Orlon was somewhere between Qiana and doubleknit, in the same way that Iowa is somewhere between Pennsylvania and Colorado (Qiana being the scariest of the miracle fabrics, it's so clingy it's almost alive). Orlon was slippery, although not as slippery as Teflon.

"Fabrics and Politics," for $800.

Who was the Orlon president?

"Fabrics and Geography," for $400.

True or false: Burkina Faso used to be Upper Orlon?

Lightning Round: Name four uses of Orlon.

1. To polish Zamfir's pan flute;
2. To coat the tiles on the space shuttle;
3. William Shatner's hair weave;
4. Miss America evening gowns.

Orlon actually was a major component in sweaters in the 1950s, '60s, and '70s. You could recognize Orlon sweaters by how limitlessly they stretched. They stretched so much you'd think that Jackie Gleason sneaked into your closets late at night while you were asleep and tried them on.

"Ever buy anything made of Orlon?" I asked someone.

"Not knowingly," he sneered.

I thought I owned an Orlon golf shirt, but on second thought realized it was Ban-Lon. And I thought I had an Orlon wind-breaker, but maybe it was Dacron. Could I have owned Orlon shoes?

Oops, Corfam.

It's so hard to keep the miracle substances straight. You never know which is which. You use one to fasten your shoes instead of laces, another glues your shoes to the ceiling, another lets you hang upside down in your shoes from the ceiling while firming and toning your abdominal muscles, and still another will convert your shoes into a playroom while-u-wait.

Orlon, of course, has become as much a part of America as sugar in the raw and diet chocolate fudge soda. It's virtually impossible to conceive of a world without Orlon. I can remember as a kid when my mom sang to me about "the train they call the City of New Orlons," chugging out of Arkansas with a new crop of Orlon from the plantations, bound for glory and the Milan fashion shows.

Du Pont hasn't announced what it will do with the remaining supply of Orlon, whether it will be donated to the Synthetic Fibers Museum in Reno—and displayed next to John Travolta's three-piece disco leisure suit—or sealed in a cylinder, and buried at sea. (It can't be put into the ground; it's not biodegradable.)

It's funny how things happen. Just the other day I overheard a conversation that started with these words: "They're not making Orlon the way they used to." And now they're not making it at all.

PG-13, NC-17, *Hike!*

Now that we've started to get used to the new NC-17, let's make sure we understand the old movie-rating system, using *Bambi* as a model.

G: No foul language. No sex. The acknowledgment of violence—Bambi's mother is shot off-screen by a hunter—but no visible bloodshed.

PG: Introduction of foul language, but delivered in a cute manner: Bambi's wise-guy kid brother calls Thumper a "----face." Introduction of mature themes: Early one morning Bambi spots a strange pair of antlers outside his mother's door. Consciousness-raising violence: Hunters are shown dropping rabbits into a stew pot.

PG-13: Escalation of mature themes: Bambi's fraternity brothers sit around discussing sex; one young buck resembling Judd Nelson unwraps a condom and shows it to the others. Emphasis on teenage concerns: The hunters—symbolizing typical adult authority figures—are depicted as mean and slothful.

R: Magnification of mature themes: Bambi is a pimp. His sister dances at a topless bar. Gratuitous violence: Bambi's mother is shot with an AK-47.

X: Total depravity: Bambi agrees to be tied up in a deer-slave love tryst. Thumper is sliced up with a chain saw and fed to wolves. Bambi's mother has graphic sex with Smokey the Bear and is snuffed.

Of course we don't have to worry about X anymore. X went poof.

Voila, NC-17.

And now for the complete score: NC 17, Duke 6.

NC-17 poses a problem for hard-core porn movies, which now advertise as XXX. NC-17 NC-17 NC-17 takes up so much space on the marquee there's hardly any room left for John "Wadd" Holmes. They could advertise as NC-51, but the higher math would confuse their audience.

Why NC-17? A Double-R, or RR, rating was rejected, because it was feared too many people would step up to the ticket window and order roast beef and cheese.

(I'll let you in on the secret: X didn't really go poof. NC-17 is X with an expensive haircut. Under the old rating system studios were afraid to make Xs because there was no profit in them—they couldn't do saturation advertising because many mainstream publications wouldn't take ads for X-rated movies. But with this happy-face NC-17, newspapers will likely take the ads. You didn't realize this was all about money? Shame on you. Soon there'll be lots more moody, dirty movies for adults. Is this a great country, or what?)

What good are ratings? As a parent, I want to know how much cursing, how much sex, and how much violence there will be in a movie so I can make an informed decision whether to allow my children to go. If there's a lot of sex—is Laura San Giacomo in the film?—my children can't go, because I'm going, and it's embarrassing for all of us to be there together. Someone should stay home with my wife.

Wouldn't it help if ratings were more specific? For example, shouldn't we differentiate between external and internal violence? Typically, external violence is a pizza-faced kid who couldn't get a date for the prom putting on a hockey mask and slashing every living thing in Toledo. This is an HEV-163: heavy external violence, at least 163 mutilated body parts. (Do not confuse this with HOV-3, a rush-hour car chase film.) Internal violence is what happens to your duodenum if you watch this film. This gets a V rating, for vomit. *The Cook, the Thief, His Wife & Her Lover* would get a V-4 rating, indicating you would rrrrralph up not only today's meals but also those from the past few days.

In terms of sex, some people may want to distinguish between quantity and quality. (To them I say, Hey, who's got time for quality?) But for most of us, the simple MSH rating—More Sex than at Home—will suffice.

The MR rating warns people this is a Molly Ringwald film.

An S rating warns that Martin Sheen or one of his sons is in the film. Avoid S-3.

The VK rating is an insider's term referring to a film that has changed its content to soften its rating: In the original *Godfather*, it wasn't a horse's head in the bed, it was Victor Kiam, wiggling his waggle. This was considered too horrible, so the scene was rewritten.

NACL contains salty language.

UL-185 is the price of unleaded gas this week.

COD is the Chill Out Dad rating, which signifies that your children believe they can handle a movie that you wouldn't even take your wife to. *Blue Velvet* is a COD.

CG-35 is a movie you need your kid's permission to see.

NA, for No Adults, is a movie with any combination of skateboarding, ninjas, bicycle messengers, and Kiefer Sutherland.

BP-160 is a movie starring Julia Roberts, and is unsuitable for men with high blood pressure.

NO-83 is the temperature forecast in New Orleans.

BW-90 is a Bruce Willis film, requiring proof that your IQ is below 90.

SAT-450 is a Stallone film.

CSNY means the movie has a strong '60s content.

MIT: Strong Nerd Content.

The I rating means you have to come alone.

NG means this film is no good.

NFG is the NC-17 version of this film.

Witless for the Prosecution

If we're lucky, by now Kato Kaelin will be finally and forever off the witness stand, and pretty much out of our lives (unless you have a guest house). But the crucial questions about Kato are left hanging:

1. Where does he go from here?
2. How does he get his hair like that?

Let's take his hair first. It is dyed and streaked and layered and razored, and the ends are perfectly curled. It's a cascade of color and texture. It's as thick as Russian dressing; I suspect Kato uses mayonnaise on it. It must take him three hours a day to get it that way. America's best-loved feature writer, Mr. Henry, calls Kato's coif "Conan the Librarian."

Being un-haired myself (memo to Robt. Shapiro: The Rogaine isn't working for you either, pal), I called my friend Nancy as an expert witness. She stared at Kato's hair, and concluded, "I guess it's cleaned and moussed, as opposed to dirty and stringy. But it's a very thin line."

As to where Kato goes from here, well, he's a very hot property as a house guest. Kato is reportedly living in Charlie Sheen's house now—I guess Judd Nelson's guest room was booked. And there are *thousands* of guest houses to go through in L.A.

County alone before he begins freeloading his way east, so I wouldn't start stocking your refrigerator yet.

I'm assuming his future is either as a continuing character in a soap opera (art imitates life) or as a beach volleyball player. He's certainly got the name for it. Karch Kiraly, Sinjin Smith, Kato Kaelin, right?

I watched Kato on the stand. He was a very accommodating witness. He could perhaps become a professional witness if the house-guest thing falls through. But . . . and let me put this as gently and respectfully as possible: He is a moron. I have leftover lasagna that is better at abstract reasoning.

There was that anxious time when Shapiro asked Kato how many hours he spent in the police station talking with the detectives, and I was afraid Kato would have to take off his shoes to count that high.

Someone in my office speculated that after the trial Kato would write a book. My response was: "Write a book? Kato can't even *read* a book. He can't even use a book to stand on to screw in a lightbulb." (It would take four Katos, by the way. One to hold the bulb, two to brush his hair out of his eyes, and one to administer CPR when he accidentally sticks his finger into the socket.)

Kato's strength is clearly the "yes" or "no" question. When he is required to say anything more expansive, he knits his brow and closes his eyes and appears to be in real pain, as if he's trying to pass a kidney stone. All this thinking must be quite taxing.

Still, I have no doubt that he is telling the truth. I base this on my keen powers of observation, honed over years as a professional journalist, plus the startling fact, discovered by my friend Gino, that *Brian "Kato" Kaelin* is an anagram for *Kaka-Brain Not Lie.*

Has there ever been a more recognizable yet insignficant figure in American history than Kato Kaelin? Even Jessica Hahn had more on the ball.

What does it say about America that this guy has become such a star? His claim to fame is that he is peripherally connected to a double homicide. Other than that he's a house pet, a cockapoo. This is no joke. Kato used to live for free at Nicole's, and O.J. apparently wasn't pleased with the arrangement, so he and Nicole dealt with Kato like community property. In the end, Kato went to live for free with O.J., and Kato the Akita remained with Nicole. I thought Nicole got the better of the deal. The dog was smarter. Kato the dog at least had the sense to alert people that a murder had been committed. Kato the person simply sat up in bed, wondering what might have made a thumping sound roughly consistent with a man strangling a yak.

Here's what we know about Kato: He lives and eats for free. He does nothing. He's thirty-six, and the only thing he's got going is his hair. Don't tell me he's an actor. Have you seen him on the stand? He makes O.J. look like Laurence Olivier. But since he was discovered sleeping in O.J.'s guest house, he has an agent, he has a movie deal, he's hosted cable talk shows, he's been invited to the Radio & Television Correspondents' dinner in Washington, where the secretary of health and human services reportedly asked him for an autograph, and he's living in Charlie Sheen's house! Hello! Hello!

Maybe this reveals my East Coast bias, but as I sat there watching Kato, I kept thinking: Is this what L.A. is really about? (I mean, like, uh, rilly.) Do people actually go to court dressed that casually, in denim work shirts, like they're appearing on *Nick at Nite*? I half expected Kato to have sunglasses perched on his head, and zinc oxide on his nose. Am I the only one flabbergasted to hear testimony about how two men went to a McDonald's drive-thru in a Bentley? In a *Bentley*?

It took just one look at Kato to put my smart friend Martha in a nostalgic reverie. Kato reminded her of all the guys on the surfing team at Marina High in Huntington Beach, California, just an hour or so from the L.A. courtroom where Kato testified.

"Those were the days we sat on the beach with olive oil on the ends of our hair to cure split ends, and lemon juice on the top of our hair to lighten it—the whole vinaigrette . . . Can you imagine showing up with Kato on your arm? He's such a loser."

In this case, so are we all.

Chic Coffee:
Say It Ain't So, Joe

In the '50s, the craze was ice cream. Every weekend the family went out for ice-cream sundaes and banana splits, and then your dad dropped dead at forty-eight, his arteries all plumped up like kielbasa, and so we reconsidered our diets and opted for something less frivolous and more nourishing, and in the '60s, the craze was . . . pizza. Pizza was also horrible for your health, inasmuch as it consisted essentially of bread (for useless bulk) and cheese (for circulatory blockage), tomato paste (for color), yeast (for infections), and those red-and-yellow-flake peppers (for boils and blisters on the roof of the mouth). Eventually, diet gurus began to enter our lives, and in the '70s, the craze was salad bars, which featured "three-bean salad" (garbanzo, fatouli, and ganoozi beans) and other fine ethnic delicacies you would not feed a hamster. No one really liked salad bars, other than the manufacturer of Plexiglas sneeze guards. In the '80s, the fad was enterprises dedicated to the production and sales of fresh chocolate chip cookies, as though chocolate chip cookies were some product of great quality and sophistication in which absolute freshness was required for the true connoisseur, as opposed to some brown glob that tastes perfectly good when it comes in a bag from Keebler.

Now it's coffee.

People actually go *out* for coffee. Like it's a movie. Like it's entertainment.

All across America, every store that goes out of business is replaced by a Starbucks or a Quartermaine's or some other fancy coffee chain featuring this week's special: Peruvian Monkeyfoot Decaf. (Which comes, by the way, with a thick foamy head that would make Budweiser jealous, and takes up two thirds of the cup, so when you pierce the canopy of foam, you realize you've paid four dollars for two sips. Which is why they call it Star-BUCKS.)

All day long there are lines out the door for coffee!

What are they putting in it, heroin? Look, coffee is black and bitter and you drink it when your eyes are red and your tongue feels like it is coated with goat fuzz, and it makes you feel momentarily better. One thing coffee is *not* is entertainment.

Still, nowadays there are only three kinds of people standing on America's streets.

1. Smokers, who are banned from every building, and forced outside, like cattle in a pen;

2. People using ATMs (and the people waiting to kill them);

3. Trendoids who have bought a container of some idiot coffee like espresso macchiato and are congratulating themselves for knowing the difference between *foamed* milk and *steamed* milk.

In the old days, and by old I mean in those days before anyone compared Keanu Reeves to Laurence Olivier, coffee came in the following varieties: black, regular, or light; "wid" or "widdout" sugar.

There were no *flavors*. This was coffee, java, joe. People only cared if their coffee was hot, not where it was grown. People saw Juan Valdez, the Colombian who hand-picked the beans with a donkey, the donkey at whose shuffling side he trudged up and down the coffee fields, picking beans—and all they really cared about was if they washed the beans at customs.

Now there are at least four hundred different coffees. It's like going to Duron.

You say, "I'm looking for something to go with a mostly burgundy Persian rug."

They say, "How about a Ugandan kona hazelnut latte?"

You say, "With foamed milk, not steamed, right?"

They say, "What do we look like, peasants?"

If that isn't pretentious enough, at Starbucks they hand you a pamphlet with mechanical drawings that opens out like the blueprints for the Louvre and assures you of "the world's best beans, roasted to perfection, and prepared at peak freshness by our professional baristas."

Baristas?

Are they, like, women lawyers?

I remember coffeehouses from the old days, when you'd take a date (who always dressed only in black) and listen to some guy who looked like Maynard G. Krebs recite poetry and play the bongos. There were tables and chairs, and you could order stale doughnuts along with the coffee. The coffee they served was Turkish, and it was so thick you could stand up a paint brush in it. After one cup you began to grow a mustache. There was a sense of community. There was commerce. . . . often people selling drugs.

Today's coffeehouse has one window bench where people drink their coffee like parolees and stare out at the street watching buses go by. They sit there burning holes in their intestines at precisely 195 degrees Fahrenheit, as it boasts in the pamphlet. There's no food to eat, just *biscotti*, the fourteenth century's version of melba toast, which tastes like a pumice stone. Hot coffee and formaldehyde are the only two solvents that will soften *biscotti*.

No seats. No food.

So why are they there, spending outrageous sums of money on what is, after all, JUST A CUP OF COFFEE?

Obviously, to show off.

There's a coffee snobbery that rivals wine snobbery. You have your foam versus steam. Your mug versus demi. Your caf versus decaf. Your New Guinea Peaberry versus Ethiopia Yergacheffe. God help you if you ask for Costa Rica Tres Rios, and you can only name dos of the rios.

To help you decide which coffee is right for you, they hand you a bean to chew on. What is *that* all about. That's like asking someone to choose a computer by licking the keyboard. Why would you chew on the *bean*? The whole purpose of grinding the hard, bitter bean and brewing the coffee is to get *rid* of the bean. If coffee beans were for chewing, we'd all be drinking Dentyne.

Anyway, now it's coffee.

But what's next?

Maybe it's outdoor cafés that sell nothing but foam.

Maybe it's the crumbs from on top of the Entenmann's cakes. You go with a plastic bag and a spoon and serve yourself. Crumbs R Us.

Maybe it's the green slime inside the lobster.

My friend Ed says the next big thing is Toast.

Just Toast. Totally Toast. House of Toast.

Seventy-five ways to serve toast. Grilled over mesquite; popped up from an old-fashioned toaster; burned on one side, like your mom used to make it; roasted on a spit; the Colonel's xtra krispy; decaf.

Hey, you know what might go great with toast?

Coffee.

IF YOU'RE GONNA HAVE A SCANDAL, DON'T MAKE IT A *BORING* SCANDAL

✳

The Packwood Papers

Dear Diary:
Routine day. Sponsored pro-choice legislation. Voted to save loopholes for timber industry. Attended surface transportation subcommittee hearing. Copped a feel from that blond page with the fishnet stockings in the mail room.

Dear Diary:
Watched tapes from the Clarence Thomas confirmation hearings. Pubic hair on the Coke can? God, that man is smooth.

Dear Diary:
The newspaper says I "made unwanted sexual advances to more than two dozen female aides, associates and lobbyists." Who said they were unwanted? *I* wanted them. What's this country coming to when a United States senator can't rub up against a young woman in the elevator and stick his tongue down her throat? What are we, in Russia?

Dear Diary:
Did a Q & A this morning at a fund-raiser. Someone asked me, "Senator Packwood, what's the secret of selecting a good

staff?'' So I told that great story about how I needed a legislative assistant: I interviewed three women. One from Harvard. One from Yale. One from Brown. Each one was smart as a whip. I said, ''This is a very difficult choice, but difficult choices are what leadership is all about.'' Then I hired the one with the biggest hooters. Ha-ha-ha. God, that's a funny joke.

Dear Diary:
Read where Bob Hope was sleeping with all the bimbo starlets he took on the USO tours. Remind me to ask William ''Not the Refrigerator'' Perry how I can get on a USO tour.

Dear Diary:
I think I'm making progress with the big redhead with the lilac perfume who lobbies for cable TV. I spotted her in the Dirksen Building, and I asked her, ''What's your sign?'' She said, ''Forty percent off everything on this rack.'' I told her I was a Taurus. She said, ''I'm a Lexus.''

Dear Diary:
Told Ethics Committee I kept a diary.

Dear Diary:
My God, they want to subpoena my diary. What do I do now?

Dear Diary:
Hmmmm: ''I fondly remember the time when John Glenn was dead drunk on the balcony of the'' . . . no, ''I fondly remember the time when Pat Moynihan was down on all fours, buck naked, pretending'' . . . no, ''I recall with great glee when Strom Thurmond first suggested we run Nancy Kassebaum through the Tailhook gauntlet'' . . . no, I've got it, ''Who would have ever believed that Alan Simpson would dress up as a Taiwanese candy striper, and'' . . . yeah, let's see them subpoena this.

Dear Diary:

Today I revealed that my diary was 8,200 pages long, single-spaced! And I've been working on it every day for twenty-five years. Well, one of my staffers calculated that's enough for thirty full-size books. Norman Mailer hasn't written that many words. That's longer than the Great Wall of China. Jeez, it's even longer than Clinton's health care bill. Uh-oh, now I have to wade through it all and get rid of any reference to cheating on my taxes, stuffing bodies in the trunk of my car, and removing the tag on my mattress. That's all I need, some two-bit Democratic senator screaming, "Criminal misconduct!"

Dear Diary:

Hit one out of the park today! Told the Senate I named names in my diary. You should've seen them scramble. Only Teddy Kennedy took it in stride; he got me in the cloakroom and said, "I bet Chris Dodd fifty bucks that my name is in there more than his."

Dear Diary:

Jesse Helms, in the Marble Room, with an air hose.

Dear Diary:

Someone asked me, given the lesson of Watergate, why I kept a diary. Why I put it all in writing. I said my diary included "the hopes, the dreams, the despairs of all of us."

Dear Diary:

Nixon sent me a telegram. Said I was a putz.

Dear Diary:

I assured the Senate this isn't blackmail. "The secrets in that diary are safe with me." They're afraid of leaks. I said: "Come on. Who in this chamber would leak anything?"

Dear Diary:
Maybe I should black out all the references to Barbara Mikulski coming over in that Daisy Mae outfit.

Dear Diary:
What is *Hard Copy*, and what do they mean by "Joey Buttafuoco says we're the only people who believed him"?

Dear Diary:
Why is everybody so upset with me? Doesn't everyone take extensive notes on his friends' sex lives?

Dear Diary:
I read Colin Powell got $6 million for his book. What's the best stuff he's got? Can he put Schwarzkopf in the Tidal Basin wearing only swim fins and a holster with the first three runners-up in the Miss Nude Cherry Blossom pageant? I can do that with two members of the House leadership!

Dear Diary:
Hired a literary agent.

By Land and Air and She

Sometimes you learn a new fact about someone you know, and instantly gain a perspective that explains everything.

Take Pee-wee Herman. You'd watch this alleged adult prancing around in his bow tie and white socks, looking like a badly drawn character from a 1952 Indonesian comic book, and you'd ask yourself: What gives? What is the *deal* with this schlemiel? Can anyone be that much of a loser? Then, illumination comes in the form of a solo performance in a darkened movie theater. Ladies and gentlemen, Misssster Pee-wee Herman! Thank you very much. Let's give him a hand, so to speak.

Or Lassie. You watch Lassie for years, and you love her daring and her intelligence, but there's something about her you can't quite put your finger on. Her courage at times seems almost excessive, almost . . . foolhardy. Also, she is never content to just save Gramps from the mineshaft, she then has to *gloat* about it in this deep, throaty triumphant bark. And she drinks water from a bowl like a slob. Then one day you find out something that puts everything in a new perspective: Lassie was a boy! A male dog. Which would explain why you never saw a fire hydrant on the set.

Anyway, I read an item in the paper last week that did the same thing for me about Hillary Clinton.

No, Hillary is not a boy. (Not to my current knowledge, anyway.) But suddenly, she seems to make much more sense to me.

It was puzzling: Here is the most competent member of the Clinton administration, who is not even technically a member of the Clinton administration, a strikingly handsome woman of astounding talents and with an awesome résumé, and yet she doesn't seem ever to be entirely satisfied with herself. She keeps changing. Her name. Her hairstyle. Her clothes designers. Her entire image! Remember the campaign? One week, she says she isn't some kind of stay-at-home wifey who stands by her man and bakes cookies. And the next week, she is *literally baking cookies* and handing them out to the press.

What gives, Hillary?

Then, last week, I was stunned to learn that in 1975 Hillary tried to enlist in the Marines. (Possibly she was looking for a few good men, as she was about to marry a man who was looking for a few good women.)

My first reaction was that it sounded like something that arose out of a drunken bar bet. You know, like when guys dare each other to do something stupid—say, take off their trousers, pull their underpants over their head and whistle the theme to *Gilligan's Island*—except this must have been a group of female lawyers. Imagine it. A bar scene. Hillary Rodham Clinton-to-be says, "Yeah, well, if you're so smart, I dare you to argue the pro-life position, that the state has the right to force women to carry unwanted pregnancies to term." And Camille O'Rourke-Lefkowitz responds, "Oh, yeah? Well, I dare you to shave your legs and join the Marines."

Hillary in the Marines? Hmmmmm.

Hillary reports that the recruiter looked at her, in her thick glasses, with her burgeoning crow's feet, and said, "You're too

old, you can't see, and you're a woman"—proving almost anybody can pass a simple multiple-choice exam.

The recruiter also allegedly said, "Maybe the dogs would
take you," apparently referring to the army, where soldiers are
called dogfaces. But Hillary was new to Arkansas then, and may
have misunderstood his dialect. He might have said, "Maybe the
frogs would take you," implying Hillary should try the French
Foreign Legion; or "Maybe the Hogs will take you," a reference
to the University of Arkansas Razorbacks; or maybe instead of
"the dogs would take you" he was saying "the dorks would take
you," a reference to a possible career in the life insurance industry. Or he might have simply said, "You make my knees knock,"
and Hillary has chosen to repress that memory.

*Note to copy desk: Have somebody call the White House and
ascertain just how inebriated Hillary was at the time. When men
enlist in the Marines, they're usually so drunk they attempt to sign
the enlistment form with their tongues. Oh, and leave room for an
insert when the White House assures us that Bill tried to enlist in the
Marines also, and was turned down during the physical when he
kept taking his pants off during the eyesight exam.*

Anyway, then I got to thinking about it. Why did Hillary
apply to the Marines? How does it jibe with her nearly neurotic
compulsion to remake herself all the time?

When you think about the Marines, you think about what?
The Look.

Marines look a certain way. They are steel-eyed guys wearing big, goofy lace-up boots and absurd camouflage gear that
looks like a garbage man's uniform that has been vomited on by
owls. Their hair looks like it has been cut by scorpions. In the
Marines, every day is a bad hair day. (Oh, you do get a cool
sword.) Here is the thing: As a Marine, you always look the
same. You are supposed to look the same. So you don't have to

worry about your clothes, or your hair, or anything. You're a Marine. You look like a wind-up doll. Any questions?

Anyway, that's my theory. Attempting to deal with her own insecurities, knowing that she faced a lifetime of personal grooming indecision, Hillary made a desperate bid for the kind of enforced structure only the Marines could provide.

They turned her down, and the rest, as they say, is history.

No More Puns on
Whitewater. Oar Else.

They're breathing a sigh of relief in the White House over the most recent Whitewater poll, which found that:

a. 4 percent of Americans believe Bill Clinton did something terrible in Whitewater and should be punished.

b. 2 percent of Americans believe Bill Clinton is being unfairly blamed for what happened in Whitewater, and should be exonerated.

c. 94 percent have no idea what happened in Whitewater, don't care, and mostly just want to know more about this member of the British parliament who was found dead, hanging from a noose, wearing women's underwear, with an orange slice in his mouth.

I am in this last group. I like the Gory Tory Story a lot. I don't understand Whitewater, and don't care. (All I know is that the president ought to sign up Tonya Harding's lawyers—they haven't missed on a motion yet.) The only people who like Whitewater are Washington political geeks, who can only get excited about any scandal if it involves the unauthorized moving of a decimal point, and *Washington Post* headline writers, because it gives them an opportunity to use phrases like BILL'S UP

THE CREEK, or HILLARY SHOOTS THE RAPIDS. This only perpetuates the notion that Whitewater is actually about a log flume ride. It gives it a Mickey Mouse quality—which some would say it richly deserves.

In an attempt to understand Whitewater, I went to a newsman who has handled a major Whitewater story and asked him what it was all about. This is what he said, verbatim: "Bill bought some land in the middle of nowhere and got some loans or something, and there were friends and shady characters all over, and maybe the possibility of a sweetheart deal, and Hillary might have been the lawyer, I think."

This man considers himself one of the nation's leading authorities on Whitewater.

People ask, "Can Clinton survive Whitewater?" Survive it? Can he *explain* it?

Wouldn't that be something—if some two-bit land deal brought Clinton down? Here's a guy who has been so coated with Teflon you could fry an egg on his big behind. He survives dodging the draft. He survives that preposterous story about not inhaling the marijuana. He survives repeated allegations about a sex life that would make Heidi Fleiss blush. He survives the general impression that right before he became president, he was pledge master at Delta House; I mean, if there were a story tomorrow involving Bill Clinton, a vat of lime Jell-O, two orangutans, and the June Taylor Dancers, almost everybody in America would:

a. Believe it, and,

b. Not care.

He survives all that—and *this* might get him?

Apparently the horror in Whitewater isn't that the Clintons were so stupid that they bought land in the middle of nowhere, and lost their pants when even people *in Arkansas* weren't dumb enough to buy it—thus becoming the only people in the 1980s to not become filthy rich while speculating. That should be the appalling thing, because, my God, look at clucks such as Donald Trump who became zillionaires in that decade. No, apparently the horror in all this is that people in the Clinton White House have held *inappropriate briefings* about what happened! The crime is procedure. Not following the regs! This is such a nerdy, bean-counter scandal. It's like charging the Menendez brothers with not having a permit for the shotguns.

Some people (Republicans are people, aren't they? Well, except maybe for Newt Gingrich) are saying this is just like Watergate. That's not so. Yes, both scandals were quite technical and complicated, but that's where the similarity ends. At the center of this is a bunch of goobers who think *barium* is something you do when the patient dies. At the center of Watergate was something exciting: a group of Cubans sneaking around in the dark carrying monkey wrenches and bags of money, led by a maniac who ate rats and toasted his hand over a candle, like a marshmallow. Whitewater is nowhere *near* as cool as Watergate. Honestly, who's cooler, John Dean or Bernard Nussbaum? If you're drafting an all-cool team, the only No. 1 pick in the whole Clinton White House is that spiky-haired kid, Snuffleupagus.

Here's something to think about: This Whitewater land deal started about sixteen years ago. It predates Gennifer Flowers! It's ages ago. In the interim the American public has elected people to Congress who didn't even bother to pay their taxes for years at a time, and has made *America's Funniest Home Videos* a smash hit show. You no longer go to jail for killing your parents or slicing off your husband's wing-ding. And G. Gordon Liddy (his hands apparently healed) has his own radio talk show.

We have a tendency to drag these things out. Somebody in a suit promises full disclosure, and we begin dropping bread crumbs in the forest as we go from special counsel to congressional inquiry to independent prosecutor to blue-ribbon review commission. By the time we're ready to wrap up the whole thing, everybody's either dead or doing infomercials. The Packwood Diaries are far less complicated than Whitewater, and Julia Roberts will be a grandmother before anybody lays a glove on Packwood.

Americans simply don't know how to conduct a scandal.

It comes down to a difference of emphasis and style.

Take underwear. The sophisticated British politician is actually caught dead in someone else's underwear. What style!

Bill Clinton would never let that happen to him. He's too busy taking tax deductions on his . . .

How the Gingrich Stole Christmas

I think I can sum up the most volcanic American election in forty years in three words:

Congressman Sonny Bono.

Yes, we've got you, babe.

What was it exactly that persuaded Californians to elect a man who makes Tony Danza sound like Sir John Gielgud? Congressman Sonny Bono! What happened, Cher missed the filing deadline?

I could slap myself silly for not seeing it earlier; in retrospect, the seeds of Sonny's political career are obvious in his lyrics. The first indication of his designs on public service was evident when he told Cher, "There ain't no hill or mountain we can't climb," a clear reference in Capitol Hill. He staked out his political platform when he told her that their love wouldn't pay the rent, and that their money was all spent before it was earned, indicating a clear displeasure with big government overtaxing citizens to pay for failed social programs. And when he wrote, "Drums keep pounding a rhythm to the brain, la-dee-dah-dee-dee, la-dee-dah-dee-die" . . . well, obviously he is a proponent of the death penalty.

Congressman Sonny Bono was part of a Republican landslide that allows the aptly named Newt Gingrich to get a table at restaurants that would normally feed him from a dish on the floor. The *Post* ran this headline the other day: GINGRICH VOWS COOPERATION. Oh, please. This is like running the headline: DAHMER VOWS VEGETARIANISM. There wasn't an English-speaking person this side of Lichtenstein who believed Newt's claim that he felt "a sense of sadness" learning of Dan Rostenkowski's defeat; Newt would have gleefully stuck Rostenkowski's head in a toaster oven. He is the Zhirinovsky of American politics. Any minute now he'll lean out the window and start pouring hot soup on anyone who was ever in the Peace Corps. The very day he promises to be bipartisan, he calls Bill and Hillary Clinton "counterculture McGovernicks." This is Newt's notion of conciliatory? What would he call them if he were angry, "Julius and Ethel Rosenberg?"

Talk about losers. What's Clinton going to do next, quarterback the Buffalo Bills? Did this guy have the smell of poison, or what? Members of his own party were afraid to stand anywhere near him. When Clinton breezed into town, they all remembered dental appointments. The only Democrat who really couldn't run away from Clinton, his brother-in-law, Hugh Rodham, got so wiped in his Florida Senate race they ought to call him "Mr. Whipple."

Every single Republican ran against Clinton, regardless of how small or local the office: Somebody running for zoning commissioner in Toledo could stand up and scream, "Clinton wears a bra," and assure himself of a landslide. (And isn't it great that Strom Thurmond, at age ninety-two, will take over as chairman of the Senate Armed Services Committee? Thurmond thinks we're still using cannonballs. And Jesse Helms will be in charge of the Senate Foreign Relations Committee? His entire concept of foreign relations is "killing Commies."

(If this all seems a little anti-Republican, I have an excuse.

The press is *supposed* to hate Republicans. It is our *job*. Wasn't it great watching the liberal media trying to cover this fantastic bloodbath as though they were completely objective? Subtle evidence of partisanship crept through, such as the lead headline in Wednesday's *New York Times:* OH, POOP. WE'RE TOAST.)

Clinton's predicament provides a very interesting lesson in the nuances of politics. Here is a man who solved the problem in Haiti, defused a potential crisis in Iraq, brought Israel and Jordan to peace, passed a sweeping crime bill, started reducing the deficit, and presided over an economy that's unarguably in the best shape it's been in years—yet head to head in popularity polls, he loses against every potential candidate, including O. J. Simpson, the late Ayatollah Khomeini, and those guys in the McDonald's ads who sit on lawn chairs in an empty football stadium parking lot and chew with their mouths open. The crack White House political staff (slogan: "Oh yeah?") has been analyzing the phenomenon and has come up with three possible explanations for why so many people hate Bill Clinton:

1. His cottage-cheese thighs;
2. That icky thing he does biting his lip;
3. The SCAN tattoo on his left biceps.

It has been suggested to Clinton that he is so unpopular with the electorate, the only way he can get Democrats elected is by becoming a Republican.

Democrats went down like dominoes. Marjorie Margolies-Mezvinsky was gone in less time than it takes to say "Marjorie Margolies-Mezvinsky." Ann Richards? Gone. Rostenkowski? Gone. Foley? Gone. Cuomo? Gone. Cuomo had been governor of New York for twelve years; it only seemed like thirty. Mario Cuomo had become the oldest Hamlet on Broadway. His administration was characterized by indecision; if he were asked today how it felt to finally be out of the public spotlight, he'd say, "Good and bad." Cuomo spent every day of the last twelve years in agony trying to decide if he should accept God's calling and run for president. Now that he has lost to someone named Pataki, Mario can run for a bus.

Not all Democrats were losers, though. Amid all this change, amid all this movement toward political and social conservatism, it's nice to see there's still room under the tent to eat, drink, and par-tay! Teddy Kennedy and Chuck Robb won—though Robb's victory might be somewhat tainted by the fact that he ran against Pinocchio. What does it say about the Democrats when their biggest stars are Teddy "Has Anybody Seen My Pants?" Kennedy and Chuck Robb-a-Dub-Dub? Who's their next bright light, Pee-wee Herman?

And lastly, how about a big round of applause for our own idiosyncratic Marion Barry, who bucked all the national trends about bashing liberals and cutting spending and getting tough on crime by running on a platform that called for letting prisoners out of jail early *and* giving them money. Yes, just like in Monopoly, you can get out of jail and collect $200. Darned few politicians were courageous enough to run on one of those planks, let alone both.

Kinda makes you wonder what Marion will come up with next time.

Let's see . . . You get out of jail, you get a bankroll—and a gun.

MY BOTTOM-LINE
APPEAL

✸

Just a Fancy Passing

A story caught my eye a while ago about J. R. Rider, a star basketball player at the University of Nevada–Las Vegas (a noted academic powerhouse whose motto is: "Dealer Must Hit on Sixteen and Stick on Seventeen"), who was involved in a grade-changing scandal. An instructor at a junior college—where Rider was taking a summer English course—grew suspicious of the authenticity of Rider's papers when three of them had his first name spelled incorrectly. (I have always thought *J* is one of the more difficult letters.)

But it wasn't the news of a college athlete getting his grade changed so he could maintain his sports eligibility that intrigued me. That happens all the time. Jocks' grades get lifted more often than Cher's butt. No, it was the reference to another course Rider was taking: Prevention & Management of Premenstrual Syndrome, which prompted me to ask:

1. What was a man doing taking that course?
2. What is a university doing *giving* that course?
3. Are you kidding me, or what?

(I take it you wouldn't cram for that final . . . you'd cramp for it.)

Initially, I was outraged at the lamentable state of modern

collegiate education. When I went to school we majored in big things, things of substance, such as history and chemistry and French. I know this is going to sound very provincial, but back then we couldn't major in Batman.

But on reflection, I love the fact that you can go to college now and major in the '60s. I'm thinking I can ace out—especially if the tests are short-answer, because I can name all the members of the Dave Clark Five. What an advantage, having lived through it. What a great break Charlemagne would have had if he took a course in the Life and Times of Charlemagne. It reminds me of a story about a journalist who'd won a fellowship at Stanford, and found herself in a class about the '60s, with an earnest group of students, one of whom actually asked about Malcolm X, "Why did he call himself Malcolm the Tenth?"

It's not that we didn't have gut courses back when I was in college, courses like Introduction to Egyptian Art ("Hi, I'm Art Farouk") and A Theoretical Approach to Mesopotamian Penmanship. College was hard. These courses were like lumbar supports. They were the soft sleeping couch in a room otherwise filled with Danish modern furniture. They were Abbott and Costello at an Ingmar Bergman film festival.

But I was one of those liberal arts snobs who disdained gut courses like Introduction to French Culture: From Fries to Toast. Instead, I took Existentialist Philosophy of Religion, which—don't get me wrong—helped me get a certain kind of babe, but which is of no practical use to me now that I have to remodel the kitchen. I used to laugh at the people who took the most notorious gut course of them all: Basket Weaving. As it turns out the guys who took Basket Weaving twenty years ago are getting $1,000 for fifteen minutes' work now. They make some sort of donkey-shaped bowl out of banana leaves, and all of a sudden they're *artistes*. Arnie Berger, who couldn't find his behind with both hands, let alone name any of the Three Musketeers, has a New York gallery that does nothing but show his cockamamie baskets. I get out of school with a 3.4 overall, and I subscribe to *Better Homes and Gardens*. Berger, a walking staph infection who thought Romulus and Remus were *planets*, is *in Better Homes and Gardens*.

My friend Gino has a friend who is dating a kinesiology major—a fancy term for phys ed. He takes a *bowling course*. He actually gets credit for bowling. Can you believe it? What's the difference between an A and a B, whether you pick up the ten pin on a 2-4-5-10 split? Do you get extra credit if the name on the pocket of your shirt is spelled correctly? It's just as well they didn't offer bowling when Gino went to school. He'd have cut it. He didn't go to any classes. One time he had a girlfriend take a class for him. There were no tests, only a paper. She went to class. She wrote the paper. Gino's only responsibility was to hand it in. How hard is that? M. R. Rider could do that. The day it was due, Gino walked to the lecture hall, stopped the first man he saw, and asked, "Where is Dr. Roussofsky's classical architecture class?" The man promptly replied, "I am Dr. Roussofsky." A one in a million, right? Gino was so ashamed, he didn't even hand in the paper. Got an F so big you could hang one of Berger's baskets on it.

I know people condemn B. R. Rider for having a tutor write his papers. But this is hardly new. I must admit I took a college journalism course for a woman whose shape made me weak. I was working at a New York daily newspaper at the time, and I was hopeful she might find a suitable way to reward my efforts on her academic behalf. I wrote all five papers for the course, including the feature story that was the final exam. The instructor, some broken-down hack who was editing a free weekly rag, gave me—or, rather her—a C–. Here I am writing for 650,000 people a day, over a million on Sunday, and I hooked an elementary journalism course at a college where most students' body temperatures are higher than their boards.

Well, I'm steamed. I'm having revenge fantasies about how I

will barge right into this moron's cubbyhole, look him right in his rheumy eyes and say, "How dare you presume to give me a C– in your lousy little course? *Do you know who I am?*"

Of course, he'd say, "No. Why, no, I don't. Who are you?"

And I'd have to say, "I'm, er, er . . . Marlene Keppelman."

The Oy of Sex

Recently I encountered two big stories concerning sex. One about the sex lives of men. One about the sex lives of cows.

In the first one, men between twenty and forty were surveyed as to how often they have sex, how many sexual partners they've had, and what varieties of sex they've experienced.

In the second one, we learn how a cow gets horny.

Being over forty, I was jazzed about the cows.

It seems that farmers want their cows to get pregnant because after giving birth they produce the most milk. So you need to know when they're in heat. So farmers have attached electronic beeping gizmos to cows' ankles and rumps, and they measure the cows' sexual excitement. (They actually record how often a cow is mounted, and for how long. Unfortunately, there is no way for the female cow to communicate the thought, "Oh, sure, thirty seconds. Do you ever think about my needs?")

Life for men in America would change irrevocably if humans wore these electronic gizmos. We wouldn't get away with anything.

She: ". . . and the defense reaction was to tell the judge I was completely out of bounds for even *mentioning* the defendant's previous arrest, since it was thrown out of court because they had no warrant. Don't you think his attitude was just a trifle insincere and patronizing?"

He: *Beep.*

Which, of course, leads me to the survey of men's sex lives, and it seems that some of us are doing better than others.

Black men, for example, tend to have their first sexual experience two years earlier than white men, and eventually, they have 50 percent more partners. This is why, when I telephone women for dates, I give my name as Jamal Kornheiser.

The average man between twenty and forty years old has had seven sexual partners over his career—forgive the sports term.

Seven.

A sportswriter friend of mine sniffed at seven. "That's a bad year for me," he said.

"Bad year for you," I said. "That's a bad evening for Wilt."

Twenty-eight percent of the men said they'd had sex with just one partner.

"Tell me you've had sex with more than one person," my smart friend Martha said.

"Oh, sure," I said.

"Good," she said with relief.

I said, "That's counting myself, right?"

My favorite finding was about religion. The survey said conservative Protestants—I guess we're talking about Bush and Quayle—reported an average of five sexual partners; other Protestants, seven; Catholics, seven; and people belonging to other religions, or no religion, eight. Which would imply that Jewish men were doing better than Joey Buttafuoco. And who's gonna believe that?

The average twenty- to forty-year-old man is said to have sex once a week. Men over forty were originally included in the survey but were later excluded after too many answered the question "How many times a week do you have sex?" by laughing and saying, "A *week?*"

The keys to understanding the survey are in the analysis of two seemingly unrelated results:

1. Only one man in a hundred said he is gay.

2. Twenty-three percent of all men said they have had sex with at least twenty partners.

These results, when analyzed carefully, have one thing in common. The respondents are—and I want to get the correct scientific terminology for this—lying. There are rugs in a basement in Marrakech that don't lie this bad.

Does one in a hundred sound right to you? Where are you living, in the Biosphere? One in a hundred? If that's true, then they're all already *in* the army.

The Kinsey Report, the bible of sexuality, which was published forty-five years ago, said one in ten men was gay. What, Kinsey misplaced the decimal point?

Now as for twenty or more partners . . .

The truth is that men have sex only one fifth as often as they say, and *want* sex only one tenth as often as they say.

After you deduct some rock stars, some actors, and the Los Angeles Lakers, that still leaves, like, 20 million guys who'd have to be bagging babes left and right. Most of the men I know can't even get a date.

The error in this survey is the respondent. Don't you know the kind of man who willingly signs up for a sex survey? He's a total dork. He lives with his mother . . . or he lived with his mother until she died—maybe a few weeks after she died. He hasn't had a date since 1972; outside of being interviewed for this sex survey, his only human contact is in a supermarket. You gonna *believe* this guy when he tells you he has women draped all over him like tinsel?

Men lie one way.

Women lie another.

When the survey about women comes out, it will say 95 percent of the women in America have had sex with two or fewer partners—the man they are currently with, and Joey Buttafuoco. The other 5 percent have only one thing to say: *Beep.*

Bok Choy? Leaf Me Alone! And That's Fennel!

Somewhere in America would it be possible for me to get a loaf of bread without sun-dried cherries in it? Or walnuts. Or basil. Or cheese. Or olives. Seriously, what bozo with a baker's hat is responsible for putting olives in bread? Would he drop a slice of toast into a martini?

I like bread the old-fashioned way—without the entire table of contents of the *Whole Earth Catalog* inside.

Whatever happened to Wonder Bread building strong bodies twelve ways? How many schoolchildren want peanut butter on tomato basil bread? What school do they go to, Our Lady of Cher?

My friend Mike walked into a deli the other day—excuse me, not a "deli," a "gourmet boulangerie"—and made the mistake of ordering ham on rye. The woman behind the counter glared at him and hissed, "Tourist."

My God, what if he'd ordered ham on *white*! Would they have called security?

Deliver me from all this food pretentiousness. When did food go from sustaining life to interior-decorating it? Have you seen what they've done to chicken lately? And I date "lately" from the time *spaghetti* was officially replaced in the language by *pasta*. You cannot get chicken salad anymore. You can get chicken tarragon, or chicken primavera, or chicken andouille, or chicken in pesto sauce. But if you ask for plain chicken, you will be hooted. They will tell you to come back when the Kmart closes for the evening.

If you want plain chicken, it has to be "free-range" chicken, which is a chicken raised by liberals. These chickens aren't cooped up in cages and pumped up with steroids. Allegedly, free-range chickens are healthier because they feed exclusively off the land. Well, have you *seen* the land lately? No way I'm eating anything that's been grazing on Route 1 near Hyattsville.

And no matter what you order, it comes with baby corn. How did baby corn become the Sinatra of Side Dish? I don't want to eat anything with the word *baby* in front of it. Not baby corn. Not baby carrots. Not baby peas. I don't even want to eat a Baby Ruth.

Man About Town Chip Muldoon is in from L.A., where you cannot order a meal without mangoes or beets—which may explain why Richard "Hello, Dalai" Gere is taken seriously out there. Mangoes you can ignore. But even if you don't eat the beets, the red stuff bleeds into everything else on your plate, and ruins it. It's like throwing a madras shirt into a white-underwear wash.

I hate beets.

The only time I've ever eaten beets as an adult was a few years ago at the world-famous Chez Panisse restaurant in Berkeley. We'd booked the reservation months in advance. Dinner was a flat eighty dollars per person. There was no menu. They serve one standard dinner a night, and the night I went, it had beets. For that money I wasn't passing on anything, so I ate the beets. They tasted like someone had opened a tin can of candied lima beans in the middle of World War I, and here I was, seventy-five years later, licking the lid.

California is the mecca of trendy eating. In California, even the public water fountains spout Evian. (And could somebody please explain to me how so many junk foods, bags of the greasiest, lardiest, straight-into-the-arteries globules, now claim to have "No Fat!" and "No Cholesterol!" How can this be? "Lite Ice Cream . . . with half the butterfat!" Half the butterfat of what, Dom DeLuise?)

Chip Muldoon says the big eating craze out there is a particular pizza, the Sunset Strip, a quintessentially L.A. concoction with pineapples, artichokes, strips of mesquite chicken, sundried tomatoes, porcini mushrooms, and chili peppers.

"That's a pizza?" I said. "It sounds like a Jackson Pollock painting."

I've tried to start eating healthy. I'm part of a weekly organic food plan. (I responded to an ad that I thought said "orgasmic" food. You know, when you get past forty you really should see an eye doctor.)

I pay approximately $399 a week, and I receive a pouch with enough fruits and vegetables to feed a family of one a light snack. But the food is very fresh. The dew is still on it. So are the bugs. An organic farmer doesn't use pesticides.

"Waiter, there's a fly in my soup!"

"Well, sir, you ordered the *organic* cream of tomato."

I was so excited about my first shipment. I felt like I was being made love to by Harry & David. I got the pouch and opened it. There were six items, four of which I recognized: spinach, broccoli, lettuce, and onions.

Bok choy, though, was new to me; I couldn't recall seeing it before—unless it was as a triple-word score in Scrabble. And fennel was a complete mystery. I assumed it was either ornamental shrubbery or organic road kill.

"Good thing you didn't get sorrel," someone told me.

Wow. Sorrel must really be scary.

Lips that touch fennel will never touch mine, so I gave the bok choy and the fennel to my friend Nancy, who quit the food plan when she felt inundated by root vegetables. "I want to be healthy," she said. "But not *that* healthy."

My children were devastated. (They go to a multicultural school; apparently, there was a bok choy and fennel festival last week. Go figure.)

The next day, just out of curiosity, I asked Nancy about fennel.

"It's like celery, but it has kind of a licorice taste. You braise it," she said. Not me. I come to bury fennel, not to braise it.

The Power of Money

Who *wouldn't* have picked 4, 8, 19, 28, 30, and 41?

Weren't they obvious?

The only hard one in the bunch was 28.

They're exactly the numbers I would have played in Powerball, had I thought it made sense to stand in a line for three hours in the broiling heat to buy a ticket, standing ten deep around the 7-Eleven among people who usually wouldn't set foot in a 7-Eleven without an immunologist: painfully thin men with bad beards and hideous skinny legs in jogging shorts, and women with those precise blunt-cut power hairdos and no behinds, wearing linen shorts and expensive Joan and David flats.

So I'm sitting here typing this column, and somebody in Wisconsin who should rot in Hell has a $100 million of my money, and what're they gonna do with it—buy cheese?

Actually, I shouldn't disparage the person in Wisconsin, who, according to the rumor that just now crossed my desk, is an unmarried woman. I just hope the money doesn't ruin her. That can happen, you know. Yeah, a young woman, out on her own with tons of money. Before you know it, some unscrupulous viper will dance her and romance her and bleed her dry just for her money.

What a shame. I wish there was something I could do, because as you know I really respect women in general, and Wisconsin women in particular. Money means nothing to me personally. I spit on money. I don't care about her money. I care about her. I would do anything to protect her identity and her privacy. Nobody should take advantage of her. Nobody should even know who she is. The only way she should have to deal with the public is by making the call herself, by reaching out to talk to someone who isn't interested in money, someone older, someone settled and established, someone who doesn't care at all about money—money, feh! patooie!—someone warm and understanding, someone, you know, losing his hair. 202-334-6000.

Wait. I just heard it might be a man.

A *guy*!

Hmm.

Okay, same deal. We are talking $100 million here.

I asked some people what they would do with $100 million. Most people think small. They think houses and cars and trips to Europe, which still leaves them with $98,674,508. *Then* what do you do? One young woman I spoke to said she would "put my dog in day care, and buy a toaster oven." With $100 million, she could put her dog in day care in Nepal.

People should think bigger, like the redoubtable Captain Airwaves, who said, "At my age, I'd think seriously about a big memorial; real marble, some of the Italian stuff. Don't paint my name on the outside—carve it. I'm even thinking of script."

But even then he's still got $94,235,091 left.

Now, what would *I* do with $100 million?

1. End world hunger;
2. Buy a yacht with bathrooms the size of my boss's lawn;

3. Arrange to send Ed McMahon five hundred letters a week for the rest of his life that begin, in screaming bold type, YOU, ED MCMAHON, MAY HAVE ALREADY WON ONE MILLION DOLLARS, YOU FAT SUCK-UP NO-TALENT GASBAG;

4. Offer to give every poodle in Ohio a buzz cut;

5. Offer Donald Trump $11 million to cha-cha down Broadway wearing only platform shoes, a pink cummerbund, and a jockstrap (now, I know what you are thinking: Donald, of all people, wouldn't do it, because he's already filthy rich. But he knows a good deal when he sees it. He could not possibly resist, and if he did, his decision would bedevil him the rest of his life, which would be almost as good);

6. Buy some small country, like Vanuatu, and declare myself its Lord High Dermatologist. At the U.N. I would bang my shoe on the table and demand kosher hot dogs;

7. Hire mimes and instruct them to follow Sam Donaldson wherever he went;

8. Buy Cal Ripken a base hit, which he can't seem to get otherwise;

9. Hire completely hairless, shockingly obese people to hang around me all the time, making me look, by comparison, like Valentino;

10. Make a movie and then pay people handsomely to see it, so that forevermore the highest-grossing film of all time would be the documentary *Bean Farming in Uruguay (Part II)*;

11. Buy the house next door to Pat Buchanan. Give it to a nice lesbian couple;

12. Build, to the dimensions of the Lincoln Memorial, a gigantic shrine to Allen Funt;

13. Hire a full-time humor clipping service, so it wouldn't come as a surprise to me—as it did this week—that there has been, living and working in Virginia for *years*, unmolested by humor writers, a judge named Michael P. McWeeny;

14. Charter a 747, paint it blue and white, park it at LAX and hire Cristophe to cut my hair for 300,000 hours, thus freezing travel to Los Angeles for thirty-five years, thus killing the movie and TV industries, thus (eventually) eliminating violence in America.

Call Me La Ishmael

I am grateful to my parents for naming me Anthony Irwin Kornheiser because it gives me license to say anything I want about other people's names. What could be more preposterous than *Anthony Kornheiser?* This is like naming someone Moishe O'Hara. Or LaToya Teitelbaum. Or Wan-fu Piscatelli.

I have never heard of another Jewish Tony, other than Tony Curtis, whose real name is Bernie Schwartz.

All ethnic groups have their conventions for naming children. Jews often name their children after Great-Uncle Yitzhak or some other long-departed relative, which ensures that Jews often have anachronistic names that are hopelessly fuddy-duddy. The first girl I ever dated chewed bubble gum like a third-baseman, wore poodle skirts and bobby socks, and was named Bathsheba Berkowitz.

Presbyterians name their male children after their fathers, so they are all named John Porter Babblington III. The girls are all named Catherine, but that doesn't matter because they never use their real names. They are all nicknamed Muffin or Cookie or Jellybean or some other light, edible confection. Bathsheba Berkowitz's college roommate was Mallomar McPartland.

There is also a trend among Presbyterians to name their children after cold, inanimate objects, like Stone, or after manly occupations, like Hunter and Tanner. The perfect WASP name: Mortuary Slab Porter Babblington IV.

Many names are pretty much the same around the world: You've got John, Jean, and Juan. And Joe, José, Josef, and Giuseppe. Or Michael, Michel, and Miguel. Or Yasser . . . uh, I guess you're pretty much out there on your own with Yasser.

One ethnic group that can't seem to get too trendy with names is the Poles, since their alphabet consists of only seven letters—Z, X, I, Y, K, C, and S—and they can only name their kids Sczyski or Skzyzicky. Other groups using the same alphabet we do somehow wind up with names we recognize as ridiculous. At my local 7-Eleven—and I swear this is true—one clerk is named Meshmoo and another is named Saliva.

Italians name their children after saints, like Saint Salvatore "Sal the Septic Tank" Spunkatello.

Some of the most exciting names lately have come from black families, who either name their children after sounds (Shrieka) or for some reason precede their names with the syllable "La." There are LaKeisha, LaPhonso, LaBradford, LaToya, LaTrina, LaDeedah. In the hope that my son would be a good basketball player, I wanted to give him a "LA" name also, so I named him Los Angeles Kornheiser.

Today's most popular yuppie kids names are Alexander, Benjamin, Nicholas, William, Beavis, and Christopher for boys; and Ashley, Amanda, Demi, Leigh, Stephanie, and Tipper for girls. Thankfully, we appear to be out of the hideous *J* phase of the '70s and '80s, when every other child was named Jennifer, Jessica, Jamie, Joshua, Jason, or Justin. My nominee for the Cultural Totem Pole Hall of Fame is actress Jennifer Jason Leigh, who touches all the bases.

Parents ought to be more responsible for what they name their children. The sins of the '60s are haunting us now. I know the hippies meant well when they named their children after their favorite things, like Sunshine, Tranquillity, and Blotter Acid—yes, Blotter Acid Blumenthal, now a senior business-and-marketing major at Dartmouth. Face it, it's wrong to name your baby when you're so stoned you can swear the cover of the Moby Grape album just winked at you. Here is what happens when you do this: I know of a kid born in 1968—this is also true—who as a teenager would introduce himself to people this way: "Hi. My name is Caribou, but you can call me Mike."

A colleague of mine is named Athelia. It is a biblical name. Athelia tells me her name is routinely mispronounced—everything from Althea to Athleria—and her one regret is that she has been so accommodating over the years, answering to every mispronunciation, never correcting anyone. "I have an eighty-year-old aunt who still calls me Azalea."

Names are cyclical. Sometimes the name you least expect turns out to be insanely popular. When my friend Gino and his wife, Arlene, named their daughter in 1981, they thought they were being wildly adventurous, even foolhardy, by choosing the name Molly. *No one* was named Molly. It was as though they had chosen the name Frigidaire or Mel Torme's Greatest Hits. They worried that in later years, little Molly would hate them for their recklessness. Now, little Molly is in seventh grade, where every girl in her class is named Mollie, Molly, or LaMollie, and most of them have a pet cat or hamster named Molly. There is only one girl in the class who *isn't* named Molly. She is named Saliva.

Of course, in sixty years or so, no one will be named Molly anymore and little LaButthead will giggle at Grandma Molly's ridiculous name.

Lard Have Mercy

My boss is very depressed. He just found out that the "low-fat" muffins he has been eating for the past year weren't so low-fat after all. They were advertised as containing two grams of fat and 150 calories. In fact, they have eight grams of fat and 530 calories.

This means that for breakfast you can either eat one of these muffins . . . or a life-size sculpted swan made entirely of processed lard. Same difference.

"I'm very upset," my boss said. "I thought I could eat these muffins and be lean and trim, and live to be a hundred and ten."

"Not a chance," I said. "Almost everyone in the office would have killed you first."

I have seen these "low-fat" muffins. They are generally the size of an ottoman. If you get fatigued eating these muffins, you can *sit* on them, like Little Miss Muffin . . . uh, Muffet, Muffet. Even if they are low-fat, you have to ask yourself: Compared with what? George Wendt's huskier brother, Wally?

I watch supermarket shoppers studying the nutritional analysis on cereal boxes. I see the ones with young children comparing Count Chocula or Lucky Charms with shredded wheat, and putting the shredded wheat in their cart, thinking they've struck nutritional gold. Have they any idea how many tablespoons of sugar it will take to cajole their children into eating shredded wheat? Shredded wheat tastes like something a donkey has slept on.

Take cookies. One box of cookies will say LOW-FAT. Another box will say LOW-CAL. A third box of cookies will say LOW IN CHOLESTEROL. The low-fat box may be high in calories. The low-cholesterol box may be high in fat. It's so confusing.

Question: How do you know which box of cookies to buy?

Answer: What's the difference? They're cookies, you bozo. They're gonna kill you. Buy the ones with the most butter, and hope that before all your arteries ice over you get hit by a bus.

It's like people insisting they can load up on the "no-fat" ice cream they've found in the store. Oh, please. Actually I have seen "no-fat ice cream." It's called water.

Now that I'm working out, I have the appetite of a water buffalo. I am sucking up food like a Hoover. I have actually *gained* weight since I started going to a gym. My trainer tells me it is better to eat a lot of little meals than a few big ones. I ask him what he means by "little meals," and he says, "A couple of rice cakes." I tell him that if I wanted to eat a couple of rice cakes, I'd work out in a gym in Bangkok.

I'm grateful to *The Washington Post* for running a big story blowing the lid off some of these "low-fat" claims. (I'm particularly grateful for a small item that said a roast beef sub contained *less* fat and *fewer* calories than a vegetarian sub: definitive proof that there's a God. Tell the truth, wouldn't you be delighted if every vegetarian got as fat as a barn? Aren't you sick of people pinching their noses and telling you they don't eat red meat, like you're a cannibal for ordering a hamburger?) My favorite part concerned the owner of a restaurant that advertised a "low-fat" dim sum that should have had seven grams of fat, and actually had fifty-four! This is no small mistake; this is like taking off for Cleveland and landing in Kuala Lumpur. The restaurant owner explained, "I don't have that much knowledge about food or nutrition." Thank you for not opening up a hospital.

The article offered some tips on how to "eat out defensively." (Of course my question then becomes: If we're already driving defensively, and now we need to be eating out defensively . . . how should we go through the fast-food drive-thru, in a crouch?) One of the tips was how to recognize fat in foods. "If a dish glistens, it probably was cooked in oil or butter." Or hair spray, I guess. What does this mean? Should we eat only foods that look as if they've been rubbed in dirt?

Advertising That's
Below the Belt

So I'm sitting there, watching the TV, not paying a whole lot of attention, when this thirtyish blonde comes on. She's got the Lauren Bacall look, she's leaning out on what appears to be a New York City terrace overlooking Central Park—it's a very sophisticated setting—and she says, "My mother always told me to look at a man's eyes first." There's a pause. Then, she knits her eyebrows in this hip, dismissive way, and purrs, "But what did she know?"

They go to a voice-over, and it turns out it's an ad for Sansabelt slacks. Men's pants. And I'm thinking, *huh?*

Several days later I'm watching TV. This time a late-twenty-ish, studious woman comes on expressing that same soft, come-hither mood. She's got the Carole King *Tapestry* look, holding a book, an NYU law grad maybe, and she says, "I always lower my eyes when a man passes . . ." Pause. A sly grin. ". . . to see if he's worth following."

Sansabelt.

Sansabelt? The pants Ed McMahon advertised for years. Your basic fat man golfer pants, right? What are those pants doing with these women?

I see another ad: Sitting on the porch of an Outer Banks–

type beach house is a windswept, milk-fed, apple-cheeked blonde, as fresh and clean as a barrel of rainwater. It takes a look like that to get away with saying, "I have always considered a man's lower half his better half."

Sansabelt.

A man's lower half.

I am not unaware that it is common practice for a man to peer at a woman's lower half. A car I see daily in my neighborhood has a bumper sticker pleading to approaching drivers, WATCH MY REAR END—NOT HERS. Size and contour are the subject of Spinal Tap's enthusiastic "Big Bottom," which proclaimed, ". . . talk about mud flaps, my girl's got 'em."

A woman's lower half; this, you'll admit, has been going on.

But gorgeous young women going on TV specifically telling men that they're looking at them, and looking specifically at their behinds, this is new. (At least I assume it's the lower *rear* half they're looking at. Am I mistaken?)

"What do you think this means?" I ask my friend Mike.

"It means you are in deep trouble," he tells me.

I'm over forty years old. I've had a tush all my life. Never once has it occurred to me that anyone is interested in it.

My tush is for grading.

Who knew?

"This matters to women?" I ask my wife.

"To some," she says.

"To you?" I ask.

She grins and turns away. When she reaches the stairs, she turns back and says, "The other day I was picking up Michael at school, and one of the mothers looked at him and said, 'That kid's going to have great buns.' "

"Buns?" I ask.

"Buns," she says.

"Michael's three and a half," I say.

Great buns!

That night I peeked at my own buns in the mirror.

I am in deep trouble.

Jerry McCann is vice president of marketing for Jaymar-Ruby, which produces Sansabelt slacks. He freely acknowledges his pants were floating face down in the water with everyone other than Ed McMahon. "Younger men had zero awareness of our product, zero." So to establish an image with younger men, they brought in younger women. "Young men are concerned with how they look to women. We are saying women look at men and the way they're dressed."

The lower half?

"There is a wink about that whole issue in our advertising," McCann concedes coyly.

The buns?

"I get nervous when people take it to the anatomical extreme," McCann says.

As you know, Sansabelt slacks (which now come—can you believe this?—with belt loops) are not the only product being marketed with sex. Calvin Klein sells perfume with incorrigibly naked, intertwined bodies. Sometimes, when he wants to sell designer underpants, he uses seminaked intertwined bodies. Blue jeans and cars are routinely sold with sex; many TV beer commercials are so sweaty, you have to towel off after thirty seconds.

However, this Sansabelt campaign is different. Not only is it a reverse seduction—what ad agency dared fuse women with lust before?—it's the deliberate slathering of sex in order to reposition a product. These were maximum polyester, middle-aged, convention-man pants. Sansabelt *was* your father's Oldsmobile! It's shivery enough to think of Sansabelt men as having behinds, let alone that any woman would be checking them out.

I peek again at my tush in the mirror.

It's lumpy and as large as a lampshade. I am way beyond buns—these are full loaves of bread. I vow to work diligently on the Stairmaster.

I am in deep trouble.

Second Thoughts on Watches

My grandfather gave me my first watch when I was five. He made quite a ceremony of handing it over. It had been his own watch, and it apparently had great sentimental value. It had a silver expandable band, and its crystal face was faintly yellow with age. I slipped it around my left wrist, and admired it. Then I lowered my arm, and my grandfather's watch, which was much too big for a five-year-old, slid rapidly off my wrist, landed face down on the thick kitchen tiles, and shattered.

"*Que sera, sera,*" I said, that being a big song at the time.

"Get a load of this kid," my grandmother said. "He drops an heirloom, and he thinks he's Rosemary Clooney."

I didn't put on another wristwatch for thirty-five years.

Everybody else wore a watch; if I needed to know what time it was, I asked. If nobody was around, I turned on the radio. If I had no access to a person, or a radio, or one of those big clocks outside a bank, odds were I was probably on vacation, so what would it matter?

"Time," for $200:

Does anybody really know what time it is?

"Time," for $400:

Does anybody really care?

Last year, as a concession to middle age, I started wearing a watch. (What if I have grandchildren? What would I give them, my Left Banke albums?) And as soon as I did, I noticed all the other watches. They're everywhere. You pick up the Sunday paper, you'll see pages and pages of watch ads. Clearly, advertising reflects what people really buy—that's why you don't see pages and pages of ant farms.

The country has gone watch crazy. People own five, six, seven watches, even though they still have only two wrists. Like fancy-schmancy cars, watches have become a way of showing off how well you're doing. Rayful Edmond III wore a $45,000 Rolex. (It's understandable Rayful would be fussy about time, since he'll be doing so much of it.) I wonder what kind of watch Leona "Hard Time" Helmsley wears.

As most of you already know, digital is dead. (It's still big in Waikiki; *Digit Goes Hawaiian*.) If you have digital watches, get rid of them immediately. Do not embarrass your family further. Digital watches mark you as a hopeless boob.

Retro is in. Today's watches strive to evoke a simpler, long-ago time—apparently a time before watches were invented, since so many of these watches employ Roman numerals. (Except some Movados, which have no numbers. You're supposed to guess the time.)

Reconditioned watches are extremely in. Yuppies rummage around their attics looking for any old watch that's been buried in a trunk for at least seventy years, then pay out the wazoo to get it fixed. (Some of these old watches have radium dials, so after a few wearings, your wrist glows in the dark, which solves the problem of buying a night light.) Since this watch was built before batteries, it must be wound every day, leading to an appreciation of the expression: "I don't know whether to spit or wind my watch." The wearer of this reconditioned gem is deliriously proud until some seventy-five-year-old with a Seiko laughs and asks, "Sonny, where on earth did you get a piece of junk like that?"

As a consequence of this nostalgia for simplicity, the multifunction watch of the '70s is passe. It's difficult to buy a big chunk of a watch with nine hundred different dials and gizmos. This is bad news for people who think a watch ought to tell you at what temperature you can fry an egg on Mars, or the latitude and longitude of Madagascar. They can buy an almanac and strap it to their wrists.

Exactly what is the deal with all these half-moons on watches? Why should I care about lunar phases? What do I look like, a guy who's going to cross the Atlantic in a rowboat? This moon stuff escapes me, unless it's part of a plot to introduce a Roseanne Barr "Butt-Face" model.

Years ago all anyone asked of a watch was that it tell time. Then it had to be waterproof, then shatterproof; a common fantasy in the '60s was to smash John Cameron Swayze with a hammer, then throw him over the side of a tuna trawler to see if his infernal Timex was still ticking after they fished him out.

There are so many more things we want in a watch now. I asked a friend what she wanted in a watch. She said, "A date." I told her she'd have to get that on her own.

I want a watch with microwaveability; I want to be able to put it in a microwave, set the dial on high power for two minutes, and when I take it out, I want it to be dinner.

I want a watch with four-wheel drive.

I want a watch that every so often bursts into music by Zamfir, Master of the Pan Flute.

I want a watch where, instead of numbers, it has the faces of all the Eastern European Communist Party chiefs who have resigned in the last thirty-six hours.

I want a watch that cleans my house; it could be the maid's watch, I don't care.

I want a watch that informs me how many bowls of various

cereals I have to eat to equal the nutritional benefit of one bowl of Total. I want the watch to tell me what my cholesterol count is at all times, and to buzz whenever I go near a patch of oat bran. (I don't know about you, but I'm getting mighty sick of Wilford Brimley hectoring me about Quaker Oats. I want a watch that sends deadly gamma rays out at that old goat.)

I want a watch that'll make me attractive to the women in the Michelob Dry commercials.

I want a watch designed so that when your watch beeps while we're at the movies, my watch launches a nuclear missile that takes you out.

Actually, I want my grandfather's watch.

MY LIFE AS A DOG

✳

Party Animals

When my son turned five, I decided to break tradition by not hiring a birthday party professional; the choice came down to two hours on Sunday afternoon or his freshman year at Yale. This was devastating news for the lady at Party Planners, who had counted on us to finance her vacation in France.

This would have been our third straight party with her. When Michael was three, she brought in a pony.

"Why does it cost so much?" I asked.

"It's a Lipizzaner. He's coming from Vienna," she said.

When Michael was four, she booked the cast from *The Heidi Chronicles*. All the kids got depressed and hid under the bed.

This year, we drew the line. She'd been planning a Gatsby theme. Cocktails and cigarettes on Long Island.

"It's a good way to introduce your son to F. Scott Fitzgerald," she insisted.

"But my son can't even spell F.," I said.

So we made him a pirate party. As the kids came in, we gave them each a pirate hat and a pirate eye patch, and sent them straight downstairs to the basement, where they began to scream. An hour later, we served cake. Now all the kids want to live at our house.

The crucial thing to understand is this was a party for boys. With girls, it's different. Girls want structure. They want activities. They want order.

Boys want to scream.

That's it. Dig a pit. Throw them in. Let them scream.

Granted, there's a risk. You throw ten boys in there, maybe only eight come out. But those eight will say they had the best party ever.

Is this just me? I tried my best to raise my children without audible oinks in the nursery. Did I blow it? Did I unconsciously set sexist roles in motion?

When my daughter was three, she began to play with Barbies. I swear this was not my doing. She'd sit for hours on the floor in her room, happily dressing and undressing her Barbies. She never looked at a truck or a gun, though I subscribed to *Off-Road* and *Ammo*. She was six years old before we ever heard the word *gun* in the house.

It was her brother who said it.

It was his third word.

First was *cookie*. Next was *Mommy*.

Then, *gun*.

One day when he was about four, he was playing with pipe cleaners, and I noticed he'd twisted one into an interesting shape.

"What's that, Michael, a pretty bird?"

"Mutant Ninja Killer Nunchucks," he said.

We gave our kids Legos. Personally, I hate Legos. Everyone who ever walked barefoot into his child's room late at night hates Legos. I think Mr. Lego should be strung up from a scaffold made of his horrid little pockmarked arch-puncturing plastic cubes. Anyway, my kids got Legos. Elizabeth built a graceful Spanish-style villa with a patio and a fountain.

Michael built a bazooka.

My daughter's favorite game is basketball. She wants me to play it with her every morning before school. I am happy to oblige.

My son's favorite game is called "I'll Kill You." I hide.

Apparently, it's the favorite game of all the boys in his class. (My friend Nancy tells me it has always been thus. She remembers recess at Blessed Sacrament almost thirty years ago, when the girls played basketball, and the boys—segregated behind sawhorses for the safety of others and confined to an alley— played something they called Maul Ball. "They'd take a hard-ball, and attempt to kill each other," Nancy recalled. "We simply assumed it was men's work.")

The principal of my son's school recently sent home a notice to all prekindergarten parents saying that the kids were specifically barred from bringing "weapons" to school for show-and-tell. This created a show-and-tell crisis in dozens of homes in our neighborhood, a frenzied 8 A.M. scramble for nonassaultive objects. For the last six Thursdays, my son has brought a hard-boiled egg. His pal Adam brings a box of Tylenol.

Surely you must have noticed the difference between little boys and girls at parties. Most girls will stand quietly on line for games such as pin-the-scoop-on-the-ice-cream-cone. Boys, in the words of my smart friend Martha, "just barge in and grab the first thing that's longer than it is wide, and begin killing people."

The gifts are different, too. Girls will settle for dolls and notepads and board games. Boys want retro-rocket phaser guns with flashing lights that make twenty-four different kinds of high-pitched, whiny sounds, including one that exactly replicates the sound of a father going stark raving mad and smashing the gun to smithereens. Someone made the mistake of giving my son a notepad for his birthday. He picked it up and hurled it at the neck of one of the other little boys at the party. I asked him why he did that, and he grinned and said, "It was a Ninja Pizza Weapon." Go figure.

I can't vouch for this story. It may be apocryphal, but I believe it has the ring of truth: I'm told there is a group of radical feminists in San Francisco who formed a cooperative to raise their children. They were adamant about raising their children without stereotyped sex roles. They made sure all the children sang songs together, and played games together, and learned that each of them was equal and had equal opportunity and responsibility. They sought to make nurture triumph over nature. Among the gifts at a birthday party for one of the boys were a starter set of tools and a beautiful set of Barbie and Ken dolls. He was no stranger to dolls. He had many of them, as did all the boys in the cooperative. He took out the starter hammer and smashed Ken's head.

Your witness, counselor.

Oh Dud, Poor Dud

Last Thursday was Take Our Daughters to Work Day. And like any sane father I dreaded it. Isn't it enough that my daughter sees me around the house in my underpants? Do I have to be humiliated further by letting her see me at work, where I appear even less dignified?

So I came up with a scheme that would make my daughter think I was important: I seriously considered renting a hotel suite and hiring a secretary for the anteroom. Then I would sit inside, behind a big fancy desk, and as I was telling my daughter how important my work was, every few minutes the secretary would urgently come in and say, "I'm sorry to interrupt, Mr. Kornheiser, but this call really needs your attention."

"Okay, put the call through," I would say.

I'd shake my head in anguish as I listened to the voice on the other end (which in reality would be James Earl Jones saying "Welcome to Bell Atlantic"), and finally I'd speak angrily, and say something like:

"Look, just get on it right away. Don't make me fly out tonight and do it myself."

Or:

"What? That material was supposed to be in San Diego at

nine A.M.! You tell Moskowitz he'll be carving soap in South Dakota if this doesn't get done by three this afternoon!" (I'd then bang my fist on the desk, because why not, it's a rental.)

I'd let this go on an hour or so, and schmaltz it up by having somebody show up and make a big fuss over me for a huge charitable donation I'd made—the $650,000 for Bosnia I'd raised personally just by calling millionaires who owed me favors. Then I'd have the secretary come in to say apologetically, "I'm so sorry, Mr. Kornheiser, I know you were counting on spending your entire work day with your lovely daughter"—and I'd look at my daughter very lovingly—"but the White House just called. The president needs you there right away. He's got to give a speech tonight at the United Nations, and he says there's only one man he'd trust to write it on such short notice: Tony Kornheiser."

I'd pause dramatically.

"It's the president, Elizabeth; I've gotta go. I'd love to bring you with me, but you need security clearance, and there just isn't time."

Then I'd walk to the newspaper, where I'm treated by everyone there—my boss, my coworkers, the copy aides, the janitorial staff—like a dust bunny. At work, basically, I slink around meekly, like a panhandler, begging people for ideas for my column, offering them money and flattering them furiously, because I never have ideas of my own and, like Blanche Dubois, I'm totally dependent on the charity of others. I am afforded so little respect that even the random lunatics who come into the newsroom complaining that the CIA has implanted electrodes in their teeth call me "cueball head" and laugh at me.

I don't want my daughter to see that.

So take *your* daughter to work. Leave mine out of this.

I'm not even going to get into the notion of how politically incorrect it is to take our daughters to work, and not our sons. What do I tell my son when he asks if he can go to work with me—wear a dress?

It's one thing if you actually *do* something at work—if you build a house, or sell cars, or you're a neurosurgeon (where you are so important that people literally wipe your brow). But I type. That's what I do, sit and type. It isn't a real action job. It's unlikely Steven Seagal will play me in the movies.

Here's my day: I come in. I sit down at the keyboard. I wait for the muse to hit me. To mug me, actually.

When the muse doesn't come, I go eat.

I talk on the phone, desperately asking people for column ideas. (I've been known to call up foreign embassies and plead, *"Quien tiene una columno para yo?"* My Spanish is terrible.)

Sometimes I eat while I'm talking.

Must I go on?

Must my child see this?

I am not the same man at work that I am at home.

At home I'm a putz. But at work I'm a putz in a tie.

But anyway, it was Take Our Daughters to Work Day in America, and since I am a loyal American, I had to do it. Here is what happened:

Elizabeth, twelve, walked into my office, and the first thing she saw was my computer screen. Crawling across the dark screen in bright purple letters, again and again, was the sentence I had typed in many months ago to use as a screen saver—a quote from the movie *Animal House* that I thought summed up almost everything in life: "You fudged up, Dorfman, you trusted us."

Only it didn't say "fudged."

"Wow, Dad, who wrote *that*?" she asked.

"Er, the computer fairy," I said, and immediately booted up my machine to get rid of the screen saver. After a few seconds of beeping there arrived on the screen my pending messages, the top one of which was from Gino, my editor, expressing his forthright opinion of my most recent piece of writing. Gino wrote that I had royally fudged up and what was I, some sort of fudging idiot?

"Wow!" said Elizabeth.

So I sent my daughter to the cafeteria.

"They've got Gummi Worms down there," I said. "Here's some money."

I gave her sixty dollars.

I hoped that would hold her until five, when Take Our Daughters to Work Day was over.

Anyway, one very nice thing happened. I dropped in on my idol, Bob Woodward, and hung around his office like a starving puppy until he sighed and let me in. Even though he was busy, he regaled us with anecdotes about Watergate and other big stories he'd been involved with. He couldn't have been more cordial, and I thanked him profusely for being so kind. The one embarrassing moment came afterward when Elizabeth asked, "Dad, why did Mr. Woodward keep calling you 'Tommy'?"

A Bright and Shining Guy

Dwight Eisenhower. Robert Duvall. Burt Reynolds. Michael Jordan. Ed Koch. Frank Perdue. Willard Scott. Sean Connery. Sinead O'Connor. Winston Churchill. Kareem Abdul-Jabbar. Peter Arnett. Elton John. Bozo the Clown. Gandhi.

Bless 'em all.

Bald like me.

(Not sure you're losing your hair? Yul know, believe me.)

What makes us so damned cool?

Is it just the fact that our brains are closer to the surface, which makes us quicker on the uptake, or that we can stick our heads out the window and find out the weather without opening our eyes? Or is it that we're so good in bed?

Oh sure, you think I'm being defensive. I can hear women now, saying it's no big deal being bald. Like it's no big deal being flat-chested, I suppose? At least you have those high-fashion models and Audrey Hepburn to make you feel glamorous. Who do we unhaired have as role models? Fred Mertz and Louie DiPalma.

My hair began falling out when I was eighteen. I asked my doctor if there was any way to save it. He said, "Sure, put it in a shoe box.'' So I switched doctors. I went to a famous hair specialist in New York, who began injecting my scalp with estrogen. He said it would help me keep my hair. The treatments were going okay until I began getting an uncontrollable urge to shop at Loehmann's.

A few years later I bought a toupee. It was curly; it looked exactly like the one Kevin Dobson has. It cost $400, and I wore it outside the house for a total of five seconds. I was going to my car when my neighbor saw me and said, "Don't move. I'm getting my shotgun. There's a yak on your head." I went back inside and put the toupee in the shoe box with the rest of my hair.

I wouldn't say I'm overly self-conscious about having this vast, blatant, blindingly reflective expanse on the top of my head, unless you think removing all the mirrors from my house or never sitting down or bending over in the presence of other people is overly self-conscious. I grew so weary of having people look at my head and say in their idiotically chipper tone, "Tony, did you know you're going bald?" Did I know? Did I know? Wow. I just thought I had an extremely robust and well-developed part in my hair.

I've compensated. I grew a beard. I wear a hat. (All the time. Even inside the house. My kids think I'm a baseball player.) You show me someone with a beard and a hat, I'll show you a bald man underneath.

I hold on to my fantasies. I still have a brush. I still have a hair dryer. I do my best to comb over; me and Sam Nunn. I still go to a hairdresser; the fabulous Barbara, bless her. I overtip her like crazy, out of gratitude for her using a scissors and not just a buffing cloth.

(Did I tell you how much I hate my father? Oh, big time. He's eighty years old, and he has a full head of hair. I look like *his* father. He tells me being bald is nothing to be ashamed of, then he whips out a comb and stands in front of a mirror and Fonzes himself. He's eighty! He tells me my hair wouldn't fall out if I didn't worry so much. I say, who died and made you Sigmund Freud? In fact, the genetic code for baldness is carried by the maternal grandfather. So I ask my Dad about my maternal grandfather. "Bald as a hard-boiled egg at fifteen," he says. *Laughing!*)

As you can tell I'm not completely at peace with my condition. I'm still in the Shame Phase. I'm not liberated, like Richard Sandomir, who wrote the book *Bad Like Me: Adventures of Baldman*. Sandomir, thirty-three, is gloriously bald. He doesn't attempt the comb-over, which he calls "turban renewal." Sandomir wants to establish the Bald Hall of Fame, and locate it in Morehead City, N.C. (Previously, he founded the Baldness Defense League. He held the inaugural press conference at the Astor Place barber shop in New York. Sandomir feared he'd "be assassinated by an overhaired zealot.")

Sandomir disdains all the rug wearers, weave dreamers, and minoxidil minions, such as Charlton Heston, Burt Reynolds, Rick Barry, and Bill Murray, who has hair patching to cover up a significant bald spot on his crown. Sandomir wants to "out" them. One of the Great Moments in Bald History was Ted Danson's recent shedding of his piece to reveal a nascent bald growth on top, a public self-outing.

"I wept," Sandomir admitted.

Among his other Great Moments in Bald History are: the scene in *The Fabulous Baker Boys* in which Beau Bridges spray-paints Rustoleum on his bald spot; Julius Caesar crossing the Rubicon; Telly Savalas's birthdate; *People* magazine naming Sean Connery the world's sexiest man ("Why did they make him wear a wig in *The Hunt For Red October?*" Sandomir asks. "Don't they think a bald man could steer a submarine?"); Benito Mussolini's head being paraded through the streets of Milan.

Sandomir is one of my idols. I wish I were as advanced as he is. Regrettably, I'm still trying for a miracle. A few years ago I got involved with a medical study, testing a drug called Viprostol. I rubbed it on my head twice a day. (I was careful to wear plastic gloves, for fear hair would start sprouting on my palms.) It didn't work. Then I tried Rogaine. It hasn't worked either. All I have to show for it is some fuzz, like you'd find on a plucked chicken. God, I hate those Rogaine commercials where some wimpy yuppie decides to do something about his thinning hair. How I wish I still had thinning hair. This guy has a bald spot the size of a dime and he's whining. I'd like to pop him in the labonza. Lemme give you some advice, pal: Get a shoe box.

Shop Till
the Mailman Drops

In the dream I am upstairs, standing in front of the linen closet, stacking the bars of soap. There are already forty-eight of them, and it's just July. An idiot has sent me a gift from the Soap on a Rope catalog: eight bars of bath soap per month for a year, ninety-six in all! Almond, ginger, and oatmeal soaps. We're not sure whether to bathe with them or serve them for breakfast.

My wife yells up, "Honey, dinner's ready."

"I can't eat," I say. "I have to take another shower."

"That's your third today."

"Fourth, actually—two more to go. I'm finally making a dent in this bar. Why would anybody make pralines-and-cream soap? Where did the guy work before he got this job, Baskin-Robbins? . . . Look, make sure to send the kids up for their baths after dinner."

"They refuse to take another bath. Kids in school are teasing them because their fingers are always puckered. We don't have kids anymore, we have baby prunes. Michael's science homework was to use the word *experiment* in a sentence. He wrote, 'I am part of a hydroponic experiment.' "

"Tell them this will stop soon. Tell them Daddy will soon

have enough rope to hang the people who manufacture the Soap on a Rope catalog.''

Every day more and more catalogs arrive at my house. They are left on my stoop because they are too thick to fit inside the mail slot. For Christmas I'm not tipping my mailman, I'm giving him a truss.

I am new to the Catalog Game, unlike my colleague Ronalie Peterson, who is legendary for getting EVERY CATALOG EVER MADE, an average of twenty a day this time of year! If there were a ''Michael Milken in Jail'' catalog, Ronalie would have had it five minutes after sentencing. When I was young, nobody I knew shopped by catalog. The only catalog I ever heard of was the Spiegel catalog, which they gave away on TV game shows. I know this sounds totally retro, but people in my neighborhood went to stores to buy their food and clothes. ''Who shops by mail?'' I asked my father. ''Farmers,'' he assured me. Now, farmers are the only ones who don't shop by mail. If they're hungry and they want a pear, they'll go out and pick it off a tree. The rest of us dial an 800 number and wait for UPS. The good news is, the pears come exquisitely wrapped and gorgeous. The bad news is, they come in three weeks.

''Your pears are here, dear.''

''Fine, set them next to the ninety-dollar orthopedic pet bed and the one-hundred-seventy-five-dollar nostalgic Air Force leather bomber jacket with the hand-painted map of the Hapsburg Empire in the lining.''

Let me make my position on catalogs clear: If I am driving, and I see you walking down the street in L. L. Bean duck shoes, I'm going to try to run you over.

Enough is enough. How obscure and limited is our taste supposed to get?

Duncraft: gourmet birdseed catalogs. *Gourmet birdseed!* What, with little flecks of Brie in it? This is what we need during a recession, birds that only eat Omaha steaks?

Almond Plaza: thirty-six pages of almonds. Okay, eight pages, even fourteen, but thirty-six pages of almonds? The "Gettysburg Address" is written on the back of an envelope, and we get thirty-six pages of almonds.

Plow & Hearth: compost heaps for college grads. Here's something from this one: the Scoot-n-Do, a little green wagon you sit on while you do your gardening so you don't get grass stains on your catalog jeans. (Also in here is the Squirrel Spinner: "Train your squirrels to be acrobats." You put corn at the end of a wooden stake, the squirrels climb down for the corn and presumably spin around until they vomit. Great fun for the whole family.) Todd, who showed me the Scoot-n-Do, also told me about the Bug Sucker, a self-explanatory tube device used to rid yourself of household bugs neatly, without squashing them on your wallpaper.

Smith & Hawken: nature junk for the environmentally guilt-ridden, including an $85 "Sardinian Fire Tool," a long, steel, confusingly needless rod.

Mission Orchards (also, Harry and David): incredibly expensive fruit, like *one pound* of Medjool dates for $17.95! I've had less expensive dates that led to marriage.

The Cockpit: macho aviation fantasy wear for desk-bound chicken hawks.

Brownstone: serious clothes for female fogies of indeterminate age.

Hold Everything: empty boxes, all shapes, all sizes. Yuppie Tupperware.

Nothing doesn't come in a catalog anymore. One man at work told me he has a catalog devoted exclusively to Soviet military insignia—apparently they're liquidating now that the Cold War is over. One woman said she'd just sent away for the Robert Redford Catalog, undoubtedly a time-share deal. Another woman told me she has inherited the catalogs of the people who previously owned her house, including a Lesbian Music catalog and a politically correct children's game catalog. "Who'd you buy the house from, Gertrude Stein?" I asked.

Soon we'll see a "Keating Five" catalog that lets you order free, laundered money by discreetly calling the Senate Office Building, a "Trump Goes Bump" catalog for slightly soiled Georgia peaches and used airplanes, and a "What's Shakin' on H Street" catalog, where you can order huge new holes in the ground.

My smart friend Martha is partial to the Miles Kimball catalog, where she once ordered the indispensable rotary nose-hair clipper for a loved one, not to mention the personalized cocktail napkins with a picture of a backyard swimming pool that say "A Sip and a Dip With the [family name]." These, Martha explains, are for "people who drown drunk in their pools," the Orange County A-list.

I notice I'm getting a classier kind of catalog lately: Ever since I let my membership in Telly Savalas's Players Club lapse, they have stopped trying to sell me vinyl jackets and felt paintings. I kind of miss the catalog that tries to sell brown, nuclear-winter sausage and quasi-edible "cheese food" in the shape of a log cabin. Hand to God, who buys that stuff, and *whom* do they send it to? Thankfully, I still get my Lillian Vernon catalog, and just like you, I search for that cute Lucite bunny with a cabbage face that I can monogram to use as either a key ring or a dinner plate, and of course I crinkle up my face and say, "Oooohhh, that's so pwecious, I want one."

I have come to view catalogs as windows to my soul. I'm the kind of guy who hopes for Victoria's Secret, and winds up with Lillian Vernon's.

Tony, Tony, Tony.

My name is Tony, and I'm an egomaniac and a TV whore. No TV appearance is beneath me. I would do the weather on the Food Channel; I'd do commercials for adult diapers. I would sing "I Love You, Pooky-Dooky" with Barney. I would even go on Sally Jessy Raphaël's show, even though she is so unbearably slimy that she has to wear spike heels or she'd slide across the floor.

I asked my dear friend Gino, who is known for his sensitivity, to help me come to terms with this problem. He said, and I am quoting this verbatim: "Your problem is that you are pretentious, bloated, and more self-absorbed than a sponge in a toilet"—I cut him off there, and told him we'd continue the discussion after I got back from lunch with Diane Sawyer's dentist.

So it will come as no surprise that last week I happily accepted hosting CNBC's *Equal Time* with Fave Rave Info-Babe Mary Matalin (the one whose lips don't move when she talks). I didn't ask who the guests might be—because I figured I could pretty much hold my own with anybody, since I got nearly 1142 on my college boards. Hey, I'm a sportswriter. Nobody's going to ask me to be a cohost and then bring on guests who are, you know, actually *smart*.

Unfortunately, when the night of the show came, I discovered the guests were:

1. A brilliant feminist author, lawyer, and Ivy League professor;

2. A genius political strategist, think-tank fellow, and PBS documentary filmmaker.

Wendy Kaminer has written a book called *I'm Dysfunctional, You're Dysfunctional*. Not only didn't I understand it, I couldn't even understand the reviews.

As a cohost I was expected to ask her intelligent questions.

One of Matalin's first questions to her went something like this: "Let's get right to the philosophical ramifications of your work, the correlation between the self-help recovery ideology and the disempowerment of women with regard to doctrinaire feminism."

Here is an actual question I asked: "So let's say you're on a bus, and you're looking at the people. How can you tell the functional ones from the dysfunctional ones? Is it something they wear?"

Wendy looked at me like I was from South Yemen and simply continued to answer one of Mary's previous questions.

I was hopelessly out of my league. I had that horrible, numbing feeling you get when the teacher calls on you to name all the provinces of Canada, and the best you can say is: "Manitoba, and, uh, the blue one."

Some people commented to me that my eyes appeared to wander during the show. I explained to them this was because I have the attention span of a prairie dog when a conversation isn't about me, and in this case not only wasn't it about me, but it wasn't even about anything I could understand.

I told myself to sit up straight and at least look like someone with a pulse. (What actually kept flickering through my head was that old Beach Boys song. I wanted to ask, "Wendy, Wendy, what went wrong, oh so wrong?")

When it came my turn to ask another question, I said, on live national television:

"So, uh, let me ask the question that every parent wants to know: We're in the supermarket. My daughter throws a tantrum because she wants Count Chocula, and I refuse to buy it for her because it's, you know, one hundred percent sugar, and this shames my daughter, and takes away her self-esteem. Years later, when she kills me with a shotgun, will a jury let her off?"

What was going through my head at this moment was: "Help. Get me out of here, God."

What was going through her head, I am reasonably certain, was: "Help, get him out of here, God."

So at least we were on the same wavelength.

My next question was:

"So many people are in Twelve Step programs now. Some people are in eight or ten of them at the same time, and that's like, what, a hundred and twenty steps? That's like a stairway to Heaven. Is there anything we can do to consolidate all their steps, so they can get out of the house before nightfall?"

Wendy thought I was kidding. People who watched the show told me they thought I was kidding.

Yeah, yeah. That's the ticket. I was kidding.

The next guest was Ben Wattenberg, the smartest man in the world. He has a job in a think tank. He thinks. This is his whole job description: Think. Someone pays him to think. Is this a great country, or what? He has come on to talk about his new PBS talk show. The only time I watch PBS is during Pledge Week, when they put on specials with Liza Minnelli.

"He's got a great sense of humor," Mary says.

I mention that I vaguely remember a column of his on the fertility crisis in sub-Saharan Africa—but I'm sure Letterman was all over that one, too.

"The man is brilliant," Mary says. "He'll love you."

So I say, "Ben, you're a real smart guy—who do you have in the NCAA pool? Your Final Four teams still alive?"

Then I ask him about his job: "Do you think with your shoes on or off?"

I press on: "Let's say you've had a real good day thinking and you come up with an idea. So you go down the hall to a colleague, and you say, 'I've got this great idea.' And you tell him, and he says: 'I already *knew* that, Ben. Everybody knows that.' Do you feel crushed?"

As soon as the show ended, I apologized to everyone in the crew for being a buffoon.

"No, you did very well with Wendy Kaminer," the producer told me.

"Oh yeah," I said. "And I suppose she'll dedicate her next book to me: *I'm Dysfunctional, You're a Moron.*"

I told the producer I had embarrassed myself beyond measure, and I was about to tell her I was done with TV forever when she said Mary was going on vacation soon, and would I cohost with Jane Wallace?

And I said sure.

The Man of Steal

Everything in here is 100 percent true. Not that funny, maybe, but true.

My car was stolen this week.

Right in front of my house in the District of Columbia. In broad daylight.

WHILE I WAS HOME!

It's probably my fault for not sitting out on the curb every second—or not hiring Peruvian illegal aliens for when I went to the bathroom. Silly me, I thought it was all right to park your car in front of your own home without consulting Steven Seagal.

At five forty-five my car was there. I saw it. Twenty minutes later, I opened my front door to drive to the bank, and it was gone.

I actually believed that either (a) my wife or (b) a neighbor had borrowed the car for a while. And I walked out to the curb to wait for the car to come back.

Which is when I started asking myself the following questions:

1. *Borrowed* the car?

2. Your wife has her own car, and her car is not here, and she

is not at home. So if she drove her car home and borrowed your car, then does that mean your car is safe and *her car* is stolen?

3. How did your neighbors get the keys to your car? You don't even speak to them.

4. Are you an idiot?

I then uttered the three words most associated with car theft, "Son of a . . ."

I called 911 to report my car stolen.

Then I called my colleague Mike "That Toddlin' Town" Wilbon, because he's from Chicago, so he's used to items being stolen—like elections. I always consult Wilbon on matters of urban terror. Last year we went to a boxing match, and there was a drive-by shooting outside the arena. I asked him what we should do if it happened again while we were on the street—should we run like hell? Wilbon insisted that we "should lie down on the sidewalk and pretend we're dead." He administered that advice as though it were obvious urban strategy, like not licking the seat of a taxicab, that should have been self-evident to anyone but a total hick.

I was still talking with Wilbon when my ten-year-old daughter came home.

"Where's your car, Daddy?" she asked.

"Stolen, honey."

"You're kidding, right?" she said, laughing.

"Nope. It was stolen."

"Daaaaaad . . ." she said.

I handed her the phone. "Talk to Wilbon."

Now my daughter believed it, and in that happy way kids have when they think they've wandered into a storybook, she said breathlessly, "Wow! This is just like Genevieve's mom. She has a Honda, and her car was stolen from in front of her house yesterday."

Just then my six-year-old son came around the corner. My

daughter gleefully ran out to tell him the news: "Daddy's car was stolen!"

To which my son thoughtfully responded, "Dad, can you make me a bologna sandwich?"

It was now six-thirty, maybe thirty minutes after the car had been stolen. The phone rang, and a woman said, "This is the telephone company operator. You should call this number right away," and she gave me a number.

I told the kids: "This is good, I may have won a lot of money."

I called the number. I identified myself and said, "So, have I won rumba lessons?"

A man identified himself as being from the U.S. Park Police and said, "Do you know the whereabouts of your 1991 Honda?"

"I do not," I said, sensing a breakthrough.

Of all the good luck in the world, the U.S. Park Police had already found my car abandoned about two miles from my house.

I asked if Hondas were stolen a lot.

Not as often as Acuras, he said. But more often than a 1974 Pacer.

"So what am I supposed to drive to be safe?" I asked.

"A Liberian tanker."

The police said the car was driveable, and I could come get it. We all piled into one car and drove over and met officers Michael Snowden and John Marsh, who brought me to my car.

"Anything missing?"

"I had a Bullets pass in the glove compartment," I said.

"They may have taken it."

I checked. No such luck.

"Nobody wants to see the Bullets," I smiled.

On the other side of my car was another Honda, and when my daughter saw it, she got tremendously excited.

"It's Genevieve's!" she exclaimed.

And so it was. I felt like I was on the set of *America's Most Wanted*. I mean, what are the odds of that? Of all the cars stolen in the entire city of Washington, that two would be recovered at the same time, side by side in a park, and they would belong to fourth-grade classmates? (Answer: Approximately the same odds as people named Zoe and Kimba being nominated for attorney general.)

"So what do I do now?" I asked Officer Marsh.

"Get the Club," he said, referring to that big metal stick advertised on TV that attaches to your steering wheel. It looks like a rectal thermometer for a brontosaurus. Come on, if this thing is so great, how come it only costs fifty bucks?

"Get it now," he said. "Before you get home."

So I drove to an auto parts store—thanking my lucky stars that my car was recovered before it was chopped into tiny pieces like fish food—and I told the clerk my sad story, about how my car was stolen from right in front of my house. In broad daylight. WHILE I WAS HOME!

"You're the fourth one today."

Alley Oops

For those of you who have breathlessly anticipated more about my son's birthday party, you're in luck.

You may remember my advice to parents who were planning a birthday party for their sons, age five or six:

1. Dig a large outdoor pit.
2. Throw all the boys in.
3. Every few minutes toss down some birthday cake and Fox's U-Bet Syrup.
4. After two hours, drag the boys out of the pit and hose them down.
5. Accept compliments.

Well, my son turned seven this year, and this time the old backyard wasn't good enough. He wanted a bowling party. I said fine, because he had fewer friends to invite this year—many of the regulars were in prison.

I was happy to take him bowling. I like bowling. I bowled as a yoot. Me and a lot of guys who grew up to be Joey Buttafuoco. They had back hair when they were twelve.

So I took ten boys, spread them over two lanes, and started keeping score.

Oh, I should tell you that it's duckpin bowling, with the real small pins, and the real small balls, and it's harder to keep score because you get three rolls per frame, not two—and the automatic pinsetter doesn't come down by itself, you have to press a button, which means that the kids have to keep track of how many rolls they've already had, and you have to keep track of the kids who are lowering the pinsetter just for laughs and trying to hit it with the bowling ball, and, well, this is what it sounded like . . . remember, I'm sitting in the chair, trying to keep track of ten small boys bowling, trying to see the lanes, add the scores, and maintain order:

"Your turn, Aaron."

"Daddy, can I have a drink?"

"I'm not your daddy, Billy. I'm Michael's daddy. . . . Aaron, how many pins did you knock down? . . . David, it's your turn on Lane Sixteen. Sixteen, David. On your right, David. Yes, David, the side with your blue sock. . . . How many, Aaron?"

"Forty-one."

"That's impossible. You can't count."

"I can too count. I can't read."

"That's three rolls, Nick. Press the pinsetter, you're done. . . . Nick, Nick, press the pinsetter on *your* lane, not David's. No, David, don't roll the . . ." *Bang* ". . . Yes, sir, I know it is expensive equipment and I will make every effort to ensure that these plucky young lads don't continue to . . ." *Bang.*

"I got four."

"Yes, Sean, I saw. Which ball was that for you?"

"This one."

"Yes, Sean, I mean, what number ball? How many times have you rolled the ball this frame?"

"Should I count the time that by mistake I dropped the ball off Nathaniel's ankle and it rolled all the way to the snack bar and the man there said you were a putz? What's a putz?"

"Daddy, I'm thirsty."

"I thought we established, Billy, that I'm not your daddy."

"Jason, how come all the other kids have bowled, and you haven't? . . . What? What do you mean, Daniel said you were too stupid to bowl? You're not too stupid to bowl. Lots of stupid people bowl. Did I ever tell you about my old friend Joey Buttafuoco . . ."

"What's my score?"

"After five frames, eighteen, Sam."

"Is that good?"

"Yes, it is very good if you were a famous bowling dog."

"What kind of cake is there? When can we eat?"

"Daddy, I'm thirsty."

"Billy, I am not your . . . Oh, Michael, I *am* your daddy, son. You're thirsty?"

"No, but Billy asked me to ask you."

I really wasn't doing well with this. The kids had bowled out of turn. Some of them had bowled twenty balls in a row and not hit anything. Others had deliberately lowered the pinsetters, and aimed at them. Few of the kids could add past ten, so scoring was impossible. All the food questions meant they were getting bored with bowling. And a few of them—my son included—had gathered around Jason and were watching him try to eat a bowling ball.

"Back here, guys," I announced. "We've only got two frames to go. Aaron, you're up on Lane Fifteen. Nick, Lane Sixteen. . . . We won't be taking any questions right now on the size or style of the cake, or the flavors of the drinks, do I make myself clear? And why, kids? Why? You got it! Because I'm the daddy and I say so."

It was at this point that a woman who is related to me by marriage came by and told me, "You know why they're acting this way? You're too structured."

"They've got two frames to go," I said. "I thought it was important that they post a score."

"Why?" she asked. "Why was it important that they post a score? They're seven. Were you thinking of sending the score to the American Bowling Congress?"

"That's good, Alice, that's good . . . *bang-zoom*, you know?"

Next year, I'm bringing back the Pit.

Mail and Female

My daughter came home from sleep-away camp, where she'd spent five weeks. She looked great. And I was so proud of her, going away by herself.

The first question I asked her was "How was camp?"

She began by saying, "Well, the day I left I got on the bus and I sat next to Ashley, and she brought Goldfish, which was good, because I forgot my Now and Laters, and then Shannon came over, and she's from Baltimore, and she gets her clothes at the Gap, and she had a Game Boy, but all she had was Tetris, which I have, so we asked Jenny, who was the counselor, if anybody had Sonic the Hedgehog, but . . ."

She went on like this for a few minutes, still talking about the bus ride up to camp five weeks ago, and I came to the horrifying realization that she was actually going to tell me how camp was MINUTE BY MINUTE. Because this is what girls do (and when they grow up and become women, they do it, too, as any man can vouch). They gather information and dispense it without discrimination. Everything counts the same!

It is not that women lack the ability to process and prioritize information, it is that they don't think life is as simple as men do, and so they are fascinated by the multiplicity of choices that they see. It is a little-known fact of American history that Paul Revere's wife, and not Paul Revere, was originally supposed to warn the Colonial militia about the British invasion. But she insisted that "one if by land and two if by sea" was insufficient. What if *some* were coming by land, and *some* were coming by sea, and some were wading in the water on horses, which is sort of both by land and by sea when you come right down to it, and what if some were being catapulted through the air . . . and finally Paul just put on his coat and galloped off.

This is why you have to be very specific about what you ask women. If, for example, you missed a Redskins game, and you know a woman who saw it, never, *ever* ask, "What happened?" Unless you have nowhere to go until Thursday.

Ask:

1. Who won?
2. What was the score?
3. Was anyone carried out on a stretcher?

You must get them to fast-forward.

Left to their own devices, girls go through life volubly answering essay questions. And boys? Multiple choice is *way* too complicated. Boys restrict themselves to true-false.

Boys do not gather and retain information, they focus on results.

My son went to camp for six weeks—one week longer than my daughter. As I had with my daughter, I asked him, "How was camp?"

He said: "Good. I busted Jason's nose."

Short and to the point.

This was followed by "Can we go to McDonald's?"

Did I mention the cheers? My daughter came back with cheers. About 187,640 musical cheers, all of which are accompanied by an intricate series of hand, feet, and hip movements. She went to camp a ten-year-old, she came back a Vandella.

It's amazing, the affinity of girls and cheers. If you've ever been to camp you know that girls have a special gene for cheers, and that even girls who have never been to camp before—or, for that matter, been to America or spoken English before—automatically know all the cheers the moment they step off the bus.

You give me a group of three or more girls at camp, and I'll give you the entire score of *Guys and Dolls*. Girls spontaneously burst into song. It's a gender thing, I guess.

As a boy at camp, I used to look at girls in amazement, wondering why they would waste their time practicing socialization skills, when they could be doing useful things like me, memorizing Willie Mays's doubles and sacrifice flys during an entire decade.

Boys don't cheer.

Even during "color war," that traditional camp competition when cheering is supposed to result in points, here's how boys cheer on the way to the dining hall:

They look at the other team and say, "Yo, Green Team, drop dead."

If I Had a Hammer, I'd Take Out an Eye

Last week, I moved. I got a house that was bigger in every area than my last house, except one—the stairwell from the lower floor to the upper floor. Unfortunately, I did not discover this until moving day. And that is why I am dressing in the dining room now. Because my dresser didn't fit up the stairs. Neither did my antique roll-top desk, which is now in the kitchen, filled with Froot Loops and Count Chocula. Neither did my box spring, leaving me with two choices: (1) buy a new bed, or (2) sleep in the dining room, near my clothes.

Humor writers sometimes make things up to be funny. Unfortunately, I am not doing that right now. The truth is, I am the kind of guy to whom this sort of thing happens *all the time*. There is a technical term for this kind of individual. I am an "imbecile."

For example, I am not particularly talented when it comes to everyday man work. (An everyday man, for example, would have used a tape measure to measure his stairwell. I do not use tape measures. I am afraid of "whiplash.")

I cannot change the oil in my car. I'm afraid to open the hood of my car because I don't know where to stick that hood-stand thingamajiggy to keep the hood from slamming down on the back of my neck and killing me.

I am the last person on earth who still goes to full-serve gas stations. Nobody goes to full-serve. They don't even call it full-serve anymore. They just nail up a sign that says TONY.

I don't go to show off. I don't enjoy paying sixteen times the normal price for a gallon of gas. If I wanted to pay sixteen times the normal price for something, I'd buy my milk at the 7-Eleven. No, I go to full-serve because I cannot use the pump at self-serve. The last time I tried, I couldn't fit the nozzle into the gas tank, and I had to get help from—oh, the embarrassment—a woman in a Volvo station wagon. The time before that, I couldn't get the nozzle out on time, and I got gas all over my pants. I couldn't go to work. I had to stop at Saks and buy a pair of pants. The salesman asked me what I did for a living. I said I was Emerson Fittipaldi.

I can't fix anything. I can't change anything. I can't build anything. The reason I don't take aspirin isn't that I can't open the childproof cap—I don't even *try* to open the childproof cap because I can always get a child to do that for me. No, it's because once the cap is open *I can't get the cotton out of the bottle.* (I once tried to use a shrimp fork to do this. I could show you the scar.)

My children are small now. But when they get older and they ask me for advice on how to make their way in the world, I will tell them simply: Belong to AAA.

I feel I have a mission in life. I was put on this earth to pay sinewy tattooed men to do simple things for me. Handymen *love* me.

To this day my eighty-two-year-old father doesn't send me a gift on my birthday. He sends me money so I can pay Ray to fix the toilet by putting a brick in it, and so I can pay Ed to hammer a nail into the wall, because when *I* do it I leave a crater the size of a large Armand's deep-dish pizza.

I can mow, but I cannot start the mower. The last time I tried I pulled the rubber thing so hard that the mower leaped into the air like a salmon, flipped over, and cracked the gas tank. So I pay Leon to cut my grass.

(By federal law, all handymen must be named Leon, Ray, or Ed.)

When I was young, I ached to be good with wood like the rest of the guys. But in wood shop I was barred from the jigsaw after a regrettable incident involving a stuffed woodchuck named Safety Sam, who was dressed up like a railroad engineer with a red bandanna and a sign around his neck that said, SAFETY SAM SEZ: I DON'T BELIEVE IN ACCIDENTS. I accidentally cut off his head.

For years I refrained from all do-it-yourself projects, until finally, when I was 24, I bought a stereo system and grew determined I'd build shelves for the speakers. I wanted each shelf to jut out twelve inches from the wall, and I went to a lumberyard and had the boards cut to the specifications. Then I went into a hardware store and asked for "four thirteen-inch nails." I had no concept of brackets. I figured you buy a nail a little bigger than your board, and keep pounding until you reach the other side. I explained this to the men inside the hardware store (Ray, Leon, and Ed, as I recall) and they laughed in my face. So deep was my shame that I haven't walked into a hardware store since, except to obtain batteries for the flashlight I keep next to the phone, in case the lights go out and I need to call Ray to change a fuse.

Fortunately, I am not the only imbecile out there. A few weeks ago, my friend Gino got a new living room couch. The night before it was to be delivered, he decided to put the old couch down in the basement. He also decided that he and his wife could do this by themselves. Like me, Gino is afraid of tape measures, and so it was not until the couch was actually *in* the stairwell that Gino discovered the couch was *bigger* than the stairwell. It got wedged so tight that it could not be budged. At the high end of the steps was Gino's wife. At the low end, in the basement, was Gino. In between: *le couch*, jammed like a cow in a phone booth. With mounting panic, my friend realized three things:

1. There was no way to get back upstairs.

2. The basement was underground, with no doors to the outside, and it was midnight. He was going to spend the night in that basement, which . . .

3. Had no bathroom.

An hour later, Gino was still in the basement, contemplating bodily functions, and nervously eyeing the washing machine.

Suffice it to say that he eventually managed to squeeze over the couch by removing most of his clothing and suffering severe couch-tack abrasions. The next day the three delivery men arrived with the new couch, and Gino did what he should have done in the first place: He slipped them thirty dollars to get the old couch downstairs. It took Leon and Ray about nine seconds. Ed would have helped, but he was busy collapsing against a wall, laughing.

Wo Fat

Every Sunday night at seven, Mom, Dad, and I would pile in the car and drive to the Bamboo Inn for dinner. In my faith, this is called a pilgrimage. Catholics have the pope. Protestants have those silly golf pants with ducks on them. Jews have moo goo gai pan. This is true: The only night all year the Bamboo Inn closed was on Yom Kippur, the one day Jews fast.

I've been eating Chinese food religiously for over forty years. I used to wonder where Chinese people ate on Sunday night, Katz's Deli? But it's not just Jewish people who adore Chinese food. All Americans love Chinese food. As a parent I love it because it's a way I can sneak vegetables into my children's dinner. They're not like the vegetables my kids reject when I cook the meals. Chinese vegetables are sliced up and coated with sauce and indistinguishable from meat or fish or noodles. It is all attractively iridescent, like the suits that Dion and the Belmonts wore on Ed Sullivan.

For a long time the only reason to stay away from Chinese food was the vast amount of MSG used in cooking it. MSG was widely thought to be the cause of everything bad in the world—other than the Village People. Women would come out of Chinese restaurants complaining about a headache or a small speck floating in one eyeball or a flare-up of hemorrhoids, and they would refrain from having sex that night. And since a lot of guys had sprung for the dinner, well, MSG had to go. Soon Chinese restaurants had signs on the walls that said: WE DON'T USE MSG. Actually, these signs said: NOTICE TO PLEASE: MS IS NO LONGER EMPLOYED HERE. RESPECTFULLY, FINE, GOOD. Chinese restaurants never really got the hang of English. But it didn't matter because they made great food that everyone loved. And now that the MSG scare was done, America was happy eating Chinese food.

Until last week, when we found out Chinese food has a higher fat content than Rush Limbaugh. The Center for Science in the Public Interest said last week that a container of kung pao chicken—a personal favorite—(the translation of *kung pao chicken* from the original Szechuan is, "giant lumpy mound of poultry grease")—has almost as much fat as *four* Quarter Pounders!

Fat in the fried rice. Fat in the beef with broccoli. Fat in General Tsao's chicken. (The corpulent General Tsao became a hero of the Ming Dynasty by exploding at the Imperial dinner table, a sign of great respect to the hostess.)

Chinese restaurant owners are throwing themselves off bridges. They spent a lifetime learning to say, "Oy, gevalt!" Now it's wiped out with one study.

I am devastated by this development. How can I give up Chinese restaurants? All I really need to know I learned at a Chinese restaurant. I learned how to drink tea from those small cups that got so hot you had to hold them with a napkin—and I admit I always wondered how people smart enough to come up with sweet and sour pork weren't smart enough to invent the handle. I learned how to read by cracking open fortune cookies. The only problem was that the first time I gave an oral report in school, the subject was "making friends," and I said, "Man who opens heart to friend builds gentle breeze to hang wash on."

(Am I the only one who remembers back in the Cantonese-only days, when Chinese restaurant menus always had a page of "American" food, which resembled American food in an eccentric sort of way, the way a lithograph of *Dogs Playing Poker* resembles *Guernica*. The American food was oddly prepared; for example, there were olive garnishes in the Jell-O. And speaking of desserts, there would always be (1) litchi nuts, which tasted like chilled eyeballs, and (2) ice cream, which was served in metal dishes and had chunks of ice in it, and which came in two recognizable flavors, such as chocolate and vanilla, and a third wildly exotic flavor, like "mung bean.")

I am so devoted to Chinese food that I spent years "seasoning" my wok. You "season" a wok by treating it with oil and then baking it. Granted, I may have used the wrong kind of oil—I rubbed in neat's-foot oil because it did such a good job on my Tommy Tresh autograph model baseball glove. As a result my wok had a rather substantial rust spot, which made it look like I was cooking in a hubcap. It took me awhile to perfect the art of using the wok. First you have to heat up the wok to the temperature of Three Mile Island, and *then* you drop in the oil. I kept getting "oil backfire," which would burn my face and hands. I now realize why the Chinese are so svelte: They run away from the wok. Hence the expression "Wok—don't run." Ha ha.

Getting back to that statistic that one container of kung pao chicken has almost as much fat as four Quarter Pounders—well, this is terrible news for McDonald's, which had cornered the fat market for so many years.

What I love about McDonald's is that they hang up a nutritional chart on the wall, breaking down the various contents of their foods. This is what I call "chutzpah": selling you for breakfast a cholesterol-laden egg, a slice of melted cheese substance, and a hunk of pork sausage on a greasy muffin and making believe you won't drop dead by the time you reach your car. If you look at this nutritional chart carefully, you'll see that the healthiest thing you can buy at McDonald's is a salad. Let me ask you something: When was the last time anybody ever said to you, "Hey, you wanna go down to McDonald's and cop some *salad*?" No way. When I go to McDonald's I'm going for something that I'd be afraid to eat with the lights on.

So in order to compete with the Chinese restaurants for the fat market, I believe we'll see McDonald's introduce Phat Foo Mac, which, translated from the original Hunan, is: "Bucket o' Angioplasty."

A Man's Home
Is His Hassle

I often find myself reflecting about why I spent so much money for rooms I never use—like the, ahem, "powder room" off the kitchen.

This is a woman's room. Gather a group of women together to talk about what they want in a house, and you'll hear "powder room on the first floor." When you ask why, they'll say, "Because it's so convenient."

However, should a man actually ever *use* this convenient room, he would be punished. ("Can't you use the upstairs bathroom?" she'll say. "I thought this was supposed to be convenient," he'll say. "But not for us," she'll say.) Particularly forbidden is the use of the soap and hand towels, which are museum pieces and not meant for human hands. Visiting women intuitively understand this, and bring tissues. God forbid you should get water on the miniature soaps and ruin the pristine detail of the small Italian shepherd eating angel hair pasta on the back of a goat.

This is life in the '90s: A couple buys a house and immediately the man finds himself banned from it.

The other day, my research department telephoned a friend

of his, a real estate agent named Eric, and asked what men and women look for in a house.

"Women are interested in the neighborhood, like if there are kids in the neighborhood, and how close the schools are, and they are looking for *flow* to a house—nice, warm, open family areas where you can keep an eye on your kids and still carry on adult conversations."

And what do men want?

"A bar in the basement."

No woman will let a man decorate a house the way he wants—black Naugahyde couches (so the food stains don't show), a big pile of newspapers in the middle of the floor, a stuffed moose head, one of those small refrigerators that you could use both as a footstool and a place to store the beer, and a urinal in the corner.

Women are completely unaware of what a man wants. It's not a den, an office, or a library. (Men over forty are very big on getting libraries, until it is pointed out to them that they can no longer read anything smaller than the big, green PHILADELPHIA 160 MILES on I-95.)

No, ask a man who lives with women to list which rooms of his own house are important to him. And he lists:

1. Garage;
2. Basement;
3. Backyard.

What these rooms have in common is that none of them are actually *inside* his house. The only real room a man values is that one small bathroom that no one else uses—the one place in a houseful of women and children where he can truly be left alone. (As his favorite room, my friend Nancy's husband listed "refrigerator." Nancy thinks this is because he stands in front of it with the door open and the light on so often that he has come to think of it as a small den.)

Let us say a house needs to be painted—and a man would recognize this only if great gobs of paint chips were falling from the ceiling and landing in his Cheerios. A painter will come and ask, "What color do you want the rooms?"

And a man will answer, "I don't know, whatever. . . ." Which means: white.

Poor schlub. It never occurs to him, as it would to a woman, that there are *hundreds* of shades of white, including, just to name four from the 1,200-page catalog of Duron paint chips, Polar Bear, Navajo, City Lights, and, so help me, Snickerdoodle.

Men fear color because they have a vague dread that it means the old furniture won't work, and they'll have to buy new. Men don't buy furniture. They inherit it from their grandmothers, and pass it along, uncleaned, to their sons—as I will proudly do. (Didn't you ever wonder why so many big, strong men with tattoos and back hair have threadbare velvet Victorian living-room couches with doilies on the back?)

Women like to buy new furniture. They like to go through those books of swatches. It usually takes them seven to eight years to decide which couch they want. By then a man wants to move. Men loathe new furniture, because it means they will no longer have a place to sit. Men know they are dirty and disgusting and will ruin the new furniture with their potato chip grease and their beer foam and their general crustaceous ooze. Every room with new furniture is more time spent in the garage for a man.

Men do not know from furniture. Take chairs. To a man there are only two kinds of chairs: comfortable and uncomfortable. A man has no idea what a Queen Anne chair is—other than it is probably unavailable unless Queen Anne and her grandmother are dead.

According to Eric the real estate agent, men are completely inflexible when buying a new house. They cannot envision change. Entire deals have been lost because a man doesn't like the wallpaper in the foyer, and when it is gently pointed out to him that he can replace the offending wallpaper for, like, a hundred bucks, he explodes. "What am I, Bob Vila? I came here to buy a house, not build one from the ground up!"

Women, on the other hand, are comfortable with change. They can see changing the wallpaper. They can see changing the furniture. They can see changing the rugs. They can even see changing husbands. But keep your hands off the soap in the "powder room."

How My Garden Groans

My tomato crop came in the other day. Five tomatoes. All ripe on the same day. I picked them, and held them up in front of my face to admire them. One had a huge, dark soft spot on the underside. One had a deep, forbidding gash along the top that looked like a tire track. One had what appeared to be a nose. So that left me with a total of two usable tomatoes, the size of kidney stones.

That's my entire yield.

It's pathetic. I feel as if the whole world is one large salad, and I'm a chickpea.

The man in the house behind me has four hundred tomatoes on six plants. They don't all ripen on the same day. He gets tomatoes from July through September. I think it goes without saying that I hate this guy.

The other day he looked over at my meager plants and said smugly, "I guess not everyone has a green thumb."

I tried to come up with a withering rejoinder. Unfortunately, all I could think of was: "Oh yeah? Well, at least I don't have to live next to *me*!"

I am so jealous of people who can grow fruits and vegetables.

I believe this is called "greenis envy."

I buy those packages of seeds, with the beautiful color pictures of what my vegetables should look like when they come up. I'll see these leafy carrots on the package, but what I grow are horribly deformed tubers that look like human pinkies. Whose seeds did I actually get, the Dahmer collection?

My friend Joel has a huge cantaloupe patch. You haven't seen melons like this since, um, a time when I could have safely completed this joke. I asked Joel how he did it. He said, "I scattered the seeds on the ground and walked away."

I knew there was a trick to it.

I probably shouldn't be so depressed about my inability to have a garden. I write a newspaper column. What do I know about digging? To me, good dirt is finding out that Dan Rostenkowski was a woman. Had God wanted me to farm, he'd have given me a better body for overalls and a name like Norbert or W.J.

Suburban gardening is about ego—like, which guy's got the biggest squash? (I believe that is called "zucchinis envy.") I'm clearly not doing it to save money. Because when all is said and done, with the tools you buy to prepare the soil, the fertilizing, the mulching, the spraying, and the dusting, each edible tomato has cost approximately $16.75. If you're gonna spend that much, Safeway will send a limo for you.

Still, I don't understand why I have no tomatoes, and my neighbor can be a wholesaler for Contadina.

"It's because he gets full sun," I told my friend Gino.

"It's because he's not *you,*" Gino replied.

By the way, Gino has a wonderful vegetable garden, which is astounding when you consider this is the same guy who got his couch wedged into his basement staircase, and had to remove all his clothes and smear himself with Mazola oil to get back up the steps. Who'd figure a bozo like him could grow anything but fingernails?

"We have so many tomatoes, we use them to play catch with the dogs," Gino bragged.

The reason Gino's garden is so bountiful, it turns out, is that his wife is the gardener. Gino's one contribution to the garden was building a picket fence around it. I have seen the fence. Think about a wino who has been down on his luck since 1957, scrounging meals from Dumpsters and consuming no liquids other than peach schnapps. Now think about the wino's teeth. That's Gino's fence.

Hearing that Gino's wife was the gardener eased my spirits. Maybe gardening was a chick thing. Maybe all a man is supposed to do is dig the holes, then go play golf . . . and when he gets back, the salad will be grown. I went to a couple of women I knew for confirmation.

"Tell me about your garden," I asked Liz, a writer who is so sensitive that she cries when a tree falls in the forest and there's no one there to hear it.

She frowned. "It's too painful. . . . I planted a lot of seeds. They came up. It was gratifying, it renewed my belief in rebirth. Then everything died."

"What happened?" I asked.

"The same as every year. I start out very excited at seeing all these green sprouts. But then it gets hot, and I stay inside in the air conditioning, and I don't water. And the plants die."

"Why do you think they died?" I asked.

"Because I'm not a good person."

Bulletin: The wires just reported that Ivan the Terrible is in fact merely Ivan the Very, Very Bad. Thank you. We now rejoin this column, already in progress.

". . . no way," said the orangutan. "Because you don't know where that banana's been!"

Anyway, my boss Mary, who wishes to be called Mitzi in this column because she's afraid she will come across as a ditz, told a similarly harrowing story, which goes like this: "I'm really unhappy. I had a beautiful garden. Then my husband went away for a month, and now the garden is gone, and I see now that it must have been because he watered it.''

Are we to assume that "Mitzi" didn't water the garden?

"Well, I thought that was the whole point. You don't have to water because they're *outside*. God has dew and rain. The plants are supposed to get down to the water under the ground, aren't they?''

You can see why she wanted to be called Mitzi.

"And anyway,'' she continued, "the hose doesn't reach. So maybe that's the problem. Maybe we need a longer hose, a hose that reaches the plants.''

Getting an Earful

A few weeks ago I began to no-
tice that something was wrong with my hearing. The tip-off was
that one night when the children were watching *The McLaughlin
Group*—not *my* children, mine were watching reruns of *The
Patty Duke Show*; I bring in other people's children to make it
appear that we are an intelligent household in case *Life* magazine
sends a photographer over—and I couldn't hear John McLaughlin. He was talking and gesturing animatedly, but no words were
coming out. It was as though he were choking on a can of Ajax,
the Foaming Cleanser.

No such luck.

I ignored the problem the first night, because it didn't seem
like a problem, if you know what I mean. But the next night,
when I couldn't hear *America's Funniest Home Videos*, I went
batzoid.

After repeated, sophisticated testing procedures (I covered
one ear with a thirty-two-ounce *Last Action Hero* souvenir Slur-
pee cup), I found I couldn't hear a thing in my right ear. It was
apparent to me, as I knew it would be to any physician with a
degree from an American medical school, that a brain tumor the

size of a fully ripened Big Boy tomato was encroaching on my brain and would kill me by Thursday.

I called my doctor, and described my symptoms, and asked him to recommend a neurosurgeon. He sent me to an ear doctor. What a moron! As though a problem with hearing could possibly be related to the ear!

The ear guy (technically, an "ornithologist") looked in my right ear and asked, in the same disapproving voice a person might use to, say, inquire whether I regularly inject heroin directly into my carotid artery, "Do you use Q-Tips to clean your ears?"

What do you say to that?

I sensed, by the way he asked the question, that Q-Tips weren't good. But I felt that if I told him the truth—that I do not use Q-Tips because they are so prissy, and instead I regularly dig my fingers into my ears and grind around in there until I relieve the itch, and that there are times when the itch is so annoying that I will gladly shove anything in there, even a shish kebab skewer—he would find me hygienically repulsive, as you are undoubtedly doing at this particular moment, poised as you are with that spoonful of Wheatena frozen at your lips. It was easier to live with his judgment that I was stupid than that I was a cave man. So I said:

"Yeah, I use Q-Tips."

He frowned.

"They're not for the ears," he said.

Q-Tips are not for the ears?

What exactly are Q-Tips for? To paint the foyer? The doctor told me to lie still. He said, "I'm going to take something out of your ear the size of the Washington Cathedral."

Ear doctor humor, I presumed. Here's another: Did you ear the one about . . .

After a few twists he removed something the size of an

eraser—no, not the small tip of a No. 2 pencil, the big, arrow-head-shaped eraser that you fit *over* the small tip—from deep inside my right ear.

He showed it to me triumphantly, holding it up like it was a bone fragment from Zachary Taylor. I feared it was alive.

I didn't know whether to step on it or put it on a leash. Have you ever seen a banana that had been lying in the street since 1989, when it was run over by an oil truck, then some dog had gotten hold of it and dragged it around, and then, in the heat, it had begun to bubble and ooze? You would sooner frame *that*, and hang it in your newly painted foyer, than look at what came out of my ear.

"I'm so embarrassed," I said.

He smiled, then worked on my left ear—my *good* ear!—and removed something similarly revolting.

"This is humiliating," I said.

The doctor assured me that he sees this all the time.

I made him promise not to tell *Washingtonian*.

"You'll be amazed at how much sharper your hearing is now," the doctor told me.

"Why are you yelling?" I asked him.

Some will wonder about the lesson in all this. (Most people won't even get this far, however. They quit when I mentioned "ooze.") There are two lessons, and they are wondrous:

a. The human body is a miraculous creation of God.

b. God has a shockingly adolescent sense of humor.

Animal House

Earlier I wrote of my son's fifth birthday party and how—despite all the preparations I had made for an orderly, intellectually challenging party with a magician and a well-orchestrated supply of board games—the boys had reverted to their natural state, which is to say feral brutes whose idea of a swell time was to attempt to gouge one another's eyes out with a stick.

The next year, because he and his friends were one year older, one year more civilized, one year closer to becoming polite, sensitive men, I had grander hopes for his party. The party would reflect this new gentility.

As a symbolic gesture I went out to buy a tablecloth.

"I'm having a party for six-year-olds. There will be fifteen of them," I told the saleswoman at the party store. "Can you recommend a tablecloth?"

"Red," she suggested. "The blood stains won't show."

As the boys arrived, I sent them down to the basement. When I followed them down, I saw they had quickly made themselves at home—if their home was Beirut. Some were using the sleep sofa as a trampoline. Some were playing hide-and-seek *inside* the dryer. The rest were climbing the walls, literally.

I noticed one boy by himself, intently constructing something out of wooden blocks.

"What're you building there, son?" I asked. "A fort?"

"A gamma death-ray hydrogen bomb," he said proudly.

I'd been warned to pay particular attention to Martin and Gil. "Do not take your eyes off Martin and Gil," I was told. "They will wreck your house."

"They're only six," I protested.

"They can strip a car."

So I was keeping my eyes on Martin and Gil . . . when Brian crashed through the window. Luckily, it was a warm day; the window was up, so he went through the screen, not the glass.

"My God!" I shouted, as I ran to him.

"Did you see that, Dad?" my son asked. "Wasn't Brian totally awesome?" And the kids gathered around Brian and sang, "Doo-doo-doo-doo, BAT-man!"

At this point I went upstairs, because somebody was at the door—it was the scientist whom I had gotten to come over to entertain the kids by making slime and exploding volcanoes out of household chemicals—when I heard my son call out urgently:

"I need ice, Dad!"

"I told you guys, no drinks in the basement."

"It's for Jerome's eyes. Stuart hit him with the big bottle of Liquid Tide . . . by mistake."

(It's always "by mistake." When you come home and see six eggs cracked on the kitchen floor, you know it's "by mistake." Or you come home and find the goldfish dead; it's "by mistake." I once saw my daughter strangling my son, and wasn't the slightest bit surprised to learn this was "by mistake.")

I'd left the boys alone for less than one minute—and gotten off easy. The other day, my friend Gene got a telephone call from the principal in his son's school, telling him to come quickly and take seven-year-old Danny to the doctor to patch up his eye.

Danny's teacher made the mistake of inadvertently leaving four second-grade boys alone in a study group, unsupervised, for three minutes, while she took a phone call.

Three minutes.

If they were second-grade *girls*, they'd have sat together quietly and stitched a quilt for world peace. If they had any time left over, they'd have washed up for lunch.

What the boys did was hastily locate the only life-threatening object in the room—remember, this is a second-grade classroom; they're not storing hand grenades in the gerbil cages.

The boys managed to find some wooden dowels about two feet long, and then quickly organized themselves into an impromptu game of Death Javelin, which consisted of the three larger boys lining up on one side of the room and flinging the dowels at the smallest boy—who happened to be Gene's son, Danny.

Danny's assignment was to hold a jacket up in front of his face and ward off the Death Javelin. Sadly, Danny's reach wasn't quite high enough. The Death Javelin came hurtling over the top and bonked him in the eye. After the doctor, the eye patch, the scratches, the punctures, and the tears, Gene adopted a grave tone, like Ward Cleaver, and formally inquired of Danny, "What have you learned from all this, son?"

Speaking like a true boy, Danny replied, "I should've been taller."

My son's party provided no such epiphany. After leading them in a primal scream—much to the chagrin of the moms upstairs, who imagined their sons being initiated into some sort of weird Robert Bly beans and barf cult—I brought them outside, where the scientist instructed them in the manly art of making slime. The slime was a clear, gelatinous hodgepodge they smeared all over themselves and each other. (It's guaranteed nontoxic, because every scientist knows that a child's first question, *after* he puts something in his mouth, is, "Can you eat this?'') Eventually, it came time to wash off the slime, and I motioned them to the garden hose, and, just for laughs—because, hey, I needed some fun, too, I was a boy once—I hosed them down.

And they loved it.

They came running over, screaming to be soaked.

I checked for moms, and found the coast was clear, so I soaked them all, then led them in another primal scream. (A neighbor told me he hadn't heard anything like it since an Iron Butterfly concert.) Then I took them inside and fed them a gooey cake covered with ice cream and hot fudge.

It wasn't until late that night, when I was cleaning up, that I realized the only thing in the room that wasn't smeared with fudge, the only articles that were still in the same pristine condition as when the table was set, were the napkins.

Geezer Pleaser

An old friend invited me to dinner the other night with the promise of good food, good wine, and good company. My response was: How *late* is dinner?

I won't go if they're serving after seven, because then they won't be finished until at least eight-thirty, and then they'll expect me to chitchat until ten . . . which is out of the question, because by ten I'll be face down in the kiwi compote.

I've written before about creeping fogyism—that condition of becoming old before your time.

Now I think it *is* my time.

I can't stay up anymore.

Letterman is just a rumor in my life.

I'm basically done after "Final Jeopardy."

"Don't you understand that all the good things happen late at night?" my smart friend Martha asked me. "You're missing them. Yet you're still alive. What should we call this horrible life you're living?"

This is my day: I get up at five-thirty, pad around downstairs while waiting for the newspaper—I like being able to wander through my house before *they* wake up. The one thing I can't figure out is: How did all those dirty dishes get in the sink between the time I went to sleep and now?

I'm up so early that when I turn my lights on, my neighbors think I'm just getting home. It's pitch-black outside. I spend the rest of the day waiting for the darkness to come back so I can go to sleep. I think I'm the victim of some mad scientist's transplant, and I wound up with the soul of a Norwegian.

Most people look forward to Thanksgiving and Christmas. I look forward to the end of daylight saving time.

I don't even bother to read about the new season on TV, because the last show I watched until eleven was *Hill Street Blues*. Tell me, is Joyce Davenport still in that bubble bath? That's the way I want to remember her.

I guess I'm beginning to take after my father more than I realized. My father, who's eighty-two, now goes to sleep so early that he's wide awake for Bob Costas. My father is the only person I know who flew to China and had no jet lag.

A few weeks ago my friend Nancy and I went to see an acclaimed production of the notoriously long *Richard III* with Ian McKellen. It began at eight, and ran past eleven.

At intermission, I said, "Superb, isn't it?"

"Stunning," she said.

Then casually I said, "I know how it ends."

And she said, "So do I. More important, I know *when* it ends."

We left without hesitation.

My friends ask me how come I look so tired all the time?

I say it's because I *am* tired all the time.

So they say, "You must be depressed."

I say, no, just tired.

They say, "Well, you must be having a midlife crisis."

And I say, then please let me spend it on a Sealy Posturepedic.

For a while I was embarrassed by how early I went to sleep—

especially when I started going to sleep before my kids; oh yeah, my nine-year-old is still doing her homework when I go up to bed. (It's beginning to make me puke when she says, "Daddy, can I tuck *you* in? And read you *Goodnight Moon?*")

But I'm not embarrassed anymore, because I know I'm part of a growing trend of Fortysomething Fogies who can't keep their eyes open. You can recognize us because we:

1. Need to agree on when we're leaving a party before we get there;

2. No longer stay more than six innings at a baseball game and never sit through a rain delay;

3. Think sex is something you awake from a deep sleep to have;

4. Live dangerously by drinking coffee after 5 P.M.;

5. Have Arseniophobia, defined as the fear of Arsenio Hall's audience whoop-whoop-whooping and waving their fists in that strange way, because something is happening and we don't know what it is.

I'm part of that trend. And as America's best-loved feature writer, Mr. Henry, points out, "If you are part of a trend, all your sins are absolved by *USA Today*. By the middle of next week you'll see it on the front page: 'We're *All* Going to Sleep Early.' "

The problem with going to sleep so early is that I am totally out of the loop when it comes to late-night TV, and friends, after eleven-thirty is where the popular culture is made and transmitted. All the new words come from late-night TV—all the new stars, all the new 900 numbers, all the cool diseases. I have seen my children contort themselves until they literally fell off their chairs, and I thought they were having seizures until they explained they were simply imitating Arsenio interviewing Sir Mix-a-Lot, whoever that is.

I am hopeless. I don't know L.A. hip because I don't watch Arsenio. I don't know N.Y. hip because I don't watch Letterman. I don't know what's happening in the world because I don't watch Koppel. Apparently the show for fogies is Carson. I must really be a fogy, because I think Carson is hip. I don't watch Carson, though. (I tape, of course. Unhappily, I never watch anything I've taped. That's how we'll all die eventually— our houses will collapse under the weight of unseen videotapes, and we'll be crushed by the first five years of *Nightline*.)

I am constantly waiting for the "best of . . ." to be on TV, so I can understand what everyone's said for the past five years.

I never heard of Wayne's World until the movie.

What do you mean, Carson's gone?

Jay who?

Well, Your Daddy Don't Rock 'n' Roll

Go ahead and exhale. You've earned it. You had your folks over throughout the holidays. And they're finally going home.

They ask if you could take them to the airport.

"What time's your flight?"

They say it's two-thirty. "But I think we should leave here by ten."

By ten? By *ten*? "Dad, the airport's only twenty minutes away."

They say, "We like to get there early, just to be sure."

"The terrorists don't get there that early. Why do you want to get there four hours ahead of time?"

They say, "It'll give us time to get settled."

"Settled? It's an airport, not the West Bank."

These are the facts of life between grown-ups and their aging parents: You invite them to stay with you because *you* think it's the right thing to do—even though you don't really want them, because they've become wildly eccentric and do things like invite the mailman in for a cup of Metamucil. They come because *they* think it's the right thing to do—even though they'd rather stay in their own home where no one will consider it strange when they walk around the living room in a mink stole and swim fins.

Your parents come in, immediately remark on how ratty your house looks—and how they can't believe *anyone* could live like this. Then they look at their grandchildren, joyfully exclaiming how much they've grown and how wonderful they look. Then they ask for a cup of coffee (if it's not too much trouble) and announce they're ready to go home. The problem is, their flight isn't for five days. The Era of Good Feeling is over. It has lasted ten minutes. The rest of the visit goes like this:

Your dad gets up at 4 A.M. every day. ("I can't sleep," he tells you. "Is it the bed? Is it something you ate?" you ask, assuming it's your fault. "No," he tells you. "I can't sleep because I'm eighty-two years old. The older you get, the less you sleep, the more you go to the bathroom. I've reached the point where I spend more time in the can than Spam.") Since he's wide awake, he wants breakfast, and he ambles into the kitchen to fix some. This is particularly frightening because he has no sense of modern technology (he still calls the refrigerator "the icebox," calls the CD player the "hi-fi," and tries to dial Cleveland on the microwave.) You vaguely hear him poking around in the cabinets and come in just in time to stop him from shoving a banana into the coffee grinder.

Your father's breakfast is interesting. It consists of juice, one piece of dry toast, and 392 pills.

"Lots of pills, Dad," you say hesitantly.

"Oh, these? They're just maintenance."

Maintenance? You're reluctant to pry, but you can't help notice his set of monogrammed acupuncture needles.

"So, uh, Dad. You're feeling okay?"

He smiles reassuringly. "Don't worry. It's nothing," he says, inserting two small red pills under his tongue.

Your mother is not a problem at mealtime, because she hasn't eaten anything in twelve years. Nothing.

"Anything you want, Mom, just tell me," you say.

She hands you a grocery list. Everything on it seems to be "extra-strength" and "extra-absorbent."

Another weird thing about your parents is the strange prejudices they have, insane unsupportable generalizations that you tolerate because they're your parents—but it would be mortifying if they were to say these things in public. Like, your mom might say, "Hungarians drink like fish." Naturally, you wonder what possesses her to say such a thing. "Your father says he learned it in the war," she says. You are astounded. "Ma, Dad's never been to Hungary. He was stationed in Fort Dix. Hungarians are fine, sober people." And your mom says, "Well, maybe it's Romanians."

My father attributes his eccentricities to growing up in the Depression. He explains this is why he is reluctant to throw anything away—because he remembers when he didn't have anything. So he reuses things. Unfortunately, one of the things he reuses is Saran Wrap. He calls this "recycling." I call it "awww, Dad . . ."

He has no china anymore, just plastic plates he steals from the airlines. He is obsessed with the supermarket Styrofoam they sell the meat in. He has them stacked up in his closet. He must have four hundred of them. He tells me he saves them because he can cut them down and use them to store individual portions of meat in the freezer. He says you never know when you'll need one. I ask, "But when will you need four hundred? Who are you having over for dinner, Up With People?" I point out he doesn't have to save them, because every single cut of meat in America comes with its own Styrofoam tray. It is an endless supply. I tell him he should throw out all the Styrofoam trays he has collected—if only to make room for his glass jar collection.

And I ask him to drive us to the airport.

And Baby Makes 2 + 1

A newspaper headline caught my eye the other day, and I will repeat it here to see if you have the same reactions to it that I did:

FIVE-MONTH-OLD BABIES CAN ADD, SUBTRACT SMALL NUMBERS, STUDY INDICATES.

In rapid order, I thought:

1. Nonsense. Absurd. Don't make me laugh.

2. What's wrong with my kids?

I have a nine-year-old and a six-year-old. It is possible that my nine-year-old, whom I will call Corinne because maybe Dan and Marilyn Quayle will read this and think she is their child and teach her some family values, since all she seems to have learned in my house is how to burp on demand, a talent much admired among her friends—it's *possible* that my nine-year-old can add and subtract small numbers. I don't know for a fact because I have never seen her add anything more complicated than ketchup to a french fry.

I feel confident saying it's completely impossible that my six-year-old can add and subtract small numbers—my six-year-old, whom I'll call Michael because he won't care if I use his real name, since he can't read anything that isn't in giant capital letters, let alone add and subtract small numbers—because the last time I asked him what time it was, he said, and I quote, "forty-three-eleventy thousand."

Until I read this story I was relatively comfortable with my children's intelligence. My son was a typical six-year-old boy. He could take all his clothing out of his drawers, and throw it into a big pile on the floor and announce he had built a volcano. And my daughter was right in step with all the other nine-year-olds. She could:

1. Change her clothes seven times a day, throw all the discards in the general direction of the hamper, and then complain the next morning that she didn't have anything to wear because all her clothes were dirty;

2. Argue passionately that *America's Funniest Home Videos* was actually an educational show, because it taught you valuable lessons about behavior—like you shouldn't let your dog drink from the toilet bowl;

3. Identify the Soviet Union as a "supermarket chain."

But the study really threw me for a loop when it said that a psychologist had proved that five-month-olds could add and subtract—or at least distinguish the difference between correct and incorrect addition and subtraction. The proof was they would stare longer at a wrong answer than at a right answer.

In the test, if you put one rubber duckie in front of them, then put a screen in front of the rubber duckie, then ostentatiously added another rubber duckie—which should make two rubber duckies—then removed the screen to reveal three rubber duckies, they would stare longer at the three rubber duckies than they would have had there been two rubber duckies in front of them. The study showed they would stare *almost two seconds longer* at the wrong amount of rubber duckies. The conclusion was that the third rubber duckie was not what they expected, and their prolonged reactions proved they knew how to add and subtract.

Now, I don't know about you, but I'm not inclined to trust any scientific experiment conducted with rubber duckies. I don't recall J. Robert Oppenheimer explaining the theory of the atomic bomb by pointing to a rubber duckie.

This is scientific proof?

Two seconds of staring?

Look, when she was one year old, my daughter stared at chocolate pudding for half an hour, and she couldn't tell the difference between it and a pile of dog poop. On the other hand, it's things like this that always make me worry that my kids are stupid. When I read about a nine-year-old chess champion I always say, "There goes my kid's seat at Harvard." So I rush up to his room with a chess set and say, "If we hurry, maybe you can still get into Dartmouth." And he takes his finger out of his nose, and looks up at me, and says, "Daddy, if I drop my troll into the fish tank, will it explode and will it get fish guts all over the walls?"

I worry that I'm not diligent enough as a parent, that I've been too lax with my kids. I should have enrolled them in advanced Portuguese. My cousin's child asked for a nuclear-powered telescope for Christmas when she was seven. My kid asked for a Barbie Pez dispenser.

Maybe I overrate these things. I was a smart kid myself. I could read when I was three. I read from my grandfather's law books. He nearly dropped dead. He called all the relatives, and told them his grandson was a genius, and he would make enough money to take care of the whole family. I ended up writing a newspaper column like a thousand other slobs. His neighbor's grandson, a schlemiel who couldn't find his *pupik* with both hands, dropped out of high school and got a job stuffing stems into Styrofoam in a florist shop, where one day he met and later married an heiress, and is now retired, at forty-five, and living in Beverly Hills. His children are idiots. If they need to add or subtract, they can use a gold-plated calculator.

The Little Car That Didn't

Some people test well. I envy them. In high school I failed every math and science test. My math boards were so low, the colleges I applied to assumed I was a basketball player. I even failed a litmus test.

The one test I did well on was the essay. If the first three words were, "Compare and contrast . . ." I was golden. I could compare and contrast just about anything. The Magna Carta and the Declaration of Independence. The Roman Empire and the Greek city-states. Sonny and Cher. I could, as they say, really air it out: write long, and write illegibly—an unbeatable combination.

Unfortunately, yesterday's test wasn't an essay.

It was my car inspection.

We flunked it.

I took the test lightly. I should have prepared more. I should have gone to a D.C. Auto Inspection remedial course. The things I did were so obvious: spray the tires with Armor All, hang an air-freshener tree from the rearview mirror, put on an I BRAKE FOR D.C. AUTO INSPECTORS bumper sticker, and refill my windshield washer fluid with some old Perrier; the natural carbonation is great on glass, and who cares if the benzene poisons the wiper blades?

Actually, I should have taken the test in someone else's car. I didn't have a chance in a Chevette. Even the cab drivers were laughing when I drove up, and most of their taxis didn't even have bumpers. One station wagon, the whole right side was smashed in, and what looked like a person's leg was hanging out of the trunk, okay? So not only should this car be impounded, the driver should be facing a felony rap. He zipped through. Afterward, this same guy tells me, "Last year they flunked me. Best move I ever made was trading in my Chevette on this wagon."

It goes without saying that owning a Chevette has its ups and downs (shock absorbers are not standard in a Chevette; the Chevette owner likes to think of driving as a test of physical endurance). And it does teach you about humility. True story: I was leaving Capital Centre a few months ago, opening the door to my Chevette in the parking lot, when a young man in his early twenties and his friend stopped me.

Pointing to my Chevette, the young man said, "That's a rent-a-car, right?"

"No," I said. "It's mine."

"You *own* that car?" he hooted.

"Yeah. I own a Chevette."

He was grinning as he walked to his car, a late-model Toyota. He high-fived his friend delightedly and howled, "I'm doing better than Tony Kornheiser."

It's bad enough owning a car people laugh at. It's doubly humiliating when the inspectors slap a scarlet diamond-shaped sticker on the windshield—and they do it with such glee—to tell the world you've flunked the test, and you've got thirty days to correct what's wrong or you'll be shot on sight.

It's so embarrassing, failing your car inspection. It's like flunking out of Clemson. What's worse is having to sit in line for two hours to take the test.

Oh sure. You don't just breeze through. You really should bring a book. Not to read—to translate. They flunked me because one of my taillights didn't work. I bet it was working when I first got in line. It probably rusted in the interim. (Though it could be worse. It could be the DMV. That's the land of lost souls. You're lucky to get out of there the same age as when you walked in. And talk about friendly service. Where did they work before the DMV, Panmunjom?)

I was surprised when they got me for a taillight. I figured they'd nail me for bad tires. After all, I had to drive through D.C. to get to the inspection station. People say our streets aren't safe; hey, most aren't even paved. These aren't mere potholes—you can drop into them and disappear forever. Generations from now archaeologists will dig under the Whitehurst Freeway and uncover a fleet of fully preserved Dodge Omnis. If any of our mayoral candidates declared war on potholes, he or she would win in a landslide.

They flunked the guy in front of me, too. He was driving a black BMW sedan with tomato-red leather seats and vanity plates: DUN GR8. I assume they flunked him for tackiness. I thought my taillight was a bad rap. It was the third taillight, the one above the rear window. It's like I'd answered the extra-credit question wrong and they flunked me for the whole exam. They just started making those taillights in 1986. If they're so important, why didn't Henry Ford put them in the original blueprint? My wife's car only has two taillights; she passed. I don't feel any safer with a third taillight. I wouldn't feel safe in a Chevette if it had armor plating.

I tried to have this conversation with the inspectors, but they're not a real talkative bunch. They just hand you the punched card with your violations and paste on the scarlet sticker. This isn't "Metro Week in Review."

Fortunately, I was able to find a bulb for a third taillight at a Capitol Hill gas station on Pennsylvania Avenue. They were nice enough to fix the light on the spot, and give me a valid inspection sticker before any of my neighbors learned I'd failed the test and disgraced the block. I'm good for a full year. And next time I'm coming back in a Yugo.

Plenty of Nothing to Do

Now that the school year is over, and my children are home all day long . . . I'm thinking of smashing my head through a plate glass window.

Stop me if this sounds familiar:

"Dad, I'm bored."

Wait, let me try it again the way it really sounds:

"Daaaaadddd, I'm booorrrrrred!"

My kids are eleven and eight, and they're always bored. Everything bores them, including the brand-new $39.95 Sega video game I bought them this morning that they traded to the kid down the street because it was so borrrrringgg. They traded it for a stick. A *stick*! I asked them what the attraction of a stick was that they thought it was worth $39.95? They told me, and I am quoting verbatim here, "It was once alive."

I tell them there's so much to do: They can read, they can play the piano, they can ride bikes, they can watch TV, they can bury the cat up to its head in the backyard and fire up the lawn mower. (It's okay for me to joke about such things because I'm a professional humorist. Do not try this yourself.)

I tell them when I was young we didn't have anywhere *near* as many options. I tell them when I was young my diversions were pretty much limited to reading comic books about GIs in World War II (where machine guns went *"Budda Budda Budda,"* and soldiers with cigars in their teeth and comical cross-hatching on their faces that was supposed to look like stubble kept saying things like, "Eat lead, you lousy Krauts") and watching black-and-white TV with sitcoms such as *The Stu Erwin Show*, starring, obviously, Stu Erwin, who, to tell you the truth, I couldn't pick out of a lineup with the Andrews Sisters. There was no Nintendo, I say. The only thing remotely interactive with TV was *Winky Dink*, which featured a plastic screen that you were supposed to put on your TV and draw on with crayon— except you kept forgetting to put the screen on, and so your dad hit you with a belt or a baseball bat, which dads used to do fairly regularly (maybe Stu Erwin even did it), AND KIDS WERE BETTER OFF FOR IT, I point out menacingly.

They tell me the story bores them.

I ask them what they want to do.

"There's nothing to do," they say.

(What they're saying is that you, as a parent, are responsible for their entertainment. If you buy into this, they begin stringing you out. Say you take a deep breath, and against your better judgment you offer to make the deadly three-hour drive, and spend the $1,480 it takes to placate your family at a big-deal water slide amusement park like Busch Gardens, your kids will immediately say, "Do we have to go to Busch Gardens *again*?")

I tell them to call a friend.

None of our friends are home, they say.

What are you talking about, I say. Your friends are nine years old. Where did they all go at that age, to the Crusades? Are they celebrating D-Day by parachuting into the Le Havre–Cherbourg peninsula?

"Can you buy me X-Men cards?" he says.

I bought you X-Men cards two days ago. They were six dollars a pack, and you got five cards. Who drew these cards,

Picasso? These are not collectibles. There are no X-Men rookie cards.

What about all your toys, I say. What about those games?

"Games are for kids," she says.

Excuse me, Jessica Tandy, I say. What about playing ball? There are 368 balls in the house. There are tennis balls, footballs, basketballs, golf balls. There's that soccer ball you have on a string, I say, the one you've almost shattered the TV screen with. There's that ball the dog ate and barfed back up that no one will go near. There's that "vortex," the football with wings that some idiot invented as though it will help a kid learn to throw a football if you put wings on it; I mean, why not invent a golf club with a pogo-stick head, for those *really* long drives? Or a basketball the size of a watermelon seed so any shot goes in?

Both my kids like sports, and I try to get them to play sports with the kids on the block. But there's no league on the block. Sports have been taken over by some league with at least nine letters in its name, like the MCFPSPBFD 7-10 Gender-Equal T-Ball Workshop. Kids don't play ball unless there's an organized league with a trophy for everyone. My son is eight, and he's already got more trophies than Willie Mays. Every time he puts on his sneakers, someone hands him a trophy. If Rodin were alive today, he'd be making plastic baseball players.

And if you put your kids into leagues, you have to drive them there, then watch them play. There were no leagues when I was a kid. I played stoop ball. My old man didn't stand around watching me play stoop ball; he did what all fathers did in the 50s—he finished the basement. (To this day I can't look at knotty pine without having flashbacks.)

If you don't stay and *applaud* your kids, they will grow up with a self-esteem problem. According to America's best-loved feature writer, Mr. Henry, that's the beginning of the end: People are going to see grades fall, and cats being tortured, and fires being set, and eventually someone's sitting in a doctor's office recovering a memory. And who are they going to blame?

You.

Which is why when my kids are bored, I immediately rush out and buy them ice cream.

Smitten

Being a shameless TV hound, I eagerly accepted the invitation to cohost *Broadcast House Live* for a couple of days last week. It never occurred to me what a tragic mistake I had made until I saw myself on the monitor sitting next to the first guest, Jimmy Smits.

Jimmy Smits used to be one of the hunk lawyers on *L.A. Law*. Now he is the hunk homicide detective on *NYPD Blue*. Eventually, if his career lasts, he will be the hunk shuffleboarder on *Miami Beach Condo 33139*. Just how hunky is Jimmy Smits? He's the kind of guy you see, and then have to blind yourself with an ice pick.

I met Jimmy Smits briefly before the show. He was in the greenroom, where the guests and staff hang out. His body was obscured by a clutch of women in various categories of personal arousal, ranging from "squealy schoolgirl" to "yes yes yes yes YES YES YES." But I could see his head towering above theirs—because Smits is a big guy, six foot three, and not your typical twerp shrimp of an actor—and I elbowed my way through to introduce myself.

I felt empowered, being the cohost and all; I could walk right up to Mr. Big Shot TV Star Jimmy Smits and say anything I wanted. I have read all the classics of literature and philosophy and am equally well versed in American popular culture. I had a veritable library of information both arcane and profound from which to draw for my meeting with Jimmy Smits. So I walked up to him, pumped his hand, and said the first thing that came into my mind, which was, I swear:

"So, do you go to a gym?"

"You said *what*?" my friend Gino asked as I proudly related the story of my encounter.

I have to admit, it didn't sound quite so brilliant, repeating it a second time, down there in the company cafeteria.

"Why did you say *that*?"

"Well, ah, I go to a gym. . . . I thought we'd have something in common."

"So if you were introduced to Gabriel García Márquez, would you ask him, 'So, do you pee in a toilet?' "

Anyway, that's what I asked Jimmy Smits: "So, do you go to a gym?"

(It made sense to me. He's a big, strong guy, you know. What should I have asked—"Do you think we're acting prudently converting our naval fleet to nuclear propulsion?")

And Smits said, and this is his verbatim answer: "No, thanks. I'm fine."

A very enigmatic answer, I thought. Until I realized he obviously (1) had not even listened to anything said by someone who looks like me. And he (2) assumed I was some kind of water boy, and I was asking if he wanted me to get him a sandwich.

I would have clarified my role, but by then the women had eased me out of the way and were back buzzing around him, as close as the shell to the peanut. Grown women actually buckled at the knees near Smits: He would walk by, and the line of women would actually undulate as their knees gave way. I've had women react strongly around me, but it's usually more of a shudder.

One of the women on the show's staff told me her friend was so excited to hear Smits would be on the show that she pleaded, "Just rub against him, and tell me what it feels like."

(Men would never do that. If Claudia Schiffer walked through an insurance office, all the men would poke each other in the ribs and ogle her, and they'd find some reflective glass and station themselves in a way to surreptitiously catch her reflection from an angle, or they'd simply squat on the ground trying to look up her dress. But they wouldn't directly approach her. Women are much more honest and direct. They go up to a hunk like Jimmy Smits and swoon in his presence. They say, more or less, Here is my heaving bosom, take me and ravish me on the linoleum, but get done before five-fifteen because I have to get to the supermarket and pick up a brisket for my fat load of a husband, who sniffs his food like a dog and wouldn't notice if I walked into the living room totally naked unless I passed in front of the TV set and blocked his view of that Olajuwon fellow, whatshisname, Raheem?)

So later I'm sitting there next to Smits, and I'm supposed to interview him. And I have all these really intelligent questions prepared, you know, about the recent shift toward conservatism among the electorate. But we start showing a film clip of the humblingly muscular Smits doing push-ups buck naked, with a big, blue TV dot covering his heinie, which makes it hard to gracefully slide into a question about the efficacy of our foreign policy in Bosnia. And it was then, coming out of the clip, that I saw myself in the monitor—this fat, bald, marshmallow-pale geezebag sitting next to this unbelievably gorgeous man. And I thought to myself:

Gaaackk! Who is that toadstool interviewing Jimmy Smits? It's bad enough to be fat, bald, and forty-five—but now I'm sitting next to a guy who's much bigger than I am, and his skin is clear, and his eyes are bright, and he's filling up the TV screen like something Cézanne painted, and next to him I look like that putz Marty Allen who says "Hello dere," AND WE'RE ON TV FOR GOD'S SAKE AND EVERYONE CAN SEE HOW PATHETIC I AM!

At this point I offered to move and let Jimmy Smits sit next to the host, my friend, the fabulous Robin Young, who had recently fainted and fallen off her stool.

"Maybe you want to sit next to Robin," I said.

Recognizing that I felt old and useless and ugly in his aura, Jimmy Smits did the kindest thing—he put his arm around me. Right there, on TV, Jimmy Smits put his arm around me.

And I have to admit, ladies, I felt a tingle.

Girth of the Blues

Photos from my college reunion came back the other day. There has to be some mistake. Everybody else looked just the way I remembered them, but somehow the pictures of me got distorted.

What kind of lens does this, gets everybody else in focus and makes one guy appear irretrievably fat?

From the front I'm pear-shaped. I look like something you win at a carnival for knocking milk bottles off a table.

From the side I look like the third leg of an isosceles triangle.

I should write Fotomat. Something must be wrong with their developer. This can't be me.

Where did that mudslide of a stomach come from?

What a lousy time I've picked to look like Dom DeLuise.

Next weekend's Memorial Day. The pools open. I'm going to have to take off my shirt. I can't afford to do that. The kids'll see me and think I'm some sort of inflatable rubber Shamu.

Luckily, I don't have any dimpling on my thighs yet, and none of that crepey skin under my arms. My midsection is a disaster. I sit down and I look like a Shar-Pei. Talk about love handles, this is some serious baggage here—the entire New York City subway ridership could hang on.

I guess it sort of snacked up on me.

I was never fat as a kid. I was one of those jerks who made fun of the fat kids. I truly didn't think I was fat now until these horribly distorted photos arrived. Okay, I'd noticed a couple of changes: I couldn't button the collar of my shirts, but I assumed it was the laundry putting in starch—I'd told them I hate starch. Then I couldn't button my suit jackets, and I told my wife, "Can you believe the laundry is putting starch in my *suits*?" She made a crack about how I'd better stop talking about buying a Miata, because they'd have to lower me in with a crane.

It's all come together.

My age.

My waist.

The amount of pounds over what it says on my driver's license.

Looking back, I should have paid more attention the night we all sat around watching *Designing Women*, and I made the comment how Mary Jo was such a foxy little thing, and three people in the room turned to me and said at exactly the same time, "I'd have thought you'd prefer Suzanne." Hmmmm, Ms. Avoirdupois. Anyway, I looked at those preposterously out-of-focus pictures— perhaps it's Kodak's fault, because I'm certain I was wearing a belt, and you can't even see it below my gut in the photos—and I wrote this song to the tune of "I'm Henry VIII, I Am":

> *I'm fat as a whale, I am*
> *Fat as a whale, I am, I am.*
> *I'm much fatter than the people next door*
> *I can't fit into my pants no more*
> *And every day I eat gobs of sweets*
> *Two eclairs, a pudding, and some jam*
> *I am infinitely larger than a porpoise*
> *Fat as a whale, I am.**

*© Tub O'Lard Tunes 1990

I've started running.

Well, not really running, more like creeping.

And wouldn't you know, as soon as I started, I got hurt. Unfortunately, it's nothing sexy like shin splints or a stress fracture—my thighs got chafed, the inside of my thighs. All that fatty tissue rubbing against itself. It's a good thing my son's only recently out of diapers; we had some Balmex at home. My thighs looked like round steak. I'm surprised people didn't stop me on the side of the road and ladle me with barbecue sauce.

"Vaseline," advised the jogger pals.

I'm so slippery when I run now that if I fall down near a storm drain I'm likely to slide all the way to Maine Avenue.

Not that jogging is going to do me any good. Because it makes me hungry. I get home and eat twice as much as before. I'm down to only one big meal a day, but I'm eating it from eight to midnight.

Around the turn of the century, those were the good old days. If a man had an ample middle then, it meant he was prosperous. Girth was respected as a sign of accomplishment. William Howard Taft, all three-hundred-plus pounds of him, was elected president. Today he couldn't win. Today he couldn't even fit inside the voting booth.

I guess I'll go on a diet.

My wife doesn't trust me when I say that. I've gone on diets before, and never even made it through one full day without cheating big time. (My idea of a diet is: I eat with a small fork.) She'll bring home diet rice cakes, and I'll slather peanut butter and jelly on them.

"You're supposed to eat them plain," she says.

"Dick Gregory wouldn't eat these plain," I answer.

My former best friend, Mike, recently went on a diet, the one Tommy Lasorda and Ed Koch shill: You drink a couple of milkshakes and eat one "modest" meal a night.

"There's a slight difference of opinion," Mike says. "My

'modest' is, I stop after four rolls and one dessert. Their 'modest' is three hundred calories. It's somewhere between three leaves of romaine lettuce and one lick of white chocolate chunk. They claim you feel full on their food. I don't. I'm living on the memory.''

Mike is my former best friend because he's lost thirteen pounds on this diet and will soon blow away in the wind. My only joy comes when I ask how he feels, and he complains, ''Extremely hungry.''

Our mutual friend Dave Kindred, whose prose once graced the *Post*, is tinkering with the thought of attempting this same diet, and has already begun experimenting with the milkshakes. ''I like them,'' he is pleased to report. ''After meals, I have them for dessert.''

ACKNOWLEDGMENTS

My special thanks to my smart friend Martha Sherrill; America's best-loved feature writer, Henry Allen; Norman Chad, who is the real Man About Town Chip Muldoon; Jeanne McManus, who said I could call her my friend Nancy, and she would call me Ramon; my friend Gino, better known as Gene Weingarten, the editor of the Sunday "Style" section of *The Washington Post*. Gino wrote much of this book, including all the columns, the introduction, and this paragraph. That's my picture on the cover, though.

Curiosity Killed the Cat Sitter

Curiosity Killed the Cat Sitter

The First Dixie Hemingway Mystery

BLAIZE CLEMENT

Thomas Dunne Books
St. Martin's Minotaur ⋈ New York

THOMAS DUNNE BOOKS.
An imprint of St. Martin's Press.

www.minotaurbooks.com

Library of Congress Cataloging-in-Publication Data
Clement, Blaize.
    Curiosity killed the cat sitter : the first Dixie Hemingway mystery / Blaize Clement.—1st ed.
      p. cm.
    ISBN 0-312-34056-7 (alk. paper)
    EAN 978-0-312-34056-8
    1. Women detectives—Florida—Sarasota—Fiction. 2. Sarasota (Fla.)—Fiction. 3. Pet sitting—Fiction. 4. Cats—Fiction. I. Title.
    PS3603.L463C87 2006
    813'.6—dc22

2005016624

First Edition: January 2006

10 9 8 7 6 5 4 3 2 1

Acknowledgments

My greatest thanks to the "Thursday Group"—Susana Gonzalez, Kate Holmes, Greg Jorgensen, and Clark Lauren—who listened to scenes from this novel as it took shape, and who are unfailingly kind even when I write trash.

Also to Pamela Strom and Dr. Everett Shocket for law-enforcement and medical information.

To Florida licensed trauma cleaner Bill Sullivan for explaining how crime scenes are sanitized. To professional pet-sitter Virginia Wilson for insider information. To Lora Garrett, crime-scene technician with the Sarasota County Sheriff's Department, for information on who does what in forensic investigation. To Dr. Reinhard Motte, Miami–Dade County associate medical examiner, who gave me some unpleasant facts involving death and pets. To Mary V. Welk, ER nurse and author, who cut to the nitty-gritty and told me how my victim would look.

And most of all, thanks to my dream team: Marcia Markland, who is such a warm and generous person that she should be in an editors' hall of fame; Diana Szu, Marcia's patient and efficient assistant; Annelise Robey, who was brave enough to become my agent, and Don Cleary, who handles all the legal stuff with wit and style.

Curiosity Killed the Cat Sitter

1

It was about 3:30 Thursday afternoon when I stopped by Marilee Doerring's house to pick up a new key. I have keys to all my clients' houses. I carry them on a big round ring like a French chatelaine. If a robber broke into my apartment, it wouldn't be to rip off my Patsy Cline CDs, it would be for my key ring.

I'm Dixie Hemingway, no relation to you know who. I'm a pet-sitter. I live on Siesta Key in Sarasota, Florida, and so do all my clients. Until three years ago, when the world crashed around me, I was a deputy with the Sarasota County Sheriff's Department. Now I take care of animals. I go to their homes while their owners are away and feed them and groom them and play with them. They don't ask a lot of questions or expect much from me, and I don't have to interact with people any more than I choose to. At least most of the time. On this particular afternoon, I was about to become a lot more involved with a lot more people than I wanted to be.

Siesta Key is an eight-mile barrier island connected to the mainland by two bridges. The Gulf of Mexico laps at the west side, and Sarasota Bay and the Intracoastal Waterway are on the east. Inside the key itself, there are fifty miles of canals, so we have almost as many boats and boat docks as we have seabirds, which is a bunch. You name it, we've got it. Terns, plovers, gulls, egrets, herons, cranes, spoonbills, storks, ibis, and pelicans all happily scoop up their favorite entrées on our beaches and in our backyards. Offshore, manatees and dolphins play in the warm water.

Counting part-time residents, the key is home to about 24,000 sun-tanned people. Except for "the season," when snowbirds come down and inflict their money on us, and spring break, when college students get drunk and pee on the hibiscus, Siesta Key is a quiet, laid-back place. On the map, it looks like an alligator's head with an extremely long and skinny nose. Siesta Village and Roberts Bay form the head, with Crescent Beach where eyes would be. The nose is just wide enough for one street—Midnight Pass Road—with private lanes and tourist lodgings on each side, along with occasional undeveloped wooded areas.

Marilee's cat was a silver-blue Abyssinian named Ghost. Awful name, sweet cat. I had taken care of him several times before, and the only thing different about this time was that Marilee had called the night before to tell me she'd had her locks changed, so I would have to pick up a new key before she left town. She lived on the bay side of Midnight Pass Road, about midway between Turtle Beach and the south bridge. Her street was curvy, lushly tree-lined and short, the house a low-slung stucco with a red barrel-tile roof and deep recessed arches over doors and windows, the kind of Mexican-Mediterranean hybrid that Floridians love. Dwarf schefflerias and pittisporum and hollies made swirling patterns of ground cover in the front yard, interspersed with clumps of red geraniums and bird of paradise plants. The front door undoubtedly had once hung on a cathedral in some South American country, and the doorbell was a deep-bonging thing that sounded like it might have come from the same cathedral. As I waited, I could hear the faint sound of classical piano music from next door.

Marilee opened the door a cautious slit and peered out at me. Later, I would wonder about that, but at the time it didn't seem unusual for a cat owner. A cat can be taking a nap on its hundred-dollar kitty pillow or watching a television program especially designed for its feline pleasure, but let somebody open an outside door the narrowest bit, and it will go streaking out like it's escaping a torture chamber.

Marilee was stunningly beautiful, with glossy black hair tumbling over her shoulders in the kind of casual disarray that takes a lot of work. It framed an oval face with skin like a cosmetic commercial, only hers wasn't airbrushed, it was really that perfect. Her eyes were dark violet blue, with thick black lashes, and her mouth had the kind of moist expectancy that automatically makes you think of sex. I could smell expensive perfume, the kind I've only worn by rubbing a strip from a magazine on my wrist. She was wearing a short pink terry-cloth robe that cost more than my entire wardrobe, including the winter coat I have salted away in mothballs in case I ever travel north. Her legs were long and slim, tanned enough to look healthy but not so dark as to look like she tarted herself up in a tanning booth.

At first she looked surprised to see me, then in that breathy voice of hers, said, "Oh, you've come for the key! I was just about to jump in the shower. Hold on, I'll get it."

She closed the door and I imagined her bare feet sprinting over Mexican tile. Next door, the music stopped and a moment later the garage door opened and a white Jeep Cherokee backed out and headed toward Midnight Pass Road. As it made the turn, I could see the driver was a young man, no more than a teenager, which surprised me. Somehow I never think of teenagers listening to classical music, which shows what a lowbrow I am.

Marilee opened the door again, wider this time, and stretched her arm out with a loop of red silk ribbon dangling from a finger. A shiny new door key hung on the ribbon like a gold pendant on a necklace.

Feeling a bit like the upstairs maid, I held out my hand and let her drop it into my palm. I said, "Don't forget to leave me a number where I can reach you, and the date and time you'll return."

I should have whipped out my notebook and made her give me the number right then. But she knew the routine, and I already had all the pertinent information in my files—her vet's name and number, the dates of Ghost's immunization shots, his medical history, his favorite foods and toys and where they were located, and his favorite hiding place in case he decided to play Where's Ghost?

I told her to have a safe journey and not to worry about Ghost, and went on my merry way. I never saw Marilee again, at least not alive.

My alarm went off at 4:00 the next morning, and I got right up. One thing you can say for me, I wake up well. I sleep in underpants, so all I had to do was pull on khaki cargo shorts and a T and lace up my Keds. I brushed my teeth, splashed water on my face, pulled my hair into a ponytail, and I was ready. Animals don't expect you to dress up for them. I could go naked for all they care. By 4:15, I was halfway to my first stop. The sky was just beginning to pink a little around the edges, and the early April air was a balmy seventy degrees.

The sea breeze freshens in the early morning on Siesta Key, tickling the undersides of palm leaves and sending orgasmic tremors through trailing bougainvillea. Snowy egrets open their topaz eyes and stretch their blue-toed feet, and great blue herons stilt-leg it to the edge of the shore to pick up breakfast coming in on the tide. The air tastes of brine and fish and sand, and throaty chants of mourning doves underscore the squawk of seagulls rising and circling on air currents. It's my favorite time of day, a time when I have the streets almost to myself and can zoom along on my bike like a gull looking for early-waking grubs and unwary snails.

I always see to the dogs first and leave the cats and occasional birds and rabbits and hamsters for later. It isn't that I play favorites, it's just that dogs are needier than other pets. Leave a dog alone for very long and it'll start going a little nuts. Cats, on the other hand, try to give you the impression they didn't even know you were gone. "Oh, were you out?" they'll say, "I didn't notice." Then they'll raise their tails to show you their little puckered anuses and walk away.

My first stop was at Sam and Libby Grayson's, a retired couple who had gone north to visit their daughter. A wooded area separated the Graysons' street from Marilee's, and with tall trees lining the street and woods behind, it was like being in the middle of a dark forest. The

Graysons' house was a two-story ultramodern built of cypress and glass, with a high vaulted cage around the lanai that gave it a look of dignified exuberance. One of the bulbs in the twin coach lights flanking their garage had burned out, and I made a mental note to replace it when I came back in the afternoon.

Until a few years ago, nobody on Siesta Key ever thought about burning security lights. But since everybody north of Georgia seems to have looked up one day and said, "By gawd, I'm moving to Florida!" we've started having break-ins here and there, even a murder now and then. So now people on Siesta Key leave night lights burning so potential burglars and rapists can see better.

I propped my bike in front of the garage and sorted through my keys. Rufus, the Graysons' schnauzer, started barking to show me he was on the job as guard dog, but he knew it was me and his heart wasn't in it. As soon as I pushed open the door, he was all over me, not the least bit ashamed to let me see how glad he was that I had come. I like that about dogs. They don't worry that you might not like them as much as they like you and hold off until they're sure, they just go ahead and declare themselves and take the chance of being rejected.

I knelt down to hug him and let him kiss my chin. "Hey, old sweet Rufus," I said, "How's my old sweet Rufus?" Dogs like you even when you say the same dumb things over and over. Cats expect you to have more self-restraint.

I got his leash out of the wicker basket in the foyer, and as soon as I opened the door, he was out like a shot. I had to hold him steady while I locked the door behind me, and then we both loped off. Rufus plunged off the pavement to pee on a palm tree, then raced on ahead of me. My Keds made smacking sounds on the asphalt, so I moved to the edge of the street where pine needles muffled the noise. I didn't want to cause some retiree to think a criminal was running down the street and haul out his handgun. Something about not having to shovel snow anymore and being surrounded by sunshine and tropical foliage 365 days of the year causes a lot of people to feel so guilty that they compensate by scaring themselves with thoughts of imminent crime. They go out and buy themselves a gun and sort of hope they'll get to shoot somebody with it, so you have to be careful.

Rufus did his business next to a hibiscus bush and I picked it up in a poop bag and kicked a cover of pine needles over the spot before I moved on. I like to be tidy. I let the leash play out so Rufus could feel independent, and he bounced into the middle of the street to check out a fluffy egret feather. He whoofed at it and nosed it around, showing off to let me see he was alert to anything new. Something caught his attention from the woods, and he raised his head and began barking loud enough to wake everybody on the block.

I jerked the leash taut and said, "Shhhh! Quiet!"

He barked again and I turned to look over my right shoulder. I could have sworn I saw a figure slip behind a tree trunk in the murky shadows.

Any number of things could have been moving around back there in the predawn shadows. A snowy egret or a great blue heron could have dived for a baby black snake from one of the oak trees. A squirrel could have awakened early and leaped from a branch with a flash of white underbelly. Or somebody returning from a middle-of-the-night tryst might have seen me and ducked into that dark thicket. God knows, there are plenty of men and women who drift in and out of one another's beds here on the key, and some of them are married to other people. But still, the skin on my shoulders puckered and I felt uneasy, with that tingly feeling that tells you unfriendly eyes are watching.

I yanked Rufus out of the street and set off for the Graysons' house so fast he had to do a scrambling dance to catch up. As we trotted up the driveway, the *Herald-Tribune* delivery man turned into the street and sailed a paper into the flower bed by the front walk. I retrieved it and put it in a wooden chest outside the front door where people leave drop-offs when the Graysons aren't home. Somebody had left a stack of paperbacks rubber-banded together, and in the pale glow cast by the lone security light I could see a yellow Post-it stuck on top with a heavily scrawled "Thanx!"

I fed and brushed Rufus and put out fresh water for him. With him following me like an aide carrying a clipboard, I did a fast check of the house to make sure he hadn't gotten bored over night and chewed up something. The Graysons' latest acquisition was a full-sized carousel horse that had once been part of John Ringling's collection—Ringling practically built Sarasota, and you can't turn around here without seeing something circus-related. The horse was mounted on a floor-to-ceiling brass pole in the dining room, and it gave the room a happy, carefree look. I took a moment to admire it before I turned on the TV in the den for Rufus. I set it on Nickelodeon so he could watch *Mister Ed*. Then I hugged him good-bye.

"I'll be back tonight," I promised. "You be a good boy, okay?" I don't know why I ask animals questions like that. If one of them ever answers me, I'll probably freak out.

Rufus was sitting in the front hall with his head cocked to one side when I shut the door behind me. I felt guilty leaving him alone, but everybody has to come to the realization sooner or later that we're all alone in this world.

2

It was almost 6:00 A.M. by the time I worked my way to Marilee Doerring's house. On that twisty street, the house next door was the only one visible, but I could see a couple of lights there. The normal world was beginning to wake up. I let myself in with my new door key and flipped on the foyer light. Abyssinians are people cats, and when I'd taken care of Ghost before, he had always come bounding to the door to greet me.

I called, "Ghost?"

Dogs come when you call, and cats answer. But there were no little *nik-nik* sounds of friendly greeting. A stack of outgoing mail was on the foyer table, with the top envelope addressed to the IRS. I figured Marilee must have planned to mail it on her way out of town and forgot. While I gave Ghost time to decide to come out of hiding, I flipped through the other envelopes, most addressed to department stores or utilities, and then slid the lot in a deep-flapped pocket on my cargo shorts. I would put it in her mailbox for pickup as I left.

The living room was to the left, and I ducked in to give it a quick once-over while I called to Ghost again. Sometimes bored animals do something naughty just to announce their annoyance at being left behind when their person leaves, but there were no overturned plants or shredded magazines in the living room. The air seemed oddly humid, with a warm breath coming from the glass doors opening to the lanai. Linen sheers hung over the sliders, and when I stepped closer, I could see that the glass slider was partially open.

I said, "Uh-oh," and hurried to the door. There were a ton of potted plants on the lanai, and a water hose had been left lying on the floor. Marilee had probably been interrupted watering the plants just before she left and forgot to close the slider. Peasant that I am, my first thought was that all that warm air would make the AC run harder and that Marilee's electric bill was going to be enormous. The second thought was that Ghost might have gone outside. The lanai was typical—a tiled pool at the far side and wicker furniture and potted plants grouped under the roof on the inner side. It was screened, of course, sides and top, to keep out insects and falling leaves. In Florida, screened lanais are called "cages," and anybody who is anybody has a caged lanai.

A screened door was at one side, opening to the yard. Most lanai doors have simple latch mechanisms that can be locked, but since a dedicated burglar can simply slit the screen, most people leave them unlocked so pool cleaners can get in. The furniture on the lanai made dark shapes in the murky light as I sprinted to the outside door. It wasn't firmly latched, and I pulled it shut, making sure the latch caught. I could see a light in a back window of the house next door, but no sign of Ghost.

I trotted back inside, pulling the slider shut and locking it behind me, and hurried toward Marilee's bedroom. Unless Ghost had gotten outside through the lanai door, he was probably hiding. His favorite hideaway was atop an immense antique armoire in Marilee's bedroom. Abys have powerful back legs that give them unusual jumping ability, and Ghost vaulted up there when he was nervous or when he was sulking, tucking himself into an invisible small mound.

Calling "Gho-oo-ost," I went down the hall to Marilee's bedroom. As I went through the door, I flipped the bedroom light switch, and the room's vibrant colors sprang alive. I stopped with the hairs on the back of my neck rising. Marilee's bedroom was like something out of *Architectural Digest,* with deep pumpkin walls and a tall dark bed that Pancho Villa might have slept in. Ordinarily, the room was fastidiously neat, but not today. The drawers on the bedside tables stood open, and all their contents had been raked to the floor.

Cautiously, I edged toward the dressing room between the bedroom and bathroom. Somebody had pulled everything crooked, as if they had jerked robes and dresses and skirts and jackets out to dig in their pockets. Handbags that were usually filed on shelves gaped open on the floor. A tall jewelry cabinet stood like a gap-toothed vagrant, with blank spaces where its drawers had been. The drawers were piled on the floor with jewelry spilling from them.

Whoever had done this hadn't been after valuables to pawn or sell, but for something that could be secreted in a small space. Drugs were the obvious first thought, but Marilee had never struck me as a user, and if she was a dealer it didn't seem likely that she would keep her supply in her jewelry cabinet.

In the bathroom, drawers had been similarly ransacked. A hair dryer lay on the counter with its cord plugged into an outlet by the door. It was a brush-type dryer that doubled as a curling iron, with a few black hairs caught in its bristles. Marilee usually left her bathroom so spotless that the errant hairs seemed almost obscenely disordered.

I must admit that while I was appropriately concerned that somebody had broken into Marilee's house, I was more concerned about Ghost. I went back into the bedroom and looked up at the carved cornice at the top of the armoire.

"Ghost, are you up there?"

A faint little *nik-nik* came from the top of the armoire, and Ghost came sailing down and landed at my feet. Cats hate for you to gush at them, so to protect his dignity, I let him wind himself around my ankles before I knelt to stroke the top of his head.

Ghost's hair was ticked, meaning it had several colors on one hair shaft. The overall effect was an iridescent sheen graduating from silver to pale lavender. He wore a black velvet color studded with miniature hearts and keys. The collar gave him a decadent look, like a charming

French roué whom you know you shouldn't allow yourself to trust, but you can't resist.

"I was afraid somebody had taken you," I said.

He rubbed his face and neck against my leg to reassure me, gently scratching my skin with the charms on his collar. Now that we had properly greeted each other and I knew he was okay, I headed toward the kitchen. I would give Ghost his breakfast first, and while he ate I would call 911 and report the break-in. Ghost trotted behind me making happy little squeaks of anticipation. I've trained all my cat owners not to leave food out all the time, but to put it out twice a day and remove it as soon as the cat has stopped eating. That way they don't get finicky or fat, and mealtime is a big deal to them.

To a dog, food is simply a necessity of life, and they're not too picky about how it tastes or what it's served in. A weighted plastic feeding bowl suits a dog just fine, and you can give them the exact same food twice a day and they'll think you're the greatest chef in the world. Cats, on the other hand, are snooty gourmands. Oh sure, they may supplement their finicky diet with an occasional mouse head or lizard tail, but that's more to satisfy their hunting instinct than for the taste. Cats like their food fresh and flavorful, and they'll turn up their noses today at what they loved yesterday. If their dishes aren't spotlessly clean, they'll even turn up their noses at food they love.

Cats don't shove their bowls around on the floor, either. They sit in front of them daintily, giving the impression of having patted a linen napkin in place. Cat owners therefore feed their cats in dishes ordinarily reserved for royalty, and the cats accept them as their due. Ghost ate from a hand-painted porcelain bowl, and he lapped his drinking water from an ornately carved silver serving bowl. It held enough water for a trio of cats, but it served the purpose well enough, and both Marilee and Ghost thought its elegance was totally appropriate.

When I stepped through the kitchen door and flipped the light switch, I instinctively turned toward the water bowl, and then did a quick backward dance. I'm not sure, but I think my legs may have pedaled the air for a moment. A man was lying on the floor with his face in Ghost's silver bowl. A strip of putty-colored masking tape ran across the top of his head to the sides of the bowl, holding his nose underwater. The back of his head was caked with dried blood, and he was entirely too motionless to be alive.

For a second, my eyes darted around the kitchen, refusing to look at the body. Everything in the kitchen was normal. A stainless-steel teakettle of Italian design, with a carved yellow bird for a pouring spout, sat shining on the immaculate stove. A yellow dish towel was on the countertop beside the sink, neatly folded so both edges were turned in the way you do with guest towels. Trust Marilee to fold her dish towel that way.

I looked back at the dead man. He wore a navy blue suit, and both sleeves showed white shirt cuffs. His shoes were expensive black wingtips, well polished, the kind pimps and undertakers wear. As well as I could tell with the dried blood on his head, his hair was dark. I couldn't see his face. I tiptoed over and knelt beside him. I don't know why I tiptoed, it just seemed the right thing to do. His body had been carefully arranged so that his arms were out to the side with the elbows bent in a kind of "I surrender" pose. I took his wrist in my fingers and felt for a pulse. The wrist was cold. The man was definitely dead.

Ghost wailed a long insistent falsetto that forced me to do what I should have done already. I got up on rubbery legs and went to the wall phone and dialed 911.

The dispatcher who answered didn't sound like anybody I knew. Old training kicked in, and after I gave her Marilee's address, I said, "I've got a Signal Five, adult male."

Signal 5 means homicide victim. With his head bloody and taped to a cat's bowl, I didn't think it could be anything else.

The dispatcher verified the address and asked my name.

"Dixie Hemingway."

"Are you sure he's dead?"

Ghost had gone into a crouching position with his body stretched long and his nose twitching toward the dead man.

"Oh yes, he's dead."

"What appears to be the cause of death?"

I cleared my throat. "He appears to have drowned in a cat's water bowl."

The dispatcher was silent for a moment, and then rallied. "Inside the house or outside?"

Ghost was slinking toward the man, and I swung my foot to distract him.

"Inside. In the kitchen. I came to feed the cat and found him."

Ghost crept closer to the man's head. I skittered toward him on my Keds and tried to block his progress with my foot. He ignored me and twitched his whiskers.

"Do you know who he is?"

"No, I've never seen him before, and the woman who lives here is out of town."

"Somebody's on the way, ma'am."

Just as I hung up, it occurred to me that the killer could still be in the house. I grabbed Ghost and ran.

I was pacing the driveway with a seething Ghost in my arms when the green-and-white squad car pulled in. The deputy who got out wasn't anybody I knew, but I knew the type well enough. Hair cut so short it was near-shaven, hard lean body under a crisp dark green uniform, black leather belt bristling with all the accoutrements of authority, and a small diamond stud in one well-shaped earlobe. I could tell from the stiff way he walked that he thought there was something fishy about a woman finding a dead body in somebody else's house before 6:00 A.M.

"You called about a dead man?"

Ghost twisted hard in my arms and glared at the deputy. Either he didn't like the tone of his voice or he was so pissed at being held against his wishes that he hated everybody on general principle. I took a moment to read the name on the deputy's ID tag: Jesse Morgan.

"I'm Dixie Hemingway," I said. "I'm a pet-sitter. The owner of the house is Marilee Doerring. She left town last night and won't be back until next week. I don't know who the dead man is."

"How do you know he's dead?"

"I tried his pulse. He's dead, trust me."

"Where'd you find him?"

"In the kitchen. I went in to feed the cat and there he was."

"And you think he . . . you think he drowned?"

I shot him a look. "Yeah, that would be my guess, since his nose is stuck in a bowl of water."

"Anybody else in there?"

"If anybody was there, they could have gone out the back door after I left. I didn't look around. I grabbed Ghost and ran."

He inclined his head a quarter of an inch toward the cat and said, "That's Ghost?"

"Yeah."

"He doesn't look happy."

"He hates being held."

"So why did you grab him? Why did you bring him outside with you?"

I blinked at him for a good five seconds before I realized he had a point. Ghost had been there when the murder was committed, and he had been there with the dead body, but I had instinctively scooped him up as if I were rescuing him. I knew the reason, but I doubted Deputy Morgan would understand how maternal impulses can kick in even when they don't make any sense.

As if he had asked a really stupid question, I said, "He could have contaminated the area for forensics."

"Wait here," he said, and walked down the driveway and through the open front door. He had a good walk, which surprised me. I would have expected a rookie's power stomp, but it was a seasoned stride—confident but not cocky.

I crooned under my breath to Ghost, and he gradually sheathed his extended claws. A frightened or angry cat can do serious harm with its claws, but I knew he wasn't that angry. His pride was hurt at being restrained and he just needed to remind me that he could hurt me bad if he wanted to.

In a few minutes the deputy came back with his phone stuck to his ear, calling for a crime-scene unit. When he tucked the phone in its holder on his belt, he said, "I'll need to get some information from you."

"Sure, but I have to do something about Ghost first. I think I'll ask the next-door neighbor to keep him until I can take him to a day sitter."

He looked at his watch. "It's pretty early. Do you think they'll be up?"

"I saw a light there earlier. They have a teenager, and he's probably getting ready for school. I'll just be a minute."

I was off before he could tell me what he thought of the idea. The house was about forty feet away, with a yard full of ground cover instead of grass, so I sprinted down the street. The house was built on the same lines as Marilee's, but the stucco was more pink than cream, and the front door was bright turquoise.

I rang the doorbell, and while I waited I met Ghost's outraged eyes. I blinked at him slowly, which in cat language means "I love you." That usually calms an agitated cat, but it didn't do much this time. Ghost definitely didn't blink back.

3

The woman who answered the door gave *stiff-necked* a whole new meaning. Her neck rose from her narrow shoulders like a soaring redwood, broader at the base and held stiffly upright by thick cords that showed bruised blue under her sallow skin. In comparison to her neck, her head seemed too small, made even smaller by the way her pale hair was pulled into a tight knot high at the back of her skull. She held her chin tilted upward, with her eyes squinted and the corners of her rubbery mouth turned down. From the deep grooves running from her thin nose to her jawbone, I surmised that her inverted mouth was a habitual expression.

I said, "Sorry to bother you. I'm Dixie Hemingway. I take care of Ms. Doerring's cat. There's been an incident at her house, so the Sheriff's Department will be working there for a while. I can't leave the cat in the house with all the people going in and out, and I don't have my car with me. I was hoping I could leave him with you for an hour or two."

She started to close the door and said, "I don't want to be involved."

Her carefully enunciated syllables oozed with barely suppressed contempt. She definitely felt she was speaking to an inferior, and she wanted me to know it.

I slid my foot in the door before she could close it. "The deputy over there wants me to leave him someplace, and there's really no place else to take him."

She frowned and allowed her eyes to open all the way.

I said, "He can stay on the lanai, and it will just be for a little while."

She spun around and walked away, managing to do that without moving her head. Since she hadn't slammed the door in my face, I assumed I was to follow. I stepped into a large square living room with a glass wall across the back. It was dark inside, not just because no lamps were burning but because the glass was covered by thick draperies. They were more appropriate for a cold clime where you need insulation against frigid winds, not for a sun-filled place like Florida.

Instead of pulling the cord to open the drapes, she pushed the edge aside, unlocked the slider, and held them back while I slipped through the opening. She watched me while I took Ghost to the far corner under the roof. I knelt down and let his hind legs touch the floor between my knees while I kept my hand under his chest to hold his front paws up.

I said, "You're just going to stay here for a little while, and then I'll come get you and take you to Kitty Haven. You'll like it there."

I lowered his front feet to the floor but kept one hand under his chest, ready to lift them if he tried to run. His whiskers were anxiously pointed up, and I talked low to him while I eased my backpack off. I got out one of my emergency Tender Vittle packets, along with a disposable bowl. Semimoist cat food is like Froot Loops for a child—both are poor excuses for nutrition, but they'll do in a pinch. Ghost eyed the pouch and made his skin quiver, either to show revulsion or enthusiasm, I wasn't sure. I emptied the pouch into the bowl and put it on the floor. Slowly, I pulled my hand away from his chest and stroked his head and neck. He dropped his eyelids to half-mast to show me he was not pleased with me, but he didn't run when I stood up.

Instead, he crouched in a martyred sulk, tail wrapped tightly to his side, paws folded under his chest, head looking straight forward. Do whatever you want, his posture said. I have to eat breakfast in a strange place and there's a dead man in my house, but don't give me a second thought. I'll be fine.

I went back inside, and as the woman let the drapes fall shut, I saw Ghost hunker over the Tender Vittles and dig in.

"I don't know your name," I said. "I should have asked."

She switched on a lamp that managed to look both priceless and ugly at the same time, and in its weak glow I noticed that a gleaming grand piano dominated the room.

"I am Olga Winnick," she said stiffly.

A tall skinny boy with white-blond hair and an innocent mouth stepped into the room with his knobby neck angled to the side trying to see what was going on. He was dressed for school in jeans and a white polo shirt with a collar. His eyes were red and puffy, as if he needed several hours more sleep. He stopped like a spooked horse when he saw me.

"Oh, hi," I said. "I'm Dixie Hemingway. Your mother is letting me leave my cat on your lanai for a couple of hours while the Sheriff's Department is in the house next door."

He gave me a tight, self-conscious grin, the way adolescents do when they can't figure out what they're supposed to do next.

Mrs. Winnick said, "My son is a pianist. He isn't interested in what happens next door."

I said, "Is that you? I've heard you. I always thought it was the classical radio station."

He didn't answer, either from embarrassment or because his mother jumped in before he could.

"He's going to Juilliard soon." From the way she said it, she might as well have added "you stupid clod."

I made appropriate noises to show how impressed I was that the kid was a musician, while he looked like he would have been extremely grateful if the floor had opened and let him fall through to oblivion. Neither of them volunteered his name, but I was afraid he would have a nervous breakdown if I asked, so I let it slide.

"I'll pick the cat up as soon as I can," I said. "Would you mind giving him a bowl of water? If he has water, he'll be okay."

Mrs. Winnick turned to look at me full on. "I am allowing you to leave that woman's cat on my lanai. That should be enough."

Her son's face flamed, and he turned and left us.

I got out as fast as I could, with the slamming front door making it clear that Mrs. Winnick felt sorely imposed upon.

Another green-and-white patrol car was pulling into the drive as I got back to Deputy Jesse Morgan, and an ambulance was slowly gliding to the curb. Morgan's eyes flicked to my braless bosom and up again. "Got the cat squared away?"

"For a little while. I have some other pets on my schedule, and I have to go home and get my car. Would it be okay if I do that before I talk to anybody?"

Morgan looked toward the street, where a third deputy was parking in front of the ambulance. Both deputies got out of their patrol cars and spoke to the EMTs standing at the back of the ambulance. An unmarked sergeant's car and a crime-scene truck with forensics people drove up and parked behind the ambulance. People swarmed into the street and up the driveway. I knew most of them. I did not look forward to the moment when they recognized me.

Sergeant Owens spoke to me first. Owens is a skinny fifty-something African-American a foot taller than me, which makes him about six three. He has a long face and droopy eyes like a basset hound. His slow and easy facade masks a lightning-quick mind. More than one person who thought it would be easy to put one over on Sergeant Owens has found themselves in deep doo-doo. I served in his unit, and I speak from experience.

Maybe he already knew I was the one who had called in the report, because he didn't seem surprised to see me. He put out his hand, cordial as if we were in a receiving line, and said, "How are you, Dixie?"

"Except for this little blip on my horizon," I said, "I'm just fine."

The last time I'd seen Sergeant Owens, he hadn't asked me how I was, he'd told me. What he'd actually said was, "You're totally fucked up, Dixie. No way are you ready to go back to work." You have to respect a man who can look you in the eye and tell you that.

Deputy Morgan said, "Miz Hemingway was just asking me if it would be okay for her to take care of some other pets and then go home and get her car before she talks to anybody. There was a cat in the house, and she took it next door. She has to come back and get it and take it someplace else."

Sergeant Owens narrowed his eyes in the exact same look that Ghost had given me from Mrs. Winnick's lanai. Both of them seemed to have expected better of me.

"How long do you think you'll be?"

"Two and a half hours, tops."

"Okay, see you then."

Another crime scene-unit was oozing down the street looking for a place to park when I pedaled away. I was an hour behind schedule, and I felt guilty about it, as if the cats waiting for me were looking at their clocks and tapping their paws. I also felt a bit of envy for the quickened adrenaline all the people at the crime scene were having. I don't care how gruesome and disgusting it is, crime is a lot more fascinating than cleaning litter boxes.

4

It was almost nine o'clock when I finished seeing to the other pets, and I had a no-caffeine-yet headache and slippery armpits. I pedaled home, tossed my dirty clothes in the washer to run later, and jumped in the shower. My hair is the drip-dry kind that I can pull back in a ponytail and forget, so all I had to do to make myself presentable was slather on sunscreen and roll transparent color on my mouth. I love the sun, but I tend to fry when I'm in it, so I pretty much keep the Beaver 43 people in business. I put on clean khaki shorts and a sleeveless knit top, this time with a bra, and in less than fifteen minutes, I was in my Bronco and headed back up Midnight Pass Road. The leather seats were already hot on the backs of my thighs, but a blast from the AC cooled my face and left my nipples pleasantly puckered.

I drove north on Midnight Pass Road to Marilee's street and parked at the curb. A second crime-scene unit had arrived, along with trucks from all the local media. A few neighbors and curious onlookers had gathered outside to stare and talk, and reporters from NBC, ABC, CBS, BLAB, and Fox were interviewing anybody who would talk to them. Crime-scene tape was stretched across the front entrance, and a contamination sheet had been posted by the front door for everybody to sign as they entered and left.

When I walked up the drive, Deputy Jesse Morgan was outside keeping the curious at bay, and Sergeant Owens was just coming out of the house. He saw me and did a U-turn, flapping his hand at me in a gesture that I took to mean "Wait here."

In a moment, he came out with a man in dark pleated trousers and an unlined teal linen jacket with the sleeves casually pushed up. Open-collared white knit shirt. Leather sandals. Smooth bronze tan, like somebody who spent a lot of time on the tennis courts or polo grounds. At first I thought they had found a rich Italian relative of Marilee's, but Owens said, "Dixie, this is Detective Guidry of CIB. He'll be handling the case."

Guidry stepped close and held out his hand. He had a nice hand-shake, firm and dry. His face was sober edging onto stern, but laugh lines fanned from the corners of his eyes, and his mouth had twin parentheses at the sides. A beaky nose and dark hair cut short, with be-ginnings of silver showing at the temples and above the ears.

Before he could speak, I said, "I hate to ask you to wait some more, but I'm really worried about the cat. I left it next door and I told the woman I'd come get it in a couple of hours. It'll take me about ten min-utes to run it over to the day-care place. Is that okay?"

He said, "You found the body a little before six this morning, right?"

"Around then."

"Have you had breakfast?"

"No, and I'm about ready to start gnawing on my arm."

He grinned. "Why don't you take the cat wherever it has to go and we'll eat while we talk."

I could have kissed him. We agreed to meet in fifteen minutes at the Village Diner and then he and Sergeant Owens went back inside the house. I went to the back of my Bronco and unfolded a cardboard cat-carrying case. I put a folded towel on its floor and loped to the Win-nicks', where a black Mercedes now sat in the driveway. The front door flew open before I got to it, and a dark-haired man in a powder blue suit came storming out with an infuriated scowl on his face.

He stopped when he saw me, and I could almost see the deliberate muscle-by-muscle transition as he got himself under control. His shoulders and chest were broad as a linebacker's, but his short legs made him eye-to-eye with me. His face was familiar, the kind you see on billboards and flyers during campaigns for local elections, but I couldn't place it.

"Good morning," he said. He reached to shake my hand, revealing a raw scratch running diagonally across the back of his right wrist. His eyes were a little too close together for my taste, and if he'd ever had a sweet mouth like his son, it had gotten narrowed into one that seemed to have forgotten how to make a sincere smile.

I gave him the tips of my fingers to shake, and he enfolded them in a hot meaty hand. "I'm Dr. Win. I understand there's some kind of problem next door."

I flinched. I knew that voice, and I knew that name. Carl Winnick was a radio psychologist beloved by people who felt they'd been cheated out of their deserved special place by single mothers, minorities, homosexuals, and feminists. He daily filled the airwaves with ranting diatribes about how public schools were teaching sex perversion to eight-year-olds, how white men were losing their jobs to illegal immigrants, and how working women were causing children to become drug addicts. He was best known for fighting to keep alive an idiotic Florida law that required unmarried mothers giving up their babies for adoption to run newspaper ads giving their names and the dates and places where they'd had sexual intercourse. Three years before, he had added me to the list of people he considered a threat to his definition of a family.

He had left the door open, and Olga Winnick stepped forward to grip its edge, as if she had to hold on to something to keep from falling. Her face was wet with tears, and her mouth was open in a rictus of despair.

I said, "I just came to pick up the cat."

He gave a false hearty laugh. "Oh, yes! The cat! Mustn't forget the cat!"

He rushed past me and got in the Mercedes and started the engine. For some reason, I imagined his fingers shaking when he turned the key. As he backed out of the driveway, he gave me a side-to-side wave like a beauty queen in a parade.

Mrs. Winnick was still hanging on to the edge of the door, mournfully watching her husband's departure the way a loyal dog watches her master drive away.

There was no use pretending I hadn't caught her crying her eyes out. "I'm sorry," I said. "This is obviously a bad time to come."

"It's nothing," she said. "We had an argument. Just a heated debate, really."

From the raw wound I'd seen on his hand, I thought it might have been more than a heated debate. I had been on enough domestic-disturbance calls as a deputy to know that husbands and wives who seem the epitome of decorum may go at each other like barroom brawlers.

As I got closer to her, I got a whiff of an odor on her breath that I remembered from living with my mother, the scent of alcohol overlaid with mouthwash. Even this early in the morning, Olga Winnick had been fortifying her courage with booze.

Inanely, I said, "These things happen."

I made a beeline to the back sliders where the heavy drapes were still drawn. As soon as I opened the slider, Ghost came running toward me making little chirping noises of relief. I squatted on my heels to stroke him, then lifted him into the cardboard case and closed it. He whined and poked a paw through one of the air holes, but it couldn't be helped. I retrieved the food bowl and checked the lanai floor for errant Tender Vittles crumbs. There were none. There was also no water bowl.

With the carrying case in both hands, I went through the living room while Mrs. Winnick tracked along behind me.

"It's this place," she said. "Nothing but cheap, predatory women living here, and half of them are Jews."

For a moment there, I had been feeling sorry for her, but the woman was as pompous and bigoted as her husband. It was a good thing they had found each other, instead of contaminating two marriages.

With my back teeth touching, I said, "Thank you so much for keeping Ghost," and bolted.

She stood in the doorway and glared at me all the way back to my

Bronco. I guess she thought I was one of the predatory women after her husband.

I put the cat-carrying case in the front seat and talked to Ghost as we drove north on Midnight Pass Road. He had got an arm through an air hole all the way up to his armpit and was waving it frantically while he made piteous mewing noises to alert people that he was being catnapped.

From the traffic light where Midnight Pass intersects with Stickney Point from the mainland, beachside condos and private clubs stand shoulder-to-shoulder behind hibiscus hedges and palm trees. They all have salty names like Midnight Cove, Crystal Sands, Siesta Dunes, Island House, Sea Club. My personal favorite is Our House at the Beach. If you spend your vacation there, you can truthfully tell your friends, "We're going down to Our House at the Beach."

At Beach Road, I turned left and slowed down so I wouldn't hit any of the half-naked vacationers crossing the street to get to Crescent Beach. It's amazing how many normally sensible women come to the key, deck themselves out in skimpy bikinis, tie a beach towel around their hips, and step out into oncoming traffic with bemused smiles on their lips. I think it's the seaside's negative ions that get to them.

Kitty Haven is on Avenida del Mare about a block off Beach Road in an old Florida-style house—yellow frame with crisp white hurricane shutters and a deep front porch. Except for areas planted with liriope and palmettos and century plants, the yard is completely covered in cedar chips. Walking to the front door through the smell of all that cedar always makes me feel like I'm inside a gerbil cage.

Kitty Haven is like a cross between a brothel and a grandmother's house, with lush velvet, soft music, and a TV screen that plays continuous films of twittering birds and darting fish. A bell tinkled to announce my arrival, and a couple of calico tabbies lolling on windowsills raised their heads to look me over. Marge Preston bustled from the back, leaving a floating wake of wispy cat hairs like the precursors of angel wings. If I were a cat, Marge is the person I'd want for my human. She's plump and white-haired like Mrs. Santa Claus, with a soft voice and a light touch that soothe the most agitated cat. She took the case and held it up to look inside the vents, and I swear Ghost began to purr.

"You'll have to keep his collar," she said.

"Oh, of course."

Marge set the case on the floor and she and I knelt to open it. I stroked Ghost's head, letting my fingers slip down the back of his neck and under his velvet collar. The collar had an elastic insert to allow it to slide over his head, and I brought it out on my fingertips and pushed it up on my wrist.

"I don't know how long he'll be here," I said. "Something happened at his house and he can't go home just yet. His name is Ghost. He hasn't had water or a litter box for over two hours. He's had a lot of stress today, so when you feed him, you might stir in some vitamin C."

Marge made tuttutting sounds as she bustled off to the back room to set things right, while Ghost told her in self-pitying yips and growls how he'd been sorely mistreated.

I got back in the Bronco and whipped around the corner, and nosed into a parking place in front of the Village Diner. Detective Guidry was already seated in the last booth in the corner with two steaming mugs of coffee on the table. I tossed my backpack onto the seat and slid in, grabbing one of the mugs and taking a big hit almost before I was settled.

"God, that's good."

The charms on Ghost's collar winked on my wrist, and I realized I still wore it. I wanted to explain that I wasn't the kind of woman who wore black velvet wristbands decorated with little hearts and keys, but explaining would make me look like the kind of woman who cared what anybody thought, so I didn't.

Judy, who's been a waitress at the diner for as long as I can remember, appeared as if by magic with a full pot and a lifted eyebrow at seeing me with a man. Judy is smart-mouthed and efficient, with an angular frame, a dusting of orange freckles over her nose, and pecan-colored eyes that have the faintly astonished look of somebody whose dreams have been worn to a nub by disappointment. We have a close friendship that exists solely in the diner. We've shared our most hurtful stories, even though we never see each other anyplace else. I know about the men who've treated her like shit, and she knows about Todd and Christy.

I put the mug back on the table so she could top it off. "I'll have the special," I said.

"Uh-huh." She didn't even write it down. I always have the special. Two eggs over easy, extra-crispy home fries, and a biscuit.

"I'll have the same, with a side of bacon," said Gruidry.

Judy splashed another bit of coffee in my mug to replace what I'd drunk while Guidry ordered, and swished away with curiosity radiating out of her like lines of light.

I took another sip of coffee and said, "Okay, I'm ready now. Ask me."

He pulled a narrow notebook from his jacket pocket and clicked a pen into readiness. "First, the particulars. Name?"

We went down the list. Name, address, phone, all those details that you give so many times it seems like they would be engraved on the air.

"Age?"

"Thirty-two."

"Occupation?"

"Pet-sitter."

He hesitated with his pen poised above the notebook. "Is that a real occupation?"

"Damn right it's a real occupation. I'm licensed and insured and bonded."

"Insured against what?"

"If I'm walking a dog and it bites you, my insurance will pay your doctor bills."

He got the kind of surprised face that people always give when they find out that pet-sitting is a legitimate profession with its own rules and ethics and legal responsibilities.

"How long have you been a pet-sitter?"

"About two years."

"Sergeant Owens said you used to be with the Sheriff's Department."

"I was."

"Why'd you leave?"

"Is that really important to your case?"

"I don't know. Is it?"

I felt rising anger and took a quick swallow of coffee.

"My husband was a sergeant with the Sheriff's Department. He was killed three years ago, along with our little girl. Sergeant Owens was my superior officer. He and I decided it would be better for me to do something else." I gave him a level look over the coffee mug. "I wasn't real good with people then, and I'm not much better now."

He nodded. His eyes were dark gray, edging toward blue. They didn't give anything away. "Tell me about this morning."

5

There wasn't much to tell, but I told him what I knew. Mostly, that consisted of the fact that I'd found the slider to the lanai unlocked and Marilee's bedroom and bathroom ransacked before I found the dead man.

"Did you notice anything missing?"

"No, but I wouldn't notice anything except the obvious. There was just one thing that struck me as odd. She had left her hair dryer behind. Most women getting ready for a trip stick their hair dryer in their overnight bag last thing after they've finished their makeup and hair. They don't leave it behind, especially when they'll be gone for a week."

"Maybe she had a spare already packed."

"Maybe, but it sort of bothers me. Marilee's an unusually neat woman. She doesn't leave her hair dryer lying out like that."

"Okay, what else can you tell me besides the hair dryer?"

I caught an edge to his voice and let the hair dryer go. I told him what Marilee had told me the day before—that she was leaving town that night and would be gone a week.

"She travels a lot on business, and the only thing different about this time was that I had to go by and pick up a new house key because she'd had her locks changed."

"Did she say why she'd had them changed?"

"No, and I didn't ask."

"Her car's in the garage. Does she usually drive to the airport?"

I stopped to think. "I can't remember ever looking in her garage when she was gone. If she was leaving from the Sarasota airport, I guess she might have driven."

"But you doubt it."

"I really don't know. It's just that Marilee is more the type to take a limo."

"Did she leave a number where she could be reached?"

I felt my face redden. "I told her to leave it for me, but I didn't look for it while I was there."

Judy slid a plate of eggs and potatoes in front of me, and put another in front of Guidry. "I'll be right back with your bacon and more coffee," she said.

To cover my embarrassment at having to admit that I'd let a client leave town without making sure she had left a number where she could be reached, I dug into my backpack and took out my client notebook.

"I have every client's information in here," I said. "When I first interview them, I get names of their vets and numbers to call in an emergency." To emphasize that I hadn't been irresponsible, I added, "Sometimes people go mountain climbing or something where I can't call them directly."

Judy plunked down a rasher of crisp bacon in front of Guidry and refilled both our coffee mugs. I eyed his bacon wistfully. It was exactly the way I like it, stiff, with no icky white bubbles on it.

Guidry moved a pair of slices to his plate and buttered his biscuit while I flipped to Marilee's page in my notebook. "She gave the number of a woman named Shuga Reasnor as her emergency number," I said.

"Shuga?"

I spelled it out for him, and forked up some egg. He had left four slices of bacon on its special plate.

"What's her number?"

I jerked my eyes away from his bacon and peered in the book. I read it off to him, and while he wrote it down, I looked at his bacon again.

He sighed and picked up the bacon plate. He raked two slices onto his own plate and then tipped the remaining two onto mine.

"You know you want them," he said.

"Well, just this once," I said. "I never eat bacon. I love it, but I never eat it. All that fat . . ."

"What do you know about Marilee Doerring?"

"Not much. She has some sort of decorating business, I think."

"Husband? Boyfriend?"

"I've never seen a man at her house, and there's never any sign of one."

"You look?"

"I don't look for man signs, but I do give the house a quick once-over every time to make sure the cat hasn't done something that needs cleaning up. Sometimes pets get bored and knock over a plant or poop in the middle of the bed. It's part of my job to check for things like that."

"How many times have you been in the house?"

"Lots. I can get the exact dates for you if you want. I keep a file at home of every visit."

"Isn't a week a long time to leave a pet alone?"

"Yeah, but cats can handle it. I go twice a day and play with them and comb them and talk to them. During the day they watch TV, and I always leave the blinds up so they can sit on the windowsill and watch the birds and squirrels outside. At night I put the lights and the radio on a timer. They get a little bored and lonely, but most pets would rather be at home alone than with strangers in a strange place."

He was watching me closely. "You really like doing this, don't you?"

"Does that surprise you?"

"It just seems like a big jump, from deputy to pet-sitter."

I shrugged. "It's really not so different. You always have to be alert, you always have to expect the unexpected, and every now and then somebody tries to hump your leg."

He laughed and then sobered. "Do you have any idea who the dead man is?"

"Not a clue. Do you?"

"We're checking it out."

That meant he wasn't going to tell me.

He said, "We'd like to keep the details of how he was killed quiet as long as we can. Have you told anybody about him being taped to the water bowl?"

I shook my head. "I haven't told anybody anything."

"Good. I'd appreciate it if you wouldn't. Some reporter will get your nine-one-one call and report it, but until somebody does, we're not going to make that public."

"Is Marilee a suspect?"

He shrugged. "Everybody's a suspect."

I had scarfed down a whole slice of bacon before I realized that included me.

Guidry tossed bills on the table and stood up. "You'll be around?"

I nodded. "I'll be on the street behind Marilee's this afternoon walking the Graysons' dog. I'll stop by while I'm there."

"Okay."

He left without any "See yous" or "It's been nice" or "Glad to meet yous."

As soon as he was out of sight, Judy plunked herself down opposite me with coffeepot in hand.

"Okay, who is he?"

"He's a detective. There's been a murder at one of my pet houses and he's the investigator. I found the body, so we ate while he questioned me."

"Well shit, I thought he might be a man. You know, a man for you. Who got murdered?"

I ignored the part about a man for me. In spite of the fact that Judy has had terrible luck with men, she persists in thinking it's time for me to get one.

"I don't know who he was."

"Shot?"

"I'm not sure. I turned on the kitchen light, and there he was, stretched out on the floor."

"No!"

"Yep, DRT—dead right there."

"Good God. Did you freak out?"

"Come on, I used to be a deputy, I don't freak out at things like that. Well, I freaked out a little, but just for a minute."

"Who's house was he in?"

"Marilee Doerring's."

"I know who Marilee Doerring is. She's a piece of work. You know her?"

"Just from taking care of her cat. She's always been fine with me. Pays on time, takes good care of her cat. I don't have any complaints about her."

Judy looked around to make sure nobody was listening, and leaned closer. "See that man at the counter reading the paper? That's Dr. Coffey. He's a heart surgeon. He and Marilee Doerring were engaged a couple of years ago."

A bell dinged from the back to get Judy's attention, and she got up with her coffeepot to go pick up an order.

I studied the man at the counter. He was lean to the point of boniness, with sharp shoulder blades jutting from his back like mountain ridges. His dark hair was shorn high, with a longer shock flopping down to meet the shaved part. It was a cut for a much younger man, a cut meant to be cool and mellow. It made him look like the nerdy kid in high school who never quite fits in, the one who's always on the sidelines watching the popular kids. He was wearing the Siesta Key male uniform—khaki shorts, short-sleeved knit shirt, and Docksiders, which exposed a lot of straight black hair on his arms and legs. For a quick second, I imagined running my hands down his bare back and felt my fingers tangle in a thicket of hair. Ugh.

Somehow I couldn't imagine him with Marilee, but if they'd been engaged, he must have known where she went on her business trips. Before I could talk myself out of it, I got up and went to the counter and took the stool next to Coffey. He turned his head just enough to give me a quick glance to reassure himself I wasn't anybody he knew, and turned back to his paper. He had a smooth rectangular face like a department store mannequin, with a high forehead and long cheeks. His sallow skin was perfect as plaster, and his dark eyes were velvety and dull, like ripe olives that have set out too long and lost their sheen.

I said, "Dr. Coffey, I'm sorry to interrupt you, but I'd like to ask you something."

He looked at me again, this time with a furrow of distaste forming on his unlined forehead.

"I'll be quick," I promised him. "My name is Dixie Hemingway, and—"

Looking flustered and anxious, Judy came trouncing to us bearing his order and her coffeepot. He moved his paper out of the way so she could set his plate down. Scrambled egg whites, dry rye toast, sliced tomatoes. I guess if you're a heart surgeon, you eat like that.

Judy topped off his coffee and looked warningly at me. "Something for you?"

"No thanks, I'm not staying," I said.

She gave an emphatic nod of her head and stomped off with her coffeepot held in front of her like a lancet.

Ignoring me, Dr. Coffey picked up his fork and cut into his egg whites. His fingers were hairy, too, with black hair sprouting between his knuckles. I watched his fork with a kind of repelled fascination. There's something unnatural about eating just the white of an egg.

I pushed Ghost's velvet collar higher on my arm and said, "The thing is, I'm a pet-sitter, and one of my clients left town and didn't leave a number where she could be reached. There's been something of an emergency at her house, and I was thinking you might have some idea where she might have gone. Like where her business takes her, or where her family lives."

He looked toward me again and then stood up so fast it seemed like his knees had suddenly gone stiff and he couldn't sit anymore. "I know nothing about this! Do you understand me? Nothing! If you bother me again, I'll have you arrested. Do you understand?" His voice was venomous, and he was shaking.

I said, "Well, actually, you can't have me arrested just for asking you a question. I'm sorry if I bothered you, but don't you think you're overreacting?"

He extended his arm with his skeletal finger pointing at me like Abraham cursing the Philistines. "Stay away from me!"

Stomping to the front door, he charged out of the diner so fast that several people in the front booths looked around.

Judy came over and leaned on the counter. "Thanks a lot," she said. "You just chased off one of my best customers. Not to mention the fact that he stiffed me for his breakfast."

"All I did was ask him if he knew where Marilee might have gone. He was going to marry her, he must know something about where her job takes her."

She groaned. "He hates her. She dumped him practically while the organ was playing the wedding march. I mean, people were in the church and everything. She just up and left him standing there."

"Well, that's sort of brave, don't you think? It must have been embarrassing, but if she realized she didn't love him—"

"No, you don't understand! She had got him to put a million dollars in her name just before the wedding. Gave him some big song and dance about how she didn't want to be dependent on him after they were married, and how she didn't want to live in fear that he would dump her one day and she'd be out on the street without a dime. How she wanted to be able to look him in the eye as an equal so they would both know she was with him because she *wanted* to be and not because she *had* to be. You know, like she was a poor little match girl out on the street getting taken in by a prince or something. The poor schmuck fell for it and transferred a million bucks to her account. In her name. Hers to have no matter what happened, like love insurance."

"And then she dumped him?"

"Like a rock. He sued her, I think, but the doofus had given her the money, so she got to keep it. He hates her guts now. It was just two years ago. I can't believe you didn't hear about it."

I didn't remind her that two years ago I'd been doing well to get out of bed and find my way to the bathroom. I wouldn't have known if they'd declared World War III.

She said, "He's got a live-in bimbo now. I saw her early one Sunday morning coming out of cocaine alley."

I knew the place she meant. Everybody on the key, including the Sheriff's Department, knows the areas where drugs are sold. There's a drug bust every now and then, but mostly it's small-time stuff not worth the time and expense to fight, especially when you know the dealers will be back on the street before the ink is dry on the arrest warrant.

"Do you think she was getting it for him?"

"Maybe, but he's never seemed coked up. She does, though. You look at her and expect her feet to be a few inches off the floor."

I looked at my watch and said, "Listen, I've got to run, okay? I'll see you later."

"Let the police handle this, Dixie."

"It's not the police, it's the Sheriff's Department."

"Whatever."

I knew she was right, but it bothered me that I didn't know how to get in touch with Marilee. I had a responsibility, and I wasn't at all pleased with how I was handling it.

6

Before I left, I ducked into the ladies' room, where two very large black women were at the sinks. One of them I recognized as Tanisha, a cook in the diner, but I didn't know the other one. I whipped into a stall, and they went dead silent, the way women in a rest room do when they've been interrupted midconversation. When I flushed, the sound seemed to release them.

"So I says to him, I says, 'You can kiss my big fat black ass.' "

"Uh-huh, that's good."

"I told him, 'You can start in the middle and kiss your way thirty-six inches to the right, and then you can go back to the middle and kiss your way thirty-six inches to the left. You can just kiss my big fat ass.' "

I went out to wash my hands, and they went silent again. I kept my gaze directed toward my hands, but I could feel them watching me. I pulled a paper towel from the holder and turned around and leaned my butt on the counter.

I said, "I absolutely cannot leave here without knowing what happened next. What'd he say?"

They both laughed. Tanisha said, "Girl, he didn't say nothing. He just stood there with his mouth hanging open, and I walked. I don't take that shit from nobody."

I grinned and tossed my wadded-up paper towel in the bin. "I wish I could have seen that."

I left them giggling and punched the door open with my knuckles—I'm squeamish about putting the flat of my hand on a bathroom door because half the women who go in there don't wash their hands—and headed for the parking lot.

The temperature had climbed and the Bronco was like a pizza oven. I started the car and let the AC run while I pulled out my cell phone and client book and flipped to Marilee's page. I read Shuga Reasnor's number while I dialed it.

The voice that answered had the husky, half-choked sound of somebody blowing out cigarette smoke and talking at the same time. "Hello, this is Shuga," she said.

I had been pronouncing the name "Shooga," but when she said it I realized the name was "Sugar," with an exaggerated southern accent. Probably a lot of people would think that was cute.

"This is Dixie Hemingway, Miss Reasnor. I take care of Marilee Doerring's cat, and she gave me your number to call in case of an emergency. Has Detective Guidry been in touch with you yet?"

"Noooo." She drew out the word while she registered all the implications of what I'd said.

Damn. I should have checked with Guidry before I phoned. Now I'd given her a heads-up that a detective would be calling her.

"The reason I'm calling is that Marilee's out of town, and I've taken Ghost to a day-care center. I expect he'll be there for a day or two, and I just wanted to make sure that was okay with you."

"You've left who?"

"Ghost. Her cat."

"Hell, I don't care. I don't know why she left my number."

"You don't happen to know where she went, do you?"

She laughed uneasily. "I didn't even know she was gone. What did you say your name was?"

"Dixie Hemingway. If you should hear from Marilee, I'd appreciate it if you would have her call me." Before she could ask any more questions, I gave her my number and thanked her, then punched the disconnect button.

"That was really dumb," I muttered to myself. "Really, really dumb."

Before I backed the Bronco out, I slid Ghost's velvet collar off my wrist and put it in my backpack. It was 11:55. I should have been at Kristin Lord's house an hour ago. A murder really screws up a work schedule.

When I got to the traffic light at Beach Road, I automatically turned my head to look at the fire station. I've done that all my life. Once when I was about seven years old, my father was in the driveway with some other firefighters polishing the fire truck when my mother and Michael and I drove by. My mother honked at him, and he gave us a big grin and waved. It's one of my favorite memories.

Kristin and Jim Lord were the kind of people who prove the theory of karma and reincarnation—they had less sense than a pair of sand fleas but were filthy rich, so they must have been really, really good in a former life. I'd known them since high school, but we'd never been friends. They ran with the kids who knew the difference between Polo and Izod—and cared—and I ran with the kids whose idea of making a fashion statement was not wearing yesterday's T. Kristin had a huge crush on my brother for a while, and I don't think she ever forgave him for rejecting her.

Kristin met me at the door of their multimillion-dollar mansion with a smile frosty at the corners. "You're a little late, aren't you?"

Kristin was slim, with glossy brown hair cut to curve around her square jaw, and heavy dark eyebrows that made straight slashes above beautiful hazel eyes. Her nose was out of a plastic surgeon's catalog, but her lips were naturally full and wide. Her upper lip was thicker in the middle, giving her a slightly rabbity look. If she were so inclined, she probably gave her husband great blow jobs—further proof of a previous life of good deeds, at least for him. She was wearing a pair of wrinkled white cotton capris and a free-hanging pink-and-white-striped shirt that covered her newly bulging tummy.

"I got tied up," I said. "Sorry."

She made a little snuffing sound with her perfect nose to show her displeasure, and spun around to walk ahead of me, her raffia flip-flops making sucking noises on the cool Italian tile.

Kristin was four months pregnant and she had developed an acute case of Fear-Of-Cat-Poop. Specifically, she was afraid of catching toxoplasmosis from her cat's litter box. Cats can only get toxoplasmosis from eating a diseased rodent, and a pregnant woman can only get it if she touches the diseased cat's feces and then eats something without first washing her hands. Kristin's cat had probably never even seen a rodent, much less eaten one, and what woman doesn't wash her hands after changing a litter box? But it was Kristin's fear and her cat and her money, so I allowed her to pay me twenty dollars a day to groom her cat and change its litter box.

The cat was an American Shorthair named Fred. Shorthairs are low-maintenance cats, so it was almost a crime to take money for what little I did. Fred's litter box was in a guest bathroom, and I kept the door closed because Kristin was so spooked about it. A litter box shouldn't have more than a quarter inch of sand in it, and flushing it away took a nanosecond. I spritzed it inside and out with my all-purpose water and Clorox mix, rinsed the hell out of it with hot water, dried it with paper towels, and spread another quarter inch of sand on the bottom. I replaced the bag of litter under the counter, and washed my hands and dried them. The whole procedure had taken two minutes, tops.

When I went out to the lanai for Fred's grooming, he and Kristin were both pretending not to be excited that I was there. Fred was doing a jug imitation, sitting tall with his long tail curled around his toes the way some executives curl a long line back under their signatures. Kristin was sitting in a cushioned redwood chair, eager to gossip. Dishing dirt was Kristin's favorite pastime. She had done it when we were in high school, and she was still doing it. She had never been fastidious about facts, and if somebody's reputation was hurt because she'd passed on malicious gossip, it never seemed to bother her.

Kristin said, "It was on the news this morning about that dead man in Marilee Doerring's house. They said you found him, but they weren't giving his name until his next of kin is notified. Who was he?"

My heart did a somersault at hearing that anything about me was on the news, but I kept my face still and lifted Fred to the table.

"They gave my name?"

"They just said a pet-sitter, but I knew it was you."

As if he sensed that a dark cloud had lowered around me, Fred looked over his shoulder with sad eyes.

Fred was large and muscular, brown, with a white muzzle and throat and white paws. Like all American Shorthairs, he was sweet and affectionate. When I ran my hands lightly over his body, telling him by touch where I was getting ready to brush, he arched his back and began to purr. I dipped a hand into my grooming kit for my small slicker brush and pulled it through the hair on the back of Fred's neck, careful to keep the brush flat so the bristles wouldn't dig into his skin.

"I don't know who the man is," I said. "Like they said, they have to notify his family before they announce his name."

Fred tilted his head back so I could get under his chin, and I made short strokes on his snowy throat and chest. He stretched his head up higher. If he could have spoken, he would have said, "Yes! Yes! Now a little to the right! Oooh, that's good!" Since he couldn't talk, he purred louder.

Kristin said, "The Sheriff's Department won't say how he was killed until they do an autopsy. Isn't that odd?"

I shrugged. "They always do an autopsy whenever a person dies in mysterious circumstances."

Kristin did a disappointed pout with her bunny mouth. "I know Marilee Doerring from the yacht club. People don't like her much. Well, men like her, but women don't."

I put a protective finger over Fred's sensitive spine and combed in short parallel strokes on each side. Fred gave a warning flick of his tail, and I went back to his neck and throat, making sure I was keeping the teeth of the brush comfortably pointed straight at his skin and not tilted to the side.

"I think it's because Marilee's so flashy," said Kristin. "Lately she's been wearing an *enormous* square-cut diamond that's *soooo* ostentatious. The thing just screams zircon!"

My experience with diamonds being limited to the small kind that nobody would mistake for a zircon, I continued combing Fred and stayed quiet.

Kristin gave a little self-deprecating laugh. "God, I sound catty, don't I?"

I don't know why people say they're being "catty" when they make unkind remarks about other people. Cats are never like that.

Kristin shifted in her chair and said, "It's not because she's pretty that I don't like her. I'm not afraid of pretty women. And it's certainly not because she has money! It's that you always get the feeling Marilee's trolling for men. If a man's anywhere in her vicinity, you can almost hear the music from *Jaws* playing."

I thought of Olga Winnick and said, "Predatory music?"

"Exactly! Marilee is a predatory woman."

I was imagining Kristin and Olga Winnick together talking about how predatory Marilee was, when Kristin's eyes settled on my wedding band.

"You're a widow. Why do you still wear a wedding ring?"

The question caught me off guard, causing my hand to jerk so the bristles of my slicker brush bit into Fred's skin. He growled a warning and waved his tail, and I quickly went back to his throat to placate him. I've never thought of myself as a widow. Widows are old women with blue hair and a lifetime of memories. I don't belong in that group, I'm just a formerly loved.

Kristin looked up at me as if she'd suddenly had an attack of sensitivity. "I hope you don't mind my asking."

I didn't answer, but just to scare her, I turned Fred so that his anus faced her while I brushed the hair around it. She watched with pale dread, so hyperalert for bits of cat poop that she forgot her question. Fred whipped his tail back and forth to let me know his patience was wearing thin. To reward him for not jumping down, I combed his neck and throat again.

He pushed his head up against my hand and purred his thanks. I picked him up and set him on the floor, packed my slicker brush away, spritzed the table with my handy-dandy water-Clorox mix, and wiped it dry with paper towels.

"I'll let myself out," I said. I had been there only about five minutes.

Kristin looked disappointed. She would have paid me another twenty dollars just to stick around and dish dirt about Marilee. Fred stuck his left back leg into the air and curved around to enthusiastically lick the inside of it. He didn't even say good-bye.

7

It was one o'clock when I put my grooming equipment in the back of the Bronco and started home. The sky was a clear Crayola blue, with a relentless white sun that lasered the top of my head. Something was nagging at me, but I couldn't put my finger on it. I'd been up since 4:00 A.M. and my brain wasn't working on all cylinders.

The lane leading to my apartment is covered with oyster shells that have leeched lime and become hardened by rain into a concrete-hard surface. Australian pines, mossy oaks, sea grape, and palms line one side of the drive, and the other side edges the sandy beach. It's a private drive with a sign at its entrance proclaiming it not for public access, but people turn into it anyway and nose down to see what lies at its end.

On most of Siesta Key, a private road like ours will take the curious to a multimillion-dollar house whose owners are readily recognizable from movies or book jackets or TV talk shows. Our road leads to a weathered two-bedroom house where my brother and his partner live, and to a detached four-slot carport with an upstairs apartment where I live. My grandfather bought the house from Sears, Roebuck in the fifties for a thousand dollars, now the house and garage apartment together are worth about fifty cents. The beachfront property they sit on is worth about five million. Or at least that's what we've been offered for it. We wouldn't sell at any price, so it doesn't matter.

Michael and Paco were in the carport putting away fishing gear, both with the bleezy, sun-blasted look that men get when they've happily spent arduous hours sweating and squinting at a blazing sea. Michael is thirty-four, blond and blue-eyed like me, but a lot taller and wider. He's a fireman, and when he's suited up in his fire-fighting gear he's roughly the size of Sasquatch. Women fling themselves at Michael the way mating lovebugs splat themselves on car windshields in the spring. I wouldn't be surprised if some of them bear razor scars on their wrists at the futility of it, because he and Paco have been together for over twelve years and counting.

As slim and dark as Michael is blond and broad, Paco is with the Sheriff Department's SIB—Special Investigative Bureau—which means he gets involved in cases that require him to take on disguises his own mother wouldn't recognize. Cases that we don't question him about. Michael is my best friend in the whole world, and Paco is my second-best friend. When I lost Todd and Christy, Michael and Paco sort of sandwiched me between them and kept the world out until I was ready for it.

Michael works twenty-four/forty eight at the firehouse, which means a twenty-four-hour shift on, followed by forty-eight hours off. He usually spends his off-time fishing. Paco works mysterious hours that nobody can predict, many of them after midnight. When he isn't working or sleeping, he goes out in the boat with Michael. I never do. I love to look at the Gulf and I love the sound and smell of it, but I don't like being on it. It's too big and willful for me. I don't much like things I can't control, at least a little bit.

I got out of the Bronco and shaded my eyes against the glare. Out in the Gulf, sunlight sparked diamonds off glittering waves undulating toward the beach where they gently exploded into lacy white froth. A few gulls halfheartedly squawked and spiraled overhead, but most of them had retreated to shady nooks for a siesta.

I said, "What'd you get?"

"Some nice pompano. A couple of snapper."

"There was a dead man in one of my houses this morning."

They both stopped what they were doing and stared at me with identical expressions of shocked concern. I felt like a kid with a great Show and Tell.

"Marilee Doerring's house," I said. "I found him in the kitchen with blood on the back of his head and his nose taped in the cat's water bowl. I'm not supposed to tell the part about the water bowl yet."

Michael said, "Well hell, Dixie. What'd you do?"

"Called nine one one. Sergeant Owens came out, and a detective I never heard of before. Paco, do you know a guy named Guidry?"

"Nope, must be somebody new."

Having delivered my impressive news, I said, "Well, I'm going to go take a nap," and left them staring after me as I dragged my weary butt upstairs to my little private world.

I have a wide covered porch, a living room with a one-stool breakfast bar and galley kitchen at the side, and a bedroom barely big enough for a single bed, a nightstand, and a double dresser. Photographs of Todd and Christy sit on the dresser. They're the last things I see before I turn off the lamp, and the first things I see when I get up in the morning.

Off the bedroom, I have a tiny bathroom, a laundry room, and a big walk-in closet that doubles as an office. It's where I handle my pet-sitting business—at a desk in a windowless cubicle in front of a wall of shelves holding folded Ts and shorts and jeans, Keds and sandals and a couple pairs of heels. A lone rod across the short end holds a few dresses and skirts.

I went inside just long enough to go to the bathroom and check my answering machine. I had three calls from women asking for my pet-sitting rates. I didn't return any of the calls. I'd already had way more than my daily quota of people, and the day was only half over.

I went back to the porch, switched on both ceiling fans, and lowered myself into the hammock strung in the corner. The surf was tumbling in its endless rhythm and gulls squawked overhead. My thoughts tumbled and squawked along with them as I let the terrible truth of the morning settle in. A man's life had been taken, and whoever did it had made sure his dignity was stripped away, too. I felt personally violated. I didn't know him, but he was a fellow human being.

I drifted to sleep and dreamed that Christy was running on the beach throwing chunks of bread to the seagulls, laughing into the sky as they swooped down to catch them in their beaks. Her hair was almost white in the sunshine, and it bounced on her shoulders from a ponytail high on the back of her head. I was thinking I'd let her play until all the bread was gone and then call her into the shade so she wouldn't burn.

I woke up without knowing I was awake, with the edges of the dream blending with the sounds of the gulls and the surf. I lay there for a moment with my eyes shut before I realized it had just been a dream.

Those of us who've lost loved ones to terrorists or religious fanatics or doped-up drivers or some other senseless violence ask, "Why? Why? Why?" But after awhile, the question becomes "Why not?" Why should we get to have our loved ones around us when people all over the world are keening the loss of mothers, fathers, sons, daughters, brothers, sisters, lovers? So many people dying for so little reason.

Todd and Christy were killed when a ninety-year-old man slammed his Cadillac into them in a Publix parking lot. If I say it fast like that, I can keep my voice even, but just.

Todd and I had talked on the phone before he left to pick Christy up at day care. "We need some milk and Cheerios," I said. "I think we're out of orange juice, too."

"Christy and I will get it on our way home," he said. "See you a little after six."

For the rest of my life, I'll play that conversation over and over in my head, wishing I could rewind it and do it over, wishing I had said, I love you, my darling, and I always will, wishing I had told him how safe he made me feel, how protected and cherished.

He and Christy were both killed instantly. Todd was thirty. Christy was three.

The man who hit them said he had accidentally hit the gas instead of the brake. He felt terrible about it. His son came to see me after the funeral and told me his father was a good man who had resisted giving up his independence even after macular degeneration had robbed him of most of his sight. Florida allows people to renew their driver's license over the phone, so he had just kept driving in spite of his family's objections. The son said he had taken the car away from his father after the accident, and that his father had wept every day since it happened. From grief and guilt, he said, not just because he couldn't drive. As if that made us even.

For a long time I was so consumed by anger that it almost destroyed me. Anger at the state for allowing people to renew their driver's license without an eye exam. Anger at a man for continuing to drive after his vision and reflexes were shot. Anger at his family for not taking his car away sooner. In the end, forgiveness came not because I stopped feeling the gash of bitterness, but because I was exhausted by it. My anger has settled down from a flaming roar to a dull simmer now, like a volcano that seems calm but may erupt when you least expect it. It's the volcanic part that's the problem, the part I can't control—especially if I see somebody abusing a child or a pet. Then I go totally apeshit, and there's no telling what I'll do.

I got up feeling flushed and swollen and went inside and stood in front of the open refrigerator and glugged an entire bottle of cold water. I carried another bottle to my closet office, and put in a call to Lieutenant Guidry. He wasn't in, so I left my number. Then I called Shuga Reasnor.

She answered the phone on the first ring, and her voice had that mix of desperation and annoyance that people get when they've been hovering around a phone for a long time hoping it would ring.

I said, "It's Dixie Hemingway, Ms. Reasnor. I just wanted to ask you something. Do you know Dr. Coffey?"

She waited so long to answer that I thought for a moment she might have laid the phone down and walked away. Then she said, "Why do you ask?"

"I saw him in the Village Diner, and I asked him if he knew where Marilee might have gone. I thought since they were engaged, he might have some idea. He got very angry. Wouldn't even talk to me. It seemed odd."

"He's odd. He's mean and he's odd. Stay away from him. Don't talk to him about Marilee."

"Do you think he's dangerous? Do you think he might have been the one who killed the man in Marilee's house? Jealous, maybe?"

"Gerald Coffey's too big a coward to kill anybody. He might hire somebody to do it, but he wouldn't do it himself."

"But you think he might do that? Hire somebody?"

"I didn't say that. I just said he didn't have the balls to kill anybody himself."

"If you think of anything that the Sheriff's Department ought to know about Dr. Coffey, I hope you'll tell them."

"Yeah, I'll do that."

We said our good-byes and hung up. I knew she wasn't going to tell Guidry about Coffey. Shuga Reasnor didn't sound like a woman anxious to help in the investigation. In fact, she sounded like a woman with something to hide.

I spent the next hour attending to business. I called the people who wanted to know my rates, which is twenty dollars a day to make a morning and afternoon visit. If they want a sitter in the house overnight, it's forty dollars. For twenty-four-hour care, the fee is sixty dollars. Most pets are accustomed to being home by themselves during the day, but I have a crew of retirees who do sleepovers and round-the-clock care.

All my fees are spelled out in a contract I have my clients sign, along with our respective responsibilities. If a pet becomes ill and needs medical care when the owners are gone, I pay for it. If some disaster happens that causes water to be shut off or the pet to have to be evacuated, I supply whatever is needed, including new quarters. When the owners return, they reimburse me for my expenses. Taking on the care of a beloved pet while its owners are away is like taking on the care of a child. I have to trust the owners, and they have to trust me.

The first woman said she had found somebody else, and the next one slammed down the phone when I told her my rates, as if I'd said something obscene. The other woman said she thought they were extremely reasonable. Everything is relative. I made an appointment to stop by the approving woman's house to meet her cat and get the pertinent information, then spent the rest of the hour entering the morning's visits into my client records.

I keep meticulous records, recording the date and time I arrived, the time I left, and what I did while I was there, along with notes about anything a pet needed or did that was out of the ordinary. If a pet has a medical condition that requires medications or vitamins or treatments, that's recorded. I have the history of illnesses, injuries, and pregnancies, along with the dates of all immunizations, the number on the animal's ID tag, and whether it's been declawed, spayed, or neutered. I know each pet's preferences in food, toys, TV programs, and music. I'm probably too compulsive about keeping all that information, but I'd rather have it and not need it than need it and not have it. Someday it might be important to know precisely when I gave a bath or a vitamin or a prescription medication.

At four o'clock, I got a banana from its special little hanger in the kitchen and ate it as I went down to the carport. A great blue heron standing on the hood of the Bronco watched me as I got a sixty-watt lightbulb out of the storage closet. I tossed the last bite of banana toward the shore, and the heron fluttered to the sand to get it. I threw the peel in the garbage can, got in the Bronco, and drove back to the Graysons' house, where Rufus was ecstatic to see me. We played a short game of roll the ball on the living room floor before his supper. While Rufus ate, I hauled out a ladder from the garage and changed the burned-out bulb in the coach light. I put the ladder away, closed the garage door, and brought in the Graysons' mail. I checked the house for any doggy accidents, giving the carousel horse a pat on the rump as I walked by. Everything was in order, and I washed Rufus's food and water bowls and gave him fresh water before we went for a walk. We walked the quarter block to Midnight Pass Road and jogged past the wooded area, where Rufus insisted on stopping to bark at unseen squirrels or rabbits. I finally persuaded him to walk with me to Marilee Doerring's street.

8

A deputy's car was in Marilee's driveway and the crime-scene tape was still on the door, but there were no CSU cars. That meant the ME had come and put the body in a bag and taken it away, but the forensics people weren't finished getting photos, latent prints, hair, fiber, and all the other evidence they gather. Next door at the Winnick house, a yard vacuum lay in the driveway with an orange extension cord snaking under the partially opened garage door.

I parked behind the deputy's car and went to his open window. He was making notes, and he looked up at me with the flat, impersonal look that law-enforcement people learn.

I said, "Hi, I'm Dixie Hemingway. I found the dead man this morning, and I told Detective Guidry I'd stop by this afternoon when I was in the neighborhood."

"He's not here."

"Okay, I'll call him later. Thanks."

Rufus was contemplating a bird of paradise plant as if he thought it needed to be peed on, so I pulled his leash and started back down the driveway. Passionate piano music started coming from the Winnicks' house, and I turned my head that way. Now that I knew it was the kid practicing and not the radio or a CD, I was truly impressed. Not that I know diddly about classical music. My taste runs more to jazz and blues and country, but I know talent when I hear it, and the kid could play. Even Rufus cocked his head and listened with doggy respect.

Mrs. Winnick suddenly rose from behind a row of low shrubs between the two lots and walked rapidly around to the driveway. She wasn't wearing gardening gloves or carrying a trowel or any other gardening tools, and I had the distinct impression that she had been hiding behind the shrubs. She seemed to deliberately avoid looking my way. Maybe she was pissed that I hadn't told her about the murder.

She leaned down to get the handle of her yard vac and switched it on, intently looking at the driveway and moving the wand back and forth over the pavement. She wore black stretch Lycra tights with a boxy white T that stopped at her hipbones. Except for her skinny butt, her body was surprisingly muscular. Her butt wasn't muscular. It was the kind that hangs in two saggy loops, like basset ears.

Rufus and I retraced our walk toward his street. At the wooded area, where an abandoned drive disappeared into the trees, he stopped and barked again, tugging eagerly at the leash. The wooded swath between Marilee's street and Rufus's street is about fifty feet wide, and runs all the way from Midnight Pass Road to the bay. A wooden fence runs along both sides to separate it from people's backyards. Originally, it spanned a private driveway to a house on a peninsular extension into the bay. The owners had died years ago and the property was frozen in some kind of litigation for so long that the house fell apart and the land leading to it reverted to its original wild state. A useless metal gate stretched across the old shelled drive as mute testimony of how quickly nature reclaims its own.

I explained to Rufus that the woods were too brambly for dogs and women in shorts, and he reluctantly abandoned the idea of exploring it. When we got to his house, I turned on some lights and the kitchen radio and he and I kissed each other good-bye.

My next stop was across Midnight Pass Road at the Sea Breeze, a pink stucco honeycomb of condos tucked into a slim slice of land at the edge of the Gulf. Every condo has a curved stucco roof over its balcony, so the balconies look like dark caves cut into the side of a mountain.

The whole thing resembles an excavated Indian ruin. Inside, it's anything but a ruin, with a marbled lobby dotted with great urns of green things and tasteful paintings by local artists. Sarasota probably has more artists per capita than anyplace in the world, so it's not hard to find good art here.

I took the stainless-steel and mirrored elevator up to Tom Hale's condo. Tom is a round man—rosy round face, warm round black eyes behind round steel-rimmed glasses, round head of curly black hair, round little belly that rests lightly on his lap. Until a wall of shelves at a home-improvement store fell on him and crushed his lower spine, Tom headed a large CPA firm. He had gone to pick up some piano wire to hang a large painting in the house he shared with his wife and two children, but you know how it is, you can't go to one of those places without wandering around looking at all the neat stuff. As he remembers it, he had no reason to walk down the aisle between towering stacks of lumber and ready-to-hang doors. Nobody ever knew what caused the shelves to topple over, but they did, spilling all their contents onto the floor and anybody who happened to be there. Luckily, only one other person was in the aisle at the time, and he escaped with a concussion and broken arms. Tom wasn't so lucky.

He sued, of course, but it took several years before the case finally settled, and by that time his CPA firm was kaput because he'd spent so much time having surgery and learning how to function in a wheelchair. The lawyers for the store claimed that he was partly responsible for his own pain and paralysis because he was an intelligent man and should have known better than to walk down that aisle. The jury didn't buy that argument, and they awarded Tom half a million dollars. His lawyers got half, plus reimbursement for all their expenses. Then his wife divorced him because she couldn't bear living with a man in a wheelchair, and she and the children moved to Boston where her parents lived. In the divorce settlement, she got most of the money that was left, and Tom got a studio apartment in the Sea Breeze. The only thing standing between him and utter loneliness was a greyhound named

Billy Elliot, a former racing dog that Tom had rescued. I suppose Tom identified with the dog.

Tom and I trade services. He does my taxes and I go by twice a day and walk Billy Elliot for him. I could hear Billy Elliot's nervous toenails skittering on the marble floor before I opened the door. He started to jump on me when I came in, then crouched in fear when I held my palm flat and said, "Down!" It always breaks my heart to see a dog cower like that, because it's a clear signal the dog has been beaten in the past.

I knelt beside him and stroked his smooth neck. "You'd feel terrible if you jumped on somebody and knocked them down," I said. "That's why jumping's not allowed."

He thumped his tail on the floor and grinned hopefully at me. From the kitchen, Tom yelled, "Hey, Dixie! Come tell me about that dead man!"

Billy Elliot followed me in and stood whipping my legs with his tail while I gave Tom the condensed version of finding a dead man in Marilee's kitchen.

Tom said, "Have they contacted Marilee?"

"We don't know where she is. She didn't leave me a number."

"Maybe her grandmother would know."

"Marilee has a grandmother?"

"Everybody has a grandmother, Dixie. Marilee has one who lives at Bayfront Village. Name is Cora Mathers."

It was news to me that Tom and Marilee knew each other, but Tom did taxes for a lot of people on the key.

I said, "Wasn't Cora Mathers the *Leave It to Beaver* mother?"

"No, that was June Cleaver. Ward and June Cleaver. The kid who played the Beaver was Jerry Mathers. Maybe his mother's name was Cora."

"I wonder whatever happened to him."

"He probably bought his own island or something. Unless somebody screwed up and he didn't get the money from all those shows."

"You think it would be okay if I called Cora?"

"Oh, sure. From what Marilee's told me about her, she's a pistol."

Billy Elliot whuffed sharply, letting us know that he had enjoyed as much of our chitchat as he could stand. He and I took the elevator downstairs, and as soon as I thought we were far enough away from the front door, I let him pee on a bush. Then he stretched his body out and took off like he was back on the track chasing a fake rabbit. Even fattened up since his racing days, he was still faster than most dogs, and I ran behind him like a maniac. When we finally stopped, I had to bend over and take deep breaths while he pranced around and gave me annoyed little huffs because I had slowed him down. We trotted back to the Sea Breeze and took the elevator back upstairs, where I unsnapped his leash and stored it away. Tom was busy with somebody's return and merely grunted and waved as I left.

It was close to eight o'clock when I fed the last cat and went home. Michael and Paco were on the terrace between the house and the carport, firing up the grill.

Michael said, "Hurry up, Dixie, we're waiting for you."

I ran upstairs, peeled off my clothes, and tossed them and my Keds on top of the things already in the washer. I took a quick shower, toweled my body and hair dry, and pulled on a short strapless cotton dress and some flip-flops. My answering machine was blinking, so before I went downstairs, I punched the play button and got Shuga Reasnor's voice.

"I've been thinking about it," she said. "And I'd like to talk to you some more about the cat. Could you come to my place? Please call me as soon as you can. Or just come on by. I'll be here all day." She left her address and hung up, and the machine's robotic voice announced that the call had come in at 4:37. I glared at the machine. I didn't want to go see the woman, and I didn't want to call her back.

I took a deep breath and dialed her number. I got her machine, which thrilled me so much that I punched my fist into the air in a "Yes!" sign.

Shuga's recorded voice said, "You have reached. . . ." and gave her phone number. Why do people give you their phone number when you've just called it?

Talking fast in case she was monitoring her calls and might pick up,

I said, "Miss Reasnor, this is Dixie Hemingway. I got your message, and I'll try to stop by your place tomorrow morning around nine o'clock."

I was so relieved that I didn't have to talk to Shuga Reasnor three times in one day that I almost skipped down the stairs to the terrace, where the outdoor table was set, the grill was ready, and the wine was chilling in a bucket.

Michael said, "Well, the queen has arrived, so we can eat."

I stuck out my tongue at him, and Paco shook his head. "You two are so mature," he said.

Michael is the cook of the family. Even when we were kids, he was the family cook. He's the cook at the firehouse, too. Michael believes that George Foreman's grill has done more for the civilized world than Einstein's theory of relativity, and he loves to do things that take a long time, like ribs and briskets and turkeys.

Michael was four and I was two when our mother left us the first time. Our father was pulling a twenty-four-hour shift at the firehouse and didn't know she had gone, so Michael took care of us until he got home. He fed us cold cereal with milk until we ran out of milk, and then we ate cold dry cereal. He climbed on a chair and got the peanut butter jar from the cupboard, and he found a jar of grape jelly in the refrigerator. We didn't have any bread, so we ate it with a spoon.

When our father came home, he found us curled up together like puppies, jelly-smeared and confused, but none the worse for wear. Our mother came back in a few days, and our life took up as if she'd never been gone. She left us for good when I was nine and Michael was eleven. Our father had died putting out a fire by then, so we went to live with our grandparents in their house on the Gulf. Now we've come full circle. Michael moved back into the house when our grandparents died, and I moved into the garage apartment after Todd and Christy died. And Michael's still feeding me.

We were so practiced at getting dinner together that we all went into action like a circus act. Michael brushed olive oil on three pompano, dusted them with salt and pepper, and stretched them on the grill. Paco brought out a big wooden bowl of salad and a tray of sliced eggplant and zucchini from the kitchen, and I slathered the veggie slices with oil. Michael laid them on the grill with the pompano, and Paco tossed the salad with olive oil and lemon juice. Michael turned the fish, and I poured the wine. Michael turned the veggies, and Paco pulled out my chair. Michael flipped pompano and veggies onto a platter, and Paco and I grabbed our forks.

If there's any better way to end a day than sitting on a terrace with your favorite people while you eat fresh-caught fish and watch a spectacular sunset, I've never found it. The men had shaved and changed out of their scrungy shorts and sweatshirts with the sleeves cut out. Michael wore white linen pants and a crisp cotton shirt with thin blue and white stripes, and Paco had on black pants and a white linen shirt. Easy with themselves and the world, they exuded that special masculine energy that goes along with vibrant health and well-honed muscles. There were women all over Sarasota who would have given one of their ovaries to be with either of them, and I had them both. I also had their undivided attention.

Over dinner, I told them everything I knew about the murder. I told them about finding the lanai door open and the bedroom and closet ransacked, and about finding the dead body. About leaving Ghost with Mrs. Winnick and how weird she was, and about meeting Dr. Win and how it had looked like the Winnicks had just had a fight. I gave them a word-by-word account of my conversation with Guidry and told about speaking to Dr. Coffey and Shuga Reasnor. I told them what Judy had said about Marilee and how she'd dumped Dr. Coffey, and about his bimbo girlfriend coming out of cocaine alley.

At appropriate intervals, one or both of them said, "Huh," and when I mentioned Dr. Win, they both twisted their mouths to simulate throwing up. They were especially interested in the gross details about the dead man, and shook their heads with prim disapproval when I told them how Marilee had conned Dr. Coffey. I guess men don't get much pleasure out of hearing how a woman has tricked a man into giving her a million dollars.

9

When I was done telling it all, Michael set his wineglass down with a firm thud. "Stay out of it, Dixie. Let the homicide guys handle it."

Paco nodded soberly. "Dixie, you can get in the middle of something you don't want to be in. Stay out of it."

"I'm staying out of it! Did I say I wasn't staying out of it? I'm just concerned about the cat. What if Marilee Doerring never comes home? Some people don't, you know."

I saw the look on their faces and stopped. Okay, so I was getting a little overheated about the cat.

"I'll stay out of it," I said. "Don't worry."

Michael smiled and said, "Okay, folks, let's get off this subject. I make a motion that we all go over to the Crab House for a while."

Paco got up and started gathering plates. "Good idea. Come on, Dixie, let's hustle."

I knew what they were doing. Neither of them wanted me to go to bed thinking about death and loss. To tell the truth, I didn't want me to do that, either. It was almost my bedtime, but the day's excitement and my long nap had left me wide-awake.

The Crab House is a bayside waterfront bar that has entertainment ranging from female impersonators to stand-up comics to rhythm and blues. It's the kind of place where you don't have to arrive on a Ducati and look fetching in black leather, but it helps. There's a wooden porch across the back where people can eat dinner beside the dock. Inside, tables line the perimeter of an oblong room separated from the porch by a glass wall. Half the patrons come from the key and half from boats that tie up at the dock. They're mostly gay, mostly good-natured, and mostly free of prejudice toward straights. My kind of place.

The bandstand and a small dance floor is to the right of the entrance, and even before we opened the door, we could hear rollicking honky-tonk piano music. Several people were dancing, and as we went toward the tables, we automatically began bobbing our heads and dipping our knees to the music. We took a table in the corner and ordered margaritas from a finger-snapping, hip-twitching waiter.

Over the music and laughter, Michael shouted, "Who's that playing?"

"That's Phil," the waiter yelled back. "A real cutie pie, and people just love him."

He sort of jitterbugged away to get our drinks, dodging around two men taking turns whirling and dipping each other in a parody of a fast waltz. The place was really jumping, mostly because of the music. All over the room, people were wagging their heads and grinning at one another like idiots.

The waiter boogied back with the drinks and did a little shimmy before he boogied off. We laughed and clicked our margarita glasses. Michael's idea had been a good one. Being in a fun place was a good way to get life back in perspective.

From where I sat, I had a good view of the pianist's back and his blond head. He had broad shoulders and wore a black jacket flocked with some sparkly designs. He was built with long bones. When he stretched an arm out to reach the end of the keyboard, his long fingers seemed to dance across the keys, lifting with playful little flips. He was obviously having fun playing, and the fun was infectious. I couldn't have said what it was that gave the music such a joyous sound. Whatever it was, it had a bouncing enthusiasm that drove deep into the psyche and flushed out every iota of cynicism.

A man in creased jeans and Doc Martens boots stopped beside my chair, and we all looked up. "Uh, I hope I'm not out of line here, but would you care to dance?"

Michael gave him a lazy grin. "Which one of us are you asking?"

The man gave him a startled blink. "Well, her, of course."

Obviously, he wasn't a native. I was guessing New York. Michael and Paco swung their heads toward me with eyebrows hopefully raised. The man met all their criteria. He was about our age and clean. His boots were polished and neither his fly nor his jaw gaped open.

I shook my head. "No thanks."

He reddened and turned away. I looked at Michael and Paco and shrugged. I knew they would both like me to meet a man and fall in love again. As much as they had liked Todd, they were ready for me to replace him, and it bothered them that I wasn't willing to entertain the idea, that I wasn't even willing to dance with a new man.

It isn't that I think love can't happen twice in a lifetime. I'm not that naïve. And I don't feel any constraint from Todd, no sense that his spirit hovers between me and a second love. If anything, Todd would want me to find somebody new and start a new family. It's the new family idea that stops me. When Todd and I had Christy, we were so caught up in the pink cloud of starting a family that we never once considered the idea that everything has its polar opposite. If a family can be started, it can also be ended. The ending is an amputation of your soul, and I can't risk that again. I also can't place that restriction on love. You either love completely and absolutely, with faith in the future, or you don't love at all. Since I can no longer have faith in the future, I choose not to love.

A little after midnight, the pianist switched moods. So softly that people stopped talking to hear, he began playing "He Ain't Heavy, He's My Brother." All around the room, people grew somber and reflective. For men who had literally carried their lovers in their arms as they died of AIDS, it was more than a sentimental ballad. Gradually, the playing grew more intense and passionate, filled with almost palpable anguish. The room had gone completely quiet and still, and as the song ended, I looked toward Michael and Paco and caught a look between them that made my heart catch. They never make a display of their feelings for each other, but their love is definitely not for weaklings.

Suddenly shy in the face of it, I drank the last of my margarita and began to scoot my chair back. I had to get up at 4:00 A.M., and Michael had to be at the fire station at 8:00. As usual, nobody knew what Paco had to do.

"We'd better go," I said.

They nodded and began to dig in their pockets for money while I headed toward the exit. The pianist got up to take a break and turned toward me. By this time, I felt as if I knew him. Through his music, he had laid himself out in a way that was almost too transparent—whether it was joy or pain he felt, there was absolutely nothing between him and his listeners. Our eyes met across the room and I opened my mouth to shout "Great music!" or "Bravo!" or something to show my appreciation. He suddenly looked stricken and turned away. At the same moment, I realized who he was. He was the Winnick teenager, the shy classical musician destined for Juilliard.

The kid took off toward the rest rooms at the back and left me rooted to the floor. The Crab House was a far cry from Juilliard, and I couldn't believe the sanctimonious Winnicks had given their blessing to their son's night job.

Michael and Paco caught up with me, and Michael took my arm as if I needed steering. Paco held the door for us, and we moved out into air that was damp and warm, with a strong briny scent from the bay. Our footsteps made crushing noises on the shelled parking lot. Somewhere in the starlit distance, an outboard motor made muffled chugging sounds and night peepers called from the dark treetops.

I contained myself until we were in the car, Michael and Paco in the front and me in the back. Then I leaned forward and said, "You know who the piano player is? He's the kid who lives next door to Marilee Doerring. The house where the murdered man was!"

Now here's one of the differences between men and women. If they had been women, both of them would have turned around with their jaws dropped and their eyes stretched wide. They would have said, "No! You've got to be kidding!"

Being men, Michael said, "Huh," and Paco didn't say anything at all.

I said, "He can't be more than sixteen years old!"

That made Paco turn. "Nah, he's older than that. He's eighteen or nineteen."

Michael said, "God, it's nearly one o'clock. We're all gonna hate getting up in the morning."

Sometimes men are just no fun.

Michael was right about hating to get up next morning. When the alarm went off at four o'clock, I crawled out of bed with a dull margarita headache and a queasy stomach. There was a time when I could stay out till after 1:00 A.M. and get up at 4:00 with at least a modicum of alertness, but no more. If I hadn't known that half a dozen animals were depending on me, I would have hit the snooze button and slept another hour. Bleary-eyed, I switched on the bedside lamp and padded barefoot to the bathroom where I automatically got myself splashed and brushed for the day. I grabbed clean shorts and a T from the closet shelf and started pulling them on as I went down the hall. Then I remembered I was going to be seeing people, so I went back to the closet and got a bra. I shook my Keds to make sure no critters had crawled in during the night, then slid my feet into them and laced them up.

Out on the porch, I stopped a minute to inhale the fresh briny odor of morning sea air. A soft breeze was cool on my skin, and I could see the dark curved backs of dolphins jumping the waves in the milky light. So long as I concentrated on my work and had moments like this, I was okay. Not great, but okay. At least I was a lot better than I had been three years ago.

I clattered down the stairs, shooed a congregation of gulls off the Bronco, and got in. I would have preferred the bike, but I didn't know what the morning would bring. I went down the drive and turned onto

Midnight Pass Road, where I didn't meet a single car. I didn't even see an early-morning jogger. I could have been the only person in the whole world.

Both coach lights were burning at the Graysons', and I mentally patted myself on the back for remembering to change their lightbulb. Rufus and I had our usual morning love-in, and as soon as we went out the front door, he started barking and straining at the leash. I had to shush him sharply to get him to shut up, and I took him toward the bay instead of toward Midnight Pass Road for his morning poop. Something was definitely calling to him from the woods.

After his walk and brushing, I put my bill on the kitchen counter, along with a note asking the Graysons to call me as soon as they got back that afternoon. Otherwise, I would make an evening call to take care of Rufus, and they'd get billed whether they were home or not. You have to be strict about these things. Sometimes people don't notify their pet-sitter that their flight has been delayed or that they've decided to extend their trip for a few days. I don't intend to neglect any of my charges, and I don't intend to pace around wondering if their owners might not have returned when they said they would. Ergo, they have to verify they've returned or pay for an unnecessary trip. I gave Rufus an extra-big hug when I left. I was going to miss him.

When I let myself into Tom Hale's condo, Tom and Billy Elliot looked up at me and Tom waved, but then their attention went back to the TV. A woman with spiky black hair and ruby red lips was holding a blue-balled microphone close to her lips and speaking low, the way sportscasters do at a golf match. Behind her was a wide wrought-iron gate, through which one could see a massive house.

"Mrs. Frazier hasn't made a statement yet, and so we're just waiting here to see what the next development will be. From what the Sarasota County Sheriff's Department has reported to us, the medical examiner's office has not yet released the body to the family."

A man's off-camera-voice said, "Any new information about the connection between Harrison Frazier and the woman whose house he was found in?"

"Well, that's the interesting thing, Joel. According to the Frazier family spokesperson, there is no connection between the two at all. The family believes he must have been killed somewhere else and moved to the house."

Tom hit the mute button on his remote and said, "Well, there's a classic case of denial."

"That dead man in Marilee's house was Harrison Frazier?"

"Yep, and if he wasn't dead already, getting caught in Marilee's house would kill him."

Harrison Frazier was one of Florida's wealthiest men, with a family that practically went back to Ponce de León. The epitome of good breeding and good taste, the name Frazier graced an opera house or botanical garden or library in almost every city in Florida.

"You think Harrison Frazier and Marilee knew each other?"

"Come on, Dixie, why would somebody dump a dead body in Marilee's house? Of course they knew each other."

"You think she killed him?"

"Marilee never seemed the type."

"Anybody's the type, Tom. Any one of us could commit murder."

His face tightened. "I've sure had moments when I could."

"We all have. Most of us are just lucky enough that the moments pass."

"Still, Marilee's a gentle soul. I just can't see her shooting somebody."

"Is that what they said? That he'd been shot?"

"I just assumed. Wasn't he?"

I shrugged. "I don't know. He might have been."

It seemed like the time to get out, before he could quizz me about what I had seen. I snapped Billy Elliot's leash on his collar and started toward the front door. Tom said, "Dixie, did you call Cora Mathers?"

I shook my head. "I haven't had a chance yet. I'll do it later."

10

illy Elliot and I took the elevator downstairs, and when we came
out the front door he leaped forward in a headlong dash. I wel-
comed the hard run. It helped get the cobwebs out of my head
from my night of dissipation. We tore around the paved parking lot
enough times to equal at least a mile before he slowed to a satisfied trot.
For once, he had been able to run as long as he wanted to. I was half-
dead and my thigh muscles were burning like a hot poker had been
stuck to them, but at least I had sweated out the vestiges of alcohol.

Back upstairs, I let Billy Elliot inside and yelled good-bye to Tom,
then drove to Marilee's house and sat in the driveway looking at the
blank house. There was no deputy in sight, but the crime-scene tape
was still up. I looked toward the Winnick house, but it looked as closed
down as Marilee's. I decided to stop by again after I'd finished for the
morning. If Guidry wasn't there, I would call him and find out when I
could bring Ghost home.

I backed out of the driveway and headed toward Midnight Pass
Road. In the rearview mirror, I saw the Winnicks' garage door rise and
a white Jeep Cherokee back out. At the intersection, I stopped, and the
Jeep drew up close behind me. The Winnick kid was driving, and his
face in the rearview mirror looked desperate. He braked and jumped

out of the car and ran to my side. I put down my window and looked into scared red eyes.

"On your way to school?"

"No ma'am, today's Saturday."

God, I had reached the age when I didn't know what day it was! Not only that, but people taller than me called me "ma'am."

The kid looked apprehensively toward his house. "Would it be all right if we went someplace and talked?"

I had cats to take care of, but I didn't have the heart to refuse him. Besides, cats don't have to be fed at exactly the same time every day. If they were living in the wild, they'd be on a random bird and rodent schedule. Okay, the truth is that I wanted to hear what he had to say.

I said, "I'll meet you at the Village Diner."

He followed close behind me and we both nosed into parking spaces in front of the diner. He opened the diner door for me without any uncertain diffidence, and I wondered which of his parents had taught him proper manners. Probably his father. The man had the soul of a sea slug, but he probably held out women's chairs. The kid was wearing jeans and a neon yellow waffle-knit knit shirt with a blue-and-white-striped collar and trimmed pocket. I would have bet good money that his mother had chosen it and that he didn't know how nerdy it was.

Judy gave me a questioning look when she saw me with another person of the male persuasion. I waggled my fingers in a wave and we took the same booth that Detective Guidry and I had sat in. Judy was right behind us with coffee and mugs.

Deadpan, she said to the kid, "You want coffee, sir?"

He blushed and shook his head. "Apple juice, please."

Apple juice had been Christy's favorite, too. For a minute, I saw him as his mother probably saw him, two or three years old and just learning to speak up to strangers. It's probably those cute overlaid memories that allow parents to look at their gangly adolescents without stabbing themselves.

Judy said, "You ready to order?"

"I'm not hungry," he said.

I understood how he felt. I never can eat when I'm worried, either.

Judy knew what I wanted, so she gave me another look and left us alone.

A woman came in dragging a whining little boy who looked about three years old. Cute kid. Skin the color of a Starbucks frappaccino and a mass of dark curls flopping over round black eyes. The woman had the same coloring and silky black hair, but she was carrying close to two hundred pounds of puffy fat on a five-foot frame, and she had sour, angry lines etched into her face. She had a death grip on the child's hand, alternately jerking and dragging him the way you have to pull a twisted garden hose. She stopped at a booth across the aisle and snarled, "Shut up and get in there!"

The Winnick kid and I watched the little boy try to scrabble onto the plastic-covered seat. His legs were too short and the plastic didn't give him anything to grab, so his feet flailed the air. The woman smacked his bottom with the flat of her hand, which caused him to jerk his head up and bang it on the underside of the table. Most kids would have cried, but he didn't, and the fact that he didn't was telling. This kid was accustomed to pain, and he knew that crying would only bring more of it.

She shoved him the rest of the way in and took the opposite seat. "Now you behave yourself," she said. "You sit there and be quiet."

Judy came to take the woman's order, and the kid and I turned our eyes away from them. I sipped coffee and watched his hands fiddle with the bundle of flatware rolled into a paper napkin. His hands were broad, with long skinny fingers and knobby knuckles.

To the tabletop, he said, "I know you saw me last night."

"I heard you, too. You were terrific."

He shrugged and blushed. It was hard to believe he was the same person as the confident pianist of the night before.

"The waiter said your name was Phil."

He blinked a couple of times and said, "It's Phillip, really." The poor kid couldn't even come up with a decent alias.

I said, "Do you play regularly at the Crab House?"

"Yeah. From eleven to one." He raised bloodshot eyes to me. "I climb out my window and walk over there."

"Ahhhh. So I guess that means your folks don't know about it."

He gave a choked laugh. "Among other things."

"You must not get much sleep."

"School will be out in a couple of months, and I'll be leaving in August."

"For Juilliard."

"Yeah."

"Are you excited about that, going to Juilliard?"

"Sure."

"Your mom's really proud of you."

"Yeah, it's all she talks about. She has lots of scrapbooks and pictures."

I had a quick image of Olga Winnick alone in that darkened house, working on her photo albums and scrapbooks, creating records of a happy family that didn't exist. Phillip was her way of vindicating herself to the world, but the woman didn't know her real son, she only knew the one she had created.

"How'd you get the job at the bar?"

He flashed me a quick look that was almost sly. "Somebody I knew told the owner about me. He had me audition and hired me."

I would have bet good money that the somebody he knew was also an older lover. He raised his head and looked at me head-on. "Are you going to tell my folks?"

I rotated my coffee mug and realized I hadn't even considered telling them. I'm not sure what that says about me, but that's how it was.

"If you were my son, I'd want to know that you were climbing out a window and playing at a bar. But you're not my son, and you're what, eighteen? Anyway, it's none of my business. I think you're probably not getting enough sleep, but other than that, I don't see anything wrong with it. It's an honest job, the place is safe, and it gives you a chance to do what you like to do."

He kept looking at me, waiting for something else.

I smiled. "That's all, Phillip."

Judy came with a coffeepot in one hand and my breakfast in the other.

Phillip said, "If it's not too much trouble, I think I'd like some pancakes."

"No trouble at all. You want bacon or sausage with them?"

"Yes ma'am."

"Which?"

"I guess both."

Nothing stimulates your appetite like finding out you're not hopelessly doomed after all.

I tucked into my eggs for a while, and he rhythmically tapped his fingers on the table. His hand span was probably twice as wide as my two hands laid side by side.

Across the aisle, the little boy said, "Look, Mama! A moon!"

He was holding up a triangle of toast with a bite mark in its center. The shape did look a little moonlike. He was a smart kid, noticing something like that so young.

With her cheeks swelled with hunks of sausage, his mother said, "Schtop playing wif your food."

His face fell and he bent his head back to his cereal.

Phillip said, "The police came and talked to my mom and dad and me about that murder."

"They're not police," I said. "They're from the Sheriff's Department."

"Oh. Well, they asked if we'd seen anything over there, or if we'd heard anything."

"Did you?"

He blushed, shifted in his seat, and looked out the window. "Not really."

Judy swished to the table with a plate of pancakes and another plate piled high with bacon and sausages. "More apple juice?"

"Yes ma'am, if it's not too much trouble."

She sped off to get his juice while I eyed his bacon and thought about what "Not really" meant.

Judy came back with another glass of juice and poured more coffee in my cup. "Anything else?"

"We're fine," I said.

Across the aisle, the woman said, "You eat every bite of that. You wanted it, you eat it. I'm not paying for shit you don't eat."

"Poor kid," said Judy, and moved on with her coffeepot.

"Phillip, do you know Ms. Doerring very well?"

"Nnnn-nnnn." He shook his head with his mouth full of pancake. I sipped coffee and watched him chew. He had put all the sausage on his plate but none of the bacon.

He swallowed and said, "My dad's helped her with some things, but I've never even talked to her."

I said, "Do you mind if I take one of your pieces of bacon? I don't usually eat bacon, but that looks so good. . . ."

"Oh, sure! Sure! That's fine!" It was like taking candy from a baby.

Perfume companies ought to bottle the smell of crisp bacon. Forget pheromones. I'll bet a woman with a little spot of bacon grease behind her ears would attract every male within a five-mile radius. Taking little bitty bites to make it last longer, I said, "What kind of things?"

It took him a minute to pick up where we'd left off. "Plumbing and stuff."

"She calls him to do things like that?"

He chewed awhile and considered how to answer. "She doesn't ex-actly call him. A few times her garage door has been open when he came home and she was out there, you know. I guess he saw her and went over to see if she needed any help."

No matter how hard I tried, I could not imagine Marilee Doerring out in her garage getting down a plunger to unstop her toilet or search-ing for a washer to fix a dripping faucet.

"That's nice of him."

"Yeah."

We both ate silently for a while, him taking huge forkfuls of food and me fighting down the rage I felt at the memory of Carl Winnick devoting an hour of radio time to say that Christy would not have been killed if I had been home where I was supposed to be instead of out acting like a man in a deputy's uniform. He had even objected to the department giving me widow's benefits, saying taxpayers shouldn't have to reward me for being a bad wife and mother.

I studied Phillip's face and reminded myself that the kid wasn't his father. The kid wasn't anything like his father. There was no reason to blame the kid because his father was an arrogant idiot.

I said, "I got the impression from your mom that she doesn't like Ms. Doerring much."

"My mom thinks she's a slut," he said. "She probably is."

The easy way he said it took me by such surprise that I choked on a swig of coffee. While I coughed and sputtered and fanned my face with my napkin, Phillip grinned. "Bet you didn't think I knew that."

I was beginning to like this kid a lot. After four years of college away from his parents, he would probably be as smooth as his dad, but he wouldn't be a phony. This kid was the real deal.

The woman across the aisle stood up and yanked her dress down over her folds of fat. "Come on," she said, "we don't have all day."

I watched the little boy slide off the seat and follow his mother to the cashier's stand.

I pulled bills from my backpack and laid them on the table. "My cats await," I said. "I'll probably see you around."

Phillip's mouth was full, and he smiled up at me with a tiny slick of syrup on his chin. I resisted the urge to spit on a napkin and wipe it off, and headed for the front door. The woman was at the cashier stand counting out change and snarling at the little boy. Outside, I stopped and put my foot up on a railing separating the parking spaces from the walk. I untied and retied my shoe while I waited for the little boy and his mother to come out.

The door opened and the woman put her hand between his little shoulder blades and shoved him forward. "Goddamn it! Go on!"

In about two nanoseconds, I spun away from the railing and pinned her to the diner's stucco wall with my forearm across her throat. "You have a beautiful child, lady, and he deserves a lot better than you. You either start being nicer to him or I swear to God I'll see that he's taken away from you and given to somebody who'll love him."

All the rage had left her face. She was afraid, and she had every right to be. Something hit my ankle, hard, and I looked down. The little boy was glaring up at me, ready to kick me again.

"Leave my mama alone!"

I stepped away from her and she grabbed her throat with both hands as if she was afraid it had a hole in it. The diner door opened and a family came out—mother, father, three preadolescent kids. They flowed around us without paying us much attention, the father teasing one of the kids and the others laughing the way close families do at their private jokes. They moved down the sidewalk to their minivan and got in, still laughing and talking.

The woman was watching me with frightened eyes. The little boy had moved to hug her leg and she had a hand on top of his head.

"Okay," I said, "that's all."

I walked briskly down the sidewalk and around the corner to my car. My hands were shaking so much I barely managed to get the door unlocked. I put my head on the steering wheel and waited for the adrenaline tremors to leave. I felt sick. I felt ashamed. Sergeant Owens had been right about me. I wasn't ready to deal with people yet.

Maybe I never will be.

11

After I got myself together and saw to the other cats, I drove to one of the ritzy streets coiling around the edge of Roberts Bay to see Shuga Reasnor. Half-hidden behind a cluster of royal palms, her house was a behemoth of glistening white stucco shaped in a wide V, its upjutting wings giving it the look of an albino frigate bird in flight.

In the circular driveway, I got out of the Bronco and pulled my shorts out of my crotch before I climbed three wide stone steps to the entrance. The front door was a thick slab of glass that allowed a view all the way through the house to the lanai. I couldn't see it, but I knew the pool would be damn near Olympic in size and either equipped with every accessory known to man or built with a cascading waterfall. Or both. I rang the bell, a brass plate the size of a turkey platter, and stood looking up at the glass door while I waited. If that sucker broke as you walked through it, a shard could slice your head right off.

Through the glass wall at the back of the house, a woman moved into view out on the lanai. She came through the slider and walked toward me, giving me a thorough examination as she came.

"Are you Dixie? Sorry it took me so long, I was watering plants on the lanai. Come on in."

Shuga was tanning-booth brown, with the kind of long blond hair that you get only by being fifteen years old or paying a bundle for extensions. Her skin was smooth and taut like a fifteen-year-old's, too, and her body was trim and youthful. She was wearing a short black tank top and low-rider white jeans that showed her flat belly and smooth swirl of navel. Only her knowing eyes and corded hands gave away her age, which I estimated as somewhere between thirty-five and forty-five. Barefoot, she led the way into her living room, her feet leaving faint damp prints on the black tile. Outside the sliding glass doors, a water hose lay coiled like a green anaconda in the midst of a jungle of potted plants.

Swooping over a coffee table the size of my bed, she plucked a cigarette out of a nicotine bouquet stuck in a crystal holder, and waved her hand at me in a gesture that managed to invite me to smoke and to sit at the same time. Her fingernails were like Porsche fenders, sleek and curved and bright red. I shook my head at the cigarette offer and lowered my butt to a curved sofa covered in a rose-colored linen. Like Shuga, the room was beautifully done, but it had a hint of street toughness that no amount of cosmetics or money could overcome.

She got right to the point. "I wasn't entirely truthful over the phone. I don't want to talk about the damn cat, it's Marilee I'm worried about. The detective talked to me, so I know about that man in her house. That what's his name person. But that's all he would tell me. You know how the police are, they won't tell you a thing, even if you're a person's best friend. You work there, you're bound to know more than the police do."

She said the last with a pasted-on smile, as if she had suddenly remembered that she needed something from me and ought to be sucking up.

"I don't exactly work there," I said. "I just stop in twice a day to take care of the cat."

"And you don't know where she went?"

"No, that's why I called you. She didn't leave a number where she could be reached."

"The detective said she was going to be gone a week."

She gave me a pointed look with one raised eyebrow, as if it was my turn. I stayed silent. If she wanted me to play coy guessing games, I wasn't playing.

She sighed and blew out a stream of smoke. "What I want to know is how they can be sure she left town? Has anybody checked to make sure?"

I thought of the hair dryer left on her bathroom countertop. "Do you have any reason to think she didn't?"

She took another hit from the cigarette and looked out at the plants on the lanai, as if hoping to find inspiration out there. Abruptly, she dropped into a chair and gave me a hard stare. "I might, but Marilee would kill me if I told anybody."

"Miss Reasnor, if you know something that bears on a crime, you should tell the detective."

"Call me Shuga," she said throatily. The seductive way she said it was well practiced.

I gave her a level stare and her mouth twisted impatiently. "People have secrets," she said. "Everybody has secrets. You probably have secrets." She slitted her eyes and peered at me as if assessing what kind of secrets I had.

"And you're afraid Marilee will be mad at you if you tell one of her secrets."

"Hell yes. Wouldn't you be mad if your best friend told one of your secrets?"

I shrugged and stood up. I didn't have time for this. "Don't tell it, then."

She crossed her legs and swung her foot like an agitated cat swinging its tail. "I made a phone call last night to the place where she might have been going. She wasn't there."

I sat back down. "I thought you said you didn't know where she was going."

"I didn't know there had been a murder when you asked me."

"And you lied to the detective after you knew."

"I'm not *sure* that's where she was going. It wasn't like she had *told* me she was going there."

Her leg swung faster, and she sucked so hard on the cigarette, it almost disappeared into ash. Then she slapped her free foot on the floor and leaned forward and looked hard at me.

"It's damn funny. It's just damn funny. The murder's all over the news, why hasn't she called?"

To tell the truth, I'd been wondering that myself.

I said, "If you're really concerned about her, you should give the investigators all the information you have."

She leaned over and stubbed out her cigarette in a crystal ashtray that already had several lipstick-tipped butts in it. She lit another cigarette, and this time her hands were shaking. "I'll think about it," she said. "I really will think about it. You won't tell them what I said, will you? I mean, I don't know that's where she was going."

I stood up to go. "Not unless I think I have to. I can't promise I won't."

She nodded, and for a moment her face looked as old as her hands.

I pushed through the great glass door and went down the steps to the Bronco, conscious all the way of Shuga Reasnor's eyes watching me. I was sure of two things—she had been hoping to use me, and she had been lying through her teeth. I just didn't know what she had lied about.

I am blessed and cursed with an excellent memory for the things people say and how they say them. It began when I was a kid and had to pay close attention to what my mother said so I could figure out which things were lies and which were the truth. It was the only way I could predict what was going to happen from one minute to the next, and even then it didn't always work. I got better at it over time, and now it's second nature to me, like having a built-in lie detector.

I threaded my way through the serpentine streets, running through the entire conversation with Shuga, hearing her voice and its inflections. I passed the village and the fire station, driving on automatic, while my mind kept going over the meeting. Then I played it again, like rewinding a tape and starting all over. She had been nervous, but honest people can be nervous when they're talking about things they don't want to talk about, and her reluctance to betray a friend's secret could account for her uneasiness.

As I turned onto the shell-topped lane leading home, a black Harley-Davidson came roaring toward me. The driver had a bandanna tied over bushy black hair. A thick beard covered the bottom of his face and dark glasses hid his eyes. He wore a black leather vest and faded jeans. Black boots. I stopped at the side of the drive and let him go by, watching his right hand. As he passed, his first two fingers extended and then folded back around the handlebar.

He sped out to Midnight Pass Road, and I drove on down the lane. The two fingers were the signal Paco and I had agreed on he'd use whenever he was working a case in disguise. Otherwise, I might have thought a serial killer was on the property.

I started replaying the meeting again, but this time seeing it instead of hearing it. Seeing Shuga's face, her swinging leg, her fingers stabbing out her cigarettes. Liars always give themselves away one way or another. Some liars sweat profusely, some raise their voices to a telltale falsetto, and some cut their eyes up and to the right, as if they're seeing a vision of the story they're inventing. I was dead sure Shuga Reasnor had been lying about something, but I hadn't caught her giveaway sign.

I pulled into the carport and sat with the motor running, staring straight ahead at the Gulf but blind to everything but the mental images in my head. Like watching a movie, I slowed it down to an almost frame-by-frame run, and then I had it. When Shuga spoke of the dead man, she had called him "that what's his name person." As she said it, she had cut her eyes for an instant toward the right edge of the ceiling, the way people do when they're inventing a lie. Now that I had the sign, I realized even her words had been a giveaway. She had tried too hard to feign ignorance of the man's name, when it was known to every Floridian who was halfway sentient. Shuga Reasnor knew Harrison Frazier. She either had a personal relationship with Harrison Frazier or she knew that Marilee did.

A little voice in my head said, "No shit, Sherlock! You just figured that out?"

I should have realized it from the beginning, the way Tom Hale had. I had been so focused on putting one foot in front of the other that I hadn't given the details of the murder much thought. Now I felt the way Snow White must have felt after the Prince kissed her and brought her out of her coma. In a way, I had been in a coma for three years, and now I was beginning to wake up.

I climbed the stairs to my porch and opened the French doors to let the sea breeze blow out all the morning's stale air while I went to the bathroom and brushed my teeth. I checked my answering machine, which had no messages, then went out to the porch and sank into the hammock.

I thought about the aura of hard knowing that surrounded Shuga Reasnor, and about her opulent lifestyle. My guess was that she had gotten her money the hard way, either on her back sequentially or in a marriage bed to somebody who had conveniently died with no other heirs. For all I knew, Marilee might have gotten her money the same way.

Had Marilee been present when somebody conked Harrison Frazier on the back of the head? Had she been there when somebody taped his face nose-down in Ghost's water bowl? Maybe Marilee had been having an affair with him and his wife followed him and killed him. If so, what had she done with Marilee? It could have been Marilee who killed him. He was big, but a woman can swing a baseball bat or golf club hard enough to knock a man out. But surely Marilee wouldn't have been stupid enough to kill a man in her kitchen and leave him with his face taped inside her cat's water bowl. Unless she'd counted on people thinking she wouldn't be stupid enough to do that and therefore they'd think she had to be innocent. And where the hell was Marilee anyway? If she had killed him, she could be halfway around the world by this time. With all the money she had, she could buy a new identity, dye her hair, lay low, and she might never be found.

No matter who killed Harrison Frazier, Shuga Reasnor was right, it was damn strange that Marilee hadn't called.

The hammock swayed ever so gently in the sea breeze and seagulls squawked and circled in the cloudless blue sky. The surf surged onto the beach in an unbroken rhythm, and I stayed wide-awake. Finally, I gave up trying to sleep and grabbed my car keys. Olga Winnick thought Marilee was a slut. Kristin Lord thought she was predatory. Tom Hale thought she was a gentle soul. Shuga Reasnor knew a secret about her that she was afraid to tell. All I knew about her was that she was neat and clean and took excellent care of her cat. I wanted to see what her grandmother had to say about her.

12

Sarasota has a slew of retirement communities and assisted-living facilities, and Bayfront Village is one of the most exclusive. Its main building is a pink brick monstrosity constructed in a vague mix of Gothic spires, Mediterranean arches, red tile roof, and Art Deco turquoise trim. I drove up a fake cobblestone drive and pulled under a portico, where a uniformed valet courteously opened the door for me. As he drove off to park my Bronco in some secret spot, wide glass doors automatically sighed open when they felt my presence. Inside, the cavernous lobby appeared to have been decorated by a committee of feverish designers who saw an opportunity to unload all the mistakes former clients had refused. Overstuffed sofas upholstered in foxhunting scenes kept company with Hindu statues and gilded rococo. Plaster cherubs with fat cheeks mingled with sleek Danish modern and ruffled chintz.

Silver-haired men and women were moving around, some going outside to cars drawing up under the portico. A lot of them pushed little three-wheeled canvas walking aids that looked like empty doll carriages. I wasn't surprised. The decor alone was enough to give them vertigo. Most of them wore sweaters, in spite of the fact that it was sizzling outside.

Feeling obscenely young and fit, I passed an easel supporting a large cardboard sign giving the week's activities. The sign was outlined in flashing lights, a tacky way of attracting attention, in my opinion, but I read it as I went by. One of the events being announced was a talk by Dr. Gerald Coffey, entitled "Help for the Heart."

I went up to the front desk and told a calm young woman in a tailored black suit that I was there to see Cora Mathers.

"Is she expecting you?"

"No, I should have called, but I just took a chance and came over."

"I'll call her. What's your name?"

"Dixie Hemingway, but she doesn't know me. Tell her I'm her granddaughter's cat-sitter."

"Her granddaughter's cat-sitter?"

"I take care of her granddaughter's cat when she's out of town. She left without giving me a number where she could be reached, and I'm hoping Mrs. Mathers knows how to contact her."

She nodded and punched numbers into a phone pad. I could hear buzzes on the other end of the line, and after nine or ten of them, I was ready to turn away. The young woman didn't seem fazed, however, so I waited. After what must have been thirty rings, a voice answered. The young woman explained my reason for coming and then listened intently while the person gave a lengthy response. She said, "Okay, Mrs. Mathers, I'll tell her," and put the phone down.

"She says to go on up," she said. "She's on the sixth floor. Turn right when you get off the elevator, her apartment is number six thirteen."

The elevator was mirrored, so on the ride up I smoothed my hair and tried to brush some wrinkles out of my shorts. At the sixth floor, I stepped out and turned right, and saw a tiny woman with wispy white hair planted in the middle of the hall waving a heavily freckled arm side to side like a highway construction worker. She wore a pair of wide-legged shorts in an exotic parrot print, with a bright red blouse that fell loosely over her thin hips. Her pale legs were as scrawny as a child's, and she would have had to get on tiptoe to be five feet tall.

"Here I am," she called. "Come on." She was beaming at me with such a sweet face that I felt a stab of yearning for my own grandmother.

When I got close, I said, "Thank you for seeing me, Mrs. Mathers. My name is Dixie Hemingway."

She turned into her doorway and crooked her finger at me to follow. "I know," she said. "Debby told me when she called. Are you related to Ernest Hemingway?"

"No, afraid not."

Taking tiny steps that moved her along in minuscule increments, she said, "I wouldn't regret it if I were you, he wasn't a man with a strong character. Oh, he was strong enough when he was young, all that swagger and boasting, but when the going got tough, he couldn't take it. Shot himself, you know. Got old and shot himself. Being young is easy, you know, anybody can do that, but it takes guts to be old."

We had now made it through a small foyer lined with framed botanical prints. Her apartment smelled like chocolate chip cookies.

I said, "Oh, this is lovely."

I wasn't just being polite, it really was. To my left was a bar in front of a small galley kitchen, and I could see a spacious bedroom to the right. Directly in front was an airy living room with a glassed wall across the back. The floor was pale pink tile and the walls were a deeper shade of pink. A pale green linen Tuxedo sofa sat in front of a glass-topped coffee table, and a couple of armchairs in a muted green and pink chintz faced the sofa. Between the kitchen and the sofa was a skirted round table with two pale green ice-cream chairs. The effect was graceful and serene, enhanced by white wicker and greenery on a narrow sunporch that ran across the back of the living room and bedroom.

"It is nice, isn't it? I'm so blessed to have it. Marilee bought it for me, you know. Sit down and I'll make us some tea. You're in luck, I just finished making chocolate bread."

I took a seat at the round table and said, "I never ate chocolate bread."

"Well, it's my own invention. Marilee gave me a bread-making machine, oh, it must have been fifteen years ago now, and I use it every week. I start it and then at just the right time I throw in some chocolate chips. I won't tell anybody when I throw them in, that's my secret."

She ministepped around the bar to the kitchen, where she clattered down two mugs from a rack and poured boiling water into a fat brown teapot. "I keep water simmering all the time," she said. "You never can tell when somebody may drop by for a cup of tea."

"You must have a lot of friends here."

"Well, not a lot, but a sufficient amount. You don't want too many people coming and going, but enough so you don't feel alone. Of course, Marilee stops by pretty often, too, and that's nice."

She put the tea things on a tray and added a plate of fist-size hunks of brown bread studded with dark bits of oozing chocolate. Next to freshly fried bacon, the scent of hot melted chocolate may be the most tantalizing smell in the world. I got up and carried the tray to the table.

"It's Marilee I wanted to talk to you about, Mrs. Mathers." I said.

"Call me Cora."

"Do you happen to know where she's gone? She forgot to leave me a number when she left."

She pulled out a chair and sat down across from me. "This is about that Frazier fellow, isn't it?"

"Sort of. I'd like to let her know about it before she comes home."

Pouring tea into our cups, she said, "Well, dear, I expect she knows by now, don't you? I'm sure it's been on all the news. Here, butter some bread while it's hot. I don't slice it, I just rip off chunks of it. I don't know why, but it seems better that way."

While Cora watched intently, I smeared butter on a hunk and took a bite. I closed my eyes and moaned. "Oh God, that's good."

"Better than sex, isn't it? Of course it's been a long time since I had sex, so I may not remember it clearly. I'll bet you have plenty of sex, pretty young woman like you."

I sipped some tea and avoided her eyes. "Cora, have you heard from Marilee?"

She swallowed a bite of bread and took a sip of tea before she answered. "I don't imagine she'll be wanting to talk to me right now. Not with that Frazier fellow dead in her house."

"You knew him?"

"I never met the man."

My head felt like it had been twisted like a doorknob and allowed to spin back into place. I buttered another bite of bread and chewed it slowly while I studied Cora's face. Her eyes were overhung by crepey eyelids, but they were bright and alert. I said, "Why don't you think Marilee will want to talk to you?"

Her lips tightened and she slapped a pat of butter on a bit of bread. "Well, Frazier's the man who ruined my granddaughter's life, isn't he? Don't think I'm saying Marilee hasn't made the best of it, because she has. But that's all water over the dam now, isn't it?"

The words lay on the table along with the bread and butter and tea. I could pick them up and learn something very personal about Marilee that she probably didn't want known, or I could mind my own business and stay ignorant.

I said, "I don't know about that, Cora. To tell the truth, I never understood what that meant, water over the dam, under the bridge, whatever."

"Well, it's just too late, isn't it? What's done is done, and you can't go back and undo it, can you?"

"I guess not. Uh, Cora, would you mind telling me how Marilee knew Harrison Frazier?"

"Well, yes, I would mind, dear. That's personal and private business of Marilee's, and I don't go around telling my granddaughter's personal and private business, now do I? Have some more tea."

"No thanks. Can you tell me where she is? I really think I should contact her."

"No, can't tell you that, either. But here's what I'll do: If she calls me—and she usually does call when she's off on one of these trips—I'll tell her you want to talk to her. How's that?"

"Cora, the Sheriff's Department would like to know where she is. It isn't just me."

"Well, I'll tell them the same thing I told you. I don't know, and even if I did, I wouldn't say, because that's Marilee's private business."

"But you're not worried about her?"

"Oh my, no. Marilee can take care of herself. I'll say that for her, she can take care of herself." She waved her arm toward the glass wall as she said that, presumably to indicate the vastness of the visible blue sky as a symbol of how well Marilee could take care of herself.

I said, "Marilee left the number of Shuga Reasnor to call in case of an emergency. Do you know Ms. Reasnor?"

"Oh my, yes, I've known her since she was a little bitty thing, only her name wasn't Shuga then, it was Peggy Lee. Her mother was a fool for Peggy Lee, so that's what she named her little girl. Poor little thing, that's about the only thing her mother ever gave her. Her daddy wasn't much better. Drunks, both of them. If I hadn't fed Peggy, I think she might have flat starved to death. She's done all right for herself, though. Last time I saw her, she looked like Miss Gotrocks herself."

"You saw her lately?"

"No, it was several months ago. Marilee had picked up my heart pills at the drugstore and forgot to bring them to me before she left town, so Peggy Lee brought them to me. I told her she looked like a movie star. Between you and me, though, I don't think that's her own hair."

"So she had a key to Marilee's house?"

"Oh my, yes. Those two have always been in and out of each other's house like it was their own."

"Cora, did you know Marilee had her locks changed? I had to stop by and pick up a new key before she left."

"Is that a fact? Well, no, I didn't know that. But then I wouldn't, because I don't have a key myself. The only time I go over there is when Marilee comes and gets me, so why would I?"

I was stumped. So far as I knew, Marilee hadn't broken any laws or done anything wrong. If her grandmother didn't want to say where she'd gone, she wasn't obligated to do so. Furthermore, I was a pet-sitter, not a criminal investigator. I had already stepped over a line by coming here, and if I went any further, I would be getting into serious unethical territory.

I stood up. "I'd better go," I said. "If Marilee calls, I'd appreciate it if you'd ask her to contact me. I've put her cat in a day-care center until the house is released, and I'd like to discuss that with her."

"I'm sure whatever you've done is just fine."

"Would you like me to put the tea things away before I go?"

"Well, if you don't mind, dear, yes, I would. Things get heavier when you're old."

I set the teapot and mugs and plates on the tray and carried them around to the kitchen counter. The refrigerator door had notes attached by magnets, and there were several snapshots of a pretty dark-haired young woman.

I called, "Are these photos of Marilee when she was young?"

Through the open space above the bar, I saw Cora's face close like a flower pulling its petals inward. She looked much older, and infinitely sadder.

"No, dear, those are not of Marilee."

Her voice held such finality that I knew I had violated some unspoken rule by asking.

"I'm sorry," I said. "I didn't mean to pry."

"Oh, of course you did, but it's all right. I'm not angry. I just can't discuss what it isn't my business to discuss, now can I?"

I reminded myself that I had no right to ask questions, and said my good-byes, leaving her hunched over the little round table.

Downstairs in the lobby, I veered behind a couple of elegantly dressed women standing in front of the blinking activities display.

"Excuse me," I said, "my grandmother is thinking about buying an apartment here. Could you tell me how you like living here?"

They turned and started talking at once, the gist of which was that the chef in the dining room put out a fabulous Sunday brunch, that there were always classes and workshops and outings planned, and that everybody who lived there was interesting. They could have done commercials for the place.

I nodded toward the blinking display. "I noticed that Dr. Coffey is going to do a talk about bypass surgery. Does he do that often?"

They sobered and nodded. "Yes, he does," said one. "I suppose he's operated on so many of the people living here that he needs to let us know that it's available for us."

I looked toward a tanned silver-haired couple striding out the door carrying tennis rackets. "Everybody looks awfully healthy. He can't do *that* many bypasses."

One woman fingered a string of cultured pearls at her throat and said, "Looks can be deceiving. Several people have been active one day and in the hospital the next. It's really alarming."

The other woman said, "Like Mary Kane. She had a big party for Sunday brunch, and that night she went into a diabetic coma. She just insisted on eating those cherry blintzes, and why not? She was eighty-five years old and she'd lived with diabetes for years and years. She knew what she could do and what she couldn't do, but I guess that time she overdid it. Two days later Dr. Coffey did a triple bypass on her."

I waited for the end of the story, and when neither of them volunteered it, I said, "And was it a success?"

"She never woke up. They had to transfer her to a hospital in St. Pete, and she was there for three months before she finally died. Dr. Coffey said she was just too frail to survive. Poor thing, and she never even knew she had anything wrong with her heart. All she knew about was her diabetes."

"Almost the same thing happened to Mr. Folsom, remember? He seemed fine too, just complained of emphysema from smoking before he knew better. And then, boom, Dr. Coffey found four of his arteries blocked and had to do bypass surgery on him. He didn't wake up, either, but he didn't suffer as long as Mary did. He passed away just a few days after the surgery."

They both fixed me with eyes frightened and resigned, while little warning bells went off in my head.

13

I said, "Dr. Coffey must be awfully busy."

"Oh, he is! At least one person a week from here has a bypass, and that's just the people living here."

"It must be awfully hard for their families, having them die so suddenly like that."

They nodded, but with a look of some disturbed confusion. "Actually, none of them has had a family. They've all been alone."

Somehow that didn't surprise me.

While the valet retrieved my car, I calculated Dr. Coffey's income from bypass surgeries. The going rate was around $150,000 per artery, so a triple bypass could bring him a cool half million. If he did just two of those a week, the million dollars Marilee had conned Coffey out of would be only a week's income. In light of the fact that she had bought her grandmother an apartment that probably cost at least a half million, and in light of the fact that it sounded like some of his patients hadn't needed the surgery anyway, it didn't seem so bad for Marilee to have taken advantage of him.

I drove south on Tamiami Trail, passing Marina Jack, where a few cotton-ball clouds were reflected in the glassy blue water and naked masts of sailboats stood sentinel around yachts sleeping in the sun. A million questions were running through my mind. Why did Cora say

Harrison Frazier had ruined Marilee's life? If Marilee knew Frazier, had she had her keys changed to keep him out? And where the hell was Marilee, anyway?

When I got back home, I put a Patsy Cline CD in the player, and Patsy and I sang together while I took the sheets off my bed and gathered up more laundry to put on top of the stuff in the washing machine. I added detergent to the wash and turned it on, and while the washer filled, Patsy and I sang another song. I got out the Swiffer and punched a clean cloth into its head, and Patsy and I sang some more while the machine started chugging. The thing about Patsy is that she kept it clean and simple. Nothing oily or mysterious. The world would be a better place if everybody thought like Patsy.

One minute I was running the Swiffer and singing with Patsy, and the next minute I was yelling *"Oh shit!"* and running to open the washer. The laundry was twisted and bloated under murky water, looking like the slimy fetuses of some horrible monster. I jammed my arm in and yanked up Ts and towels, Keds and shorts until I hauled up my khaki cargo shorts with the flapped pockets. I spread them over the washer's agitator head to hang in sodden folds while I fumbled the Velcro flap open and fished out Marilee's letters that I'd taken from her hall table.

Making moaning noises, I laid each wet, ink-smeared envelope on top of the dryer. I imagined myself explaining to Marilee that I'd had good intentions about mailing the stuff, but just, you know, forgot. I imagined myself telling Marilee that I would pay her IRS fine for being late. Then I started getting mad and imagined myself saying, "You didn't actually tell me to mail it, you know. You went off and left it, and a lot of people wouldn't even have noticed it. It's really not fair to expect *me* to pay the penalty!"

I went to the kitchen for paper towels and blotted as much water from each envelope as I could, but they were all a sorry sight. Some of them had more or less disintegrated over the checks and invoices they held. I recognized the familiar Florida Light and Power envelope, and also Verizon and Teco, but not the others. One bedraggled check was made out to a pool-cleaning service, but the ink was too blurred to make out the name, and another check was stapled to an invoice from a home-security company. The check was a loss, but the print on the soggy invoice was clear enough to see that it was for $785, for the installation of a Centurian wall safe.

"Huh," I said brilliantly. Marilee must have had something she deemed important enough to hide in a wall safe. Something she wanted to keep close at hand instead of in a safe-deposit box at the bank. Perhaps the person who had trashed Marilee's bedroom had been looking for whatever it was.

All the envelopes were business size except one pale blue square of heavy linen-woven stock. The dark blue ink of the address had run badly and the flap had come unstuck, but the thickness of the envelope seemed to have kept the paper inside relatively dry. I raised the flap all the way, just to see how wet the letter inside was, just to see if it might be salvageable. Well, okay, I raised it to see if I could see anything written on it. I know I shouldn't have, but I did.

Marilee's handwriting was round and girlish, with little hearts dotting the *i*'s. The sentence at the top of the opening in the envelope said, "I can't wait to see you!"

Carefully, I extracted the damp letter from the envelope and gingerly carried it to the kitchen and laid it out on paper towels. It was two pages long, and I laid each page out as precisely and clinically as a pharmacist laying out prescription pills. So long as I focused on drying these moist sheets, I could ignore the fact that I was tampering with the U.S. mail, violating Marilee's privacy, interfering with a homicide investigation, and generally sticking my nose into things that were none of my business.

I left the pages drying and went back to the washer and restarted it, then finished Swiffering and dusting and plumping up the cushions on the living room furniture. I have one chair in my living room. It matches a rattan love seat with dark green linen cushions patterned with bright red and yellow flowers of a purely artistic species. Originally, both love seat and chair sat in my grandmother's little private parlor off the bedroom she shared with my grandfather. The idea had been that she could retreat there when she wanted privacy or just to get away from the noise of a man and two children—the two children being me and Michael. But she never found time for privacy, so the furniture stayed like new. When I moved into the apartment over the carport, I appropriated it for myself. Like my grandmother, however, I'm not very good at just sitting, so when I die, my living room furniture may still be as good as new. But of course I won't have a granddaughter to inherit it. Unless Michael and Paco adopt a child, there won't be any relative to inherit anything. We'll all just die without leaving a trace, like sculptured sand people obliterated by the tide.

By the time I put clean sheets on my bed and cleaned the bathroom, the wash was ready to go in the dryer. I tossed it all in and turned it on, then went to the kitchen to check on the letter. Most of the ink was too blurred to read, but I took it to the porch and sat down at the table.

Dearest Lily,

It still seems strange to call you Lily! It's a pretty name and I like it, but I had intended to name you Bonnie, and that's what I've always called you in my mind. My Bonnie. I guess when you're only fifteen, you aren't real good at naming babies. Ha! I guess I know why they named you Lily, but that's something else I'll tell you when we're together.

The next paragraph was blurred, then some clear lines: "You have a right to know all the truth, not just part of it. Honey, please don't feel bad about keeping it a secret that—"

That was the only legible but except for "I can't wait to see you!"

I read those few lines over and over, and each time I had to blink hard to keep from crying. Obviously, Marilee had given birth to a daughter when she was only fifteen, and evidently she had found her. Finding a daughter you gave up at birth would be like having a dead child returned to you, a fulfillment of the heart's deepest yearning.

I leaned back in my chair and looked out at the sea. Sunshine sparked diamonds off the glittering waves. In the distance, triangular sails moved slowly along the horizon. A few shorebirds were leaving tracks down on the sand. A snowy egret, perched on one leg on a mooring post, was blissfully turned the wrong way to the breeze so his feathers could ruffle. From the rooftop, a pelican sailed to the edge of the shore and gulped something from the lapping water. No matter what happens in the world, the ocean keeps rolling. It's the one thing you can depend on.

I went inside and got an apple from the fridge and went back to the porch and watched the waves rolling in while I ate it. I thought about calling Guidry and telling him about the letter, but I didn't. I didn't want to explain about reading it, and it might not have anything to do with Harrison Frazier's murder. I thought about what Shuga Reasnor had said about Marilee having a secret, and this was probably it.

I was beginning to feel very protective toward Marilee Doerring. I didn't want to give her secret away unless it became absolutely necessary. I'm a real pushover for people who are good to their pets and their grandmothers and the babies they gave up when they were fifteen.

I threw the apple core down to a congregation of black gulls and went inside to get my things for the afternoon pet visits. I locked the French doors when I left, even though any dedicated intruder could easily burst through them. I drove down the tree-lined lane to the street, where a vacationing couple on the sidewalk paused to let me pass. The woman was short and round and sun-pinked, with a mass of curly brown hair sticking out in all directions from a tennis cap. She wore flower-printed shorts and a yellow spandex bandeau stretched over breasts as big as honeydews. Her arms were held out chest-high like chicken wings, with wrist weights attached like cuffs. As I drove by, she marched in place with her arms swinging and her cheeks puffed out while she energetically whooshed air in and out. Her husband was almost two heads taller, and he was ambling along behind her with his hands in his shorts pockets. They were so cute that I waved at them as I turned onto Midnight Pass Road. The husband waved back, but the wife gave me a startled look and resumed her power walking.

The Graysons hadn't called, so I went first to their house. One of their three garage doors was up and Sam Grayson was standing beside the driver's side of his BMW. Sam was a sexy, seventyish Cary Grant look-alike with a high forehead and silver hair cut in an almost military burr. Tall and lean, he moved with a loose-limbed grace that always made me wish I could dance with him just once.

I parked behind one of the closed doors so he could back out, but he walked out to meet me. "We forgot to call you, didn't we?"

I said, "Welcome home. How was your trip?"

"Oh, it was great. Just great. We got to spend time with our daughter and the grandkids, and we've got enough snapshots to bore our friends for months."

"That's true friendship."

"Yeah. Come on in and say hello to Libby."

We went up the front walk and he opened the door and stood aside. Rufus came galloping to kiss my knees, and Libby Grayson came from the kitchen, drying her hands on a dish towel. As beautiful as Sam was handsome, Libby had shoulder-length silver hair and brilliant blue eyes that sparkled with intelligence and good humor. Together, they looked like the couples in retirement community ads—the ones who are so fit and sexy, they make you wish you were that old so you could look so good.

"Oh, Dixie, I'm sorry I didn't call! Oh well, it gives us a chance to thank you for taking such good care of Rufus. Look how he loves you! I'll bet he didn't even miss us."

I leaned down to stroke Rufus, wishing he wouldn't act so happy to see me.

Libby said, "Sam, pay Dixie."

He took the bill from her and read it, then got out his wallet.

While he counted out twenties, Rufus trotted over and sat next to Libby and smiled at me, as if he understood it wasn't polite to two-time her to her face.

I said, "I love the new carousel horse."

Sam handed me a neat stack of twenties and said, "He's a rare one. Made of cast iron instead of the lighter stuff. You wouldn't believe what a project it was to get him mounted on that brass pole!"

Libby said, "He's so heavy, the brass pole had to be lined with galvanized steel. First we had to find a brass pole that was exactly one and a quarter inches in diameter, because the holes in the horse are one and a half inches. Then we had to find galvanized-steel pipe the right diameter to fit inside the brass pipe. It took *weeks* of phone calls!"

Rufus yawned and trotted away toward the kitchen. I knew just how he felt. This was way more information that I needed about pipes, but they were getting such a kick out of telling it that I tried to look interested.

Sam said, "We hired a guy to cut the pipes and fit them together. He had to drill a hole through them and attach the horse. When he fitted them into the brass plates on the floor and ceiling, it was like watching brain surgery. If he'd cut either pipe a quarter inch too short or too long, we'd have been back to square one."

I started edging toward the door. "Well, I'd better run. Oh, by the way, somebody left some books for you in the chest."

We all said our good-byes, and as I backed out of the driveway, Sam was leaning over the chest digging out all the accumulated newspapers. I wondered if he and Libby would actually read them or toss them in the trash. My bet was that they would trash them. Who needs so much news?

At Tom Hale's condo, I found Tom reading in his wheelchair and Billy Elliot lying on the floor with his head propped on Tom's feet. Both man and dog looked up at me when I walked in. As if we were in the middle of a conversation, Tom said, "Dixie, do you know what a fewterer is?"

"It sounds like something dirty."

"In medieval days, a fewterer was the keeper and handler of the greyhounds."

"So you're a fewterer?"

"I guess you're one, too, Dixie. We're two fewterers."

"Well, that was always my ambition, Tom, to be a fucking fewterer."

I got Billy Elliot's leash and he and I went downstairs to run. As I ran down the edge of the parking lot behind him, a dark Blazer pulled to my side and eased along with me. I looked over and saw Lieutenant Guidry eyeing me with that calm level look that only cops have. I could have been jogging along stark naked and he probably wouldn't have changed expression. I pointed to the building's front door, and he nodded and pulled away, making a U-turn and parking by the entrance.

14

illy Elliot barreled along like he was back on the track with his greyhound buddies, and my muscles burned with the effort of keeping pace. We rounded the end of the parking lot and thundered around the central esplanade of palmettos and hibiscus. At the entrance, where Guidry waited, I pulled Billy Elliot to a halt but left him enough leash to explore a bit. I dragged my aching legs to Guidry's window, panting like Billy Elliot but managing to keep my tongue from lolling out the sides of my mouth.

Guidry grinned at me. "Now I see how you can get away with eating all that bacon."

I made a wheezing sound.

"I got a message you'd called," he said.

"Yeah, I wanted to know when I can bring the cat home."

He gave me a blank look for a moment and then remembered. "Oh, the cat. Well, the forensics people are finished at the house, but the crime-scene tape will have to stay up until I get the ME's report."

"When do you think that'll be?"

He looked at his watch. "I'm on my way to the morgue now. It'll just take a few minutes. Wanta come with me?"

I stared at him. Was he nuts?

"The time comes when you have to get back on the horse," he said. "Maybe this is your time."

"Maybe you're way out of line, Lieutenant."

"Could be. Or I could be right."

"This conversation is over."

I spun away from him and jerked Billy Elliot out of the esplanade. I pulled him short and opened the front door.

"You can't hide out indefinitely," yelled Guidry.

I pulled Billy Elliot into the elevator and leaned against the wall while it climbed to Tom Hale's floor. My heart was pounding hard and a surge of adrenaline had made me start trembling. Guidry had no right to tell me what to do with my life. He had no right to tell me anything.

By the time I got Billy Elliot settled in his apartment, I was trembling not only with anger but also with embarrassment for letting Guidry get to me like that. I was the tough one, the one who kept her cool in an emergency. At least that's who I used to be. Now I was quivering like a wuss because a detective had suggested that it was time for me to stop hiding from the world. My shaking continued all the way down in the elevator, so hard that my teeth were clamped hard together. The worst thing in the world is knowing that somebody else is right and you're wrong. It was time for me to stop hiding. I just wasn't sure I was strong enough.

When I went out the front door, I made a little involuntary groan. Guidry was still sitting there with the car idling.

He said, "You ready to go?"

I clomped down the steps and went around the back of the car to the passenger side and got in. Guidry looked straight ahead as I opened the door.

"We have to make this fast," I said. "I have other pets to take care of."

"Half an hour, tops," he said, and put the car in gear.

Sarasota County doesn't have its own morgue, they use Sarasota Memorial Hospital's facilities. We were ten minutes away, and neither of us spoke a word the entire trip. I sat with my arms crossed across my chest and hoped Guidry believed I was trembling from the air-conditioning vents blowing on me. He kept his attention on the traffic, and if he noticed my shaking, he didn't mention it. We parked in the back parking lot at the hospital and took the rear entrance into the maze of hallways that make big hospitals seem like cities. If I ever commit a major crime, I'm going to head straight for the nearest big hospital. You could spend an entire day in a waiting area pretending to be a relative keeping vigil on a loved one, every day moving to a different area. You'd have plenty of bathrooms, you could sleep on the couches, and if you had money to put in food-vending machines, you could hide out indefinitely.

Guidry and I still hadn't spoken. It was as if we had a tacit agreement that we would do this thing without conversation. He led the way to the autopsy room and opened the door for me to go in first. There was a small square waiting room with scuffed beige linoleum floor and a few plastic molded chairs. A battered wooden coffee table heaped with dog-eared magazines with torn-off rectangles where addresses used to be, and a TV monitor mounted on the wall like in a hospital room. A half wall separated an attendant in green surgical scrubs from the waiting room. He stood on his side with his fists pushed against the counter and stared suspiciously at us. On the wall behind him, a filing cabinet held a coffeepot and some mugs and a jar of Cremora, but he didn't seem inclined to offer refreshments.

Guidry gave his name, and the young man picked up a phone and spoke briefly. In a few seconds, the inner door opened and a tall Cuban-American woman came out carrying a manila envelope. She had warm almond eyes and white hair cropped tight against her skull.

She and Guidry shook hands, and Guidry said, "Dr. Corazon, this is Dixie Hemingway."

We shook hands, and if she thought it strange that Guidry had brought along somebody in rumpled shorts and a T, she didn't show it.

15

D r. Corazon pushed a pair of reading glasses to the top of her head. "Your man had a subdural hematoma that would have resulted in his death, but he probably died of a laryngeal spasm. Officially, he drowned."

Guidry frowned. "I don't understand."

"If a person dies within forty-eight hours of being immersed in water, it's officially called drowning. Fifteen percent of drowning victims don't have water in their lungs, but die of hypoxia caused by a laryngeal spasm. In other words, they choke to death. Mr. Frazier had enough water in his lungs to kill him, but he also had a laryngeal spasm. It's impossible to say which killed him, but the hematoma would have caused his death if he hadn't had a laryngeal spasm or taken water into his lungs."

Guidry said, "I guess it doesn't matter. Whether it was the blow to the head or drowning or choking to death, it was still homicide."

"Well, that's the problem, Lieutenant. It does matter. The blow to his head was inflicted by a blunt object moving in a right-to-left trajectory. The tape applied to his head to keep his nose and mouth underwater was done left to right."

Guidry and I both stared openmouthed at her. I found my voice first. "You mean he was killed by two people?"

"I mean he was first struck in the back of the head by a right-handed person, and then taped to the cat's water bowl with his nose and mouth underwater by a left-handed person.

Guidry said, "Maybe it was one ambidextrous person."

"That's possible too."

"Any idea what hit him?"

"Blunt instrument, Lieutenant. You know what that means."

We all knew. A blunt instrument can be just about anything.

"Here's another thing," said Dr. Corozon. "He was nude when he was struck, and there was a time lag before somebody dressed him and tried to drown him. I know that because there was dried blood on his body, under his clothes."

I said, "If they let him lie around long enough for blood to dry on his body, maybe he was already dead when they stuck his nose in the cat bowl."

She shook her head. "No, he had some water in his lungs. He was still breathing when somebody taped him down in the water, but he wasn't fully conscious. I know that because there are no petechiae, little broken blood vessels from struggling to breathe."

Guidry said, "Can you give me a time of death?"

"This isn't TV, Lieutenant. He died between the time he was last seen alive and the time he was found dead."

He grinned. "Can't you narrow it down a bit more?"

"From the lividity, best estimate is around two A.M."

"Any idea how much time elapsed between the time he was hit and when he died?"

"Several hours, probably."

Guidry thanked the ME and took the manila envelope from her. She said, "Good luck, Lieutenant. Nice meeting you, Ms. Hemingway."

We smiled at each other and she bustled off to her grisly inner sanctum. Guidry held the door open for me, and I went through like an obedient puppy. We retraced our way through that peculiar combined odor of chemicals and putrefaction and body wastes that permeates every hospital, both of us with our heads down to keep from breathing deeply, both of us thinking hard. I suppose Guidry was thinking about his case, but I was thinking how strange it was that I had stopped trembling the minute the medical examiner had come out to talk to us, when it was the ME I had been dreading so much. The last time I'd spoken to an ME, it had been to get the details of the autopsies on Todd and Christy, but somehow that memory hadn't surfaced while Dr. Corozon had spoken. Instead, I had snapped into cool, objective detachment.

We went through the exit and stepped into the heat of the parking lot. I said, "I looked through the house before I found the body. I didn't see any blood spatters."

Guidry said, "He was probably taking a shower when he got hit. Forensics found blood traces in the bathtub drain."

"Somebody had cleaned the tub?"

"Yeah."

We trudged across the hot pavement to Guidry's car, and he beeped it unlocked. We slid into its stifling heat and he started the engine and turned the air conditioning up high. I looked at my watch. We had been inside the hospital only fifteen minutes.

I said, "When I stopped by to pick up her house key, Marilee said she was just about to take a shower."

He turned his head and gave me a look. "You think that's significant?"

"Not unless she was about to take a shower with Harrison Frazier."

"Do you have any reason to think she was?"

"Come on, Lieutenant, they were bound to know each other. Harrison Frazier wasn't the kind of man to go around breaking in a woman's house."

"Not unless he was accustomed to using a key and she'd had the locks changed."

Right then and there, I should have confessed that I had read Marilee's letter to her daughter. I should have told him that Shuga Reasnor knew things she hadn't told. But Marilee was a kind woman who gave her grandmother bread makers and expensive apartments, and she deserved a chance to have a relationship with a daughter she'd given up when she was fifteen without it becoming public knowledge. Besides,

Shuga Reasnor was right. If Marilee was okay, she would be pissed sixteen ways from Thursday if she came home and found her most intimate secrets blabbed to the world.

For all those irrational reasons, I kept quiet.

Guidry said, "Do you happen to know whether she's right-handed?"

I shut my eyes and replayed her arm stretching toward me with the door key dangling from her fingers. "She handed me the new key with her left hand."

He nodded and didn't say anything else. I didn't, either.

At the entrance to the parking lot at the Sea Breeze, Guidry stopped to let a woman on a yellow three-wheeler cross in front of us. Red-faced under hair dyed an improbable shade of magenta, she was leaning over the handlebars and pedaling with grim therapeutic exertion. A pole jutted at an angle from the rear of the trike, with a triangular orange alert flag attached to its end like a waving tail. We watched her move down the sidewalk the way jungle animals might watch a lioness chasing prey.

We pulled into the parking lot, and I pointed silently to the spot where my Bronco was parked. When Guidry stopped behind it, I said, "So when can I bring Ghost home?"

He gave me an "Oh for God's sake" look.

I said, "Come on, the cat didn't do anything wrong. Let him come home."

"Maybe late tomorrow."

"You'll let me know?"

"Yeah."

I shut the door and walked to my own car, beeping it unlocked as I went. Guidry drove off without saying good-bye, which suited me just fine. I was glad I'd gone with him, but I didn't want any conversation about it.

By the time I finished with the last cat and drove home, it was after 8:00 P.M. Before I went upstairs, I stood a few minutes looking out at sailboats silhouetted against a sky so clear and blue, it caused my heart to swell with inchoate longing. Sailboats always seem carefree to me, even though I know a lot of them are manned or womaned by people who are anything but carefree. I went upstairs and unlocked the French doors, tossing my shoulder bag on the desk in the closet-office as I walked to the bathroom. In the kitchen, I opened a bottle of cold Tecate and poured it in a wineglass. I added a wedge of lime and took it out to the porch to drink while I watched a brilliant orange sun sink toward the horizon.

When it touched the rim of the earth, pulsating for an instant on the water, a shimmering gold ribbon moved over the sea to the shore beneath me. When I was little, I believed that golden path was stretching out especially to me. I thought that if I were brave enough, I could step out on it and walk to the edge of the sea where I would find an enchanted world. I was never brave enough, so every sunset was an occasion of both wonder and chagrin.

When the sun had slid under the horizon and left only a faint reflection of itself behind, I went inside and took inventory of the refrigerator. With both Michael and Paco away, I would have to fend for myself. Except for mayonnaise and mustard and pickles, about all I had was some sliced cheese and beer and a package of corn tortillas. The freezer section held a box of Boca burgers, some ancient hamburger buns swathed in a thick layer of ice crystals, and some Ziploc bags holding mystery leftovers.

I thought about having a bowl of Cheerios, but except for breakfast twelve hours ago, all I'd had to eat all day was an apple, and I was famished. Also, the shrink I saw after I lost Todd and Christy said it was important to eat a real meal when I was alone—if you don't take good care of yourself when you're alone, you'll end up thinking you're only important when you're with another person.

There was a little Greek place in the village where I could get great lamb shish kebab if I could get there before they stopped serving. I jumped in the shower, and then ran still damp into my office-closet to pull on a short denim skirt and a white stretchy T. I dug my feet into a pair of white canvas mules, grabbed my shoulder bag from my desk, and was on my way out when I noticed the blinking red light on my answering machine. The strap on my bag must have been covering it before. I hesitated a moment, then punched the playback button.

"Um, Miz Hemingway? This is Phillip Winnick? Uh, would it be okay if . . . I'd like to talk to you about . . . you know, the club and all. It's very important. Ah, you can't call me, so I guess I'll try to call you later? And would you mind not mentioning this to anybody? Please? Thank you. Ah, it's Phillip Winnick." Then in an anxious rush, he said, "I'll talk to you later. It's Phillip Winnick." Somebody must have told him it was important to give his name more than once when he left a message.

I threw my bag over my shoulder and went downstairs to the Bronco and headed for the Crab House instead of the Greek place. Phillip wasn't there when I arrived, but the waiter who led me to a table on the back porch said he was due at 11:00.

The waiter said, "Would you like a drink?"

"A margarita, please, but I'm starving, so I'll go ahead and order."

"Stone crab?"

"Absolutely."

"Fries?"

"Extra-crispy."

"Salad?"

"Please, with blue cheese dressing."

"Caesar or house?"

"House."

"What kind of dressing?"

"Blue cheese." There must be a law that says waitpersons must ignore you if you tell them what salad dressing you want before they specifically ask you.

He flashed a wide grin and buzzed off. Without Phillip's music, the Crab House was quiet. Two guys at a table next to me were being so careful and polite that it was clear they were on a first date. On the other side of me, a man and woman were leaning forward with their elbows on the table and their hands interlaced. They had drinks on the table, but from the way they were gazing into each other's eyes, they were already intoxicated by romance. A motorboat chuffed up to the dock and a man in cutoffs jumped out to tie it up while two women and a man stood up and made tugging and fluffing motions to clothes and hair before they climbed over the side and stepped onto the dock. They all trailed onto the porch and took a table at the side, laughing and talking amongst themselves with the kind of easy camaraderie that old friends have.

The waiter brought my margarita and a board holding a miniloaf of hot bread that had a big lethal-looking knife stabbed into it. He said, "A guy at the bar paid for your drink."

I looked through the glass wall and saw a large ruddy man at the bar grinning at me. He had a bullet-shaped bald head and eyes like black ball bearings. He raised his glass to me and began to slide off his bar stool with the clear intent of coming out to the porch.

"Take it back," I said.

"It's paid for. You might as well drink it."

"Take it back, and tell the bartender to make me another one."

He set the glass on his tray and hightailed it away to the bar. My admirer turned to him and asked a question, and then looked out at me with a dark scowl when the waiter answered. The bartender looked out at me, too, and his lips firmed into a tight-mouthed smile as he dumped the margarita and whipped up another one.

I cut a thick slab of bread with the giant knife, and was using the knife to smear butter on the bread when the waiter brought a new drink. He carried it out on a tray held shoulder-high and set it down with a flourish.

"He says you've got an attitude."

"Tell him I've also got a sharp knife."

"Whoa, hon, just take it as a compliment. Men are gonna hit on you. That's just life."

He left and I looked toward the two men on my right. They had forgotten their first-date anxiety and were grinning at me. When they caught my eye, they raised their wineglasses in a toast. I smiled back and sipped my margarita. Inside, the bullet-headed man put money on the bar and stomped out, his pants creasing around a thick wad in his crotch.

By the time I got the stone crab, I had eaten enough bread and salad to be in a better mood. Stone crab is probably what God eats every night of the year, but in Florida we mortals only have it from mid-October to mid-May. Florida law prohibits fishermen from killing the crabs, but stone crabs can regenerate lost claws, so fishermen break one off and throw the crab back into the sea. That only leaves them one claw to defend themselves with, but they're not boiling to death like they would be if they were lobsters.

The claws are steamed right there on the boat, and then they're chilled and delivered to restaurants like the Crab House, where people like me eat them without giving a thought to the crab's trauma. Mine came with mustard sauce and a wooden mallet for cracking the claw, and I happily cracked and slurped away.

16

While I ate, I watched boats bobbing at the dock and idly listened to bits and pieces of conversation from neighboring tables. I learned that somebody named Tony was a real bitch and a half, and that somebody named Grace had finally gotten the money she had married for when her husband's rich and ancient mother died. Grace, they said, was hell-bent to move back east where people would be impressed with their new wealth, but the husband was refusing to give up his golf and tennis life just to hobnob with some snooty New Englanders. Poor Grace. All that money and no place to flaunt it.

It was almost eleven o'clock when I ate the last morsel. I put some bills on the table before the waiter came back, adding a hefty tip to make up for being churlish earlier, and stood up and started inside. The waiter saw me leaving and scurried over with a questioning look.

I said, "I'm going to sit at the bar and listen to the piano player."

He looked over my shoulder at the money on the table and smiled. "No prob," he said. "The pianist should be here any minute."

"You know him?"

"Just to speak to. Seems like a real nice guy."

"He is."

"Oh, he's a friend of yours?"

I smiled, suddenly feeling proud to know Phillip. "Yeah, he's a friend."

Inside, only a few people were at the bar. All men, and all with the appraising look of people who realized the evening was growing old and if they hoped to hook up with somebody, they'd better do it soon. None of them gave me a glance. I took the stool at the end near the bandstand and ordered another margarita.

The bartender grinned when he set it in front of me. "This will be your third, right?"

"Counting the one I didn't drink."

"That guy, what an asshole! What'd he think, anyway?"

"Maybe that works for him sometime."

"Not with a woman like you. He shoulda known that."

Behind me, Phillip's voice said, "Miz Hemingway?"

I spun around, to see him standing there looking at me in disbelief, as if I were a genie he had conjured up from a bottle. Up this close, I could see the black flocked jacket he wore had been made for a much larger man. He looked like a little boy dressed up in his father's suit coat.

"Gosh, you snuck up on me, Phillip!"

"Oh, I'm sorry! I didn't mean to scare you."

"You didn't, I just didn't see you come in."

"I came in the back."

"Can you talk a few minutes before you start playing?"

He grinned nervously, and I wanted to hug him. He was all wrists and ears and cheekbones, too ill at ease to know how to handle this unexpected moment.

"Come on," I said, "let's go sit at a table for a minute. You want something to drink?"

He shook his head, then licked dry lips and nodded. The bartender, who had been silently watching us, filled a glass with club soda and handed it to him.

"Okay," I said briskly, and walked the length of the bar to a tiny two-top in the back corner. Phillip trailed along behind me carrying his club soda, and we both dropped into chairs like falling rocks.

He still seemed nonplussed that I was there, so I leaned toward him and said, "You left a message on my machine that you wanted to talk to me."

"Oh. Yeah. That. Well, see, I got to thinking and all . . . you know, about what happened next door. You know, how the policeman asked if I'd seen anything?"

"Uh-huh. And did you see something?"

"Well, that's just it. I mean, I should have told him, but my mother was there and I didn't want her to know I'd been outside at that time, you know. But the cops probably should know . . . I thought maybe you could tell that detective guy."

I could tell this would take all night if I didn't prompt him. "Okay, what did you see that you didn't want to talk about in front of your mother?"

A deep port-wine blush rose from his throat and suffused his face. "It was when I was coming home Friday morning. I was crossing behind Miz Doerring's house and I saw a woman come out of her house and get in a car in the driveway. A black Miata. The car swung in the driveway, the woman came out of the house and got in, and it drove off. I thought it was Miz Doerring, but now I'm thinking maybe it was somebody else. You know, like the killer."

I waited, but he seemed unable to continue. I said, "Could you see the driver?"

Phillip's flush deepened. "The top was up, so I couldn't see. I just saw the woman."

I took a sip of my drink and pretended not to notice his discomfort. "And you could see her well enough to think it was Marilee Doerring?"

He looked down at his plate, and for a moment I thought he might cry. "Not really. I guess I didn't really look good. It could have been her or it could have been some other woman."

He averted his eyes and his throat bobbled in a nervous swallow. I tried to put myself in his place, a kid coming home after an evening that

had to be kept secret from his parents and seeing a woman he thought
was a neighbor get into a car and drive away.

"Did the woman see you?"

He bobbled his head in a staccato motion I took to be an affirmative
nod. "I think maybe she did. She looked over her shoulder toward
where I was and it seemed like she jerked a little bit—you know, like she
was surprised or scared or something."

"And then what?"

He looked directly at me for the first time. "Then she got in the car
and left."

Carefully, I said, "What time do you think this was?"

"I don't want to get anybody else mixed up in this."

"I'm not asking you where you'd been or who you'd been with, just
what time you saw a woman leaving Marilee Doerring's house."

"It was a little after four."

I remembered the flash of movement in the woods that morning
when I was walking Rufus. That had been around 4:30.

"Did you see me that morning?"

He blinked at me. "You? No, ma'am, I didn't see you."

Poor kid, he was obviously terrified, and with good reason. If the
woman he saw thought he could identify her, he could be in a lot more
trouble than his family finding out how he spent his nights.

"Phillip, if we're going to be friends, you have to do something for
me."

"What?"

"You have to stop calling me 'ma'am.' And my name is Dixie, not
Ms. Hemingway. Got that?"

He gave me a weak smile. "Okay."

"You were right to tell me about the woman, and it's something
Lieutenant Guidry needs to know. I'll tell him what you saw, and he'll
probably want to talk to you again. If he does, don't be scared. I'll tell
him to be sure and talk to you in private, and he's not going to repeat
anything you say to your parents or to anybody else. He's a nice guy,
you can trust him."

"Okay."

I was so proud of him for having the guts to confess what he'd seen that I didn't check his story with my built-in lie detector.

We looked at each other for a second, sort of cementing a new friendship, and then he gave me a genuine smile. "I have to go play now. Are you going to stay for a while?"

"I'd love to, but it's way past my bedtime."

We got up and walked together down the aisle toward the piano. Before I left him, I turned and gave him a hug. "I'll come back another night, when I can stay."

He was blushing and smiling when he waved good-bye.

When I stepped outside, all the lights were out in the parking lot, the only illumination coming from a waning moon. Nobody else was around, and the spaces between the cars were black wells where anything could have been hiding. I stood a minute outside the door, wondering if I should go back inside and tell the manager about the lights, then decided to let it go. My footsteps made quick scrunching noises in the loose shell as I stepped across the dark lot toward my car.

Part of me was proud that Phillip had trusted me enough to confide in me. The other part was dismayed. Now I knew something that could get the kid in a lot of trouble. If he had seen the killer leaving Marilee's house, he would most likely be called upon in the future to say so in public, bringing upon himself the full glare of media attention that would inevitably reveal that he was gay. He was a good kid, and I didn't want to be the one who outed him. But I had to let Guidry know about the woman he'd seen.

A pair of egrets fluttered low over my head, making those guttural egret sounds that always remind me of somebody trying to cough up a popcorn husk. I turned my head to look over my shoulder, and realized with a sense of shock that I was afraid. That's the trouble with allowing yourself to start feeling emotions after you've been closed down for a long time. You can't feel selectively. You have to let the whole gamut of feelings in, even fear.

As I started jogging toward my car, a form detached from the shadows and ran after me. I picked up my speed and ran like hell. Thanks to Billy Elliot, I had recent experience in covering ground fast. I beeped the car unlocked, tore the door open, and leaped inside, pulling the door shut and locking it a second before the man slammed a fist against the passenger window and pushed his face against the glass. Even with his nose and mouth mashed flat in a grotesque mask clearly intended to frighten me, I recognized the bullet-headed man from the bar. I threw the Bronco into reverse and whipped out of the parking space, almost hoping the man would be foolish enough to run after me so I could run him down. He didn't. He ran behind the row of cars and ducked out of sight. I sat with the motor churning for a couple of minutes and then pulled out of the lot.

Driving north on Midnight Pass Road, I watched the rearview mirror for headlights in case the man was following. At the drive to my house, I passed it and drove straight ahead to the firehouse, where I backed into a parking place across the street. From where I sat, I could see all the traffic on Midnight Pass Road, and I could also see the firehouse where Michael was sleeping. Just knowing Michael was nearby made me feel calmer. Traffic was sparse, and after awhile I decided I hadn't been followed, so I drove home. Paco's car was in the carport, but his Harley was gone, so I knew he was still on an undercover job. I ran up the stairs to my apartment two at a time.

Everything in the apartment seemed exactly as I had left it, but I still felt jittery. The malevolence of the man's eyes looking at me through the passenger window weren't what scared me. What had me feeling uneasy was that he had seemed so determined, as if he had a particular goal and I was it. I lowered the metal storm shutters, checked the answering machine, brushed my teeth, did a few turns around the apartment to work off my nervous energy, and finally went to bed with a million questions buzzing in my head.

If the woman Phillip saw had been Marilee, she would have been leaving Harrison Frazier dead in her house. Did that mean she had killed him? And if she had, who had been driving the car she got into? If it hadn't been Marilee, who was it? It could have been Shuga Reasnor.

She knew Harrison Frazier, and maybe she had some personal reason to kill him. Maybe she had lured Frazier to Marilee's house on some pretext and killed him there. Maybe Marilee had a good alibi of where she was at the time Frazier was killed. Maybe she and Shuga had planned it together, thinking nobody would connect Shuga to the killing. I wondered if Shuga had an alibi for that night. I would ask Guidry when I talked to him.

I turned over and pounded my pillow and tried to go to sleep. It wasn't my job to find Harrison Frazier's killer. My job was to take care of Ghost. But who the hell had killed Frazier? Maybe his wife had followed him to Marilee's house and conked him on the head and had somebody pick her up afterward in a black Miata. That didn't seem very likely, though. And why did Marilee have her locks changed before she left town? It had to have been because somebody had a key to her house and she didn't want that person to go in, but who? And why? Maybe she and Shuga Reasnor had had a falling-out and she was making sure Shuga couldn't get in while she was gone. Maybe Dr. Coffey still had a key to her house from when they were engaged and she'd just gotten around to making sure he couldn't use it. Maybe Coffey had hired a woman to go in and kill Harrison Frazier. No, that was dumb. Why would he do that? If he wanted anybody killed, it would be Marilee, not Frazier.

I turned on my back and took deep breaths. Why had that man in the parking lot been after me? Had he been so pissed off that I'd given him the cold shoulder that he'd waited out there for me all that time? Surely it wasn't the first time he'd been turned down by a woman. Surely he wouldn't have let something like that cause him to become so violent. Maybe he had been on something. Maybe he had snorted or shot up or ingested his drug du jour after he left the bar and got so high that he came back for lust revenge. Maybe it was just coincidence that he had chosen me, maybe he had just been there to go after any woman coming out alone.

My eyelids popped open. Oh shit, I should have called the Crab House and warned them that a psycho was loose in the parking lot. I should have told them to be sure no woman went out by herself. I turned over again and smacked the pillow. It was too late now, it was after two, and the Crab House was closed. But if somebody had been raped in that parking lot, it would be all my fault.

On that cheerful note, I finally drifted to restless sleep.

17

Thunder woke me in the night. Hard rain was pelting the roof and making drumming music on the storm shutters. It was a comforting sound. I love sleeping in a storm, safe and dry while a deluge rages outside. I went back to sleep, and when the alarm sounded at 4:00, I smacked it off and groped my way to the bathroom to splash water on my face. I estimated that I'd had all of two hours sleep, tops.

The rain had stopped, so I left the Bronco at home and took my bike, riding out into a glorious Sunday morning. On the lane to the street, I stirred up a flock of wild parakeets in the damp treetops, and their chattering brought answering cello tones of mourning doves from their hiding places. The temperature was around seventy degrees, the humidity low enough to be tolerable, and the air had a fresh, just-washed smell. Even with a sluggish brain from last night's fear and sleeplessness, I loved the feel of the day.

With the Graysons back home, I only had Billy Elliot to dog walk. The rest were all cats, which was good. Cats are a lot easier than dogs, and I needed an easy day. My plan was to wait until eight o'clock and call Guidry with last night's information, see to all the cats, and go home and sleep. Michael would come home this morning, which meant we'd have a good dinner at home tonight. Maybe Paco would be home, too, and I could catch them up on everything that had happened.

Tom Hale was asleep when I went into his condo, but Billy Elliot met me at the door. We went outside and ran like idiots, and then I kissed Billy Elliot good-bye inside the condo and panted my way back to my bike. It was still dark, but the sky was taking on a vanilla tinge of false dawn, and birds were beginning to wake in the trees and call sleepily to one another.

My next stop was at the home of twin calico tabbies named Stella and Marie. If they had been humans, they would have been lounge singers. Stella spent her time on the windowsill, looking longingly at her reflection in the glass, and Marie lolled on the sofa, waiting for somebody to come do her nails. When I groomed them, they preened and posed with delicious self-absorption, and when I ran the vacuum to pick up hair they had flung on the carpet, they both turned their heads and gave me languid looks of total disinterest.

I cleaned their litter box while they ate, then washed their food bowls and put out fresh water for them. "I'm leaving now," I said. "I hope you won't miss me too much."

From the windowsill, Stella lowered her eyelids to half-mast in grudging acknowledgment of my existence, but Marie merely flicked the tip of her tail and yawned. I was still grinning when I got on my bike and started to the next stop. A pale coral tint was washing over the sky by then, gilding the eastern edges of puffy little clouds with a darker salmon pink. In another hour, the sun would be fully up and traffic would get thicker.

As I pulled onto Midnight Pass Road, a bakery truck coming back from making a delivery of breakfast croissants and bagels sped by, barely swerving enough to avoid hitting me, and sending a fine spray of puddle water onto my legs. Unnerved, I jerked onto the shoulder and planted my soaked Keds on the ground. I was in the entrance to the old abandoned road leading into the woods behind Marilee Doerring's house. Muttering words that would have made my grandmother wash my mouth out with soap if she'd heard, I took some deep breaths to get my heart quieted down.

A faint sound caught my attention and I looked toward the rusty metal gate stretched across the old road. The road had once been paved with crushed seashells, but time and weather had taken its toll, and now weeds and low-growing vegetation covered most of the shell. The sound came again, low and urgent. Thinking an animal had been hit by a car and had crawled into the bushes, I got off my bike and walked down the road.

As I got closer, I glimpsed a flash of blue fabric, and realized it wasn't a hurt animal moaning in the bushes, but a person. I stopped. The odds were against it, but this could be somebody pretending to be hurt and I might be walking into a trap.

I called, "Is someone there?"

The moaning sound came again. I went closer, and then rushed forward. Phillip Winnick, caked with blood and dirt, lay sprawled in the tangled wet underbrush. Somebody had worked him over good.

I knelt at his side. "Phillip? Phillip, it's me, Dixie. I'm going to call for help. It's okay now. Phillip?"

His bruised lips struggled to form a word, but it was so faint, I couldn't hear. I leaned close to his face and said, "Tell me again, Phillip. I didn't hear you."

Weakly, he breathed a prayer into my ear. "Please don't tell my mother." Then he passed out.

I called 911 on my cell and gave them the location. Then I sat cross-legged beside Phillip and talked to him while I waited for the ambulance. I wanted him to have a voice to hold on to for the moments that he floated to awareness.

"This is a shitty thing somebody did to you, Phillip, but it's not the end of the world. You'll get over this, and you'll be good as new."

A surge of alarm went through me and I looked quickly at his hands. They didn't appear to be injured, and I sent up a silent thank-you for that.

"Your hands aren't hurt, Phillip, and you'll be playing the piano again soon. I know this is a terrible experience, but you'll get through it. People get through these things, and you will, too. I'll help you, and so will a lot of other people."

I babbled on, as much for myself as for him, until the ambulance came. Two EMTs jumped out and lifted Phillip onto a stretcher so quickly and so gently that I wanted to hug them both. A deputy's car was just behind the ambulance, and Deputy Jesse Morgan came and stood beside me while the EMTs eased the stretcher into the back.

"Miz Hemingway," he said. I wondered if he had talked to some of the other deputies about me.

I said, "Can I ride to the hospital with Phillip?"

"You know him?"

"He's Phillip Winnick. He lives next door to Marilee Doerring, where the man was murdered Friday." I was trying to be as cool as he was, but my voice cracked a little bit when I said that.

He gave me a slow, level look. Oh yeah, somebody had been talking to him about me.

"How long have you known him?"

I read the look in his eyes and said, "I met him that morning when I took the cat over there."

"So he's not a close friend?"

One of the EMTs got in the back of the ambulance with Phillip and hooked him up to oxygen and some kind of IV, while the other came back to talk to Deputy Morgan. They stepped away and spoke out of my hearing, then Morgan came back to me and the EMT got in the ambulance and drove away.

"I'll notify his parents," he said. "You'll have to get permission from them to visit him in the hospital."

Defeated, I clamped my lips together and forced myself not to yell at him. Morgan was right. Phillip's parents were the only people with the legal right to be with him in the hospital, and they had to be notified. But the thought of how his judgmental parents might react made my heart hurt.

Morgan pulled out his notebook. "How did you happen to know he was here?"

"I didn't. A truck almost ran me down and I pulled into the road and heard him moaning."

"He say anything to you?"

I shook my head. "I don't think he was conscious."

"So you don't know why he was out here at this hour?"

"I have no idea."

He looked down at me with coolly appraising eyes. "You seem to be having a run of really bad luck. First finding a dead man and now finding somebody beat-up."

"Is that a question?"

He flipped his notebook closed. "You'll be available later?"

"Sure."

He got into his car to go to ring the Winnicks' doorbell and tell them their son wasn't in bed asleep like they thought he was, but in an ambulance going to the emergency room at Sarasota Memorial Hospital. I started back down the old road toward my bike. As I did, something caught my eye at the end of the gate where a stunted key lime's branches pressed against the upright supports. I walked to the end of the gate to get a better look.

Key limes have long, lethal thorns, and this one had a wad of black human hair snarled on a thorny limb. The hair was long and curly, and it appeared to have been left there recently. I thought of Marilee's shiny black hair caught in the brush of her hair dryer, and a cold snail trailed down my spine.

When Christy was barely walking, I went to pick her up at the day-care center one day and found another mother raising hell because her little girl had a bald spot on her head. The day-care women were red-faced and almost in tears. They said another toddler had just reached out and grabbed a handful of the child's hair and yanked it right out. They said he had never done anything like that before and he had done it so quickly, they hadn't been able to stop him. The mother threatened to sue, and she was weeping when she took her child home. I didn't blame her. Who wants their baby yanked bald-headed, even if the yanker is just a baby, too?

I leaned my elbows on top of the gate and looked into the woods, where the tracks of the old road ran about fifteen feet before they disappeared into a tangled mass of live oaks, palms, hibiscus, lime trees, palmettos, ferns, and twisting potato vines. The foliage was so thick, I couldn't see anything except green. Steam was beginning to rise from the damp ground and the thick foliage absorbed it and breathed it out again.

I put a foot on one of the gate's crossbars and boosted myself up. I told myself to mind my own business and let Guidry investigate. I answered myself back that I only wanted to have a look beyond where the road became obscured. I slung a leg over the gate and scaled it. My Keds made gritty sounds as I walked down the devastated road to the spot where it disappeared into the brush. With both arms stiff, I parted the foliage hanging in front of my face. The road was visible for another few feet and then disappeared again in leafy branches. I let the branches close behind me and walked to the next barrier.

It was like being in the Amazon. Thick branches joined overhead to make a canopy that blotted out the early-morning sky, and I could feel the surrounding foliage exhaling its hot breath. An odor of decay or of something dead rose from the steaming thicket. I've never been claustrophobic, but this was nuts. There was nothing to see here, no reason to be here. I had to get out of this place and go take care of my pets. But first I parted the next tangle of branches and got a stronger whiff of the odor—a sweet, heavy smell that reminded me of something, but I couldn't remember what. I pushed a branch aside and looked ahead at the exposed road. More long black hair fanned out on the shadowed ground. For a second, that's all my brain allowed my eyes to see. But you can only hide from the truth for an instant when it's stretched out in front of you. Marilee lay across the road. She was faceup, with her arms slung out to the sides and her legs bent in an awkwardly lewd way. She wore a white skirt and a navy shirt tied at the waist. Animals had eaten away some of the flesh on her arms and legs and the entire lower part of her face. Her eyes stared upward in horror. I gagged and covered my mouth, then turned and ran, batting at the closed branches hanging over the road and making whimpering sounds deep in my throat.

I scrambled over the gate and ran to my bike. I made a diagonal cut across Midnight Pass and pulled into the parking lot of the Sea Breeze. Then I got my cell phone out of my hip pocket and dialed 911.

The operator who answered was cool. I gave her my name and location, and told her what I'd found. She kept her voice at a level monotone. "Please remain where you are," she said. "Somebody will be there in just a few minutes. Can you describe yourself, please, so they'll recognize you?"

That was smart. She was getting me to talk about how I looked, not how the corpse looked. She was also keeping me on the line while she sent somebody out, just in case I was a psycho who had dumped the corpse in the woods myself and was planning on pretending to be an innocent bystander when the deputies hauled it out.

"I'm on a bike," I said. "It's okay, I'm not leaving. I'm an ex-deputy."

She and I both knew that could be a lie, too, but she stayed cool. "That's good," she said. "I'll tell them to look for a woman on a bike in the Sea Breeze parking lot."

Just as she said it, a green-and-white patrol car pulled in. Deputy Jesse Morgan parked and got out of the car and walked to meet me.

"Miz Hemingway," he said. Carefully, as if I were a bomb that might explode any minute. "You've found another dead body."

18

Morgan tilted his head toward the Sea Breeze. "Is the body in there?"

I pointed across the street. "No, it's in the woods behind that gate. It's Marilee Doerring. That's the woman whose house the other body was in. Animals have been at her, but I recognized her."

I was trying to be as cool as he was, but my voice cracked a little bit when I said that.

Flat-voiced, he said, "What were you doing in the woods?"

I could feel my face getting hot. "After you left, I saw some hair hanging on a key lime branch. I went back there to check it out."

"Uh-huh." He gave me that slow, level look again. "Can you show me the body?"

"I can show you where to find it, but I'm not going back there again."

He looked down at me with the same coolly appraising eyes and then nodded. "Fair enough," he said. "Let's go."

We walked across the street and down the stretch of road to the gate. I pointed to the hair on the lime tree. "Somebody must have been carrying her body around the end of the gate and her hair got caught in the thorns."

"Don't touch it," he said. "Did you touch it?"

"Of course I didn't touch it!" That felt better. Anger always makes me feel stronger.

I said, "Just climb over the gate and walk straight back. I'll wait for you, but I need to get to my animals, so don't take too long."

He gave me another level look and climbed over the gate. His legs under his dark green shorts were muscular and tan. He walked like a man who was at home in the woods, pushing through the branches without any tensing or awkwardness. He disappeared from view and I waited, imagining him pushing through the next branches and seeing Marilee the same way I'd seen her. When he stepped back through the branches, he was calling for a crime-scene unit. He rang off, put the phone back in its holder on his belt, and fixed me with a penetrating look.

"You'll be available later?"

"Sure. I just have to see to my animals first, and then I'd like to go home and soak in Clorox for a while."

He grinned. He had a nice grin, he should have done it more often. "Where will you be after you soak in Clorox?"

I sighed. "I'll be wherever Lieutenant Guidry wants me to be."

I gave him my cell phone number again so they could get in touch with me. When I left him, he was climbing over the gate again to guard the body until the CSU people arrived.

For the rest of the morning, images of Phillip's beaten body and Marilee's mutilated body sprawled on the musky ground alternated in my head. I kept remembering how Rufus had barked at the wooded area every time we went walking. I should have known he was trying to tell me something. Dogs can smell dead bodies from a distance, even bodies that have been buried in shallow graves. If I had investigated the first time he barked, if I had told Guidry about Rufus barking, if, if, if . . .

Death has a way of forcing us to look at the ultimate question that hovers just below our consciousness. That pitiful body in the woods was no longer Marilee's home. It was just rapidly decaying flesh, no more human than a fish carcass rotting at the edge of the sea. So where was Marilee? Where was the mind that had informed her body when its heart beat?

When Todd and Christy died, an astonishing number of people said stupid things like "They're with Jesus now," as if Jesus was making Christy's breakfast in the morning and brushing her hair into a ponytail, or that Jesus and Todd were hanging out together and watching old movies on TV. I didn't want them to be with Jesus, I wanted them to be with me. I hoped nobody would say inane things like that to Cora Mathers. Oh God, had anybody told Cora Mathers that Marilee was dead? It would be terrible for her if she learned of it on the news, but I didn't know if Guidry even knew that Cora existed.

I called Guidry and left a message about Cora on his voice mail, giving him her address and phone number. The Sheriff's Department has a Victim Assistance Unit staffed by the kind of people who know how to help you through those first few days when you keep thinking it's all a nightmare that you'll wake from any minute now but you don't.

When I thought about Phillip, I couldn't keep from empathizing with the pain his parents would feel when they saw him. They were bigoted idiots, but they loved their son. Maybe this awful thing would make them realize how much they loved him, and maybe when they learned the truth about why he had been out that morning, they would be so grateful he was alive that they would let all the other crap go.

The big question, of course, was why Phillip had been beaten. Oh, I knew well enough that ignorant young men who are so horrified and ashamed of their own homosexual urges go out gay bashing just for the hell of it. People who are filled with self-loathing need to find a target for their hatred, and now that lynching black men has become socially unacceptable, hurting gay men has taken its place. But the timing of Phillip's attack made me suspicious. It seemed almost too coincidental that he'd been attacked right after he'd told me about seeing a woman leave Marilee's house on Friday morning. I couldn't shake the feeling that his attack had more to do with what he knew about a murder than because he was gay.

At eight o'clock, I called Guidry again and left a message for him to call me. At nine I called the hospital and asked about Phillip. The receptionist said there was no patient by that name at the hospital. They were either shielding him from publicity or he wasn't in the system yet. At ten, I called again and got the same answer. I called Guidry again. He wasn't available, so I left my name and number again.

Feeling cut off from the world, I pedaled home through church traffic. At the Summerhouse, I pulled my bike to a stop to allow a wedding party to spill over the walk. The bride and groom were young and laughing, the bride radiant in miles of lace and tulle, the groom tall and gallant, all the wedding guests gazing after them with the bedazzled smiles that wedding guests always have—hoping this union would live up to the fairy-tale wedding promises of happy ever after but knowing full well that nobody really lives happily ever after, not even beautiful young people who are truly in love.

One of the bridesmaids saw me waiting and gave me a little shrug and smile, meaning "I'm sorry you're inconvenienced." I smiled back and shook my head slightly, meaning, "It's okay."

When the walk cleared, I pedaled on, grinning a little bit at how we two-legged animals aren't so different from the four-legged kind. If that bridesmaid and I had been dogs, we would have wagged our tails and sniffed each other's butts to communicate our friendly feelings. Instead, we wagged our heads and smiled.

Michael's car was parked under the carport with its trunk open, showing about a zillion paper bags from Sam's Club. That meant he had made his weekly run to stock up on food for us and for the firehouse. Michael loves Sam's the way women love shoe stores, and he buys as if he's preparing for marauding invaders who will cut off every supply of sustenance.

I got a couple of bags out of the trunk and started to the house with them and met Michael coming out. When he saw me, the grin on his face faded and he gave me a look that can only come from a big brother who bathed in the same tub and peed in front of you for the first years of your lives together. "What's wrong?"

For a second, I felt like bawling. "You know the kid we saw at the

Crab House Friday night? The one who lives next door to where the man got killed? He was beaten up this morning, really bad."

Michael gathered up bags from the trunk and slammed the lid closed. "How'd you hear about it?"

"I found him. He was in the bushes there on Midnight Pass where the old road goes into the woods. I called nine one one and they sent an ambulance."

"Poor kid. Is he going to be all right?"

"I don't know yet. But there's more. After the deputy left, I noticed some hair on a lime tree, and I went into the woods there where that old road is, you know, and Marilee Doerring's body was in there."

Then I did bawl. Just stood there with a bag of groceries in each arm and cried like a baby. "Animals had been at her, Michael."

"Good God. That's awful. Come in the house, I've got coffee on."

I trailed behind him with the bags, and we both deposited our loads on the kitchen counters. The house Michael and I grew up in is pretty much the way it was when we came to live in it, except for the kitchen. Michael and Paco knocked out a wall where a bay-windowed breakfast room used to be, so it's a lot bigger and sunnier now. They also installed commercial ovens and a Sub-Zero refrigerator and freezer. A butcher-block island sits in the middle of the floor, with a salad sink on one side and an eating bar on the other.

Michael heaved a spiral-sliced ham from one of the bags and set it aside, then made short work of stowing the other stuff away, while I splashed water on my face at the sink and mostly got in the way. He slit the wrapper on the ham and motioned me to the bar.

"Pour us some coffee," he said.

While I got out mugs, he deftly peeled off several slices of ham and threw them on the big griddle between the rows of burners on the stove. I carried two mugs of steaming coffee to the bar while Michael got eggs from the refrigerator and cracked a bunch of them one-handed into a mixing bowl. The ham on the griddle was sending up clouds of damp steam and beginning to smell divine.

He said, "Why do you think the kid was beat up?"

I shrugged. "Either the obvious reason or because he saw the murderer leaving Marilee Doerring's house Friday morning."

He stopped whisking eggs and looked hard at me. "How do you know that?"

"He told me last night. I ate dinner at the Crab House and talked to him before he started playing. He said a woman left Marilee's house around four o'clock and got in a black Miata that had just pulled into the driveway. He thinks she saw him watching."

Michael turned the ham slices and got butter and a slab of Parmesan cheese from the refrigerator. "Have you told the detective?"

I watched his serrated knife cutting thick slices of sourdough bread. "I've left several messages for him to call me, but I haven't heard from him."

He threw a wad of butter on the griddle, smeared it into a big puddle, and flopped the slices of bread in it.

I got up and held out two plates, and he flipped ham slices on both of them. I said, "I knew all along that Marilee wouldn't have left her hair dryer behind like that."

Michael grunted and put another glob of butter on the griddle next to the frying bread. As soon as he turned the beaten egg into it, he sliced transparent shards of Parmesan on top and started lifting and turning it with a spatula. All that golden brown fried bread and dark red ham and bright yellow eggs was making my taste buds itch. I got forks and knives and hurried to pour more coffee to replace what I'd drunk.

Michael topped the ham slices with scrambled eggs, flopped the fried bread on the side, and slid the plates onto the bar. We sat side by side and dug in, neither of us speaking until we'd finished eating. Then Michael got up and refilled our coffee mugs and sat down with a sigh.

"I wish you weren't involved in this, Dixie."

"I wish I weren't, too, but maybe I'm supposed to be. Maybe this is how I'm supposed to start getting my life back together."

"How? By finding dead people and a kid beaten up?"

"Guidry said something yesterday that may be true. He said I couldn't hide forever. I can't, you know? I have to come out some time and start living again."

"Hell of a way to come out."

"This morning when I was coming home, there was a wedding party just leaving the Summerhouse. The bride and groom were so happy and young, you know? Just looking at them made me wish I could turn back the clock and be that innocent again."

"Feeling jealous?"

"I guess so, a little."

"Of what, that they were happy and young, or that they were in love?"

"Don't start that, Michael."

He raised his hands, all innocence. "Start what? I just asked a question."

I got up and carried our plates to the sink and rinsed them and put them in the dishwasher. Michael came behind me and squeezed my shoulders.

"Go take a nap," he said. "You look like shit."

I turned and hugged him hard, my love for him a shining sun in my heart.

19

I slept in the porch hammock until almost three o'clock, and woke up feeling dehydrated but less fragmented. I'm always relieved and grateful to find myself sane when I wake up, because for a long time I wasn't. For the first year after Todd and Christy were killed, I was a mess. Too tired to breathe, with every cell in my body bruised and aching. My nose ran for an entire year, and I barely had the energy to wipe it. I slept whole days, and when I was awake, I stared at the TV without changing stations. Just watched whatever was on, because I couldn't absorb words anyway. I didn't dress or bathe. Didn't answer the phone. I would go for days without eating and then have a giant pizza delivered and eat it all at one sitting.

Michael and Paco tried to get me to eat, to get out of my house, to wake up, but I couldn't. I just flat couldn't. Then one day in the spring, when Todd and Christy had been gone a full year, I caught sight of myself in the bedroom mirror and stopped cold. I looked awful. I looked unhealthy. I looked like a wraith. If Todd could have seen me, he would have said, "For God's sake, Dixie, what good is this doing?" If Christy could have seen me, she would have been afraid of me, I looked that scary.

That was a turning point. I got myself and my house cleaned up and went out and got my hair cut. I sold the house where I'd been so happy with Todd and Christy, and got rid of all the furniture. I donated Christy's toys to Goodwill, except for her favorite, a purple Tickle Me Elmo, who now sits on the pillows of my bed, fat and silly. When I look at his goofy face, I hear Christy's laughter spilling out like silver coins. I suppose I will keep Elmo with me forever. More than Christy's photos, and even more than my memories of her, Elmo keeps her close and keeps me sane. Mostly.

For a while, I thought I might like to move away from the key and all its memories, but Michael and Paco talked me into taking the apartment over the carport, and I'm glad they did. This is where my heart is. It's where I belong. Now occasional rips in the fabric of reality come when I least expect them. I can be going along minding my own business, attending to responsibilities, bathing and dressing and feeding myself like a normal person, and then one day I'll see Todd walking down the sidewalk ahead of me. I'll know it's him, the same way I recognize my own reflection in a mirror. It's his hair, his shoulders, his long legs. I know his walk, the way he swings his arms a little off rhythm with his steps. I'll open my mouth to shout to him, my heart flowering with a burst of pure joy, and then he changes into somebody else—a man I don't know at all, a man totally unlike Todd, and I am weak-kneed and dizzy with disappointment and fear.

It has been three years. I am long past the time grief experts allow for normal grieving. Mine is pathological, they say, and it's time I got over it. They don't explain how to do that. They merely look at me with tight lips and annoyed eyes and tell me I *have* to. I would if I could, believe me, because every time it happens, I fear that next time I won't realize it's a delusion and that I'll actually rush up to a stranger and throw my arms around him and take comfort in his foreign smells, his alien substance. If that ever happens, I may never return.

I drank a bunch of water and called the hospital again, and this time they gave me the nurses' station on Phillip's floor. A harried nurse told me he was "resting comfortably"—whatever that meant—and got off the phone before I could ask if I could see him. I called Guidry again and left another message for him to call me on my cell, then I ate a little tub of yogurt from the fridge while I stood on the porch and looked out at the glittering waves in the Gulf and told myself everything would work out all right. Phillip would recover from his injuries, Guidry would find whoever killed Marilee and Frazier, and I would find a good home for Ghost. Life would go on, and so would I.

After I took a shower and put on fresh shorts and T and Keds, I went to my office-closet and took care of business, entering records on my file cards and returning calls. A man had left a message asking me to take care of his python, and I called him up and gave him the name of another pet-sitter, one who isn't squeamish about feeding live mice to reptiles. Somebody else wanted to know if I knew how to hatch eggs laid by a dove on their front lawn, and I gave them the number of the Pelican Man. I figured anybody who has devoted his life to rescuing injured pelicans must know how to hatch dove eggs. When I'd gotten my books in order and all my invoices ready, I got in the Bronco and drove to the Kitty Haven to visit Ghost.

He was in one of Marge's private rooms, which is to say he was in a cubicle about three feet wide, six feet deep, and eight feet tall, with a sleeping basket, a scratching post, padded shelves at several levels, and a kitty door low in the back to his private toilet. A screened door across the front had a hinged insert to allow the attendants to move food and water in and out without letting Ghost escape. It was an ingenious setup, but it was still a cell, and he knew it.

Like all Abyssinians, Ghost had a muscular body and the slender head and almond eyes characteristic of cats that originated in Asia. Abys are a highly intelligent breed, and once an Aby falls in love with you, it's one of the most loyal animals in the world. Ghost had been with Marilee since he was twelve weeks old, and as far as he was concerned, she was his everything. I took him into the visitors' room and brushed him and played chase the peacock feather with him, but both of us were off our game. I finally sat down cross-legged on the floor in a dejected heap, and Ghost climbed into my lap and curled himself between my legs. Without his charm-trimmed velvet collar, he looked even more forlorn and orphaned.

I ran my fingertips over his ticked silver fur and said, "Things are bad, Ghost. Really bad. Marilee's not coming back, and Phillip has been beaten up. Maybe to scare him so he won't tell all he knows about what happened at your house. You know what it is, don't you? You know who he saw that morning."

He sighed and closed his eyes and laid his chin on my knee, as if he were worn-out from the heaviness of knowledge he couldn't express. He had known all along that Marilee was dead. As an eyewitness to two grisly murders, he could identify the killer or killers of both Marilee and Harrison Frazier. He just couldn't do it in words.

"Don't worry," I whispered. "I'll make sure you have a good home."

He opened his eyes and gave me a look of hurt accusation, and I couldn't blame him. This had happened on my watch, and I had let him down.

I slipped him some kitty treats when I left, and promised him I would come back and get him as soon as Lieutenant Guidry said I could. Even with Marilee dead, there was no reason he couldn't stay in his own home until I could find him another one. He gave me a glum look and whirled his head to the base of his tail and gnawed at it. I wasn't sure what that meant in cat language, but I was pretty sure it wasn't something nice.

Just as I was getting in the Bronco to make the rest of my afternoon visits, my cell rang—Guidry finally returning my calls.

I said, "Phillip Winnick saw a woman leave Marilee Doerring's house about four o'clock Friday morning. He says she got in a black Miata and drove off. He didn't tell you before because he doesn't want his parents to know he was out of the house at that hour."

"When did he tell you this?"

"I saw him at the Crab House last night and he told me then. But there's more. Did you know I found him beaten up this morning?"

"Yeah, I know."

I didn't ask him if he knew about Marilee. Of course he knew.

I said, "I think somebody didn't want him to tell what he saw."

Guidry was silent for a moment, and I could almost hear his brain digesting what I'd told him, along with its implications.

He said, "Can you meet me at Sarasota Memorial in the next ten minutes?"

Before I could stammer out an answer, he said, "In the main lobby," and hung up.

I stared at my phone for a few seconds, then flipped it closed and started the Bronco. Guidry always seemed to be one step ahead of me, and I wasn't sure whether I liked that or hated it.

At the hospital, I left the Bronco for a valet to park, then hurried past a group of hospital personnel out on the sidewalk for a cigarette break. As I veered round them, they all gave me the defiantly sullen looks that smokers have acquired. Wide automatic glass doors slid open for me, and I went through to the lobby, my eyes searching for a man who looked too rich and well dressed to be a homicide detective. A hand touched my arm and Guidry said, "He's on the fifth floor."

He steered me to the wall of elevator doors, and when one opened and vomited a gaggle of glassy-eyed people, we took their place. Some other people got on with us, and we all stood tensely silent as the elevator began its smooth upward glide. Guidry and I stood at the back, not speaking or touching as some people got off and other people got on at every floor.

Finally, Guidry said, "This is our floor."

He touched the small of my back with his fingertips, and I moved forward. A glass wall on our right showed a large waiting room where people were sitting staring straight ahead, each of them caught in a timeless worry.

I followed him down the hall to the ICU wing, where glassed cubicles were arranged in a circle around a busy nurses' station. A uniformed deputy sat in a straight wooden chair outside Phillip's cubicle. Phillip's bed was slightly elevated so his face was visible. It looked like a cut of raw meat. His eyes were swollen shut, his nose was bandaged, and his cheeks were wider than his head. A ventilator's blue accordion hose was taped inside his mouth, and an IV stand stood beside his bed. A couple of machines that looked like apartment-sized washer-dryer combinations stood behind him. Tubes snaked from them and disappeared under the sheet covering him.

I made a choking sound and covered my mouth.

"He looks a lot worse than he is," Guidry said. "He has some broken ribs and a broken nose, but his lungs weren't punctured and he only has a moderate concussion. He'll have a headache for a while, but nothing vital is damaged."

"His mother must be going crazy to see him like this."

"Actually, she hasn't tried to see him, and Carl Winnick keeps calling to warn us not to leak anything about the attack to the media. Says it's a liberal conspiracy to push an agenda of a perverted lifestyle and ruin his reputation."

I felt a little sick.

Guidry took my arm and said, "Let's go find a place where we can talk."

I got myself under control as we left the ICU unit and walked down the wide hall. Guidry tilted his chin toward a small waiting area where some overstuffed chairs were pulled around a coffee table. "Go sit down," he said. "I'll get us some coffee."

He went into the glassed room where a coffee urn had been set up for visitors, and I went to sit in the waiting area. In a minute, he came out carrying two Styrofoam cups with plastic stirrers jutting from them. He set them on the coffee table and pulled out a handful of sugar packets and tiny creamers from his pocket.

"I couldn't remember if you took anything in yours," he said.

I shook my head. "I drink it black."

He sat down in the chair opposite me. "This morning, a call came in a little after five o'clock from a man named Sam Grayson. He had been out walking his dog, headed toward Midnight Pass Road, and he had let the dog off his leash. The dog started barking and then took off in the other direction, chasing a man running behind the houses, headed toward the bay. Mr. Grayson managed to call the dog off, but he called nine one one to report a prowler in the area."

"I know that dog."

"That doesn't surprise me. A deputy went out, but the man had disappeared and everything looked quiet. Then your call about the Winnick boy came in. More than likely, his attack was what the dog had been barking at. He may have saved the boy's life."

"Good old Rufus! Did Sam get a good look at the man?"

"No. It was dark, and the guy was half-hidden by trees. He thinks he was bald, but I don't know if he'd be able to identify him if he saw him again."

"Last night at the Crab House, a man with a bald head chased me in the parking lot. I barely got in my car before he got to me."

Guidry leaned back and looked hard at me, assessing me the way dogs do when they smell something new. "Was this before or after the Winnick boy told you about seeing a woman leave the Doerring house?"

"After. He tried to hit on me at the bar before I talked to Phillip. Sent me a drink and then got huffy when I refused it. I'd know him if I saw him again."

I put my coffee back on the table and leaned forward. "Phillip crawls out his bedroom window after his parents are asleep, and walks to the Crab House and plays piano until it closes at one. He probably goes home with somebody from there, but I don't know who, then he goes home and crawls back in the window again in the morning. My guess is that somebody drives him to that spot on Midnight Pass Road, and then he walks alongside the woods to his house. Whoever attacked him must have known his routine and waited for him."

Guidry was watching me closely, putting together all the pieces. "His parents know he's gay?"

"I don't think so. *He* doesn't think so, and he's scared to death they'll find out. When I got to him this morning, he said one thing before he passed out. He said, 'Please don't tell my mother.' "

"Shit. Poor kid."

"Yeah. He's leaving for Juilliard in August, and I suppose he's gotten more careless as the time grows nearer that he can be open."

"I'm not letting anybody talk to him until I can question him, and that includes his parents. I think I'd like you to be there when I ask him about the woman he saw. If he's up to it, I'd like to do it tomorrow morning."

I hesitated, wondering what Guidry's real reason was, but knowing that Phillip would be less nervous if I were there.

"Okay."

"Is there anything else?"

"What do you mean?"

"Do you know anything else you haven't told me?"

"Nothing except that I found Marilee's body this morning in the woods. I'm sure you already know that."

Guidry's eyes were calm and expectant. I had a momentary flash of what it would be like to be his kid. He would be the kind of father you couldn't lie to. You wouldn't even try, because you would know he could see right through you.

I said, "Marilee's grandmother lives at Bayfront Village. She's a sweet lady, and whoever tells her about Marilee needs to be very careful with her. She knows who Frazier is. She said he ruined Marilee's life, but she wouldn't say what she meant by that."

Guidry carefully put his coffee cup on the table. "When did you talk to the grandmother?"

"Yesterday. I went to see her because I thought she might know where Marilee was. She knew all about Frazier's murder from the news, but she wouldn't say what his relationship had been to Marilee."

"You talk to her very long?"

"A little while. We had tea and some fresh chocolate bread she'd just made. She uses a bread maker Marilee gave her fifteen years ago. Marilee bought her the apartment she lives in, too, and Cora said Marilee came by to visit real often."

For some reason, I wanted Guidry to know that Marilee hadn't been just a gold-digging bimbo who got herself murdered and thrown in the woods. She had also been a loving granddaughter who bought her grandmother a bread-making machine and a nice apartment.

He gave me a lifted eyebrow. "You get around, Dixie."

I thought about the letter I'd put in a folder in my desk—the letter Marilee had written to her daughter. I thought about the invoice for installing a wall safe in Marilee's house. I even opened my mouth to tell Guidry about them, but instead I shrugged.

"It's just that I find out things about people from taking care of their pets."

His expression changed, and I suddenly felt chilled.

He said, "Dixie, how did you know that Marilee's body was in the woods?"

20

My mouth went dry. I didn't need him to spell out his real question. He was asking me if I had anything to do with Marilee's murder.

"I got curious when I saw a strand of hair caught on a tree. I've always thought it was odd that she didn't take her hair dryer with her, and when I saw that hair, it reminded me of the hair in her brush. I just had a feeling I should look farther back in the woods."

"You didn't already know she was there?"

"Of course I didn't!"

"But you see how it could look, don't you? You had keys to the house where both murders were probably committed. You found Hamilton Frazier's body, and then you went straight to where Marilee Doerring's body had been dumped in the woods, even though she hadn't been declared missing. You talked to Phillip Winnick and he tells you that he walks home before dawn every morning, and that he saw a woman leave the Doerring woman's house the night Frazier was killed. The next morning, he's found badly beaten, possibly with the same blunt instrument used to kill both Hamilton Frazier and Marilee Doerring."

I felt dazed and confused, and at the same time intensely aware. The dark blue of Guidry's shirt seemed to brighten, and I could detect the musky fragrance of his aftershave. Guidry seemed on high alert, too.

His gray eyes were wide and watchful as a hunting cat's. If he'd had cat whiskers, they would have been pointed forward and his ears would have been up.

My fingers were gripping my Styrofoam cup so tightly, the coffee was shivering. Just the thought of being a suspect caused a slick of hot guilt to coat my throat.

"Guidry, I never laid eyes on Hamilton Frazier before I found him dead."

"I believe you, Dixie, but you have to admit that logic would put you at the top of the list of suspects."

"Why do you believe me?"

"Motive, Dixie. You had opportunity, but I don't think you had reason to kill anybody."

He sounded like a professor lecturing a class of would-be homicide detectives. Or like somebody giving me a friendly hint of an effective defense to use in case I was arrested for murder.

Stiffly, I said, "This has been very interesting, Lieutenant, but I have to get back to work."

When I got to the elevator, Guidry caught up with me.

"Can I ask you a favor? Would you tell Cora Mathers that Marilee is dead?"

I stared at him, ready to tell him that I was a pet-sitter, dammit, not a member of the Sheriff's Department. But I knew why he wanted me to notify Cora. I had already made a connection with her, and she was more likely to give me information that might help the investigation.

"You owe me," I said.

"Big time. And you'll talk to her about Frazier's relationship with Marilee?"

"Sure, Guidry. I'll go tell a sweet old woman that her granddaughter's body has been lying in the woods with animals eating her, and then I'll ask her a lot of questions. Are you nuts?"

"I didn't mean it that way, Dixie."

The elevator doors opened and I stepped in. "I'll go see Cora," I said. "That's all I'm promising."

He put his hands in his pockets and stood silently watching me until the elevator doors closed.

At the Sarasota Bayfront Village, the woman at the front desk called Cora's apartment and told me to go on up. In the elevator, I tried to find the right words to say what had to be said, but there is no right way to tell somebody about death.

Cora was standing outside her door again, waving at me like a little girl excited to have company. "Did you come back for some more of my chocolate bread? I don't have any fresh today, but yesterday's is still good. It doesn't have to be hot, you know. It's good cold, too. I keep it in the refrigerator and just heat it up in the toaster oven. Sometimes I don't even heat it, I just eat it cold."

"I have something to tell you, Cora."

"Well, come on in. You can tell me while we have some tea."

She scuttled ahead of me, talking a mile a minute. "I don't think there's anything that don't go down better with tea, do you? A lot of people here are drinking green tea. I never saw any green tea, did you? I just drink plain old brown tea. I don't think I'd like to drink something green. Would be like drinking hot lime Jell-O. Yuk. Here, you sit down while I make us some brown tea. I've always got the kettle on, you know."

I edged into one of the ice-cream chairs at her round table and watched her totter into the kitchen area. She turned up the heat under a steaming kettle and put teabags into a teapot, then clattered down cups and saucers while she continued to talk.

"A lot of people say they can't sleep at night if they drink tea after noon, but it never hurt me none. I drink tea all day long and I sleep just fine. If I don't, I get up and watch TV. Some of them shows are dirty, got people doing it right there in front of your face. You ask me, there's some things people ought not do in front of other people, and that's one of them. You ever see any of them dirty shows?"

I got up to get the tea tray and said, "I've seen some of them, but just for a few minutes. I don't much like watching other people having sex."

"Well, that's how I feel, too. What good does it do you to watch? If

I'm not going to do it, I sure don't want to watch somebody else doing it. What did you want to tell me?"

She had caught me off guard, and when I looked at her, I realized she had been babbling because she was scared. I probably wore the same face that Sergeant Owens and Todd's lieutenant had been wearing three years ago when they came to tell me about Todd and Christy. They didn't have to say a word for me to know that my life was over.

I said, "I think you'd better sit down, Cora."

I've seen greyhounds who have been pulled from the track to be destroyed, and their eyes had the same defeated look as Cora's.

"Is it about Marilee?"

"Yes."

"Has something happened to her?"

"I'm afraid so."

"She's dead, isn't she?"

"I'm sorry, Cora. Yes, she is."

Her face imperceptibly crumpled, its thin skin suddenly cracking into an infinity of tiny lines. But her blue eyes remained blazingly dry, and she straightened up in her chair.

"How did he kill her?"

"I don't know, Cora. Her body was found this morning, but I don't know how she died. She was in the woods behind her house. I suppose she was killed about the same time Harrison Frazier was killed."

She closed her eyes at the image I had conjured, but mercifully didn't ask who had found Marilee's body or its condition. She was a sharp old lady, she probably knew the things that would happen to a body left lying in the woods for several days.

"I always knew he would be the end of her. I knew it from the first day."

"They don't know who killed her, Cora."

"I know. It was Harrison Frazier. I knew he would."

"Harrison Frazier was killed, too, Cora."

"I know that, and I'm glad. That's a terrible thing to say, isn't it, to be glad that another human being is dead, but I am. The world's a better place without him, if you ask me. But it's not a better place without Marilee."

The tears came now, spilling down her ravaged face. She didn't bow her head and she didn't wipe the tears away. She cried defiantly, as if her weeping were an accusation.

I reached across the table and took both her hands. "Cora, I'm so sorry."

"Oh, don't think this is the first time I've cried over what Harrison Frazier did to Marilee. This isn't the first time, and it won't be the last."

"What did Frazier do, Cora?"

"Turned chicken, that's what. His family thought Marilee wasn't good enough for him, and he didn't have the balls to stand up to them. That's what hurt her the most. The way he let them drag her through the mud."

"When did this happen, Cora?"

"Marilee was fifteen. I guess Harrison was just fifteen, too. Lord knows they weren't either of them old enough to take on a baby. I don't fault Harrison for that. But the way he acted later, that was the thing that just killed Marilee."

"Are you talking about Marilee's daughter?"

She sighed. "I'm not supposed to talk about her, but now I don't guess it matters. It wasn't right, what they did. I don't care how much money they paid Marilee, it wasn't right."

"What who did?"

"The Fraziers. They wanted Marilee to put the baby out for adoption, and that was all right with me. I didn't want Marilee to be tied down with a baby to raise and her just fifteen years old. I'd already been through that with her mother. If my daughter had given Marilee to some nice folks, Marilee might have been better off. I did the best I could for her, but I had all I could do to keep food on the table for us. If I had it to do over again, I'd have tried to get my daughter to let Marilee be adopted, and she wouldn't have ended up hanging herself, God rest her sweet soul."

My heart did a little slide. Cora Mathers had lost more than any woman should have to endure.

"So Marilee's baby was adopted?"

"Bought is more like it. The Fraziers came up with the idea of their daughter taking the baby, and Harrison talked Marilee into it. His sister had been married a good while and I guess she couldn't have one of her own. You know how that goes. Them that wants them can't get pregnant, and them that can't handle them get pregnant if a man so much as looks at them. Anyway, Harrison told Marilee if she let his sister have the baby, they would always know she was being taken care of, and that after they married, they could get her back."

"He said they'd get married?"

"That's what he claimed. He said they'd finish school and then they'd get married. His family probably told him to say that, and Marilee believed him. She was just fifteen years old, she didn't know how men lie to you."

"You don't think he ever planned to marry her?"

"Not for a minute. They had Marilee sign a bunch of papers. She had to promise to stay away from the baby and never let on she was hers. They paid her to do that. If you're rich enough, you can pay somebody to do just about anything."

I poured her a cup of tea and waited while she took a shaky sip. I said, "The photograph on the refrigerator—"

"That's Lily. That's what they named her. She's nineteen now, and she got in touch with one of them places that find your real mother for you. I don't know for sure how it works, but they called Marilee and then she and Lily talked on the phone. Marilee thought since Lily had found her, it wasn't like she was breaking her promise to the Fraziers. They've been writing, and Lily sent her that picture. She looks exactly like Marilee. Marilee was so excited about meeting Lily. Now she never will."

"How old was Lily when Harrison's sister took her?"

"Oh, just hours. When the baby came, the Fraziers were right there with a lawyer and she signed papers and they took her."

"And Marilee thought one day she would get her back?"

"That's what Harrison told her. And he said it didn't make any difference what his folks said, he wasn't going to let Marilee go."

"But he did."

"Well, he did and he didn't. He didn't marry her, if that's what you mean, but he never let her alone, neither. He was a fool for her, was what he was. Went crazy mean if she got mixed up with any other man. He told her one time he would kill her if he ever caught her with another man, and that's what he's done. Killed her."

"Wasn't he married?"

"Married and with kids. Marilee was just the woman he had on the side. He thought it was enough that he paid her. How do you think that made her feel? I tell you, all the money in the world won't make up for a man treating you like a whore. He ruined her life, and then he killed her."

"Did Harrison Frazier know that Marilee and Lily had found each other?"

"Oh my, no. She had promised, you know, and they'd paid her all that money. No, she couldn't let Harrison know."

Cora looked up at me and gave me a wry smile. "If I keep talking, this won't be true, you know? It'll all turn out to be just a bad dream."

"I know. Talking helps to let bad news settle in slowly instead of all at once."

"Well, I'll just tell you this, and you can pass it on to whoever it is that's looking into this. Harrison Frazier was the one who killed Marilee. Now I think I'd like you to leave me alone."

I understood. I had been like that, too, wanting to burrow into a hole and suffer by myself. I thought briefly about alerting somebody, but then decided to honor Cora's request to be left alone.

"Do you mind if I come by tomorrow?"

"That would be nice of you, Dixie. If it's not too much trouble, I'd like it if you'd stop by."

"Just one more thing, Cora. When the investigators are finished at Marilee's house, it will have to be cleaned. I need your permission to call the special cleaning people." I couldn't think of any other way to describe the professionals who clean and sterilize a house where blood and body fluids have been spilled.

She flinched a bit and then rallied. "You do whatever you need to do, hon."

I made fresh tea for Cora and left her sitting at the table warming her hands on a steaming cup.

Before I drove away, I called Guidry on my cell phone. He answered on the second ring with a clipped "Guidry here."

"Marilee had a baby when she was fifteen. Harrison Frazier was the father. His older sister adopted the baby, and his family paid Marilee to stay away and keep it a secret. But Frazier kept seeing her on the sly, and he told her he would kill her if she ever had another man. Her grandmother thinks he murdered her."

For a moment, the line was silent, and then he took a deep breath. "Does the grandmother have any ideas about who killed Frazier?"

"No, but there's something else. The daughter is nineteen now, and she found Marilee. They've been corresponding and they were going to meet."

Okay, now I'd told him everything I knew. Well, almost everything.

21

I said, "If Frazier was insanely jealous like Cora says he was, maybe he killed Marilee when he caught her with another man."

"And what was the other man doing while Frazier was killing Marilee, standing by watching?"

"Frazier could have knocked him out first."

"And who took Marilee's body to the woods? Do you think Frazier did that while the second guy was unconscious and then went back to get himself killed? Damned cooperative of him if he did."

"Well, I don't know, Guidry. I'm just passing on what Cora told me, so don't give me attitude."

"I appreciate the information, Dixie. Like I said, you get around."

"Yeah. Now, when can I get a haz-mat crew in Marilee's house so I can bring Ghost home?"

"Who?"

"Marilee Doerring's cat. We talked about him, remember?"

"Dixie, the Doerring woman is dead. You can't bring a cat back to her house."

"What's the difference in her being dead and off on a trip?"

"A pulse, for starters."

"No, I mean what's the difference to a cat? The contract I had with Marilee Doerring gives me temporary custody of her cat, with the obligation to do whatever is necessary for his welfare in an emergency. This is an emergency. There's no reason why he can't stay in familiar surroundings while I look for a new home for him. He'd be a lot happier."

"That's what I live for, Dixie, to make a cat happy."

I batted away a floating cat hair and said, "Okay, that was snide, because I really do live to make a cat happy."

"Crime-scene tape should come down some time tomorrow. It's all yours after that."

"Just until I can find a home for Ghost. Would you and your wife like a nice cat? Absyssinians are usually good with kids. If you have some, that is."

There was another pause while my face got hot. I couldn't believe I'd just said what I'd said. He was going to think I was trying to find out if he was single, which was ridiculous. When he spoke, I could hear the grin in his voice. "I don't happen to have any kids, Dixie, never have. Don't have a wife, either, although I did once."

My lips were tingling like I'd had a shot of niacin. It was really stupid. I didn't care whether he was married or not. I said, "A cat would be good company for you, Guidry. Cats don't have to be taken for walks, and they don't bark and disturb the neighbors. They're really ideal pets. Research shows that people who have pets are healthier than people who don't. Did you know that?"

This time, he outright laughed. "I'll think about it, Dixie, but don't get your hopes up."

He clicked off and left me holding an empty phone.

I muttered, "Fuck you very much, Lieutenant," and started the Bronco.

Talking about Ghost had helped me get my priorities straight. I had to find a new home for Ghost, and I had to do it quickly. He was not only cramped in his private room at Marge's, but it was costing me forty dollars a day to leave him there.

I didn't want to leave him with just anybody, either. Pets are like surrogate children. Now that I knew how Marilee had been denied her own daughter, I understood a little better why she had lavished so much love and attention on Ghost. Unable to choose the most nutritious food for her child, she chose it for her cat. Forbidden to buy pretty clothes and toys and baubles for her daughter, she bought them for her cat. Even Ghost's collar with its silver hearts and keys was like a charm bracelet she might have given her daughter. I felt a new affinity for Marilee, a kind of mother-to-mother rapport. Marilee had entrusted me with her substitute child, and I wanted to carry out her wishes.

I was already late making my afternoon pet visits, but I turned the Bronco toward Roberts Point Road and Shuga Reasnor's house. I pulled up in front of Shuga's glass doors and slammed out of the car into the suspended heat peculiar to late afternoon on Siesta Key.

Shuga was home. I could see her through the glass doors. She was sitting on one of her rose linen sofas with a phone stuck to her ear and one long bronzed leg swinging like a nervous pendulum. She saw me when I got to the top step, and even that far away I could see her eyes widen. She got up and started toward the door, still talking on the phone. I put my fists on my hips and stood without ringing the bell while she ended her conversation and flipped the phone shut.

She pulled the door open and stood looking at me. At first, I thought she had two black eyes, but it was smeared mascara. She said, "I know she's dead. The detective called me."

"Can I come in?"

"What do you want?"

"You're the person Marilee authorized to make decisions about her cat."

"Oh, for God's sake!"

Rolling her eyes, Shuga stepped out of the way and pulled the door shut behind me. We walked silently to the living room and sat down across from each other.

"I just have a few minutes," she said. "I have to take care of things a lot more important than a damned cat."

"Things like calling Marilee's daughter and telling her that her mother's dead?"

Her leg stopped swinging, and she gave me a level look.

"Yeah, things like that."

"That's who you called, isn't it? That's where you thought Marilee was going when she left here."

"Okay. Is that a crime?"

"Why didn't you tell Lieutenant Guidry that you'd talked to her daughter? Why didn't you tell him you knew Harrison Frazier?"

Her head snapped up then and she jumped to her feet. "Get the hell out of my house, lady. My best friend just died, and I don't have time for this shit."

"Your best friend didn't die, she was murdered. Did you kill Marilee, Shuga? Were you involved with Frazier and got jealous because he had the hots for Marilee?"

She barked a loud laugh, then sat down and took a cigarette from the crystal holder on the coffee table. She stuck it in her mouth and talked around it while she lit it from the silver lighter on the table. "That's rich. Me involved with Harrison Frazier? I don't think so."

She sucked smoke deep into her chest and slumped back on the couch, looking at me the way a cobra looks at the man playing the flute, wondering whether to be nice or lunge for my throat.

I said, "Let me make it easier for you. I know that Harrison Frazier was the father of Marilee's daughter, and I know he's been seeing her for years. Did he come here to Siesta Key to see her?"

Through a fog of exhaled smoke, she said, "Oh, God no. Too close to Orlando. No, they met in other places. Every month or so, she would fly off and spend a few days with him. They always went to some out-of-the-way place where nobody would recognize them. Harrison would rent a cabin in some godforsaken spot in Louisiana or get a room in a mom-and-pop motel in Bumfuck, Nebraska, places like that. He could have taken her to the penthouse suite at the finest hotel in the world, but he took Marilee to dumb places like that. She was so crazy about him, she thought she had a good time. I think they spent all their time fucking, so I guess maybe she did."

"If they always met someplace else, what was he doing here when he was killed?"

"I don't know. That's why I got scared that something had happened to Marilee when you found him in her house."

"Marilee's grandmother thinks Harrison killed Marilee. Cora says he was crazy jealous and that he threatened to kill her if she got involved with another man."

"He was jealous. Marilee thought jealous meant he loved her, the dumb cluck. But he couldn't have killed her, he was dead. Somebody killed both of them."

"You said Dr. Coffey wouldn't kill her himself but that he might hire somebody to do it. Who else had reason to kill Marilee?"

"I don't know anybody who would kill her. I'm telling you the truth."

I wasn't sure I believed her, but I let it go. "How did Marilee get involved with somebody like Harrison Frazier, anyway?"

"Cora was a cook at the grade-school cafeteria in Orlando. She barely made enough to scrape by, so she was always looking for ways to make money. The summer Marilee and I were fourteen, Cora got a job cooking at a ritzy camp for rich Baptist families outside Orlando. It was more of a resort than a camp, but it was supposed to be a way for families to have a clean, wholesome vacation with their kids and still give them a chance to swim and hike and hang out like normal kids. They let Cora bring Marilee and me with her, and we waited tables in the dining room. The rest of the time we were free to walk around the camp. If we were at the lake and one of the rich boys decided to come down and sit with us, we couldn't do anything to stop them."

"Harrison was one of those boys?"

"So far as Marilee was concerned, he was the only boy. She was nuts about him. If he'd asked her to drown herself in the lake, she would have jumped right in. She thought he was in love with her, the dumb dope, but I think he was more excited about the idea of easy sex. He was just fifteen, and she was probably his first. With all the things going on, it was easy for him to slip off to meet her, and neither of them knew jack shit about condoms or had any way to get any. By the time camp ended, Marilee was pregnant."

She shook her head and stared at the floor for a moment, lost in the memory. "Harrison hadn't even given her his address, but Cora tracked down his family and contacted them. She was smart enough to know they would pay for Marilee to go someplace and have the baby, but I don't think she ever expected them to want it. Poor dumb Marilee thought Harrison would marry her." She wiped away sudden moisture on her cheek and said, "What an idiot!"

"Did Harrison know how she felt?"

"Oh sure. Marilee never was good at keeping her feelings hidden, at least when it came to Harrison. She kept thinking one day he would leave his wife and marry her. Then their daughter turned eighteen, and Marilee got a letter from Harrison's attorney saying there wouldn't be any more money. It was like somebody had dropped a bomb on her."

"How much had they been paying her?"

She gave me a tight grin, exhaling a cloud of smoke and curling the tip of her tongue to touch her upper lip like a smirking dragon. "A quarter mil a year."

"Wow."

"Yeah, wow is right. They got her used to that kind of lifestyle, and then they expected her to go back to living in a trailer park?"

I had to agree that the idea of Marilee Doerring in a double-wide was a stretch of the imagination.

"She called Harrison when she got that letter. He said she'd had a free ride for eighteen years and now it was time she grew up."

I could almost hear Harrison Frazier's bitter voice speaking the words, the voice of a man who had been caught fooling around with trailer-park trash when he was fifteen and had been paying the price ever since, literally and figuratively.

"I heard she got some money from Dr. Coffey, too."

"Yeah, but every cent went to buying that place for Cora and setting up a fund that will take care of her if she ever needs a nursing home. Cora worked her ass off raising Marilee, and Marilee never forgot it."

"So when Frazier cut her off—"

"She went totally bonkers."

"Is that when she got in touch with her daughter?"

Shuga leaned forward and jabbed her cigarette out in the ashtray.

"She had a plan to get close to the girl and make the Fraziers squirm. Harrison has other kids, he wouldn't want them to know he had raped Marilee when she was fifteen and got her pregnant."

So much for the story Marilee had told Cora about her daughter finding her through an agency.

"She was going to say she was raped?"

Shuga nodded, her eyes bright with grim shrewdness. She wasn't disappointed in Marilee the way I was. She understood how Marilee's mind worked. She had pulled herself out of the same environment, told the same lies, created the same illusions, made the same place for herself in the world of money and possessions. She and Marilee had both played the hand nature had dealt them, the same way I had and everybody else does.

I stood up to go. "I have to find a home for Marilee's cat, and I need your approval of whatever I do."

"Hell, I don't care what you do. If you're thinking about sticking me with it, forget it."

Shuga didn't get up, and I didn't say good-bye. I felt her eyes boring into my back as I went out the glass doors and got in the Bronco.

I drove down Roberts Point Road, pulled into a driveway, and dialed Guidry again. This time when he snapped "Guidry," I said, "Dixie Hemingway" just as crisply.

"What have you got, Dixie?"

"Shuga Reasnor says Marilee and Harrison Frazier went away for a few days almost every month for eighteen years. Marilee was in love with him and thought he loved her. Then she got a letter from his attorney saying the quarter of a million she had been getting every year was over. The lady was pissed. She got in touch with her daughter, whose name is Lily. She was going to pressure Frazier to keep paying. Her plan was to claim he raped her when she was fifteen."

"Interesting. Have the reporters got to you yet?"

"Reporters?"

"You know, the people who shove microphones in your face and yell questions at you."

"You think they'll do that?"

"Come on, they've already figured out that Marilee and Frazier had something going, and nothing sells like sex. Now that Marilee's dead, they'll really be licking their chops. You found both bodies and you take care of her cat. Hell, the *Today* show will probably want to interview you."

My throat closed up and for a moment I couldn't breathe.

"Dixie?"

I clicked off without saying good-bye. I knew Guidry was right. Just the fact that I was a pet-sitter who'd found the dead body of one of Florida's first families was enough to make me fodder for reporters, and somebody was bound to do a story about Marilee and her orphaned cat. While they were setting up that story, they'd probably dig up footage of me going crazy wild three years ago while cameras rolled. And the worst of it was that I wasn't sure I wouldn't do it again. Put me under enough stress and I could blow like Vesuvius.

22

Grimly, I pulled out of the driveway into traffic. I had to go on. Not just go on with my afternoon pet visits, but go on with my life. I couldn't let fear rule me, not even fear of myself.

My mouth still had the bitter taste of the hospital's coffee, and my mind jumped to the coconut cream pies that Tanisha makes at the Village Diner. Late as I was, I rationalized that except for a little bitty tub of yogurt, I hadn't eaten anything since breakfast. It would only take a few minutes to have pie and good coffee, and then I would be stronger and braver.

Judy was pouring coffee at a table near the front door when I walked in, and a look of surprise crossed her face when she saw me. I waved to her and plucked a Sunday *Herald-Tribune* from a thin stack by the cashier stand before I slid into a booth. Judy went to the back to get a coffee mug and setup for me, and I spread the paper on the table and scanned the article headings. The President had just issued a denial of something his opponents had accused him of, a CEO had just been indicted for cheating thousands of investors, some scientists had developed a way to alter another seed to make it sterile, and a question had been raised in Sarasota about the way the Sheriff's Department was handling the investigation of the murders of Hamilton Frazier and Marilee Doerring.

Judy plunked a mug on the table and poured coffee in it, but my eyes were locked on the article. It seemed that popular radio psychologist Dr. Win was claiming the Sheriff's Department was showing undue bias toward a former deputy by not arresting her. The woman in question was me. The article went on to say that I was known to have been dismissed from the department because of emotional instability following the tragic deaths of my husband and child, and that I had started taking care of pets after being declared unfit for law enforcement. The author of the article said he had interviewed Dr. Win but had not been able to locate me. Without coming right out and saying so, the implication was that I was hiding.

My heart was pounding hard. In a related article, other people had been interviewed for their opinions about me. As Marilee's ex-fiancé, Dr. Gerald Coffey said I had accosted him while he was eating breakfast on the morning of the murder, and that my behavior had been irrational and alarming. There were even quotes from a couple of people whose pets I had taken care of. They said they probably wouldn't hire me again because it was just too creepy the way I'd found two dead bodies, and how could they be sure I hadn't had something to do with them being dead. There were also several quotes from clients who said they thought the whole idea was ridiculous and that I was an excellent pet-sitter. But you could almost read a hint of doubt in their words.

Judy said, "You just now seeing that?"

I nodded, struck dumb with sick apprehension.

"Don't let it get to you. Stupid son of a bitch didn't have anything real to write about, so he made up a bunch of shit. Nobody'll pay it any mind."

"Yes, they will. Who wants to give their house key to somebody who's accused of murder?"

"You should sue that bastard," she said. "Sue him for slander and libel and defamation of character and loss of income and loss of reputation."

"Maybe I could sue him for my wrinkles while I'm at it."

"I'm serious," she said. "Don't let this go by without a fight, Dixie. This is your *name* we're talking about."

I swallowed the lump in my throat. "That wouldn't stop people from wondering about me."

"People who know you won't believe it, and that's all that matters. What do you want to eat?"

"I can't eat now."

"Yes you can, Dixie! Now you listen here, if you let that slimeball make you go crawling back in your shell, then he's killed you. You want to let him kill you?"

"No."

"Then hold your head up and go on about your business. That cop will find out who killed those people, and everybody will know you didn't have anything to do with it. Now I'm going to bring you some eggs and bacon, and you're gonna eat every bite of it, and you're gonna like it."

I looked up at her flushed face and had to laugh. "I don't want breakfast, I want some of Tanisha's coconut pie."

"That's more like it. If we let fuckers like that make us stop being normal people, then we might as well crawl in a hole and die."

She flounced off to get my pie, and I folded the paper and laid it on the seat beside me. My hands were shaking so bad I had trouble folding the paper. One thing kept running through my mind. While I had the greatest respect for the guys with the Sarasota Sheriff's Department, I wasn't so naïve that I didn't know they were under pressure to make an arrest. And if they decided to go with the obvious, it would be me. I had found Frazier's body, I had led them to Marilee's body, I had a key to Marilee's house, and I was known to be a mental case, no longer fit to wear a deputy's badge. If I had been conducting the investigation, I would have already arrested me as the prime suspect, and now Dr. Win had gone on the air demanding just that. If they arrested me, I didn't have a shred of an alibi. My only witness would be Rufus, and juries aren't known to pay much attention to what a dog has to say.

There were people who thought Carl Winnick walked on water. He was a pillar of the community, rich, educated, with plenty of well-placed contacts. I was a pet-sitter with two years of community college and a dubious medical leave of absence from the Sheriff's Department. An emotionally unstable woman who couldn't be trusted with a gun or with public safety. Which one of us would people believe, me or Winnick?

For a moment, I felt like going home and crawling in bed and pulling the covers over my head and hope it would all straighten itself out. But Judy was right. I had come too far to do that. I had faced things a lot tougher than Carl Winnick accusing me of being a killer.

Not a *lot* of things, maybe, but some.

One or two.

Okay, one. Losing people you love is harder than anything.

As Judy put my pie on the table, Tanisha moved her wide smiling face into the square opening between the dining room and the kitchen and waved at me, her jowls jiggling and her black eyes almost lost behind her round cheeks.

Judy said, "Tanisha says to tell that reporter to kiss your big fat ass."

It surprised me so that I laughed, a big belly laugh from deep inside. Tanisha winked at me and withdrew her head.

Judy said, "Why's she saying you've got a fat ass?"

"It's a private joke," I said. "We were in the ladies' room one day and big fat asses came up."

"Uh-huh. Well, she's got a big one, that's for sure. You know, she cooks for somebody that lives around Marilee Doerring's house. I heard her telling somebody she was that close to the place where the woman was killed."

"Lucky them. She's good."

Judy splashed more coffee in my cup and left me making love to my pie. The crust was crisp and flaky, the filling rich and smooth, and the meringue was exactly right, not weepy or dry or too sugary, with flakes of fresh coconut making sweet little explosions in my mouth. I managed to eat almost a whole minute without thinking about the newspaper article. Instead, I thought about how a good cook like Tanisha could pick up big bucks cooking for parties or just making occasional meals for a family. I mentally ran down the houses near Marilee's, wondering where Tanisha cooked. I'd never seen her in Marilee's neighborhood, but most likely we were there at different times.

My cell phone beeped just as I downed the last pastry crumb. The ID readout showed Michael's number, so I answered.

He said, "Have you seen today's paper?"

"I saw it."

"Are you okay?"

"Yeah. I just had coconut pie. I'm at the diner."

"That asshole at the paper has been calling me, looking for you."

"I'm sorry, Michael."

"Not your fault. What does your detective say about it?"

"He's not my detective, and I haven't talked to him."

"Maybe you'd better. Tell him I'm going to stick my foot up that reporter's ass if he writes any more shit about you."

"It'll blow over, Michael. Any response from us will just give him something else to write about."

"You sound pretty cool about it."

There was a note of admiration in his voice. I took a deep breath and realized I *was* rather cool about it. No more hammering heart. No more fast, shallow breathing. No more fine hand tremors.

I gave a shaky laugh and said, "I guess I am. Who would have thought?"

"So when are you coming home?"

"I'll be late. I haven't even started my rounds yet. I had to talk to some people first."

"Well, be careful."

"Yeah, I love you, too."

I felt calmer after I hung up. I had a big brother who cared about me, and I had handled a lot of stress in one day with only a couple of minor breakdowns. I was making progress.

As I was leaving the diner, I saw Tanisha heading for the ladies' room, so I made a U-turn and followed her. She was already in a stall when I got there. I washed my hands and dried them while I waited. When she came out, she grinned shyly at me. I watched approvingly as she lathered her hands, then handed her some paper towels.

I said, "Judy said you did some cooking for somebody in Marilee Doerring's neighborhood—where that man was killed."

"Not no more I don't."

"Oh."

"Hunh-uh, I wouldn't set foot on that street again, no way, hunh-uh. Bunch of stupid people live on that street, and that man's the stupidest."

"What man?"

"You know, that one I told to kiss my ass, that's who."

"I didn't hear you say his name."

"I guess I didn't say it. Come to think of it, I don't believe I did."

"Tanisha, could you say it now?"

She laughed, but looked at me warily. "Why you want to know?"

I was stumped. I didn't know why I wanted to know, I just did. I said, "I guess I'm just nosy. I work around there, too, and I'd just sort of like to know who to watch out for. I don't know what the guy did to piss you off so much, but you seem pretty easy to get along with, so whatever it was must have been something I wouldn't like, either."

She pushed out her lips and furled her brow while she considered my reason, and then nodded. "I guess you got a right to know if you work around there. He accused me of stealing something, like I gave a rat's ass about the stupid thing, and it wasn't even his."

"Why'd he do that?"

"He seen me getting this little piece of pipe out of the trash when I was on my way to the bus stop. Somebody had put it out at the curb, and I saw it. It's at the curb, it's the trash, it ain't stealing to take it, right? Somebody threw it away, it's for anybody to take that wants it. Short little piece of brass pipe about two feet long."

"That must have been the Graysons' house. They hung a carousel horse on some brass pipe."

"Uh-huh. I don't know who's house it was. It's on the other side of the woods where that man got killed. They just put the pipe out and I saw it and picked it up. I thought maybe I could make a towel rack or something out of it."

"And somebody accused you of stealing it?"

"Yeah, this little runt drove in the driveway and yelled at me like I was some kind of criminal. He said, 'What you doing with that, girl?' Called me *girl*, the old fool. I said I wasn't doing nothing with it and he come over and yanked it out of my hand. Took it *away* from me! Then he said, 'You go on home now, girl. You got no business here.'"

Tanisha's eyes were snapping with humiliation and anger. "I guess he thinks he lives on some kind of plantation and I'm one of his slaves. But them days are over, honey! Ain't nobody gonna talk to me like that. That's when I told him to kiss my big fat black ass, and I waggled it at him when I said it, too. I left and I ain't never going on that street again."

She threw her wadded paper towel in the bin and headed for the door. "I gotta get back to the kitchen or they're gonna send somebody looking for me."

"Who was he?"

She paused with one hand holding the door open. "I don't know who he was. Never saw him before, and hope I don't never see him again, neither."

"Was he bald?"

"Bald? I don't think so. I didn't notice him bald."

"His car, was it a black Miata?"

She shrugged. "I don't know cars. It was black, one of them little low cars."

"When did that happen, Tanisha?"

She frowned. "Thursday night. Why're you so excited about it?"

"Because whoever killed the man in Marilee Doerring's house cracked his head with a blunt instrument. Like a piece of brass pipe. Somebody saw a black Miata around there that night, and later there was a bald-headed man acting suspicious."

Her eyes grew wide. "You think that little pig that hollered at me killed that man?"

"I don't know. Maybe. Would you recognize him if you saw him again?"

"Oh yeah, I won't never forget him."

We gave each other solemn stares just thinking of all the implications, then she moved on and let the door swing shut behind her enormous backside. After a few moments while I let it sink in, I followed her. Hot damn, maybe Tanisha and I had solved the murders.

23

A s I went around the end of the diner's counter, I glanced toward the empty stool where Dr. Coffey had been sitting when I talked to him. Suddenly, a piece of our conversation fell into my brain as if it had been poised above my head, just waiting for me to return to the scene. I had said, "My client left town and didn't leave a number where she could be reached." I had said, "I was thinking you might have some idea where she might have gone. Like where her business takes her, or where her family lives."

When he jumped up and threatened to have me arrested, I had assumed he was jumpy about the possibility of getting involved in a murder investigation. But I hadn't mentioned a murder, and I had never used Marilee's name. All I'd said was that I was a pet-sitter. Surely Marilee Doerring wasn't the only woman he knew who owned a pet. I wasn't even sure the news of the murder had been on the news yet, and even if it had been, how could he have been so sure that's what I was talking about?

My hand was reaching for my cell to call Guidry and tell him all my brilliant deductions, when I caught sight of the wall clock behind the counter and changed my mind. I was over an hour late with my pet visits, and if I didn't get my mind back on my own business, I could lose it.

Like a robot on bunny batteries, I got in the Bronco and started my afternoon rounds, apologizing to each cat for being late and promising to make it up to them later. I left Billy Elliot's run for last, rapping on Tom's door to alert him that I was there and then using my key. Just as I stepped inside, a loud TV voice said my name. Tom and Billy Elliot were parked in front of the TV, and Carl Winnick's infuriated face filled the screen.

"The woman has a key to the house where at least one of these murders took place, and possibly both of them. She has a history of emotional instability that caused the Sheriff's Department to dismiss her, and is clearly the most obvious suspect. Yet the Sheriff's Department has not arrested her, and I want to know why."

Both Tom and Billy Elliot felt me behind them at the same moment and swung their heads. Tom grabbed his remote and clicked off the TV.

"Shit, Dixie, I didn't know you were here. I'm sorry you heard that."

I wasn't sure my voice would work, but it did, even though it came out a rusty croak. "Tom, do you believe what he said?"

"Good God, Dixie, of course I don't. Carl Winnick is an officious, self-righteous idiot."

"Then why were you watching his show?"

"That wasn't his show. That was the evening news with a clip of what Winnick is saying on his show."

My knees bent like Silly Putty. I sank onto a chair and stared at Tom. "So it's not just Dr. Win's usual fans who got that?"

"Don't let it get to you, Dixie."

I stared at him. Why did everybody keep telling me not to let it get to me? How could I not let it get to me that a talk-show celebrity was getting airtime to accuse me of murder?

He said, "Have the reporters found you yet?"

"Not yet."

"Would you like to hide out here until this blows over? Billy Elliot and I would be proud to have you as our guest."

I took a tremulous breath and stood up. "Thanks, Tom. I appreciate the offer and the vote of confidence, but I'm not going to hide."

"Well, if you decide to just lay low for a while—"

"Okay."

I got Billy Elliot's leash and he and I went downstairs and ran as if it were a normal day. A casual observer wouldn't have known that I was beginning to be mad as hell. If Dr. Win had been there, I would have told him to kiss my big fat white ass.

It was a little after 8:30 when I got home. The sun had just set, dropping abruptly below the line of the sea as if it had been treading water and at the last minute had gone under. The sky was streaked with waving banners of cerise and turquoise and lavender, and a couple of brave stars were showing their faces. On the beach, the tide was spreading lacy ruffles on the sand like a lone flamenco dancer entertaining herself.

Michael was on the cypress deck with the hood of the smoker open, scenting the sea air with the aroma of smoking meat. He waved a long fork at me and yelled, "You're timing is perfect. Are you hungry?"

"Are you kidding? I'm starving."

Gingerly, he transferred a slab of brisket from the grill to a big platter and closed the smoker. "I've got potato salad and beans inside," he said.

I happily trotted ahead of him to hold open the kitchen door, then got down plates while he slid the hot brisket onto the butcher block. I opened the lid of a pot simmering on the stove and moaned like a cat in heat. Michael's pinto beans with hot peppers and garlic and tomato are good enough to make strong men weep with unabashed joy. I ladled some beans on each of our plates and added potato salad from a big bowl sitting on the counter. Michael's knife made thin diagonal slices across the tender brisket and transferred them to our plates, where they oozed their succulent juices.

I set our plates on the eating side of the counter and got silverware and napkins while Michael popped us both a beer. Then we both dug in, and for a while the only sound was my little whimpers of contentment.

We didn't talk until after we'd finished eating and got the leftovers put away. Then we took coffee out on the deck and sat in the redwood chairs our grandfather had built with his own hands—chairs so sturdy they'll be here long after Michael and I are gone. We waited awhile, letting the sea's breath cool our faces, before we talked.

"Dixie, I have to tell you something."

"What?"

"Somebody was in the house today while I was gone. There were tire prints in the drive, and more prints of somebody walking across the sand to your place, then to the back door here. Whoever it was broke the lock and went inside, there were footprints all over the place. I didn't find anything missing, but I guess something could be gone and I just don't know what to look for. I went inside your place, and it's the same. Nothing messed up, but sandy tracks on the floor."

I was sitting stiffly upright with the back of my neck tingling. Michael's house was old and the back door didn't fit well. My French doors would be child's play to an intruder.

"Did you call nine one one?"

A mosquito buzzed around Michael's head, and he waved at it in the reflexive way Floridians do, not really expecting to remove it but needing to show some resistance so the mosquito wouldn't think it had clear title to a particular piece of flesh.

"Yeah, they came out and dusted for prints, but I think they were just going through the motions to satisfy me."

"You think it could have been a reporter?"

"No reporter would stoop that low. Well, they might, but I doubt it was a reporter."

We sat silently for a few minutes. A muscle in Michael's jaw was working, and I knew he was forcing himself to stay calm for my sake.

He said, "I had left the brisket cooking. At least the bastard didn't take that."

I grinned at his forced joke. "What makes you think it was a man? It could have been a woman."

"Dixie, until they catch whoever killed those people, I want you to keep the hurricane shutters down when you're home by yourself. There are too many crazies out there, and with that son of a bitch Win splashing your name all over the news, somebody's liable to decide to come looking for you just for the hell of it."

I said, "Winnick hasn't even tried to see Phillip, and neither has his wife. He's afraid the media will find out what happened to him and hurt his reputation. His own son! Can you believe that?"

"I can believe most anything, Dixie. But my main concern is you. I want you to stay out of all this. Don't talk to anybody else. Don't listen to anybody else's sad story. Let the cops handle it by themselves."

"I haven't talked to anybody. Not really. Well, a little bit."

"Just promise me you'll back off, okay?"

"Okay. Come upstairs with me while I look around?"

He stood up and reached a hand to haul me to my feet, then put his arm around my shoulder and squeezed me to his side. "It'll be okay, Dixie. Just be careful."

Together, we went up the stairs to my apartment, but Michael had swept up all the sandy footprints, and nothing looked as if it had been disturbed. I stood on tiptoe to kiss his cheek, thanked him for dinner, and promised again that I'd stay out of the investigation.

When he left, I closed the hurricane shutters and hurried to the desk in my closet-office to see if the mail I'd taken from Marilee's house was still in the manila folder in the top drawer. It was, and I felt a little chagrined that I'd thought somebody had been looking for it. Meaning I had a guilty conscience. Not so guilty a conscience that I was ready to tell anybody about the letters, but guilty enough to be jittery about having them.

I put the folder back in the drawer and went in my bedroom and pulled my bed away from the wall. The bed is built on a wooden frame that has two storage drawers for linens on one side, but the side against the wall has another drawer that nobody knows about. It's not exactly a secret, it's just that nobody has ever asked and I've never mentioned it. When I pulled the drawer open, its contents were exactly as they had been when I put them there three years ago.

When a deputy quits or retires from the Sheriff's Department, she can either purchase her department-issued gun or let it go back to the department. Todd's 9-mm Sig Sauer went back when he was killed, and mine was turned in when I went on indefinite leave of absence. But almost every deputy qualifies for two or three personal backup guns as well as a department-issue weapon. Todd's primary personal was a Smith & Wesson .40, and mine was a .38. Both guns were fitted into a special case in the drawer on the dark side of my bed.

During the six months I trained at the Police Academy, they kept score of who put the most bullets in the head or heart region of the cardboard targets. The rule was that out of forty-eight shots, a minimum of thirty-eight had to hit dead center. The person who most consistently hit on target got a plaque at the end of the six months. It surprised a lot of people that I got that plaque. I still have it. They called it a "marksmanship award," but I was never able to forget that was a euphemism for "accurate killer." Most people don't know this, but it's against the law for a law-enforcement officer to shoot to maim or disable. By law, a law-enforcement officer is obligated to shoot to "eliminate the threat"—which means to kill. People who can't accept that shouldn't go into law enforcement.

It had been three years since I'd handled my .38, but it felt familiar and right in my hand. I sat at my kitchen bar and took my gun apart and cleaned and oiled it. When I was done, I popped a magazine in the butt and put two extra magazines in the pocket of the cargo shorts I would wear the next day. I laid the gun on the bathroom counter while I showered and brushed my teeth. When I went to bed, I put it on the bedside table where I could get it quickly.

Somebody had already killed two people and had tried to kill a third. I didn't intend to be next.

I drifted to sleep and dreamed that Marilee was clutching a cat exactly like Ghost to her voluptuous bosom, but his name was Phillip. She was pleading with me to save him. "You have the key, Dixie. All you have to do is use it."

When the alarm sounded, it took me a few seconds to remember where I was. I went to the bathroom and stared at myself in the mirror. Was it possible that my dream had actually been a message? If not from Marilee's spirit, then from my own subconscious? Crazy as it seemed, I thought it was. Somehow, I had the key to solving the murders and to fingering the person who had attacked Phillip. I just didn't know what it was.

I brushed my teeth, splashed water on my face, and pulled my hair into a ponytail. I pulled on a knit top and the cargo shorts I'd laid out the night before, and stepped into my Keds. Holding my .38 ready, I raised the storm shutters. The porch was empty, and I slid the gun into the right pocket of my shorts, where it made a satisfying pressure on my thigh. I had no idea what I was going to meet, or if, in fact, I needed to take a gun with me, but I wasn't taking any chances.

By 4:15, I was halfway to my first stop, and the morning went smoothly. I didn't find a single dead body, nobody got beat up, no reporter accosted me, and none of the cats on my schedule had done anything naughty that I had to clean up.

While I fed cats and groomed cats and changed cats' litter boxes, my mind was on the strange message I'd gotten in my dream. I take dreams seriously because they're the only way our subconscious can communicate with us. I went over the dream again and again—Marilee holding Ghost, except it wasn't Ghost, but a cat named Phillip. Was that because I saw Phillip as a pet? No, I really didn't. Was it because Phillip was similar to Ghost in some way? Maybe, but how? Ghost knew who the murderer was because he had been in the house when both murders happened. Did Phillip know, too? Had he recognized the woman he'd seen that morning and wasn't saying? What was the key that I was supposed to have to all this? A key is like a code breaker, something that unlocks secrets, but if I had such a key, I didn't know what it was.

At Kristin Lord's house, she greeted me coolly and left me alone while I groomed Fred. She didn't mention anything about Dr. Win's allegations, but I wondered if she had been on the phone trying to find another cat groomer.

Guidry called a little after nine o'clock, just as I was leaving Kristin Lord's house. "Can you be at the hospital in fifteen minutes? I'd like to talk to Phillip Winnick now."

I thought about my promise to Michael to end my involvement in this case. I thought about the two cats still on my morning schedule. I thought about how Guidry seemed to think that I had nothing to do except jump when he called. For all those reasons, I knew I should say no.

I said, "Okay."

24

When I got to the hospital, I stashed the gun and the spare magazines in the glove box after I parked. I stopped in the gift shop to get some reading material for Phillip, then took the elevator up to his floor. In the ICU unit, Guidry was outside Phillip's glassed cubicle, talking to a nurse. Beyond him, I could see Phillip. He no longer had the ventilator, but his swollen face was a mass of purple bruises.

Guidry didn't speak to me, just held his hand out and took my arm while he finished his conversation with the nurse.

He said, "Is he medicated?"

The nurse raised his eyebrows and gave Guidry a tight smile, the kind you'd give the village idiot. "Of course he's medicated. He's able to talk, but it will hurt. Try to keep it to a minimum."

The nurse followed my gaze toward Phillip and shook his head. "It's hard to take in, isn't it? You just never dream that somebody would deliberately do this much damage to a kid."

Guidry said, "Come on," and gave my arm a firm tug.

Phillip's eyes were closed, and when he heard us enter, he opened them with a hopeful look that quickly changed to polite disappointment. I felt like apologizing for not being the person he hoped to see.

I said, "Hey, Phil, good to see your eyes open. You look like hell. Blink twice if that's how you feel."

He managed a weak smile, winced at the pain it caused, and slowly blinked two times.

"I brought you some things to read," I said. "But they didn't have much of a selection. You have a choice of *Reader's Digest, House & Garden,* or *Sarasota Today.* When you've enjoyed as much of those as you can stand, I also got you a Carl Hiaasen book."

I was prattling to cover my dismay at how devastated he looked. Even without the ventilator down his throat, he looked pathetically vulnerable and ravaged. He closed his eyes, either from exhaustion or the effects of his medication, and I shut up. I knew he would recover from his injuries, but the sight of his sweet face so swollen and bruised made me want to go find the person who had done this to him and hurt him really, really bad.

I took one of his big hands and stroked it, wishing I could make all his pain go away just by rubbing him. The normal reaction to being beaten around the head and shoulders is to hold your hands over your head to protect your skull. I suddenly realized that Phillip must have tucked his hands under his armpits during his attack. Awed, I couldn't even imagine the incredible willpower it had taken to protect his hands and leave his head exposed.

I said, "Phillip, I know you didn't see the person who attacked you, but was there anything at all about the person that seemed familiar? Footsteps, scent, sound of his breathing, anything?"

His eyes opened, and for an instant the look he gave me seemed absurdly hostile, the way a drowning animal looks at its rescuers. He rolled his head side to side in slow denial, then closed his eyes again.

On the other side of the bed, Guidry cleared his throat meaningfully, and I took my cue. "Phillip, Lieutenant Guidry wants to hear about the woman you saw leaving Marilee Doerring's house. Just tell him about it in a few words, okay?"

He opened his eyes and gave Guidry a somber look. In a husky whisper, pausing to take shallow breaths, he said, "Black Miata came . . . woman got in . . . drove off. Top was up . . . couldn't see . . . driver."

Guidry said, "Was she carrying any luggage?"

Phillip's eyes widened. "No."

"You remember what she was wearing?"

Keeping his eyes fixed on Guidry, Phillip said, "Pants . . . light color."

"High heels? Low heels?"

"High . . . they . . . made a noise."

"What about her hair? Was it up or down?"

"Down, I think."

"Black hair?"

"Dark."

"You're sure it was a Miata? Couldn't have been an MGB or a Mercedes or a Toyota?"

"I'm sure."

"When the car door opened, did a light come on inside?"

Phillip's eyes grew wide again, and it seemed to me there was a flicker of fear in them. "I guess."

"But you didn't see the driver?"

"No."

"Do you think you could identify the woman you saw? Would you know her if you saw her again?"

"Didn't see her . . . that well."

"Where were you when you saw her?"

Phillip cut his eyes toward me and then swung back to meet Guidry's penetrating gaze. "My window."

"By your window, outside your house?"

"Yes."

"Did the woman see you?"

"I think so . . . she looked . . . over her shoulder . . . jerked . . . like she was . . . surprised."

Guidry's questions had come in rapid-fire sequence. Now he stepped back from the bed.

"Okay, Phillip, thanks. You've been a big help, and I won't make you talk anymore, at least not today."

This time, I was positive I saw fear in Phillip's eyes.

I squeezed his hand. "You just concentrate on healing. By the time you leave for Juilliard, you'll be fine."

He gave me a ghost of a smile, but the fear was still in his eyes.

Guidry was quiet as we walked down the hall toward the elevator. I didn't speak either. Something was bothering me about Phillip's account of what he'd seen that morning. Eyewitnesses are usually uncertain about a lot of details. They change what they say from one time to another, adding some elements and altering others. Phillip hadn't changed a thing. In fact, he had used almost the exact words that he'd used with me. That could either be because he had an unusually vivid recollection, or because he was repeating a rehearsed story.

I said, "It's probably a guy thing, but could you tell the difference between a Miata and some other sports car in the dark?"

"Sure. Why? Do you think the kid's lying?"

"I just wondered about the car."

He didn't answer me, and we got in an elevator full of people and went down without speaking again. In the lobby, he said, "Thanks, Dixie. It was easier for him with you there."

I gave him a half wave and went through the doors to the parking lot, half relieved and half annoyed that he hadn't mentioned the accusations Carl Winnick was making about me. The fact that he hadn't probably meant he hadn't been influenced by them, which was good. But he could have spoken a word of support.

Damn, now I was wanting Guidry to prop up my ego with nice words of encouragement.

I wrenched open the Bronco, flung myself in the seat, gripped the steering wheel, and gave myself a good talking-to. Mostly, that consisted of telling myself that the last thing I needed was to start caring what some man thought about me, and to get my head out of my butt and go take care of the other cats on my schedule.

It was 11:15 by the time I groomed the last cat, and I still hadn't checked on Cora. I was starving, but I knew I couldn't eat until I was sure she was okay. This time, the concierge at Bayfront Village recognized me and called Cora before I got to the desk. We both waited while the phone rang, the concierge counting the rings by little nods of her head while she smiled at me and rolled her eyes toward the ceiling in a show of amused patience. When Cora answered, the concierge said, "You have a visitor down here. Shall I send her up?"

She replaced the phone and said, "She's waiting for you."

From the casual way she acted, I gathered that reporters covering Marilee's murder hadn't yet discovered that Cora was her grandmother. I took the elevator up and found Cora's door open a crack.

I knocked and pushed the door open. "Cora?"

"I'm in here," she called.

I followed her voice, making a right turn into a short hall that led to a large sunny bedroom. Cora was sitting upright in a bed that looked big enough to play hockey in. She wore a white pleated nightgown with a high collar and long sleeves, and her wispy white hair stuck out in all directions, like a newly hatched chick's.

"I'm sorry, Dixie, I just don't feel like getting up today."

"Well, of course you don't, Cora. Have you had anything to eat?"

"I'm not hungry, dear."

"I know, but you should eat anyway. I'll make you some tea."

I didn't give her a chance to argue, even though I remembered how she felt, throat closed tight with grief, stomach roiling in angry waves, lips compressed to keep from howling like an animal. I filled the teakettle, and while it came to a boil, I found bread and eggs in the refrigerator. I made buttered toast and a poached egg, poured a small glass of juice, and put together a breakfast tray that I carried into the bedroom.

"Oh, Dixie, honey, you didn't need to do that. And anyway, I don't want anything to eat."

I poured a cup of tea and paraphrased what Judy had said to me. "Cora, if you let the slimeball who killed Marilee make you stop living, then he's killed you, too. You need all your strength now to help put him behind bars, so eat the damned breakfast."

Her head jerked up at me, eyes blazing, and then she suddenly laughed. "You know, you're a lot like Marilee. She's bossy, too. Was."

She only picked at the egg, but she ate all the toast and drank the juice. When she was finished, I left the tea things on the tray and washed the dirty plate and glass in the kitchen.

Cora was out of bed when I went back into the bedroom, her bare toes peeking from under her nightie.

"Here," she said, "you can have these. I was saving them to leave to Marilee, but now that she's gone . . ."

She held out a pair of red glass earrings, the kind you see in a jumble of junk jewelry at a garage sale. My eyes misted as I took them. I wouldn't have worn them to a rat-turd exhibit, but I knew they held memories that made them beautiful to her.

"Thank you, Cora. Is there anything I can do for you before I go?"

"No, dear, I'm fine. I'll just rest for a couple of days and then I'll be ready for whatever comes next."

"I'll drop by tomorrow, if that's okay."

"That's fine, Dixie. You're a sweet girl."

I didn't feel so sweet when I drove away. I felt pretty sour, as a matter of fact. Both Phillip and Cora, two people I had come to care about, were going to have to face harsh realities in the coming days and weeks, and it wasn't fair.

It was noon, and I was starving. I don't do too well without food administered prior to 10:00 A.M., preferably with lots of black coffee. I took Tamiami Trail, passing slumbering boats in the marina and following the curve of the waterfront, where large sculptures were lined up like unexpected rib ticklers. I turned right on Osprey and took the north bridge to the key, going straight to Anna's Deli on Ocean Drive, where you can get the best sandwiches in the world.

Halfway to the take-out counter, I realized the couple ahead of me were Dr. Coffey and a young woman with frizzy blond hair hanging halfway to her butt. Her hand was raised to fiddle with a piece of hair at the back of her head, and a diamond the size of a doggy liver treat caught the light—a reminder to the rest of us that being a rich man's bimbo might not get much respect, but it paid well. I turned aside and pretended to study the menu on the blackboard on the side wall while Coffey paid for their sandwiches.

As they walked out, I looked over my shoulder at the woman. She turned full face toward me, and I could see what Judy had meant about her probably being a doper. Glazed eyes with pupils expanded so wide they looked like black holes you could get sucked into, skin slightly sallow under her salon tan, a general look of being lost in some private space. Coffey didn't see me, and he put a proprietary hand on the small of her back to propel her forward.

I went to the counter and ordered baked turkey with tarragon mayonnaise on a pumpernickel roll. "And a big dill pickle and two bags of chips," I said.

The woman at the counter laughed, showing a row of glistening white teeth that went well with her ginger skin and hazel eyes. "You sound like you're hungry."

"I went past hunger a long time ago. Give me a brownie, too. A big one."

"Coffee or tea?"

"Coffee. A triple, black."

She walked to a butcher-block counter in the back and turned in the order to a person of indeterminate sex who had dreadlocks and wore an oversized white shirt. She came back and rang up the sale while I watched the sandwich person slather tarragon mayonnaise on two thick pumpernickel halves.

Keeping my mouth firmly under control to keep from drooling, I handed over some bills and said, "You know that couple that just left?"

"Dr. Coffey? Yeah, he comes in here every week on his day off. Always gets the same thing, ham and Swiss on rye. I don't know how people eat the same thing all the time like that. I like a little variety in my life."

"You know her too?"

She made a mouth and counted out my change. "Not really. Don't want to, neither. Frankly, I don't know what he sees in her."

She leaned over and put her elbows on the counter, ready to get down to the nitty-gritty. "If you ask me, she's bad news for him. He seems like a pretty nice guy, but who wants to have a man cut open your chest and mess with your heart when he's dumb enough to hang out with a junkie like her?"

Personally, I didn't want anybody cutting open my chest and messing with my heart, no matter who they hung out with, but I could see her point.

I said, "That's funny, I've only heard about her two times, and both times people mentioned that she was a junkie."

"Well, you can tell just by looking at her, can't you?"

"You don't think he uses, too?"

"He don't seem the type, you know? That's why it's so weird that he's with her. You'd think he'd have better taste. I mean, that woman is pure trash."

The food-prep person had my sandwich assembled and was slicing it in half. He or she then wrapped it in that gray kind of waxed paper that you never see anyplace except in a deli, giving it a neat fold to keep all the goodies inside. The sandwich went in the bottom of a paper bag, with a dill pickle the size of a man's dick wrapped and placed on top of it. Two bags of chips went in last. I was ready to leap over the counter and snatch it up, but the counter woman must have had eyes in the back of her head, because the second a stack of napkins was thrown in and the bag was neatly folded down, she went and got it.

"Enjoy," she said.

I grabbed the giant-size coffee on the counter and headed for the door. "Thanks a lot," I said. "See you."

That's the nice thing about living on the key. It's small enough that when we say "See you," we really mean it.

25

I drove half a block to the Crescent Beach parking lot, parked under some live oak trees, and jogged to the steps leading to the main pavilion. Ask anybody who lives on Siesta Key and we'll proudly tell you that Crescent Beach was entered in the World Sand Challenge in 1987 and named the finest and whitest sand in the world. Heck, we'll tell you even if you don't ask. We'll also tell you the sand is made of ancient quartz crystal, and that even when the temperature is hot enough to make your brain boil, the sand on Crescent Beach is still cool to your feet. Some people claim the beach has healing properties, and that Siesta Key is one of the energy centers of the planet. I don't know if that's true, but if you live on the key, even if you have surf at your front door like I do, you get a compulsion every now and then to go to Crescent Beach and scuff your bare feet in the sand.

I climbed the steps with my precious deli sack in one hand and coffee in the other, bypassing the vending machines and snack bar and going to a picnic table under the shade of a soaring roof. I put my coffee and deli bag on the table, swung my legs over the bench, and took a seat facing the ocean. Down on the white sand, broiling tourists were laid out like meat on a grill. A few children were splashing around in the waves while their parents sat under umbrellas and watched them.

Except for a young man at a table about ten feet from me, I had the area to myself. He was swarthy and bearded, in dirty cutoffs and a floppy dress shirt with the cuffs suspiciously buttoned. With a faded bandanna tied over a mop of black curls and his eyes hidden behind dark reflective shades, he looked like a wanted poster for a Middle Eastern terrorist. He was staring out at the water and muttering to himself in the way of people who've stopping taking their medication, but he wasn't speaking English, and I couldn't tell if his foreign tongue was an actual language or one he'd invented for his personal world. A canvas bag sat on the pavement at his feet, most likely holding books or food or all his worldly possessions. Or a bomb.

I laid out my lunch like a priest preparing Communion. I unwrapped my sandwich and pickle and opened the chips, placing them at exactly the right spots. Placement of food is important. You don't want the important stuff to be over on the side. The main stuff should be in the upper middle, with accompaniments to the side or slightly below. I've been known to rearrange a plate several times before I get the order just right. Eating in the right order is important, too. First a bite of the main stuff, then one of each of the side things in turn. If you take two bites of something in a row, you'll screw up the whole rhythm. Not that I'm a control freak or anything.

I took a bite of sandwich and closed my eyes, making an *mmmm-mmm* sound, like a baby nursing. There is nothing in the world as good as one of Anna's turkey and pumpernickel sandwiches with tarragon mayonnaise. If there were a sandwich hall of fame, it would be in it.

A faint breeze moved the shadowed air, and a couple of black gulls sailed in and landed a few feet away to look hopefully at me. Not to be selfish, I left two little corners of bread for the gulls, tossing it as far away from me as I could so they would move away. They went for it with a loud flutter of wings, and didn't even notice that I also had a brownie. The young man took no notice of me or of the gulls, but continued to look fixedly at the ocean. I was glad he was ignoring me. I much prefer being ignored.

Just as I took the last bite of brownie and was ready to take the last sip of coffee—I plan these things so they work out like that—there was a commotion over in the snack bar area. A security guard trotted past my table to see what was happening, and the young man at the adjoining table got up to walk a few steps away from his table and stare. I half-turned on the bench to look, too, and met the gaze of the bald-headed man who had tried to attack me in the Crab House parking lot. A crowd of people pushed between us, but I was positive it was the same man.

A woman separated herself from a group of passing tourists and walked briskly to the young man's table, where she swooped down and grabbed his canvas bag and walked away with it. The young man kept staring toward the dustup at the snack bar.

I jumped to my feet and yelled, "Hey!"

The woman broke into a run and disappeared down the steps to the parking lot. The security guard had been swallowed up by the crowd in the snack bar, so I stepped over the bench, ready to chase after the woman.

Without looking toward me, the young man stretched his arm out at shoulder level. His hand was clenched in a fist, with the first two fingers stabbing a stern V. Then he turned and walked rapidly away, going toward the beach.

I stopped and turned my gaze back to my own table. Trying to act as if nothing had happened, I gathered up my lunch refuse and carried it to a trash bin. The young man who seemed out of touch with reality was Paco, and he was telling me to butt the hell out. He had just made a drop in a drug sting, and I had almost ruined it.

Whatever had happened over in the snack bar area had apparently been resolved, and the crowd there began to drift away. The bald-headed man had disappeared, and I was left wondering if I had imagined him. Maybe the stress of everything that had happened was making me see danger where there wasn't any. Paco was moving along the edge of the shore, most likely headed toward one of the beach accesses where his Harley would be parked.

I walked to the steps leading to the parking lot and started down, my thoughts swirling with visions of Phillip's beaten face, the bald-headed thug, and the drug sting I'd just witnessed. I was tired. I wanted to go home and take a shower and crawl in bed and let this excess of reality recede a little bit.

On the way home, I swung onto Marilee's street. Jake Anderson, the trauma-scene cleanup guy I had called, was in the driveway next to his big white van with a bio-hazard icon on its side. He and a couple of other men in blue haz-mat suits were just loading their equipment into the truck. They had taken off their headgear but still wore vinyl gloves to their elbows.

I pulled up behind them and stuck my head out the window. Jake grinned and pulled his gloves off and tossed them into the back of the truck.

"All done, Dixie. It'll smell like cherry syrup for a while, but you can go in."

"Okay to take a cat in?"

"Sure."

"Thanks, Jake."

I backed out, knowing the house had been cleaned and sanitized the same way operating rooms are cleaned. Ghost might not like the lingering odor of ozone or the final deodorant fog, but he would be safe from any biological pathogens that are the natural aftereffects of a murder. I turned the corner onto Midnight Pass Road, and at the Graysons' street I saw Sam and Rufus out at their mailbox. I turned and drove to the curb beside them and parked. Sam looked up from a stack of mail with a questioning look, then smiled.

I got out and squatted beside Rufus and exchanged kisses while Sam looked on like an indulgent father.

When I stood up, I said, "Sam, I hope you and Libby haven't lost faith in me because of the things Carl Winnick has been saying."

"Oh good grief, Dixie, of course not! You know, Libby and I were just talking this morning about that, and we think he's off his rocker. His wife drinks, you know. She and Libby belong to the same Great Books club, where they talk about Virginia Woolf or somebody, and she says Olga Winnick has always had a nip or two before they meet. Her husband's on the radio yapping about how wholesome he is, and his wife's a lush."

"I guess you know about their son being attacked."

Sam shook his head. "It makes me sick that I didn't know the boy was lying out there when that man ran by. I thought he'd been trying to break in somebody's house. I never dreamed he had just attacked somebody."

"The detective told me Rufus may have saved Phillip's life."

Sam leaned to scratch Rufus behind the ears. "You hear that, boy? You're a hero."

Rufus wagged his tail and grinned modestly, basking in the pride Sam and I were lavishing on him.

I said, "Sam, before you and Libby left last week, did you put a piece of brass pipe at the curb for trash pickup?"

"Yeah, a piece left over after they got the carousel horse up. Why?"

"The cook at the Village Diner works part-time for somebody on this street, or at least she did until last week. She said that she picked up a piece of brass pipe in somebody's trash last Thursday night."

"There was a piece of galvanized steel, too, the pipe they used for lining the brass."

"She didn't mention that, but she said a man drove into the driveway and took the brass pipe away from her. He was pretty nasty about it, and she's hurt and angry. Do you have any idea who he might have been?"

"Drove in *this* driveway?"

"That's what she said. She said he drove a black sports car, but she didn't know who he was."

"I don't know anybody who would have done that, Dixie."

"Do you know anybody who drives a black Miata?"

"I don't think so. Can't think of anybody." Sam was standing like a soldier at attention. "Does this have anything to do with that killing? Do you think that's what the killer used? My brass pipe?"

"I don't know, Sam. It just seems odd for somebody to make a big scene over a piece of pipe that was left at the curb for trash pickup one night, and then the next morning a dead man is found in a neighbor's house with his head bashed in."

Sam winced. "God, that must have been awful for you, Dixie, finding that body."

Apparently, he didn't know I'd found Marilee, too.

I said, "Not as bad as finding Phillip beaten up. That was the worst."

I gave Rufus another hug and got back in the Bronco. "I'll see you, Sam."

He and Rufus watched me drive away, both of them with sad expressions on their faces.

At the meandering driveway to my place, I started to make the turn and then straightened the wheel and drove straight ahead. There was one more thing I had to do before I went home.

The Crab House doesn't open until five o'clock, so there were only a few cars at the far end of the lot, probably belonging to cooks or staff. I parked by the front door and crunched over loose oyster shell. The door was locked, and when I rapped on it, a young Latino with liquid black eyes and a scraggly attempt at a goatee opened it a crack and peered out.

"We're not open," he said.

"I know, I'm here to see your manager. One of your employees has been badly hurt."

His eyes rounded and he looked uncertainly over his shoulder.

"I don't know," he said. I wasn't sure if he meant he didn't know what to do about me, or if he meant he hadn't understood what I'd said.

"I have to come in," I said.

He shrugged and opened the door wider, stepping aside with a shy smile as I passed him. A slight blond man in the waiters' uniform of black trousers and white shirt was putting little vases of flowers on the tables. He saw me and stopped what he was doing, looking at me with a question on his face.

"Can I help you?"

"Are you the manager?"

"He's not here right now. Did you want to apply for a job?"

"No, I wanted to tell him—you—something."

I walked closer to him and saw a name tag reading RAY. I said, "Ray, Phillip Winnick was beaten up Sunday morning on his way home."

"Who?"

"Phillip, the young man who plays piano."

"Oh my God! Phil?"

"I found him near his house early yesterday morning. He was in pretty bad shape. He's in the hospital now."

He sat down at a table and stared up at me, the implications of what I was telling him playing over his face.

I took a chair across from him and said, "Do you know who Phil leaves with when you close?"

His face tightened and he shook his head. "Nobody here would have done that. Nobody who knows Phil would have done that. Everybody who knows him likes him."

"I'm not suggesting that the person he leaves with was the one who beat him up. I'd just like to talk to him, find out if he saw anybody around when he dropped Phil off."

The door opened and the bartender from Saturday night walked in, going straight to the bar and beginning to set out bottles and glasses. He was a tall, bookish-looking man with rimless round glasses and a frieze of short beard around his cheeks and chin. Except for shirtsleeves that bulged with muscles, he reminded me of a chemistry teacher I'd had in high school setting out Bunsen burners and vials of smelly chemicals.

Ray got up and went over to the bar and spoke quietly to him. The bartender turned and looked at me with a frown, then recognized me. He put down the towel he was using to polish a wineglass and came over to shake my hand.

"I remember you," he said. "You're Phil's friend. I'm Dennis."

"Dixie Hemingway, Dennis. The reason I'm here is that Phil's been beaten up. I want to find out who did it."

26

Ray said, "I was just telling her nobody from here would have hurt Phil."

I said, "I think Phil leaves here with somebody who takes him home. I'd like to talk to whoever that is. He may have seen somebody in the area yesterday morning."

Dennis got the impassive look that people take on when they have information they don't want to divulge.

"Look," I said, "I'm not a cop. I'm not here in any official capacity. I'm just Phil's friend, and whatever this person told me would just be between him and me."

Dennis and the waiter exchanged a wary look. I completely understood their reluctance. Phillip and his unknown friend were gay. Phillip was still in the closet, and the other man might be, as well. To give me the man's name was not only to involve him in a crime, but to out him. Given the level of hysterical homophobia that still exists in this country, with its coy "Don't ask, don't tell" silliness, no ethical or responsible person would do that.

Dennis said, "Tell you what I'll do, if I see somebody I think might have given Phil a ride, I'll tell him you're looking for him. If he knows anything, he can give you a call. How's that?"

His voice was smooth and friendly, but I knew he would close me out if I pushed. That's all I was going to get.

I stood up and put my hand on his arm. "Thanks. I appreciate that Phil's a good kid, and I'm really upset about this."

Ray whipped out an order pad and I wrote my name and business phone number on the back of a slip.

I nodded good-bye to them and started for the door. Behind me, Dennis called out, "Hey, I just remembered something. You know that bald-headed guy that tried to hit on you the other night? He was back last night, and he asked about you."

I turned and stared at him. "About me?"

"Yeah. He wanted to know if you came here often. I told him I didn't know you."

"Did he know my name?"

Dennis grinned. "He just called you the blonde bitch."

"That guy's bad news. He chased me in the parking lot that night. I barely got in my car in time."

"You call the cops?"

"No. I just went home. I guess I should have."

"Damn right you should have. I'll pass the word about him."

I started to leave again, then turned back. "Does he come here often?"

"Never saw him before that night when you were here."

"When he came back, did he try to hit on any other woman?"

"Not that I noticed. He stayed at the bar by himself, left when we closed."

"Okay. I just wondered."

I went outside and got back in the Bronco, wondering why the man had picked me out to try to pick up. Or stalk.

I finally left the *whoosh* of traffic and drove under a blessed quiet canopy of green oak branches to my apartment. When I rounded the last curve, I saw Paco in front of the carport. Still in disguise, he was holding a man to the ground with one hand while he held a phone to his ear with the other.

I pulled into the carport and got out.

Paco snapped his phone closed and flashed a white grin up at me. "Got a friend of yours here, Dixie."

The man was facedown with his hands cuffed behind him. His head was smooth and shiny as a dolphin's, and his piggy black eyes were spitting venom.

I said, "He's been following me. He chased me at the Crab House the other night and he was at the beach this morning."

Paco took one of the man's ears and twisted it. "How come you're following the lady, *pendejo*?"

"Fuck you, asshole!"

"Don't you wish."

Paco got to his feet and put one foot on the man's butt to hold him down. "I'll let you in on a little secret, amigo. The lady used to be a deputy, and she's still got a lot of friends in the department, and they're gonna be real mad when they find out you've been stalking her. They may decide to dump you in the surf and let the sand crabs crawl in your eyes."

Any other time, I would have enjoyed listening to Paco pretend to be a zonked-out bum who had no connection to law enforcement, but I hadn't had a shower all day and I knew company was coming.

I said, "Excuse me, I'll be right back."

I ran upstairs and took a two-minute shower. Just as I was pulling on underpants, I heard tires crunching the shelled driveway. I shimmied into a short skirt and T, stepped into sandals, ran lipstick over my mouth, and sprinted for the French doors.

Downstairs, Paco stood on one side of the downed man, and Lieutenant Guidry stood on the other. Guidry said, "Dixie, I'd like you to meet Bull Banks, a freelance thug who'll do anything for a buck. He was recently released from one of our penal hotels for beating up an elderly couple."

Paco said, "I was just asking him nicely to tell us who hired him to attack the kid."

Bull said, "I don't know what you're talking about. What kid?"

Guidry said, "Bull, it's not like it was when you started your career. Now we've got all kinds of technologies. When we get DNA results from what we found on Phillip Winnick, I think we'll find that you're our man."

"Don't give me that shit. You gotta have hair or something for a DNA test."

"Oh, we can use lots of things. Little skin cells from your fists maybe."

"Fists! Ha, that's a good one."

"Oh yeah, we got good skin cells from your knuckles, Bull. Little knuckle cells were all over the kid's face."

"Didn't use my fists!"

Guidry and Paco exchanged looks and grinned. Just at the instant I realized they knew each other, Bull Banks realized he'd just made a tactical error.

"You can't prove a fucking thing! Anyway, the kid's a goddamn queer!"

My head exploded, and the next thing I knew, I was on top of Bull Banks like a rodeo cowgirl, using his ears to slam his face in the sand and yelling words at him that would have made my grandmother ground me for a year. I didn't know how long I'd been on him, but Bull was howling and sputtering and choking from all the sand in his mouth and nose and eyes. From the looks of his face, I'd been at him long enough to cause him some serious discomfort.

Paco pried my hands off Bull's ears, and Guidry hooked an arm under my waist and lifted me up. Guidry was grinning, and when they stood me on my feet, he kept one arm around me to keep me from falling on Bull again. I kicked Bull in the ribs and yelled, "Who paid you to beat him up? You tell me who, or so help me God, I'll kick your teeth down your throat!"

It felt so good to kick him that I kept doing it.

Bull yelled, "Stop it, bitch!"

Guidry said, "Now Bull, that's not a nice way to talk to a lady, especially when she's going to press charges against you for stalking her.

When they add that to attacking the Winnick kid, you'll get the 'three times and you're out' life sentence. If you're nice to Ms. Hemingway, she might be persuaded to forget about the fact you've been stalking her."

Paco said, "The way you're protecting him, you must be a good friend of whoever hired you."

I turned at the sound of a marked squad car scrunching over the shell toward us. A uniformed deputy got out and took in the scene. When I turned my head back, Paco had disappeared.

Guidry spoke to the deputy. "This is Mr. Bull Banks. He needs to be Mirandized and taken in for the assault of Phillip Winnick."

The deputy nodded and hauled Bull to his feet. Guidry touched the small of my back with his fingertips and said, "Let's go upstairs and talk."

Feeling more surreal by the moment, I climbed the stairs ahead of Guidry. At the porch, he turned the umbrella in the table so it shaded us from the midday sun. "Sit down, and I'll get us something to drink."

I sat as if I were a guest and he was the one who lived in my apartment. He went inside as if he owned the place, and in a minute he came out carrying two bottles of water from my fridge. He sat down in the chair opposite me, unscrewed the cap on his water, and took a long drink. When he put the bottle on the table, his eyes were calm and expectant.

I said, "Do you think Bull killed Frazier and Marilee?"

"We'll look into where Bull was Thursday night, but I doubt he's our man. Not that Bull couldn't be bought to do it, I just don't think he did."

"He's the man who was at the Crab House Saturday night before I talked to Phillip, the one who chased me in the parking lot. This afternoon, he was watching me at the pavillion at Crescent Beach. He must have left about the same time I did, but I stopped by Marilee's house and the Graysons' on the way home, so he got here first. I think he was here yesterday, too. Somebody broke into my brother's house and then into my apartment upstairs. They left sandy footprints, and whoever it was drove a car down the drive."

"Any idea why he's stalking you?"

"He could have seen me talking to Phillip, I guess. I thought he'd left, but he could have come back without me seeing him. If the woman Phillip saw knew he was watching her, and if Bull had anything to do with killing Frazier and Marilee, he may have followed Phillip to the Crab House, intending to kill him. Then he saw Phillip talking to me and guessed he was telling me about the woman, so he decided he had to kill me, too."

"If he was going to kill you, why didn't he kill Phillip?"

"Because Rufus sensed what was going on and barked. That scared him away. Do you know what kind of car he drives? Is it a black Miata?"

"Bull might drive a *stolen* Miata, but he doesn't own a car."

"He must have had a car that night, because he probably waited in the Crab House parking lot and followed Phillip when he left. Then he followed him again when his lover drove him to that spot and let him out of the car."

Guidry rotated his water bottle on the table. "That's where your theory breaks down, Dixie. Bull's the type who would beat the kid up just because he's gay. It may not have anything at all to do with the murders."

"Then why was he after me?"

"You turned him down at the bar, and you chatted up a gay guy. In Bull's world, that's plenty of reason to hurt you."

"Guidry, you know Sam Grayson? The man whose dog barked and scared Bull away when he was beating Phillip? The dog's name is Rufus. Well, Sam put a piece of brass pipe at the curb before he left town last Thursday night for the trash people to pick up Friday morning. A little piece about two feet long. Tanisha saw it when she was walking to the bus stop, and she picked it up."

"Tanisha?"

"The cook at the Village Diner. She'd been cooking for somebody on the Graysons' street, and she saw the pipe and got it. She said a man drove in the Graysons' driveway and took it away from her, sort of accusing her of stealing it. *And* he drove a black car that may have been a Miata."

For a second, Guidry looked like he needed to put his head between his knees and take deep breaths.

"And you think . . ."

"Maybe that was Bull. Maybe he used the pipe to kill Frazier and Marilee."

"He got inspired when he saw the pipe and decided to go kill somebody with it?"

"You have to admit it's a strange coincidence."

"Somebody had to have a damn good reason for killing Harrison Frazier and Marilee Doerring, and unless we turn up some compelling evidence, I don't think Bull Banks had anything to gain by their deaths."

"Somebody could have hired him."

"Yeah, but who?"

"Shuga Reasnor said Gerald Coffey wouldn't kill them himself, but that he might hire somebody."

"That's just gossip, Dixie."

"Guidry, you didn't just meet Paco for the first time today, did you?"

"Who?"

"Paco, the guy downstairs, the one who called your private line when he caught Bull Banks."

"Is that his name? Nobody introduced us."

The guileless look he gave me would have fooled the most confirmed cynic, but it didn't fool me.

"Dixie, before you arrived at Marilee Doerring's house and found Harrison Frazier, where had you been?"

My heart skipped a beat. "Why are you asking me that? Do you believe that crap Winnick is saying?"

"That's irrelevant, Dixie. Where had you been?"

"I told you that before. I walked the Graysons' dog about four-thirty, and then Billy Elliot, the greyhound at the Sea Breeze. After that, I went to a house to take care of a cat. Marilee's was my second cat of the morning."

My voice was tight and curt. I couldn't believe Guidry was asking me for an alibi.

He said, "Any humans see you? Anybody who can verify that you were where you say you were?"

I could feel my jaws clenching and my hands making fists. If there's anything I pride myself on, it's honesty. Having my honesty questioned was like jabbing me with a sharp stick to see how much pain I could take.

"That's the whole point of my work, Lieutenant. I wouldn't be going to those houses if people were home. Tom Hale was home, but he was still in bed."

"He lives where?"

"At the Sea Breeze, with Billy Elliot."

"The greyhound."

"Yeah."

"Besides Tom Hale, nobody else saw you that morning?"

"I don't know, Guidry, I guess somebody could have seen me, but I don't know who."

"Okay."

I stared at him a moment, feeling a confused mixture of anger that he'd asked me for an alibi, and a rational understanding that he was just doing his job.

I said, "This has been really fun, Lieutenant, but I need to take a nap so I'll be awake for my afternoon pet visits."

He stood and handed me his empty water bottle. "Thanks for the refreshments."

I watched him walk down my steps and then went inside and lowered the storm shutters against the glaring western sun. Amazingly, I was fairly calm. A year earlier, I might have curled up in a corner and sucked my thumb if in one ninety-six-hour period I'd found two murdered bodies, been accosted by a psycho in a parking lot, been vilified on radio by a radical hatemonger, stumbled on a kid I liked a lot who'd been badly beaten, and had a homicide detective question me as if I were a possible murder suspect. Now I was just pissed. A little jumpy, true, but mostly pissed.

It was true that I needed a nap, but first I went in my closet-office and checked my messages. One was from somebody named Ethan Crane, who claimed to be Marilee's lawyer but was probably a reporter trying to trick me.

"I need to speak to you about Miss Doerring's will," he said. "Please call me as soon as possible."

"Yeah, sure," I said. There was absolutely no reason why an attorney would need to talk to me about Marilee Doerring's will, and reporters will stoop to anything to get an interview.

I went in the bedroom, kicked off my Keds, and fell on the bed, lying with my toes pointed toward the ceiling like a body in rigor mortis. I wanted to be in the hammock on the porch, but now I didn't feel safe to sleep out there. Some creep like Bull Banks could sneak up the stairs and stand looking down at me sprawled out with my mouth open and drool running down my chin. A reporter could tiptoe upstairs and take photographs of me and run it with the caption "Is she a murderess being coddled by the Sheriff's Department?"

I got up and looked up the name Ethan Crane in the phone book. There really was an attorney by that name. The phone number was the same, too, but that didn't mean the call was legitimate.

I padded barefoot to the French doors and looked through the square glass panes. The sky was a clear and innocent blue. A young snowy egret stood one-legged on the porch railing, his yellow beak pointing upward and his raised foot invisible in his underfeathers. A soft breeze gently ruffled his fine feathers, and he seemed to be smiling. Why not? He didn't have to worry about reporters or public opinion or homicidal thugs.

I went back to my office-closet and dialed Ethan Crane's number. A receptionist answered in a nasal singsong: "Ethan Crane's office."

I gave my name and said, "I'm returning Mr. Crane's call."

She immediately put me through, which told me two things: She had been told to be on the lookout for my call and Ethan Crane wasn't very busy.

His voice was a smooth burr. "Ms. Hemingway, thanks for calling.

I'm sure you're aware that Marilee Doerring is dead. We need to meet and discuss her will."

"Why?"

"That's what we need to discuss. I'd rather not get into it over the phone, but you are one of the principals named in the will."

I shook my head like a boxer taking one punch too many. "Mr. Crane, I hardly knew Marilee Doerring. I take care of her cat when she goes out of town, but that's my only involvement with her."

"Can you come to my office?"

Still dazed, I said, "When?"

"How about right now?"

I still felt like I was being set up for something, but I told him I'd be there in fifteen minutes. To make myself feel more like a grown-up, I put on a white linen skirt with a toast-colored cropped top. I put on high-heeled sandals, too. If you're going to match wits with a lawyer, you need to stand tall and stick your tits out.

27

E than Crane's office was in a narrow building on a side street in the cluttered business section of the key. The building was old and crumbling, set so close to the sidewalk that dark fingerprints and smudges from palms and shoulders spotted it. Down at ground level, chunks of stucco had flaked off like scabs from an old sore. The doorway was recessed in an alcove lined with wooden benches like church pews, on which a vagrant and a couple of tourists too tired to go on sat mutely staring at one another.

Old gilt paint on the glass door had faded so the words ETHAN CRANE ESQ., ATTORNEY AT LAW were barely discernable. Feeling like a character in a gothic novel, I pushed the door open and went up a flight of worn wooden steps rising from the linoleum-floored vestibule. Why in the ever-lovin' blue-eyed world would a woman like Marilee Doerring choose an attorney in a dump like this?

At the top of the stairs, a door stood open at the far end of a wide oaken landing, with two closed doors on either side. A man sat at a desk watching my approach. He wore a white shirt with the sleeves rolled up, and a dark tie that had been loosened and thrown over one shoulder. He stood up, rearranging himself with amazing speed and grace, so that by the time he was fully erect, his tie was hanging true and knotted firmly under his collar, and his shirt cuffs were buttoned. He was fortyish, ruddy-complected, and extraordinarily good-looking. The reason for Marilee's choice of attorneys might not be so mysterious after all, I realized.

He said, "Ms. Hemingway?"

I nodded and we shook hands. He had a nice handshake, not the sweaty clasp I'd have expected from somebody in such a sleazy office. He was also a lot younger than the aged sign on the door had led me to expect. He gestured to a leather chair with a seat hollowed and darkened by decades of rear ends. I sat down and crossed my legs, giving the room's drab walls and musty bookshelves a quick once-over. I hadn't spoken yet, and that seemed to amuse him.

Before he sat down, he leaned forward to hand me a brown leather folder, and I caught a whiff of lime and musk and sweet cigar.

He said, "I think this will clear up some of your questions."

He leaned back in his chair with his hands clasped behind his head and watched me. Like a blind woman expecting Braille, I ran my fingertips over the folder before I opened it. It had a grainy texture like painted-over grit. Slowly, I opened it and read the heading on the first page: "The Marilee Doerring Living Trust."

The first few pages were standard explanations for a revocable living trust, and I skimmed through them quickly. Florida probate laws are so complicated and expensive that most Floridians have revocable living trusts instead of wills. A revocable living trust holds whatever assets a person chooses to put in it until the person either dies or revokes the trust. If it hasn't been revoked when the person dies, an assigned trustee carries out the wishes expressed in the trust without having to pay probate fees or being under the constraint of a court's supervision.

After the explanatory section, there was a quitclaim deed to Marilee's house, and then four more pages of legal explanation. On page five, under a section headed "Trust Income and Principal Distribution," were instructions for the trustee in the event of Marilee's death. Mainly, the instructions specified that all listed assets were under the control of the trustee, to sell or maintain as the trustee saw fit, for the benefit of the named beneficiary. Listed assets were Marilee's house, her car, and all personal possessions within the house.

I was named trustee.

The beneficiary was Ghost.

At Ghost's death, any remaining assets would go to me.

I looked up at the attorney and caught his amused look.

"This can't be right," I said. "What about Marilee's grandmother?"

"Ms. Doerring had a separate irrevocable trust set up for her grandmother," he said, "fully funded with enough to take care of her for the rest of her life. The revocable trust for the cat will hold up, don't worry."

"I'm not worried! I don't want it. I don't want Ghost, and I don't want the responsibility of handling all that money."

He shrugged. "Sorry. You've got it anyway. The cat and the money."

"Can she just do that? Without asking me?"

"Can and did," he said.

"Can I refuse it?"

"Yes. If you refuse, everything in the trust reverts to the state."

"Including the cat?"

"Including the cat."

I shuddered. That was pretty much the same thing as saying the cat would be euthanized.

"When did you draw this up?"

He pointed at the folder. "It's dated there. I didn't draw it up, my grandfather did. He passed away a few months ago, and I've taken over his practice. I never met Ms. Doerring."

I flipped some pages to find the date the trust had been signed. It had been a little over a year before, shortly after I'd begun taking care of Ghost when Marilee went out of town, when Ghost had been still a kitten.

"You're not Ethan Crane?"

"I am, but not the same Ethan Crane who drew up that document."

He really was a handsome man, and it annoyed me that I was aware of that, especially when I was seeing my life pass before my eyes like somebody going down for the third time.

He leaned across the desk and clasped his palms together. "Look, it's not as bad as it sounds. There are no bank accounts involved, no stocks or bonds or cash other than what's in the house. You've got complete power of attorney, so you can do whatever you want to with the house, the car, the jewelry, whatever her personal possessions were. If you want to, you can move into the house with the cat and use the car and everything else as if it's your own. If you don't want to do that, put the house on the market and let an estate-liquidation company sell the rest of it. So long as you see that the cat's well cared for until it dies a natural death, you can do whatever you want to with the assets in the trust. It's a pretty sweet deal."

I could feel my lower lip creeping out like a sulky four-year-old's, and I felt like throwing myself on the floor and kicking and screaming. A healthy, happy, active cat can live twenty years or more, and Ghost was less than two. The last thing I wanted was to complicate my life for the next twenty years with a dependent. I didn't want Ghost for my own. When Michael and I were growing up, we'd always had pets, but I didn't want a pet now. Owning a pet requires a committment. It forces you to have a close relationship with a living being with needs and feelings. I didn't want to make that kind of committment. I didn't want a close relationship with anybody, no matter how many legs he had.

I stood up. "What do I do now?"

He rose to his feet and held out his hand. "Whatever you want to do. That's the beauty of a living trust. You're the trustee, and that's that. Get a death certificate from the Sheriff's Department, and then all you need is the power of attorney in that folder."

His hand felt so warm that I knew my own must be frigid. I tucked the folder under my arm and walked out of his office like a condemned woman on her way to the execution chamber. I could feel him watching me, and for a humiliating moment I hoped my butt looked good.

In a bemused daze, I drove home. Michael's car was still gone, but Paco's Harley was under the carport. More than likely, he was in bed catching up on lost sleep from whatever job he'd been doing—a job that had involved a drug sting at Crescent Beach. I might never know what had been in the canvas bag I'd seen a woman pick up because Paco's life could depend on my not knowing. I accepted that the same way I had accepted department secrets that Todd hadn't told me. It comes with having detectives and undercover cops in the family.

What I didn't accept was what I'd just learned from Ethan Crane.

I kicked off the heels and changed clothes again, pulling on a clean pair of shorts and a sleeveless T. My brain was screaming for sleep, but I was too disturbed to lie down and shut my eyes. I stripped my bed and threw the sheets in the washer with some towels and dirty clothes. While the washer chugged away my body's cells and scents, I attacked the bathroom like an avenging Fury until every square inch sparkled and smelled of bleach. I love the smell of chlorine bleach. Breathing it makes me feel I'm cleaning my brain of old gunk while I'm destroying germs and stains. By the time I put the last polishing rub on the sink's water spigot, I felt cleaner inside, as if all the images of violence and ugliness of the last few days had been polished away.

I padded barefoot to the office-closet and read the living trust again. It still said the same thing. I was now Ghost's legal keeper, and I had complete control over Marilee's house, her car, and eveything in her house.

Boy-howdy.

Whoop-de-do.

Shit.

My office phone rang and I froze, waiting for the answering machine to click on. It was a man, and not a voice I recognized. This one was sure to be a reporter. He said, "I called before. I'd like to talk to you, Miss Hemingway."

I made a face at the phone and said, "I'll just bet you would!"

Then he said, "I got your name from Ray at the Crab House," and I snagged the phone before he could hang up.

"Hello, this is Dixie."

"I'm calling about Phil. Do you know how he is?"

"He's going to be all right, I think. He has some broken ribs and a broken nose, but he's not terribly hurt."

"His hands?"

"His hands weren't hurt. I think he must have tucked them under his arms to protect them."

"Oh God."

"Yeah. His head was totally uncovered. But it could have been a lot worse. A dog started barking and the attacker ran away."

"I've called the hospital several times, but they wouldn't tell me anything."

I said, "Did you drive Phil home yesterday morning?"

I could hear a quick intake of air, and for a moment I was afraid he wasn't going to answer.

He said, "Phil told me about you. He likes you. He said you weren't going to out him to his folks."

"I wouldn't have either."

"Do they know yet?"

"I really don't know what they know. Look, could we meet and talk someplace?"

There was another long pause and then he sighed. "Do you think it would help Phil?"

"I don't know. It might, and it certainly won't hurt him."

"Where would you like to meet?"

"How about Bayfront Park in twenty minutes?"

"How will I know you?"

"I'll be the blonde sitting on a bench facing the waterfront. You can't miss me."

"Okay."

Almost exactly twenty minutes later, I drove under the arched entrance to Bayfront Park, a hiccup of land jutting into Sarasota Bay. I parked in a space facing the bay and followed the sidewalk that curves around the park. Bayfront Park had been Christy's favorite place in the whole world. She and I had spent a lot of time at the Steigerwaldt-Jockey Children's Fountain, her favorite, and we'd both loved the wonderful flying dolphins on the Dolphin Fountain.

Benches line the walkway, and on any day people are sitting on

them, mesmerized by the view of Sarasota Bay. I found an empty one
and plunked myself down and waited. A thin young man in chinos and
a white knit shirt turned from where he'd been standing looking out at
the moored boats, then looked around to see if anybody was with me.
After a minute or two, he walked toward me. He was younger than I'd
expected, twenty-two maybe, and had pale skin that wasn't well ac-
quainted with sunshine. His hair was sandy brown above dark sunglasses that I suspected were worn more to hide his eyes than to shield
them from the sun.

He stopped in front of me and said, "Miss Hemingway?"

"It's Dixie," I said, and put out my hand.

He had a nice handshake, firm and dry. He sat down beside me and
said, "I'm Greg."

I nodded, wondering if it was his real name.

"Greg, I appreciate your meeting with me. I'm just trying to help
find out who hurt Phil."

He took a deep breath, the way people do when they've been holding
their breath, and gave a shaky laugh. "I don't know why I'm so nervous."

"You don't know me from Adam," I said. "Of course you're nervous."

He grinned and nodded. "I guess you'd like to know how I know
Phil."

"If you don't mind telling me."

"We met at summer music camp a couple of years ago. I was a counselor, and Phil and I just hit it off. When I graduated from Juilliard, I got
a job with the Sarasota Symphony Orchestra and looked Phil up. I'm a
violist."

"Do all you musicians go to Juilliard?"

He smiled. "No, just some of us."

"Juilliard's very important to Phillip's mother."

"I know. I think that's the main reason he's going there. He says
she's had her heart set on Juilliard for him since he first started playing
piano."

"You think he's just going to please her?"

"Not completely. But he'd like to do something that would make her happier. He feels protective toward her. From what he says, she's pretty depressed. Phil's her whole life."

"I'd been thinking you two might have met at the Crab House."

He laughed. "No, that place is too noisy for me."

"But you do go there and pick Phillip up when he's through playing?"

He colored. "We have a late supper and spend some time together, then I take him home. Well, not home exactly. I take him to that spot where you found him there on Midnight Pass Road. He walks the rest of the way home."

"Had you ever noticed anybody there at that time? An early jogger maybe, or somebody walking a dog?"

"Never. There's never a soul out at that hour."

"Somebody was there yesterday. Did you see anybody then?"

He shook his head. "He must have been hiding in the trees and grabbed Phil after I left."

"Did you see a car parked on the side of the street? Anything?"

"Nothing. Absolutely nothing."

"Greg, do you know anybody who drives a black Miata?"

"I don't think so."

"When you go to pick Phil up at the Crab House, have you ever seen a bald-headed man hanging out in the parking lot?"

He frowned and took off his glasses. He had intelligent green eyes, and without his glasses, he looked no older than Phillip. "You know, I *have* seen a man like that. I noticed him the first time because he was standing next to a car, looking into it like he might be thinking about breaking into it. When I drove up, he walked off and went around the corner to the side of the building. Then I saw him again a couple of nights later. He was just leaning against the wall near the front door like he was waiting for something. Not like he was waiting for some*body*, but for some*thing*, like something to happen. Why? Was that who beat Phil up?"

"It might be. Somebody in the neighborhood saw a bald-headed man running along beside the woods right after Phillip was attacked."

"Do you think he was hanging around the Crab House to watch for Phil?"

"I think he might have been, yes."

"But why?"

"Greg, has Phillip talked to you about the murder that happened in the house next door to him?"

"A little."

"He saw a woman come out of the house on the morning the murder was committed. I think somebody wants to make sure he doesn't tell who the woman was. Do you have any idea who it might have been?"

He looked shocked. "He hasn't said a word about it."

His surprise seemed genuine, and so was mine. I thought Phillip would have confided that secret.

Greg said, "You know, he's been awfully quiet since that happened. Maybe that's why."

"Quiet?"

"Withdrawn, not himself. I was afraid it was something to do with us, but maybe it was because of the murder."

"Did he mention seeing a black Miata next door?"

He shook his head. "I can't remember anything about a Miata ever coming up. All he said about the murder was that you'd found a dead man in the next-door neighbor's house and took the woman's cat over to his house to stay for a while. He said his mother was annoyed because she not only hates the woman, she hates cats. That's when I understood what a cold woman his mother must be. I know some people like dogs better than cats, but to *hate* cats?"

I studied him for a minute. He had a kind, intelligent face that I liked. "You have a cat?"

"Not anymore. I left her with my mother when I went off to school, and now they've bonded and Mom won't let me move her. Actually, she was supposed to be the family cat when we got her, but she sort of adopted me, and after awhile the whole family thought of her as my cat. She got really depressed when I left for college, but my mother spent a lot of time with her and she got over it. We got her when I was eight, so she's pretty old now."

"Maybe it's time for you to get another cat, one that's all your own."

"I've thought about it, but I'll have to wait until I can afford one. You know, the vet bills and the food and all. I still have a school loan to pay, so it may be a few years before I can take on that kind of responsibility."

The more I knew about this young man, the better I liked him.

"Greg, if Phillip knows who the killer is, his life is in danger. I don't want to alarm you, but if the killer has seen you and Phillip together, he may think Phillip told you what he knows. Until this whole thing is over, make sure you're not alone in a secluded spot."

He gave me a wide-eyed stare. "I can't believe all this is happening."

"It should be over soon. Just be careful."

28

reg and I promised to stay in touch, and I left him staring out at Sarasota Bay. For the next couple of hours, I was too busy with my afternoon pet visits to think about everything that had happened. To tell the truth, I was on sensory overload. I couldn't take in much more. The wonder was that I had been able to withstand as much as I had. I took it as a good sign. I must have gotten stronger without even knowing it.

It was almost sunset when I got to Tom Hale's apartment and ran with Billy Elliot. When we got back upstairs and I took his leash off, I went into the kitchen and sat down at the table where Tom was pushing buttons on a calculator and writing numbers on a form of some kind. He gave me a puzzled look over his glasses, and then laid down his pen.

"What's wrong, Dixie?"

"Tom, did you know that Marilee Doerring had a living trust that left her house to her cat?"

He did one of those blinking head jerks that people do when they hear something shocking, and then he laughed.

"I didn't know it, but I'm not surprised. She had a kind heart."

"You were her CPA. How come you didn't know that?"

"Because it had nothing to do with how she paid taxes."

I picked up a pencil on the table and studied it intently. Nice point. No teeth marks.

I said, "She made me trustee."

"Why is it that I don't think you're happy about that?"

"Because it sucks, that's why. I don't want that responsibility, Tom. I don't want the house, I don't want the car, I don't want the cat. I don't think it's fair that she could just dump it on me without my permission."

I sounded a lot like Shuga Reasnor, but it was how I felt.

"Being trustee doesn't mean you have to take care of the cat personally. You can hire somebody else to do it. There must be a thousand people right here in Sarasota who would jump at the chance to move into that house and take care of the cat for you. Hell, if I didn't think Billy Elliott would be jealous, I'd do it."

Hearing that affected my brain like I'd just had a slug of double-caffeine coffee.

"Are you sure?"

"Absolutely. You're only responsible for seeing that her wishes are carried out. You don't have to take on each responsibility personally."

"Will you take care of all the financial stuff for me?"

"Sure. You decide what you want to do and how you want it done, and I'll take care of it. I'll pay myself a fee from the estate. I'd recommend that you sell that Ferrari right away. I can handle that for you."

I was feeling better and better. Maybe Marilee hadn't played a dirty trick on me after all. Except that a lot of people would consider having the trust a huge bonanza for me. A lot of people might also think I had known about the trust all along. A lot of people might consider it a motive for murder.

When I left Tom, I drove to Bayfront Village. The woman at the front desk saw me when I came in the door and immediately picked up the phone to call Cora. Cora must have answered on the first ring, because the woman waved me on before I got to her desk.

"She's waiting for you," she chirped, as if my visit were a magnificent gift. I suppose in a retirement home, all visitors are considered a magnificent gift.

Cora had opened her door a crack again, and I rapped on it with my knuckles and pushed it open. No lights were burning, and the apartment had the dreary look of space where sunlight had recently withdrawn its warmth. Cora was sitting in a wing-back chair by the glass doors to the sunporch, still in her nightgown, her wispy white hair sticking up in the gloom like apparitional floss. I switched on a lamp and sat down in a chair at an angle to her. Neither of us said anything for several minutes, just sat there in the half-lit room and breathed in and out.

After awhile, Cora sighed. "They say God never gives us more than we can handle, but sometimes I think God has overestimated what I can take."

I said, "Have you eaten anything since this morning?"

She looked startled, as if the idea itself was foreign. "Well, hon, I don't remember if I did or not."

I got up and went in the little kitchen, switching on fluorescent lights that made harsh reflections on the white countertops. I found a can of vegetable soup, and while it heated, I made a pot of tea and got out cups and saucers for two. I poured the soup into a pretty blue pottery bowl, added crackers and butter, and carried the supper tray to the living room.

Cora eyed the tray with a flicker of interest. "There's a TV tray behind the sofa there," she said. I put the tray down on a lamp table and looked behind the sofa, where a wooden TV tray was folded flat. I pulled it out and set it up in front of Cora's chair, put a napkin in her lap, and arranged her meager meal.

"You'd make a good waitress," she said.

I poured myself a cup of tea and sat down and watched her take a few tentative spoonfuls.

"It's good," she said. "I didn't think I was hungry, but I guess I am."

For a few minutes, the only sound was the click of spoon against bowl and Cora's faint slurping noises. She ate the entire bowl of soup and several buttered crackers before she pronounced herself full.

I removed the TV tray and poured us both another cup of tea. Her color was better now and her eyes had lost some of their stunned dullness.

I said, "Cora, do you know an attorney named Ethan Crane?"

"Well, I did, Dixie, but Ethan's been gone now for a good while, a year maybe. Did you know him, too?"

"No, but his grandson called me today and asked me to stop by his office. It seems he has taken over Mr. Crane's practice. His name is also Ethan Crane. Do you know the grandson?"

"No, I can't say as I do. He's taken over Ethan's practice?"

"That's what he said. He had a living trust that his grandfather had drawn up for Marilee. Do you know about that?"

She frowned. "A living what?"

"A trust. It's a kind of will. According to the younger Mr. Crane, Marilee had two trusts, one for you and this other one that he talked to me about. Do you know about the trust she set up for you?"

"Oh my, yes, I know all about it. I have a copy of it. It's personal, dear, so I won't tell you what's in it, but I won't ever have to worry about running out of money."

Her face crumpled and she sobbed quietly with her hands over her face. I waited, knowing that tears would come like that for a while, just spring out when she least expected them, as if there were a well of tears inside her that had to pour out on their own time. When she was cried out, I got up and got Kleenex for her from the bathroom and sat back down.

"Cora, the trust that Mr. Crane wanted to talk to me about was different from the one Marilee had for you. This one was for her cat."

Cora stared at me wide-eyed. "Her cat?"

"The cat that I take care of when Marilee leaves town. His name is Ghost. She made this trust about a year ago, right after I started taking care of him. I didn't know anything about it until Mr. Crane told me, but she put her house and car and everything in her house in this trust."

Cora looked as if she was about to smile. "For her cat?"

I nodded. "For her cat. And she named me the trustee."

Cora put her head back against the chair and laughed. Then she looked at me. "This is the truth? Marilee left her house and car to her cat?"

"It's the truth."

She laughed again, a girlish laugh of pure delight. "That's Marilee," she said. "Lord, that girl was always dragging home every stray cat she saw. She wanted to give a home to all of them, and some of them didn't even want a home, they'd rather be roaming the alleys. But no, she couldn't stand it, she had to take care of all of them."

"It's an awful lot of money, Cora."

"Well, don't worry about it, hon. Marilee must have trusted you to take good care of her cat or she wouldn't have named you that whatchacallit."

"Under the terms of the trust, when the cat dies, all the money that's left goes to me."

"And it should. Cats live a long time. You ought to get paid for all that time."

"But I don't want it, and I'll get somebody else to take care of Ghost."

She smiled at me with a new sparkle in her eyes. "Well, you'll have plenty of time to figure out what to do with it when the time comes. And by that time, you might want it."

"This doesn't bother you?"

"Land no, it don't bother me one bit. It tickles me, is what it does. You know, Marilee was a good girl. Lots of people might look at her with all the money she made and think she was something else, but she was a good girl, and her leaving all that to her cat just proves that she was. Now when I think of my baby, I won't be thinking of how she ended her last minutes on this earth, I'll be thinking that up to the very end, she was a little girl wanting to take care of all the cats in the world. A generous, loving little girl. That was my Marilee."

I leaned over and patted her veined hand. "The apple doesn't fall far from the tree, Cora."

"I guess that's true. We never had much, but I always gave what I had."

Carefully, I said, "For such a young woman, Marilee acquired quite a lot."

She nodded proudly. "She did, that's a fact. Marilee always had a head for figures. When she started getting the money from the Fraziers, she wasn't old enough to take care of it herself, and Lord knows I didn't know how to handle that much money. We wanted to get away from the Fraziers, so we moved here and she went all by herself to Ethan Crane and got herself declared a grown-up. I don't remember what he called it, but I signed some papers and he had her something or other removed through the court."

"Disabilities of nonage."

"I guess so. Anyway, after that she could handle all that money by herself, and she did right well. She bought us a house first off, a nice little frame house in Bradenton, and then we went out and bought everything new. New refrigerator and new stove and new beds and mattresses. Oh my, we had a time doing that. First time either one of us had ever had a whole houseful of new things. She spent over half of the first money she got on the house and furniture and a new car for herself and one for me. But the money was going to keep coming in, every year, you know, so Marilee would sit up every night studying about how to invest it."

I did a bit of fast calculation of what half of a quarter of a million dollars invested twenty years ago would be worth today at 10 percent compounded interest, and my head got swimmy. If the same amount was invested every year for twenty years, the total value would be more than I could count. Even accounting for Marilee's expensive lifestyle, she had made herself an extremely wealthy woman.

Cora was watching me figure it out. "When I die," she said, "all the money she made goes to help other poor girls get an education or start their own businesses. Ethan Crane set it up that way for her."

"I never realized," I said.

"Well, you wouldn't, would you? Marilee never forgot where she came from, or how hard it was for us before the money. I kept working for a couple of years, but she wouldn't hear of it, and so I finally quit. It was about time, too, my ankles were going real bad. I haven't worked a lick since, and Marilee's always taken good care of me. She was a good girl."

Feeling chastened and slightly guilty, I got up and washed the supper dishes. I wondered if I would have been half as responsible as Marilee had been if I had started getting a quarter of a million dollars every year when I was sixteen. Marilee continued to surprise me.

On my way home, I turned on impulse and drove around the curve to Marilee's house. A white Jaguar sat in her driveway, and I pulled up behind it and got out. When I rounded the corner of the garage, I saw Shuga Reasnor at the front door, trying to unlock it. She looked around at me with a dark expression of frustration and resentment.

"Have you had the damn locks changed?"

I shook my head, all innocence. "Doesn't your key work?"

"I don't know what's wrong with it! You must have a key, let me in. I need to get some of my things."

"I'm not authorized to let anybody in, Miss Reasnor."

"Oh, bullshit! Who's going to authorize you? Cora? The police? I have a right to go in and get my personal property before they send in some estate liquidator to haul everything off."

"I'd have to make a list of everything you took and you'd have to sign a statement saying you took it. Otherwise, I can't let you in."

"Oh, for God's sake! What difference does it make to you? It's not your house."

It didn't seem the time to tell her the house now belonged to a cat.

I said, "I'm responsible for it, though, at least for the time being."

She stretched her mouth into a semblance of a smile. "Look, it's worth a couple of hundred dollars to me to get my things now. What do you say?"

"I say you'd better leave."

"What's the problem? You said Marilee left my name to call in an emergency."

"An emergency involving her cat, not something you left in her house."

"I'll call Cora. She'll let me in."

"If Cora gives me permission to let you in, that's fine. I just can't do it on my own."

She turned away from the door and clumped past me on her high heels. "Of all the stupid, idiotic, ignorant . . ."

I waited until she was in her Jag before I ambled past her to the Bronco and pulled out, backing up by the curb to let her exit the driveway and drive off in front of me. She gave me a murderous glare as she spun out and away. We both knew that she would come back, but only she knew why.

I waited until she'd had time to get onto Midnight Pass Road before I pulled back into the driveway. Marilee's yard was freshly edged and the walk and driveway blown clean. Even after death, yards get maintained and pools get cleaned on Siesta Key. The Winnicks' house was blank-faced and silent. I imagined Olga Winnick inside grieving the loss of innocence—either her son's or her own.

Shuga obviously hadn't known that Marilee's locks had been changed, and that was surprising. If she'd always had a key to Marilee's house, why hadn't Marilee given her a new key when she had her locks changed? And why hadn't she known about the change? That's the kind of things that women tell their friends, but Marilee hadn't told Shuga. Maybe Shuga had been the reason she'd had them changed. Maybe it was Shuga she didn't want goming in her house while she was gone. But why? And why now, after being friends for so long?

Whatever it was that Shuga had hoped to get was something very important to her, and it seemed strange that she hadn't said what it was, the way one woman would tell another. "I loaned her my best shirt and I want it back." Or "I took a bracelet off the last time I was here and forgot it." Instead, she had looked pinched and grim when I told her she'd have to reveal what she took and sign a statement listing everything. Shuga didn't want anybody to know what she was taking from Marilee's house. I wondered if this was the first time she had come looking for it, or if she had been the person who'd ransacked Marilee's bedroom and closet.

Phillip had said the woman he'd seen had dark hair, but in the dark Shuga's hair might have looked dark. Maybe Shuga had entered through the lanai and killed Frazier and Marilee, searched for whatever it was she wanted, and then left in a black Miata driven by an accomplice. But who was the accomplice? And who took Marilee's body to the woods? Marilee was small, but Shuga didn't seem muscular enough to carry her body that far.

I finally got out of the car and used my key to go inside. I flipped the switch to bathe the foyer in muted light, and sniffed at the cherry-scented air. I made a tour of the house, ending up in the kitchen, where I stayed clear of the spot where Frazier's body had lain. It was the first time I'd ever been the first person in a house after the crime-scene cleaners, and I found the experience more disquieting than finding the dead body. Crime-scene cleaners remove not only spilled blood and body fluids but every living microbe, which leaves a house strangely absent of life. I had never realized before how invisible agents in our homes are constantly throwing off subtle scents and energies that create the essence of our interiors. Without them, a house is as impersonal as a tray of surgical instruments.

I went to the garage, where Marilee's Ferrari took up half the space. The other half held a plastic garbage can, empty red and blue recycle bins, a stepladder, some stacked paint cans, and a few folding chairs propped against the wall. I knew the investigating team had thoroughly checked the car, but I opened the passenger door anyway. The Ferrari had creamy leather seats, so soft you could have made underwear from them. I ran my hand inside the storage pocket and under the seat. I opened the glove box and took out the sole content, a thin leather folder which held registration and insurance information. Otherwise, there was nothing. No maps, no sunglasses, no boxes of Kleenex or breath mints or leftover napkins from a fast-food drive-through. Not even a CD in the CD holder.

I opened the trunk and shined my penlight inside. As far as I could tell, there wasn't a speck of dust in it. I hadn't learned a thing except that Marilee had been an extremely tidy woman who'd kept her car as fastidiously neat and clean as she'd kept her house and person. The remote control for the garage door was clipped to the sun visor, and I slipped it into my pocket. Before I went back in the house, I positioned the recycle bins and garbage can against the garage wall, next to the folding chairs and stepladder.

29

When I got home, I saw Michael's car, but neither he nor Paco was outside, and their house was dark. It was close to nine o'-clock and I'd been up seventeen hours. It seemed like a week since I'd eaten my turkey sandwich at the beach.

Forlornly, I went upstairs and cleaned up a bit, then went back down to go someplace for dinner. Paco called to me from the cypress deck, and I made a detour to where he was sitting in the waning light nursing a beer. He had removed his bushy beard and mop of unruly hair, and only a redness along his jawline betrayed the spirit gum that had held his beard firm. Nobody would dream this smooth-shaven guy with short-cropped hair and John Lennon eyeglasses was the same person as the scruffy beach bum he'd been at noon.

I went inside and got a beer and some cheese and crackers and joined him. We sat watching the light fading on the horizon while baby wavelets sucked at the shoreline.

Paco broke the silence. "Are you okay?"

I took a bite of cheese and chewed it morosely. I was way hungrier than cheese.

"I guess. I haven't done anything too outrageous, so I guess I'm cool."

"You want to talk about it?"

"Talk about what? The thing at the beach or the thing here?"

"The thing at the beach didn't happen. The thing here did."

"How did you catch him? Did you know he was coming here?"

"I noticed him watching you at the beach, and I thought I recognized him. After the thing that didn't happen was over, I got the Harley and left. Later, when I was driving home, he pulled out of a parking lot in front of me. I followed him, and when he turned into our drive, I went on past and then doubled back and walked down the lane. He had pulled his car into the trees, but he was an easy mark. He's not the brightest bulb in the string, believe me. He was looking around trying to figure out where to hide when I rushed him."

"If you hadn't come home when you did—"

"Dumb luck."

"I don't think so. I think somebody was watching over me."

He gave me a searching look, knowing I meant Todd. "Okay."

"What will happen to Bull Banks now?"

"Unless they can hold him on something more than beating up a gay kid, he'll be out on bail in no time. With luck, he'll get sent up as a three-time loser, but in the meantime he'll be out, without a whole lot to lose. Which is why I want you to be extra careful, Dixie. Bull Banks wouldn't be following you just because you're a hot babe, somebody's paying him."

"You think I'm a hot babe?"

He gave me an exaggerated leer. "Hon, if I was straight, I'd jump your bones in a minute."

"Do you think I should be scared?"

"You think I'm in danger of becoming straight?"

"No, I mean should I be scared of Bull Banks."

"Damn right you should. Dixie, can you find someplace else to stay for a while? Until this whole thing is cleared up?"

I started to tell him about Marilee's trust, then decided to wait and tell him and Michael at the same time.

"Paco, where is Michael?"

"In bed with a headache. Too much sun today. He's sort of lobster-colored."

"Tom Hale invited me to stay at his place for a while."

"He's the guy at the Sea Breeze? That's a fairly secure place. Do it. I'm leaving in a little while and I don't want you here alone. Especially with Michael out like a light."

I got up and gathered our empty bottles. "I'll get my things together."

"Dixie? It'll just be for a couple of days."

I heard the concern in his voice and smiled back at him.

"I know. I'll be fine."

It took me less than fifteen minutes to throw some clothes in a duffel bag and copy Marilee's Social Security number and birth date from her tax return. Then I drove straight to Marilee's house. I used Marilee's remote control to open the garage door, and pulled the Bronco inside. Funny how things have a way of working out the way you intended all along.

My heart was jumping like crazy against my ribs. If Guidry knew what I was doing, he would have my head on a platter. If Michael and Paco knew what I was doing, they would have my whole self on a platter. I intended to find Marilee's new wall safe, and I intended to open it. Call it intuition, a hunch, or an informed guess, but I was convinced that whatever was in that safe was the reason Harrison Frazier and Marilee had been murdered.

A little voice sitting on my shoulder yelled that the killer had trashed Marilee's bedroom, looking for whatever was in the safe, and might come back to try again. I could imagine newspaper headlines screaming "Curiosity Killed the Cat Sitter!" But I had been cowering from danger too long, protecting myself from ugly reality like I was a delicate flower that would wither at a breath of hot air. If I went on like that, I might never get back my courage or my ability to live in the real world. Besides, I kept seeing the words Marilee had written to her daughter, and imagining how awful it must have been to miss seeing her daughter grow up. This was something between Marilee and me—mothers banded together against everything and everybody who would take our children away from us.

My bet was that the code to open the safe would be one of the numbers I had copied, and that the safe would be hidden somewhere in Marilee's closet. Women always keep valuables in places that feel intimate and inviolate to them, places like their underwear drawer or under their mattress. The killer had looked in those obvious places, but he—or she—hadn't known about the wall safe. I, on the other hand, not only knew about the safe but was a pro. If a safe had been hidden behind a baseboard or in the floor or in a wall, I would find it.

Two hours later, hot and sweaty from crawling around Marilee's closet, I gave up. I hadn't found a thing. So much for being a pro.

I showered in Marilee's guest bath and crawled into bed in her guest room, first sliding my .38 under the pillow. My stomach was gnawing on itself, my knees hurt from thumping around on the Mexican tile, and my head ached from hunger and anxiety. It was after midnight when I finally fell into exhausted sleep. It didn't seem that I'd been asleep five minutes when a scream rang out in the darkness, and it took me a full minute to realize I had made it. I lay with my heart pounding, trying to get oriented.

Okay, I was at Marilee's house, in Marilee's bed, and something—a sound of somebody breaking in the house or a nightmare I couldn't remember—had caused me to scream. The red numbers on the bedside clock read 3:34. I got my gun from under the pillow and slid out of bed. Holding the gun in the stiff-armed position and hugging the wall as much as possible, I moved to the open bedroom door. If somebody had broken in, my scream had already clued him that I was on the alert. It had also told him exactly where I was located. Arms stiffly extended, I flattened myself against the wall beside the door, ready to take out anybody who entered.

For a terrible second, I remembered an exercise at the Police Academy that tested our physical and emotional reflexes—not to mention our gag reflexes—by having us handle the aftermath of a mock terrorist attack. We had to pick up body parts and lead hysterical survivors away from the severed heads of their loved ones. Even though we all knew the body parts were plastic covered in fake blood, they felt and looked real enough to make us feel horrified sympathy for the actors who played their roles so convincingly. I had nightmares about that exercise for months, which was the whole point of it. Life is precious, and the obscenity of willful destruction of human bodies is an affront to the soul. We should never forget that, no matter who we are. People in law enforcement, with the legal *obligation* to blow people away if they're a threat, need to have it indelibly seared on their brains.

I wasn't a deputy anymore, so I didn't have the sworn duty to kill a person threatening me. I could legally clip them in the leg or arm just to stop them. But my police training told me that doing that would almost surely get me killed. Criminals have a way of shooting back even when they're wounded. They have a way of playing dead and then turning their guns on you when your guard is down. So would I shoot to kill, or would I shoot to maim?

The truth was that I didn't know.

Minutes passed without a sound, and then the alarm sounded and made me jump a foot in the air. I flipped on the light and padded down the hall, holding the gun ready but now acutely conscious that I was naked except for underpants. Turning on lights as I went, I checked the entire house, feeling more foolish with every closet door I opened. All the doors and windows were secure, and I didn't find any evidence of a break-in. I probably had just scared myself with a bad dream.

I finally went to the bathroom and got ready for the day. Now I would be late getting started because I'd let fear get in the way. I drove the short distance across Midnight Pass Road to Tom Hale's condo, where Billy Elliot was pacing behind the door, waiting for me. We ran for about fifteen minutes and I took him back upstairs. He wanted more, but I didn't have the stamina. All the cats on my schedule got the same short shrift. I was too wasted to give them what they deserved. I promised I would make it up to them in the afternoon, and as soon as time came for the diner to open, I sped there like a winter bird to a feeder.

The diner was moist with biscuit heat and coffee steam. I waved to Tanisha behind the cook's window and took a stool at the bar. Judy raised her eyebrows at me from across the room and I nodded. She stopped at the cook's window and put my order in before she came with a mug and the coffeepot.

She said, "Everything okay?"

I said it was, because that wasn't the time or place to tell her everything that had happened since we last talked. Besides, if I told her about Phillip, I would probably break down and blubber all over the counter.

"The regular?"

"With two biscuits. And bacon."

She said, "Baaay-connn," as if I'd had some kind of epiphany, and went off to turn the order in.

I pulled my cell phone out of my backpack and looked at it. I knew I should use it to call Guidry and tell him where I was staying and why. Knew I should tell him about the safe, and about the trust. I put the cell phone back in my backpack and drank coffee instead. I couldn't talk to Guidry until I'd had food.

When Judy plunked down my breakfast, I went about eating it with serious efficiency. Tanisha's biscuits are like her piecrusts—light, flaky, and delicious. I ate one with my eggs and bacon and saved the other to eat with jelly, like a dessert. I was just about to eat the jelly one when a man slid onto the bar stool next to me and spread a *Herald-Tribune* on the space in front of him. His hands were pale and bloodless, with stiff black hairs between his knuckles. I saw Judy do a double take, and I looked sideways to see who it was. Dr. Gerald Coffey was so intent on an article he was reading that he didn't notice who was beside him.

Judy did the same quick question and answer routine with him that she'd done with me, then brought him coffee and topped mine off. She gave me a hard look while she poured mine, like she would pound me into the floor if I caused him to leave again. She needn't have worried. I wasn't up for another confrontation with him. I just wanted to eat my biscuit and drink my third cup of coffee and go back to Marilee's house.

I was eating the last crumb when Judy brought his scrambled whites and dry rye. I carefully kept my gaze straight ahead while she set it down, and shook my head when she asked if I wanted anything more.

For a minute or two, Coffey ate silently. Then he cleared his throat. "I think I owe you an apology, Miss Hemingway."

I still didn't look at him, and for a moment I couldn't think of anything to say.

He said, "I don't blame you for being angry. I was pretty unreasonable when you spoke to me before."

I turned my head then. "Marilee's dead, you know."

His face reddened and for a second his eyes shone with unshed tears. "Look, could we go someplace more private and talk?"

I nodded and slid off the stool. He followed me, and we both left bills with the cashier and went out the front door. I pointed to the Bronco and said, "We can talk in my car."

I beeped it unlocked and got in the driver's seat. After a momentary hesitation, he opened the passenger door and got in. We both sat staring straight ahead at people going in and out of the diner. I was too wiped out to do anything except wait for whatever he planned to say.

"I loved Marilee," he said softly. "You probably don't believe that, but I did."

"Why wouldn't I believe it?"

"You've talked to Shuga Reasnor, haven't you? I'm sure she's told you that I hated Marilee. She's told everybody that, but it isn't true."

"Dr. Coffey, I don't really give a gnat's ass whether you loved Marilee or not. What I'd like to know is how you knew I was talking about Marilee when I told you I was a pet-sitter. I didn't mention her name, and nothing had been on the news yet about the murders. Not hers and not Frazier's. So how did you know I was talking about Marilee's cat?"

"You think I killed her, don't you?"

"I think it's a definite possibility."

He gave a laugh that sounded more like a sob, and pounded his fist against his khaki knee several times to get himself under control.

"I think it was her skin that I loved most," he said. "She has the most fantastic skin, so smooth, you just want to—"

He broke off and blushed, caught in the act of reliving how Marilee's skin had felt under his hands. "I'm sure I seem pathetic to you," he said. "Hell, I seem pathetic to myself. She was like a disease I'd caught, you know? I didn't intend to start anything with her, it just happened."

I said, "I'm not making any judgments."

"Oh, of course you are. And I don't blame you. I'll tell you something I've never told another soul. I used to look in her windows at night to see if she was with somebody. I would actually hide in the bushes and spy on her." He shook his head sadly, as if he were watching himself doing that shameful thing and couldn't get over how dumb it was.

"Love makes people do crazy things," I said.

"The craziest thing was that even when I saw other men go into her house, I'd still believe her when she told me they didn't mean anything to her. That I was her only one."

"Were you watching her when Harrison Frazier went in? Did you go in and bludgeon them both?"

He raised trembling hands in front of his face and looked at them. "Just telling about this makes me shake. But all this was two years ago. If I'd been going to kill her, I'd have done it then."

"Maybe you waited so nobody would suspect you, and then hired somebody to do it for you."

"No."

"You still haven't explained how you knew it was Marilee I was working for."

"I recognized the cat's collar on your wrist. I was with Marilee when she bought it. We got it in New Orleans from a silversmith. It's one of a kind, I'd know it anywhere."

"So why did you go apeshit just because you knew I was taking care of Marilee's cat? You said, 'I know nothing about this!' What was it you knew nothing about?"

His Adam's apple did a nervous bobble, and I got a whiff of sour breath. "Marilee and Shuga sometimes got involved in moneymaking schemes that turned out to be bogus. I guess I thought they were doing something shady again, and that you thought I was involved in it, too. Because I'd been involved with Marilee."

I turned the key and started the Bronco. "Dr. Coffey, that's about the lamest lie I've ever heard in my life. Now if you'll excuse me, I have work to do."

He gave me a long-searching look, then opened his door. "I didn't kill her," he said. "I really did love her."

I didn't answer, and he shut the door softly and walked across the parking lot. I watched carefully, but his car wasn't black. It was a red Porsche that fairly screamed *man with little dick*. Dr. Coffey might have been telling the truth about being with Marilee when she bought Ghost's collar. He might even have been telling the truth about recognizing it on my wrist. But he sure as hell wasn't telling the truth about why he'd jumped up and threatened to call the police when I spoke to him. He'd had some other fear in mind.

30

I still had two more cats to see, and then I drove to the hospital to visit Phillip. I took the elevator to his floor and followed the arrows to the ICU. Even before I got there, I could hear the beeps of heart monitors and the occasional squeal of an IV or blood bag that had emptied. Doctors were making rounds, and the head nurse darted from cubicle to cubicle as private duty nurses stood aside like penitents at Mass while the doctors leaned over their patients. Fluorescent lights gave everybody a washed-out look. I turned toward Phillip's cubicle, hoping he'd look better than he had before.

He wasn't there. His entire room had been stripped, even to the wall cabinet unit that had held medical supplies.

I must have looked stricken, because the head nurse jogged over and put his hand on my shoulder.

"It's all right," he said. "He went home."

"I was afraid he had—"

"I know. It's this place. It makes you expect the worst. To tell the truth, I don't know why they put him here. His injuries weren't that critical."

"It was for the extra security. I'm surprised the doctor dismissed him so soon."

He looked uncomfortable. "Well, she didn't. His father came and took him against the doctor's advice. He said he could recuperate at home just as well as here, and he took him. We couldn't legally keep him."

I could feel myself going pale. I felt as if I'd just heard Phillip had been shipped off to hell.

The nurse read my face and shrugged. "We did all we could to change his mind, but once the Sheriff's Department removed him from protective custody, we were helpless."

"Did anybody contact Lieutenant Guidry?"

An alarm sounded in one of the cubicles, and he skittered backward a few steps with an apologetic smile. "I'm not sure. We're so busy."

He ran to help somebody whose condition was truly critical, and I retraced my steps down the hall, dialing Guidry as I walked. He wasn't in, so I left a message on his voice mail, telling him that Phillip wasn't safely tucked away in the hospital any longer, but with his parents.

Morosely, I drove to Bayfront Village, where I found Cora up and dressed. She looked worn, but a lot stronger.

"I decided to go downstairs and have a bite in the dining room," she said. "I guess I've been in this room by myself long enough."

"That's good, Cora. Is there anything I can do for you while I'm here?"

"No, dear, I'm all right for now. You've been very sweet to look in on me, Dixie. You're a good girl."

We went into the hall, and as I helped her lock her door, I said, "Cora, what do you know about Dr. Coffey?"

She smiled. "Oh, he's a strange man, dear. I don't go to him anymore, not since he and Marilee split up. They were engaged, you know."

We started walking toward the elevator, Cora taking teensy steps and me slowing down to such a slow pace that I felt off balance.

I said, "I talked to him this morning and he said he had been so jealous of Marilee that he would hide in the bushes and watch her house. I'm wondering if he kept doing that even after they broke off their engagement."

"You're wondering if he killed Harrison and Marilee?"

"I've thought about that, yes."

"Dixie, I told you before, Harrison Frazier killed Marilee. Now I don't know who killed Harrison, and I can't say that I care a whole lot. That's awful, I know, but it's the truth."

"Was Dr. Coffey always your doctor?"

"Not my regular doctor. He just does hearts, I think. No, I had some chest pain and nothing would do Marilee but that I see a heart specialist. She took me to him, and he did some tests. At first, he thought I needed one of those operations where they take a detour around your heart. I don't know how they do that exactly, but people get it done all the time. But then he decided I didn't need that after all, and I just went back a few times. Him and Marilee were pretty hot and heavy there for a while, but then she got mad at him about something, I never did know what, and quit him."

Ahead of us, the elevator doors opened and two elderly women got off and looked around like migrating geese after a landing. One of them said, "Oh, this is the wrong floor," and they giggled like girls. They turned back to the elevator and pushed the button.

Cora and I continued our snail walk toward them. I said, "I heard she and Dr. Coffey were actually in the church about to get married when Marilee called it off."

Cora laughed. "It wasn't that bad, but almost. They were supposed to have a rehearsal for the wedding and she told him before they went. But they weren't in the church, they were at her house. I thought it was just wedding jitters, you know, but she was serious."

The elevator doors opened and the two women hopped inside. They didn't even ask if they should hold it for us. We were moving so slowly, they could have taken several trips before we got to it.

"I also heard a rumor that Dr. Coffey gave Marilee a million dollars just before she called off the wedding. Was that an exaggeration, too?"

"Well, I can't rightly say about that. He may have, I don't know. He's pretty rich, you know, I guess he could have given her some without missing it."

Her voice had taken on a serenely hard edge, and I remembered that Shuga had said it was Cora who had demanded money from the Fraziers when Marilee was pregnant. She apparently found it wholly appropriate that Dr. Coffey might have given Marilee a million dollars, just because he had it to spare. I didn't ask her anything else, and we finally reached the elevator and went downstairs. I declined an invitation to have brunch with her and hugged her good-bye outside the dining room.

The doorman had left my Bronco parked near the front door with the keys in it, so I didn't have to wait for him to get it. I waved to let him know I was the one taking it, then headed toward Marge Preston's Kitty Haven. The time had finally come that I could bring Ghost home, only now the home he was going to was truly *his,* not just where he lived with his owner.

I paid Marge for the time Ghost had been with her, and carried him out in one of my cardboard cases. I could see through the air holes that he was hunkered down in a depressed rabbit pose. Neither of us was holding up well.

At Marilee's house, no reporters lurked in the bushes, and Bull Banks's ugly face wasn't anywhere in sight, but I slowed down when I saw Carl Winnick's black Mercedes in the driveway next door. I could imagine the kind of conversation going on in that house, and it made me sick. Carl Winnick would be spouting his twisted hate for homosexuals, and Olga would be bleating about Phillip's future musical career.

I wanted to call Guidry and yell at him for allowing Phillip to leave the hospital, but I knew he had no reason to hold him there. And if I told him that Phillip shouldn't be with his god-awful parents, he would tell me they had the legal right to take him home. I told myself Phillip's parents loved him. I told myself they wouldn't hurt him any more than he was already hurt, but I didn't believe myself for one minute.

I opened the garage door and pulled inside. When the door shuddered down behind me, I took a deep breath—either of relief or apprehension, I wasn't sure. I got the .38 out of the glove box and put it in my pocket, then carried Ghost into the house through the kitchen door. When I opened the carrying case, he bounded out like a demented gazelle and made several mad careering turns through the house.

When he was run out, he began aggressively sniffing at the walls and making the peculiar face that cats do when they smell certain chemicals. It's called "doing flehmen"—stretching the mouth in a tight little smile, front teeth covered by upper lip. The purpose is to expose pores in the upper gum and palate, where a cat's vomeronasal organ is located—the organ that gives cats a sixth sense, along with the five that humans have. All cats have it, from lions and tigers in the wild to the tamest domestic pussycat. The more they hate a scent, the more pronounced they'll do flehmen. Sometimes it's the only warning an animal or person gets before they're attacked. Tigers, for example, will attack somebody with alcohol on his breath and rip them to shreds.

I never wear any kind of fragrance when I'm working with pets, but watching Ghost's reaction to the odor of chemicals on the walls made me remind myself to be extra careful with scents for a while. Ghost was going to be supersensitive until he got used to all the changes in his life. That made two of us.

I got down an ordinary ceramic bowl—Ghost's silver bowl being not only impounded by the Sheriff's Department but forever rendered too gross to drink from—and put out fresh water for him. He brushed his cheeks and rubbed his ass against all the cabinet doors to leave his scent and reclaim his territory from the haz-mat crew.

I knew he hadn't been eating much at the Kitty Haven, so even though he had already had breakfast, I got out his food dish. Ordinarily, I preach a daily diet of dried organic food, because it contains all the nutrients a cat needs to stay sleek and healthy. But a constant healthy diet gets pretty boring, even for cats, so an occasional dish of canned stuff is okay as a special treat. Ghost loved sliced beef in gravy the way I loved bacon, and after all he'd been through, I thought he needed sliced beef. I wouldn't have minded some myself.

Marilee kept a ten-pound bag of dried cat food in the pantry, along with stacks of canned food. I opened the pantry door and did a double take.

"Huh," I said. When you're all by yourself with a cat, you can make an intelligent comment like that without having to explain yourself.

The pantry was L-shaped, with the short end at the left of the door.

In the past, the sack of dried food had sat on the floor under the long shelves, and stacks of canned food, jars of catnip, boxes of special treats, and some kitty toys had taken up a long shelf facing the door. Now they took up two shelves on the short end. Marilee had apparently re-arranged the pantry since I'd last seen it.

As I moved cans of veal and lamb and chicken around on the short shelves, looking for sliced beef, I realized the shelves were now only half as deep as they used to be. Marilee hadn't just rearranged her shelves, she had remodeled them.

"Huh," I said again, my repertoire of intelligent exclamations being somewhat limited by then.

I got out a can of sliced beef and opened it for Ghost. He began to swoon with ecstasy even before I put the bowl on the floor. Then I went back to the pantry and removed everything on the newly foreshortened shelves so I could get a better look at the back wall.

It looked like all the other wallboard unless you looked closely, then you could see it was freshly painted hardwood. I got a knife and slid it in the crack on the left. I moved the knife up and down without hitting any resistance. I did the same thing on the right side, and hit resistance at the top, middle, and bottom.

"Bingo," I whispered. The back of the shelf was a hinged door.

Right then, I should have got on the phone and called Guidry. I should have confessed that I had an invoice to a wall safe in a folder in my desk drawer. Should have admitted that I had opened Marilee's mail and found the invoice. I should also have told him I had been keeping this information from him, and that I had no earthly reason for doing so except that Marilee had lost her daughter, too. Even I knew that was an irrational reason to hide evidence, but it seemed logical at the time. If I could protect her secrets, she and I wouldn't be so vulnerable.

I tried prying the door open with the knife, but it didn't budge. Thinking it must have a pressure-sensitive latch, I pushed my fingers all along the top edge of the door. When I got to the left side, I heard a click, and the door swung open.

"Oh gosh," I whispered, because a cream-colored safe was set flush inside the wall.

"Oh hell," I muttered, because the safe had both a combination and a keyed lock.

To open this sucker, you not only had to get inside Marilee's mind and figure out her code, you also had to have a key.

My cell phone rang and I froze. Only two or three people in the world had my cell number, and I wasn't looking forward to talking to any of them. It was Michael, calling from the fire station.

He said, "Are you okay?"

"Yeah, I really am."

"You're at Tom Hale's, right?"

I twisted the toe of one of my Keds into the floor, exactly the way I used to do when we were kids and Michael quizzed me about something we both knew I'd done and I was denying. I took a deep breath and straightened my back. I was thirty-two years old and I could do anything I wanted.

"Actually, I'm at Marilee's house. I'm going to spend a few days here. I'll explain about it later. It's a long story."

He said, "Are you crazy?"

"I think that's still to be decided."

"Aw shit, Dixie, I don't like this one bit. That asshole Dr. Win is right next door. He'll have every reporter in town over there."

"I don't think so. I think this is the last place anybody would think to look for me. I'll be back in a day or two. After this blows over."

He warned me about a hundred times to call if I needed anything, and I promised I would.

He said, "I don't like it, but I guess it's okay."

"I love you."

"Love you, too, Dix."

That's my big brother, the gentle giant.

Ghost was still hunkered over his sliced beef, blissfully chewing with his eyes half-closed. I went back to the pantry and and fingered the safe's keyhole. I hadn't expected to need a key. People usually select a birth date or address or Social Security number for a numerical code, so I had thought I had everything I would need to open the safe when I found it. Needing a key was a major problem.

I looked around the kitchen. If Marilee had chosen the pantry to hide the safe, maybe she had hidden the key in the kitchen, too. But before I started searching, I needed to take care of my primary business of pet-sitting. I sat at the kitchen bar and used my cell phone to check phone messages at my apartment. A few more reporters had called, and one client had called all the way from North Carolina to say she had heard the news about me and didn't want me going back in her house. She had called another sitter, she said, and she would never hire me again.

That really hurt my feelings. I felt like a little kid whose best friend had just told her she didn't like her anymore.

The last call was from Phillip Winnick. His words were slurred, but more intelligible than they'd been the day before. It wasn't how he talked that alarmed me, it was what he said.

"Um, Miz Hemingway . . . I mean Dixie . . . this is Phillip . . . If I don't see you again . . . I just want to say . . . thank you . . . That's all. Oh, and . . . I'm sorry I lied."

I played the message several times, and every time he sounded terrified and desperate. Something was going on, and whatever it was had made Phillip think he might not see me again. I put the phone down with a chill running down my spine.

31

Feeling leaden and dull, I took a shower and changed clothes. No matter how hard I tried to convince myself that the Winnicks loved Phillip, I couldn't shake a feeling of impending doom. Phillip was about as scared and miserable as a kid could get, and it sounded as if he was feeling guilt for not being honest about being gay. I knew his family wasn't likely to give him the love and support he needed. If anything, they were more likely to add to his despondency. Phillip needed a friend, and right now I might be the only one he had.

I finally couldn't stand it any longer, so I marched out the front door and down the street to the Winnicks' house.

I could hear voices shouting even before I got to the front door. Olga Winnick shrill and pleading, Carl Winnick harsh and threatening. Under their harangue, a tortured undertone that was Phillip. It was exactly what my worst fears had been, and maybe even worse. I didn't care if Phillip was their son, I was going to take him out of there. He was over eighteen, they couldn't keep him if he wanted to leave.

I jabbed the doorbell and then banged on the door for good measure. Once I could have yelled, "Sheriff's Department, open up!" but I couldn't do that anymore. Anyway, I wasn't there in any official capacity. I was there as a friend, which takes precedence over all other reasons.

The door didn't open, and the yelling continued. I rang the bell again and banged harder on the door. Olga screamed, a long wail that brought fine bumps to my skin. Carl Winnick shouted something that sounded like "What the hell are you doing?"

Faintly, I heard Phillip reply, but I couldn't make out the words.

Something was terribly wrong. I grabbed the handle on the door and tried the thumb latch. The door wasn't locked. I rapped on it one more time and pushed it open, calling out as I did.

"Hello? Phillip?"

Olga and Carl Winnick stood in the shadowy living room with their backs to me, their postures strained and stiff and angry. Phillip stood beyond them in front of the closed drapes. I couldn't see him very well in the murky light, but he seemed to be in dark pajamas almost the same shade as the bruises on his face.

Olga whirled and shrieked, "Get out of my house!"

I didn't try any pretense. I said, "I've come to get Phillip."

Olga came at me like an avenging Fury, actually running with her arm held out stiff and her fist closed like a battering ram. The woman was nuts if she thought she could scare me with that fist.

I grabbed her wrist and twisted it, then got her other wrist and locked it behind her back. The woman was wiry, and stronger than I'd expected, but I knew I could have her on the floor in a second. She seemed to know that, too, because she didn't kick at me, just twisted her stiff neck and panted like a tethered dragon, sending out hot air and the odor of liquor.

Carl Winnick ran past us toward the kitchen. Without his executive suit jacket, his barrel chest and short legs made him look almost pathetically misshapen.

Olga said, "This is all your fault! You and people like you, filling his head with filthy ideas!"

I called to Phillip over her head. "Phillip, you're a good, decent, talented young man, and you don't have to stay here. Come with me."

He shook his head. "It won't . . . make any difference."

"It will! Of course it will. You're hurt now, but you'll heal and every-thing will be okay. You don't have to live a lie anymore."

"Just . . . live with my parents hating me."

"They don't really hate you. They just don't know you. They'll change, you'll see."

Carl ran from the kitchen and jammed his red face close to mine. "I've called the police, girl, so you'd best leave before they come and arrest you."

I stared at him, and something clicked into place in my brain.

Phillip took a couple of steps forward and said, "Leave her alone, Dad."

That's when I saw the gun. The barrel was dark, like his pajamas, and he carried it with the muzzle pointed down by his thigh. In his large hand, the stock was almost invisible. But I could see the telltale red pinprick that showed the safety was off. I should have known. In addition to teaching his son to open doors for ladies, Carl Winnick had taught his son how to handle a semiautomatic.

I said, "Phillip, what are you doing with a gun?"

Too calmly, he said, "I'm going to kill myself with it."

Most of the time when people threaten to kill themselves, you can hear in their voice a silent plea to talk them out of it. To bargain with them. To promise them that things will change, that their lives will get easier, that some injustice to them will be righted, that somebody will listen to them and actually hear what they're saying. Phillip wasn't do-ing any of those things. He was stating a cool intention, one that he'd al-ready worked out in his head, one for which he could see no alternative.

Carl said, "Didn't you learn anything when you got beaten up?"

"I learned how ashamed I make you. I learned I'll never be the son you want."

Slowly, Phillip's arm raised so the gun's barrel was at the side of his head. I heard a silent whimpering inside my own head, and a sick metallic taste coated my mouth. I had to stop him somehow, but every idea carried the possibility of making him pull the trigger.

Even Carl seemed to understand that something had to be said that would change Phillip's mind.

"I'm not an unforgiving man, son, you know that. You can make me proud of you again!"

Phillip's voice took on a new irony. "Sure, all I have to do is kill myself."

"Do you have any idea what that would do to me and your mother? Do you want to heap more shame on us?"

I lost hope then. Just completely lost the last thread of thin hope I'd been clinging to.

So did Phillip. Wearily, he said, "There's more than one way to kill myself. With a bullet, or living the way you want me to live. Either way, I'll be dead."

I had loosened my hold on Olga, and she suddenly twisted free.

"Phillip, we're going to send you to a hospital! They'll cure you! When you're yourself again, you can still go to Juilliard!"

Phillip barked a hoarse laugh that jerked his head backward, and the gun sounded with a roaring blast. He crumpled to the floor with blood spilling around his head in a bright pool. Olga screamed and covered her face with both hands. Carl gripped the door frame and stared goggle-eyed and frozen. I tried to push past them, my cell phone in hand, already dialing 911.

I didn't realize I was sobbing until Deputy Jesse Morgan gently shoved me aside.

"Somebody already called," he said.

He had his own phone out, calling for an ambulance, then he rushed to Phillip and blocked my view.

The thin wail of an ambulance's siren was already cutting through the midmorning heat, and I knew that several more cars from the Sheriff's Department would soon arrive. I walked back to Marilee's house and closed the door.

I didn't want to see them take Phillip's body out in a bag. I was afraid I might kill Carl Winnick if I did.

Back in Marilee's guest room, I crawled into bed. With the wooden blinds closed, the room was dark as a cave, and the stucco walls were thick enough to muffle sounds from outside. If I covered my head with a pillow, I couldn't hear any noise at all from the Winnicks' house.

I knew how to do this. I knew how to numb myself from horror. I knew how to withdraw into myself so the sharp edges of reality wouldn't scrape me and jab me and cut me. I had thought I could face life, but I couldn't. I didn't even want to.

Ghost slithered under the covers and pushed himself into the crook of my body, sending his body heat into my stomach. Instinctively, I cupped my hands around him and felt his heart beating. His rough tongue lapped at my wrist, and he began to purr. Dumb animal to dumb animal, he was sending me love in the only way he knew how, and gradually it crept into my cold veins and to my anguished heart.

I finally had to admit to myself that it wasn't the world I was retreating from, but my own rage. I truly and sincerely might take my .38 in hand and go over and fill Carl Winnick with bullets. I truly and sincerely might go over and pistol-whip Olga Winnick to death. I had it in me to do that, and I knew it and was terrified by it. I also knew there's nothing so paralyzing as unexpressed fury.

My cell phone rang in my pocket and sent Ghost scrambling out of bed. I checked the ID and groaned. It was Guidry.

Without any preambles, he said, "Dixie, the Winnick boy is alive. He's on his way to St. Pete's trauma center. I don't know how badly he's hurt, but he's alive."

I sat up and wiped at the tears on my face with the edge of the sheet. "Carl Winnick was the man who took the pipe away from Tanisha. He either clubbed Phillip himself or he hired Bull Banks to do it for him."

"How do you know that?"

"I just know. He used the same words to me that he used to Tanisha, called us both 'girl.' I know it was him."

"Deputy Morgan says you were at the door when Phillip shot himself. The Winnicks say they don't know why he did it. Do you?"

"Sure. He told them why. They didn't want the son they had, and he couldn't live with that. His mother's response was that they were going to send him to a hospital to 'cure' him."

"Jesus. Poor kid."

"You'll go after Carl Winnick, right? Because if you don't, I will."

"No you won't."

The phone went dead, and I slammed it against the covers.

"Son of a bitch! Egotistical bastard! Shithead!"

Yelling is always good when you feel totally helpless.

But Phillip wasn't dead. Maybe a miracle would happen and he would be okay.

I got out of bed.

My cell rang again, this time Michael calling from the firehouse. "Dixie, I just heard about the Winnick boy."

I collapsed right where I stood, crumpling to the floor and sobbing into the phone. "Oh Michael, that sweet, gentle boy! His beautiful face!"

"I know, Dixie. I know."

"It's not fair!"

"No, it's not."

Huddled on the floor, I clutched the phone to my chest and cried so hard it seemed I was stripping out the lining of my throat. I cried for the horror of what had happened to Phillip, for what had happened to Todd and Christy, and for every other senseless tragedy that destroys the light of the shining young. I don't know how long I cried, but when I was able to hear again, I lifted the phone to my ear and Michael was still there, still holding me from his end of the line.

I said, "I'm okay."

"If you need me, I can take a sick day and be with you."

"No, I'm fine, really."

"Call me in a couple of hours, okay?"

I wiped my wet face and nodded at the phone. "I will, but don't worry. I really am okay. Or at least as okay as anybody would be after . . . you know."

"Yeah. I'm not worried, but call me anyway."

I got up and washed my face. What I'd told Michael had been true. Anybody would be disturbed by watching a boy shoot himself in the head, and the fact that I wasn't any more upset than the average neurotic was encouraging.

Ghost trotted after me and patted at my ankles. I knelt to stroke his silvery fur, and he nosed his head into my hand and arched his back, insistent as a needy baby. I went to the Bronco and got my grooming kit out and took Ghost to the lanai. Pulling my slicker brush through his hair until his coat was smooth and shiny calmed us both down.

As I brushed him, I looked toward the Winnicks' house. I could see a back window that was probably in Phillip's room. He had been outside that window when he saw a woman get into a car in Marilee's driveway. I had been sure that was the reason he had been beaten up, but I had been wrong. Phillip had been beaten because Carl Winnick had hired somebody to scare him straight, to punish him for being gay, to destroy his burgeoning self-esteem . . . who knew what Winnick's sick reasons were?

I don't often use the word *evil*. It smacks too much of wild-eyed fanatics eager to control the world by imposing their skewed ideas of right and wrong. But when I thought about the kind of mind that would hire a thug to beat up his own son because the kid was gay, the only word that came to mind was *evil*. Carl Winnick was truly an evil man, and the fact that he presented himself to the world as the voice of morality made him all the worse.

When Ghost was combed and feeling sleek again, I left my grooming supplies on the lanai table and carried Ghost through the slider before I pulled it closed. I've learned not to try to coax any cat through a door, because they will always get halfway in and decide to contemplate the secrets of life while you stand there like an idiot telling them to please get a move on. Instead, I carry them over the threshold like brides.

It took two hands to securely lock the slider, so I put Ghost back on the floor before I locked it. Then with Ghost trotting by my side, I went back in the kitchen and made a cup of tea. I drank it sitting at the snack bar while I imagined what was happening to Phillip at the trauma center. Doctors would be fighting for his life. There might be surgery, blood transfusions, ventilators, and all the other modern techniques that exist to preserve life. But no matter how many devices I could envision working for him, I couldn't escape the reality of what a bullet does when it explodes inside a skull.

I washed Ghost's food bowl and my teacup while Ghost twined in and out between my ankles, arching his back and rubbing against me with his tail held high. I was touched. Cats have tiny scent glands on their faces and at the roots of their tails. When they rub against you, it's their way of mixing their scent with yours. You can't get any closer to a living being than sharing odors, and Ghost was telling me that he and I were now bonded as one. He was signing on as my closest friend, my confidant, and my protector.

Even domestic cats can be vicious, and Ghost was also letting me know that if he and I went hunting together in the wild, he would pounce on a rodent, stick his daggerlike eyeteeth in it, and sever its spine for me. He would shred its flesh into bite-size chunks and share them with me. Since we weren't in the wild, he would have to content himself with bringing me the occasional unlucky lizard caught on the lanai. All that bonding behavior made it even more imperative that I find a new owner for Ghost before he became too attached to me. He had already lost one person he loved, I didn't want him to lose another one.

I left our dishes draining on the counter and went back to the pantry and looked at the safe again. It didn't seem so important anymore, but I had to get my mind off what was happening to Phillip. I fingered the keyhole again. It was small, so they key would be small, too, and easily concealed. Just the thought of looking in all the possible places Marilee could have hidden it was mind-numbing. Guessing the numbers for the code would be a lot easier.

I got the numbers I'd copied from Marilee's ruined tax return and went back to the safe to demonstrate my savvy knowledge of how people use their birth dates or Social Security numbers or house numbers for codes they commit to memory. Easy for them to remember, but also easy for a burglar to figure out. Not that I was a burglar. I was more of a protector.

Ghost watched intently while I tried the first six digits of Marilee's Social Security number. I tried the last six digits. I tried them both backward. I tried her birth date, first by month and year, then by day, month, and year. I tried them backward, too. I tried her house address and her zip code and various parts of her phone number. Nothing worked.

I closed the wooden door over the safe, replaced the cat food on the shelf, and crawled back in bed. Ghost joined me, staying politely down by my feet but close enough to warm me. Immediately, visions of Phillip shooting himself swam before my eyes. I hadn't seen Phillip's injury before Deputy Morgan pulled me aside, but I had seen the gun and I knew what an exploding bullet does.

In the trauma center at St. Pete, doctors were working to save Phillip's life. But if they succeeded, would he be Phillip or a pitiful shell without a mind? Without consciousness of his surroundings, without the ability to think or create, without the ability to live with any degree of joy? To me, such a life was not a life, but a breathing death.

I hadn't been on speaking terms with God since Todd and Christy were killed, but now I had a little talk with him. Or her, as the case may be. I said, I'm still mad at you for taking Todd and Christy, but maybe you did that because they were hurt so badly that they wouldn't have been *them* if they'd lived. They would have hated that, so I guess you did the right thing. Now Phillip has been hurt, and he would hate having to live not as himself. He would hate not being able to play the piano, not being able to have fun, not being able to love and be loved. So I just want you to know that if you decide to take Phillip, I'll understand. I won't like it, but I'll understand. Not that you need me to okay what you do. But if he can have a good life in spite of what happened, then I ask you to help the doctors save him. That's all. Amen.

It probably wasn't much of a prayer by most people's standards, but it was the best I could do and it made me feel better.

I slept for a little while, and when I woke, I was ready to take care of the cats and dogs on my schedule. Ghost was sunning himself on a window ledge when I left, and he blinked a couple of I love you's when I said good-bye. We were making progress.

32

Tom Hale was hovering near the door waiting for me when I got to his condo. He had heard about Phillip's suicide attempt on the news, and he was determined to find out everything I knew. I gave him the short version, but it was still a lot to condense. When I told him what I suspected about Carl Winnick, he shook his head in disgust.

"That's always the way," he said. "Those sanctimonious holier-than-thou types are always covering up something rotten. I hope they roast his balls over an open flame."

"First, they'll have to prove he did it."

"The boy, how bad is he?"

"It was to his head, Tom."

Tom looked down at his ruined legs. "It would be better for the kid if he doesn't make it. Not if it's to the head."

I felt tears coming, so I stood up and got Billy Elliot's leash and snapped it on his collar. Tom rolled his chair toward me and fixed me with a stern look.

"Dixie, don't try too hard to make sense of any of this. Life doesn't make any sense. Like they say, bad things happen to good people. It's like chaos theory. You know chaos theory?"

I considered my options. If I was honest and said I didn't know diddly about chaos theory, Tom would tell me everything about it twice, and I'd never get away. If I lied and said chaos theory and I were old friends, he'd catch me in my ignorance and I'd still end up hearing all about it.

I sighed. "Tom, I really have to go. I've got a million things happening at once and none of them make any sense, and so far as I can tell, they're all impossible."

He smiled and gave me a thumbs-up. "You've got it, Dixie! That's chaos theory!"

When I got back to Marilee's house, a green-and-white vehicle from the Community Policing Unit was in the Winnicks' driveway—either to gather information or to offer the services of the Victim Assistance Unit.

I laid my .38 on the kitchen bar, and sat on a bar stool to use Marilee's phone to call the trauma center at St. Pete. A woman told me she could not provide any information about any patient, period.

I said, "I just want to know if he's still alive."

"I'm sorry. I can't tell you anything."

I had known before I called that I wouldn't get anywhere. To the woman answering the phone, I could be a ghoulish reporter following up a lead on a kid who'd committed suicide, or I could be the person who had pulled the trigger, checking to see if I'd been successful.

I called Guidry to see if he knew anything, but he didn't answer his cell, so I left a message.

I fed Ghost, showered, and changed clothes, then went out to the lanai to get the grooming supplies I'd left on the table when I combed him. Phillip's window was dark. I walked to the side screened door to look at it, as if the window held some secret that might help Phillip live. Phillip's phone message now made perfect sense. He had already decided to kill himself when he called. He had wanted to thank me and to apologize for lying before he died. He should have known he didn't need to apologize to me, especially not for lying about being gay.

A coil of surprise moved at the base of my skull, and I looked at Phillip's window again. Drought-tolerant Bahia grass grew from Marilee's lanai to the wooden fence that marked the back boundary at the woods, with a bed of low junipers separating her yard from the Winnicks'. I opened the lanai's screened side door, stepped out onto the grass, and went to stand at Phillip's window. From that spot, I looked toward Marilee's driveway. It was completely hidden from view by the corner of her house. Even the street in front of her house was invisible from Phillip's window. I walked down the side of his house until I came to a spot where I could see Marilee's driveway and the walk from her front door. It was at the very front of the Winnicks' house, next to their garage. If Phillip had seen a Miata pull into Marilee's driveway, it hadn't been from his window.

With my mind whirling, I went back to Marilee's lanai and picked up my grooming supplies. As I was going through the glass door, my cell phone started beeping from the kitchen bar and I hurriedly pulled the slider closed and sprinted to answer it. It was Michael, his voice anxious because I hadn't answered promptly. I told him I was absolutely jim-dandy and not to worry. I still hadn't told him about the safe, but now didn't seem the time. I also didn't tell him that I'd just discovered that Phillip had lied to me.

I put my grooming supplies in the Bronco and went back to the kitchen. I was hungry, but there was still the danger of being caught out by a reporter or by Bull Banks out on bail, so I toasted some waffles from Marilee's freezer and ate them dry while I thought about Phillip's lie. He had lied either about where he'd been when he saw a woman leave Marilee's house or about what he'd seen. I tried to put myself in the shoes of an eighteen-year-old kid who had seen something connected with a murder. Could he have heard a woman's footsteps and a car's engine and then exaggerated, saying he'd seen a woman walking and a black Miata pulling in the driveway? Maybe. Or maybe the Miata pulled back far enough for him to see it in the street when it drove away. It made me too sad when I thought that Phillip might not live to explain what he'd lied about, so I wrenched my mind away from the lie and focused on the combination to Marilee's safe.

I hadn't given up on the expectation that it would involve numbers most familiar to Marilee, but I had already tried the obvious ones. I got a bottle of water from the refrigerator and leaned on the bar to drink it, staring blindly at the phone on the counter. Ghost came and wound sinuously around my legs, rubbing his silky hair against my bare skin. Marilee had probably stood in exactly this spot a million times, talking on the phone while he rubbed against her ankles.

Marilee had loved Ghost. She had chosen a strange name for him, but I supposed it had meaning to her. Thinking about that made the hairs on the back of my neck rise to attention. What if Marilee hadn't been thinking of numbers when she chose a combination for the safe? What if she had been thinking of a word? I grabbed a pen and wrote *Ghost*. Then I looked at the phone's keypad and put the corresponding number under each letter.

I went to the safe and punched in 1 1 6 7 8. A satisfying click told me I had guessed right. The combination to the safe was the name Ghost. Now that I had figured it out, it made perfect sense. All I had to do now was find the key to open the second lock.

I toasted some more waffles and tried to think where I would hide a key if I were Marilee. The killer had ransacked her closet and the drawers in her bedroom and bathroom. I had assumed he'd been searching for the safe, but maybe he'd known where the safe was and had been searching for the key. If that were true, maybe he'd had reason to search where he did.

I got a black plastic garbage bag and went into Marilee's bathroom. Ghost sat on the countertop and watched me empty bottles of lotions and boxes of powder, throwing the empties in the trash. I checked for a key inside every bottle and jar in the medicine chest and tossed them, too. Except for some aspirin and several bottles of vaginal gel guaranteed to feel like natural secretions, Marilee's medicine cabinet was as innocent as a twelve-year-old girl's. No prescription painkillers, no tranquilizers or antidepressants, no stimulants or hormones. Except for an occasional headache or dry vagina, Marilee had apparently been bloomingly healthy.

I gathered up some unopened bottles of perfume and cologne and bath oil to take to Cora along with a bunch of scented candles with virgin wicks. The rest went in the trash bag, including half a dozen sticks of mascara and enough lipsticks to paint the lips of every woman in Sarasota and still have some left over for Bradenton. Ghost followed me when I hauled the bag out to the garage and stashed it in the garbage can. I made a mental note to remember to put the can out at the curb Thursday night, then went back into the kitchen.

Getting rid of the bathroom trash had made me feel more organized. I hadn't found the key, but at least I was doing something constructive.

I stood in the middle of the kitchen and looked around. Get focused, I told myself. Think.

I put a colander in the sink. Then I went through all the cupboards and got out every sack of flour and sugar and cornmeal, every box of cereal, every jar of spices, every opened package of anything. Ghost sat on the counter, intently watching my every move, his head turning like somebody watching a tennis match while I sifted everything through the colander. I ended up with a sinkful of dry stuff that would probably stop up the drains.

I looked at Ghost. "I should have done this over the wastebasket, shouldn't I?"

He looked at me and let the vertical aperture in his eyes widen, but not in a judgmental way.

I scooped the mess into a big bowl and dumped it into a garbage can under the sink, but I hadn't given up yet. I got out all the jars in the refrigerator and lined them up next to the sink. I stuck my hand inside jars of jelly and jam and pickle relish and mayonnaise and mustard. All I got for my trouble was yucky fingers and gross condiments which I then tossed in the trash. Ghost's whiskers wavered and he scooted back from the sink's edge, disgust written all over his face.

Pointedly, he got to his feet and arched his back and yawned. I knew what he was saying: It was bedtime, and I was wasting my time. But I couldn't stop. I searched the refrigerator's vegetable drawer and meat drawer. I got out every opened bag of frozen vegetables and dumped them in the colander, running hot water on them in case the key was frozen inside a solid mass of peas or carrots. At least I could get rid of the ruined vegetables by pushing them down the disposal.

Ghost left me when I turned on the disposal. He had been loyal, but even an Abyssinian's loyalty has its limits.

I sat down at the bar and glumly considered my options. If I told Guidry about the safe, he could have somebody from the department crack it. But that would mean I'd have to tell him about the invoice I'd found in Marilee's mail. And then I'd have to come up with a good explanation for not telling him before. And what if the safe held a wad of cash or valuable jewels? Common sense told me I was still a possible suspect. The same common sense told me that nobody considered me a strong suspect, because I'd had nothing to gain by the murders. But if there was a chunk of money in the safe, Guidry might think I'd known about it all along.

See how the mind works when you have an overactive conscience? Not to mention a guilty secret.

In my dream, Marilee had said, "You have the key." I had thought she meant it in a metaphorical way, but maybe I was trying too hard to read symbols into something that was literal. Like Freud said, sometimes a cigar is just a cigar. Maybe she meant a real key. Maybe I had the key to the safe in my possession and my subconscious was trying to remind me of that.

Thinking of the dream brought back the image of Marilee holding Ghost. Maybe that was the dream's message—the key had something to do with Ghost. Marilee had chosen Ghost's name as the numerical code for the safe, so maybe the key was hidden with something of Ghost's, too. With a burst of inspiration, I sprinted to the pantry and grabbed the bag of dried cat food and dumped it into the sink. I searched through it, stirring it and turning it with both hands, but I didn't find a key. Guiltily, I put it back into the bag handful by careful handful. Ghost came back in the kitchen and jumped on the counter while I did that, giving me a look that suggested he would eat food that had been roiled around in the sink when hell froze over.

I went back to the bar and drank some more water. Ghost hopped down from the counter and meowed up at me. In the bright kitchen light, his shiny fur gleamed like silver. I knelt and stroked his head and neck.

"I wish you could talk. You probably know where the key is."

He gave me a couple of I love you blinks, and in the next instant, I was racing for my backpack. I rummaged inside and pulled out Ghost's velvet collar with its little silver hearts and keys. A silly, frivolous thing for a cat to wear, a one-of-a-kind item made by a silversmith in New Orleans and bought on a trip Marilee had made with Dr. Coffey. I turned it around, examining each silver key, and then found the one that was heavier and thicker than the others.

"Hot damn," I whispered.

It was a real key, not just a charm, and I had been carrying it around all week in my backpack. I cut it off with Marilee's kitchen shears, and went back to the safe. The key glided into the lock like a hot knife into butter. I wiped my hands on my shorts and pulled the door open. Inside the safe was a stack of manila envelopes.

Carrying the stack with both hands, I went to the bar and put it down as gingerly as I would lay a ticking bomb. The stack tipped over and envelopes fanned out beside my gun and cell phone. I took a deep breath and moved the gun and phone over a bit. A thin thread of warning spiraled across my cortex like a figure skater making frantic figure eights, but I ignored it. If the contents of the envelopes held information vital to the murder investigation, I would most certainly call Guidry and turn them over to him. But if these were records having to do with Marilee's daughter and her relationship with Harrison Frazier, I would protect them. For Marilee's sake. For Lily's sake. For Cora's sake. Maybe for my own sake.

The envelopes were the kind that have a metal clasp to hold the flap down, and my fingers trembled a little when I pulled up the prongs on the first one and opened the flap. I upended the envelope and let its contents slide out onto the bar. They were photographs, all turned face-down. Expecting a photograph of Lily in her formative years, I turned over the one on top. It wasn't Lily. It was definitely not Lily.

It was a view of a large naked man laid out on a messy bed. His arms were spread across the rumpled sheet and his hairy legs were open. Incongruously, he wore black dress socks. A black-headed woman lay prone between his legs with her face shoved into his crotch. A blond woman hovered above him with her breasts dangling above his head, and his lips had a firm hold on one of her nipples. Neither woman's face was clear, both being shrouded by long hair, but the man's face was clearly visible. He could not have looked any sillier.

All the other photographs were of the same man, and some of the poses made the first one seem innocent. The man had been caught in every conceivable obscene position with two hookers. He had not only made a complete and total fool of himself, he had exposed himself to eighteen kinds of blackmail, loss of respect, ridicule, and perhaps loss of his loved ones. Each photograph bore the date and time, as if the photographer wanted them to have every possible stamp of validity. A ruled sheet of paper was folded with the photographs. In her rounded handwriting, Marilee had recorded a column of dates, with numbers beside each date. The dates went back over five years, regular as a calendar every month. The amounts were regular, too. Five thousand, five thousand, five thousand. There were no dollar signs, but I assumed the numbers referred to money received.

I put the photos back in the envelope and washed my hands at the sink. Before I went back to the other envelopes, I drank a glass of water. Revulsion really dries up the mouth. The next envelope held almost identical photos, but the man was different. This one was a squat, round man with a receding hairline. He looked vaguely familiar, but I couldn't place him. The two women were the same blonde and brunette, and the man's look of mindless bliss was also the same. Another ruled sheet of paper with a column of dates and figures, but this one had started only two years ago. The numbers were greater, though. Eight thousand every month. Next to the dates and amounts, Marilee had noted where the money had gone, always distributed in amounts of one or two thousand dollars to several mutual funds. Marilee had apparently believed in diversity. Cora had been right, Marilee *had* been good with numbers. Big numbers. She had also had a savvy sense of how to invest small amounts of cash without attracting attention.

I had to wash my hands again before I opened the other envelopes.

It wasn't that I found the graphic sexual images so shocking, it was the reason for the photographs being taken that made me feel like I'd been dipped in a vat of congealed chicken fat. The reason was obviously blackmail. And while the two women were always careful to keep their faces hidden from the camera, I was almost positive they were Marilee and Shuga. At least one mystery was solved. Now I knew how two women without any marketable skills could make an indecent amount of money. Literally.

I went through the other envelopes with increasing horror, revulsion, and reluctant admiration.

The photographs of Dr. Gerald Coffey were in the fourth envelope, and they confirmed my first mental image of his hairy back. The pose that exposed it was a special one, involving the insertion of a large dildo into his equally hairy backside while he knelt on all fours and apparently howled like a wolf. It was not the sort of pose that would inspire confidence and trust in heart-surgery patients. Which was no doubt why the column listing his payments culminated in the number one, followed by six zeros. The million he had paid Marilee before she jilted him at the altar had been hush money, not the love money he claimed. Wondering briefly why she had ever considered marrying him in the first place, I moved on to the other envelopes.

33

The photographs seemed almost commonplace now, all of naked men made hopelessly vulnerable by lust and stupidity. Some of the faces looked faintly familiar, and I assumed they were in the public eye in one way or another. Each of them had been paying Marilee between five and ten thousand dollars a month for years. Even splitting the take with Shuga, she would have been raking in a considerable amount of money. With the quarter million she got every year from Harrison Frazier's family, she surely had never worried about paying the rent.

The vulnerable fifteen-year-old girl who had been tricked into giving her baby to Harrison Frazier's sister had grown up to be a woman who extorted money from a lot of men for the sheer pleasure of it. The money the Fraziers had given her had been more than enough for her and Cora to have a good life. It had been enough to live well in the present and also invest for the future. But it hadn't been enough to fill the need Marilee had nurtured, the need to have control over men and to make them pay. And she had been aided and abetted by her friend Shuga, the poor girl who wouldn't have had enough to eat if Marilee's grandmother hadn't fed her. I wondered if all the money they'd taken had ever made up for what they thought they'd missed out on.

Now I knew what Shuga had come to get, and why she had been so frightened. If Marilee had the only copy of the photographs, Shuga's blackmail income was now up shit creek. From what Cora had said, Marilee had always been the cleverer of the two, the one who had led the way. It made sense that she would have controlled not only the money but the photographs. I wondered if Marilee and Shuga had had a dispute that made Marilee change her locks to keep Shuga out. If Marilee had decided to cut Shuga out of her share of the blackmail income, Shuga might have come for the photographs, gotten into a fight with Marilee, and killed her. But where did Harrison Frazier fit into that scenario? Had he simply stumbled into a situation by accident and been killed because he knew who killed Marilee?

I spilled out another photograph and my heart jumped crazily. I should have known he would be included, but I was still shocked. It was Carl Winnick, apparently photographed so recently that there were no payments listed yet.

There were still some unopened envelopes, but I had a question that interested me more than seeing the rest of them. Who had been taking the pictures? Who was the third party to this blackmail ring? I shuffled through another collection, this time searching for clues to the place where they'd been taken. In every photo, the camera had been positioned so nothing was visible inside the frame except the sheets on the mattress, the two women, and the victim. Such consistency suggested a tripod holding the camera, but surely none of these wealthy men would have cavorted in front of a camera he could see.

I left the photos on the bar and went down the hall to Marilee's bedroom, flipping lights on as I went. It was past midnight now, and I should have been in bed two hours ago, but I was wide-awake and curious. When I flipped the switch in Marilee's bedroom, the bedside lamp on the far side of the bed lighted up, and Ghost lifted his sleepy head from his spot in the middle of the bed and gave me an annoyed look.

The armoire faced the foot of the bed, and I supposed they could have left the doors ajar and positioned a camera on one of its shelves. I opened both doors and looked for a spot where a camera might have been placed, but the shelves were filled with a large-screen TV, a VCR, a

DVD and a CD player, not to mention speakers, along with filed videos and CDs neatly organized according to musical category and artist. Somehow, the idea of Marilee disturbing the neat order of her entertainment center for a smut-capturing camera didn't fit. And even if she'd been willing to lower her neatness standards to accommodate her lack of moral standards, it would have been too risky. Even with all their blood pooled in their penises, the men would have noticed the open doors to the armoire and gotten suspicious.

I looked toward the top of the armoire. It was a perfect place to hide a camera, using one of the remote controls in Marilee's night table to turn it on. I dragged a high-backed Spanish Colonial armchair from the corner of the room over to the armoire and climbed on it. From that height, I could see a camera mounted behind a perfectly round lens-size hole drilled in the carved cornice. I felt a tug of reluctant admiration for the way Marilee had gone about the business of blackmail. She had been resourceful, efficient, and organized, all marks of the true professional.

Ghost suddenly sat upright with his ears and whiskers pointed toward the door. At the same moment, I smelled the reek of alcohol behind me and whirled to see Olga Winnick in the doorway, her eyes blood-red with fury and despair, her mouth a rectangular gash of malicious rage. She held a butcher knife in her raised hand, with an unmistakable intention to kill me with it.

Suddenly, it seemed inevitable that she was the one. I said, "I should have known it was you."

She swallowed with a convulsive movement of her neck, which made me think of pythons swallowing mice. "I will do anything to protect my family. Anything!"

"Let me guess. You thought Marilee Doerring was after your husband, so you killed her."

"Don't be stupid! I would not dirty my hands on that woman."

For a woman who must have consumed a lot of alcohol before she came, she spoke with amazing control and clarity. The only thing that betrayed how much she'd had to drink were her red eyes and the odor she radiated.

She took a step forward and Ghost sailed over my head to the top of the armoire. She flinched and looked up at him, interrupted for the moment. Ghost crouched at the edge of the armoire and peered down at her, his mouth making the peculiar little smile of a cat smelling something highly offensive, every muscle in his body quivering, his whiskers pointed forward and his ears on alert. With all the chemical odors in the house, the alcohol she radiated was too much for him to stand.

My mind was scrambling, screaming at my body to *do something*, but I was paralyzed. My gun and phone lay on the kitchen counter with the photographs, and she had me cornered. Marilee's big bed blocked me on one side and the bedroom wall was at my right. The only possible weapon was the nearest lamp. The lamps were tall and made of what appeared to be heavy cast iron. If I could grab the closest one and unplug it before Olga Winnick stabbed me, I might be able to stun her with it and run.

As I edged a half step toward the table, she looked back at me.

In that split second, I understood why she was there. I said, "You're protecting your family right now, aren't you? You're here to stop me from telling the truth about who killed Marilee Doerring and Hamilton Frazier. It wasn't you, it was your husband."

Tears filled her eyes and spilled unheeded down her cheeks. "She lured him into her perversions! She was an evil, evil woman."

I thought of the photographs on the kitchen counter. "She did lure him and trick him and use him. How did you find out?"

She wiped at her eyes with her free hand. "A wife always knows. He would leave our bed and come here, he was obsessed. Night after night, I saw him go through her lanai to her. She was here waiting for him, here with all her filthy practices."

Her voice broke and she shut her eyes for a second to compose herself. I took the opportunity to scoot a few steps closer to the lamp. If I could keep her talking, I had a chance.

She opened her eyes and looked at me with renewed determination.

I said, "He came here Thursday night, didn't he? And found Harrison Frazier with Marilee. That must have been a shock to him."

She shook her head, quick to support her husband's intelligence. "He already knew. He saw him when he arrived. He kept watching the house, pacing back and forth, acting as if I wasn't even there, didn't see, didn't understand. Men can be so blind where predatory women are concerned."

I nodded sympathetically, thought about saying "Ain't it the truth," then decided against it. Instead, I said, "Did you know when he came here Thursday night?"

"Oh yes, I knew. Carl didn't know I was awake, but I knew when he got out of bed and left the house. I stood in my kitchen window and watched him go to her lanai just as he always did, saw him disappear into her house just as I'd watched him many times before. He carried a weapon in his hand, a piece of pipe he must have had in the garage. My heart was breaking, but I could not stop him, you see, because it would have led to a scene that might have wakened Phillip. I did not want him to know what his father was doing. A boy should look up to his father as a role model."

"So you stood at the window and waited and watched."

Her breath shuddered, sending out more intense waves of alcohol. "Yes."

"And what did you see, Mrs. Winnick?"

"I saw my husband come out of this house with something in his arms. He carried it across the backyard and walked along the fence beside the woods, and then he disappeared from my view. I didn't know what it was that he carried. Then he came back here to the house again. In a little while, he went out to the driveway and got into that man's car and drove away."

I pushed my foot a few inches to the left and said, "What time was this?"

Wearily, she said, "It was exactly five minutes past one. I know because I looked at the clock on the microwave after he left."

I pulled my right foot alongside the left one, trying to make it look as if I were just adjusting my posture, and said, "You must have been extremely concerned. I mean, it didn't look good for your family, did it?"

"I had to do something. A woman like you can't understand what it is to be a good wife and mother. You can't know how a real woman will go to any length to save her family."

For a minute there, I'd been feeling sorry for her, but that brought me back to reality. "What did you do, Mrs. Winnick? How did you save your family?"

"I came over here and saw what had happened. Saw the mess here. The shower was still running, that naked man hanging out of the tub and blood on the floor. That piece of pipe next to him. It was awful. I turned off the shower and put the man on the floor while I cleaned everything. I went out the side door and put the pipe in the garbage can at the street. Then I went back home."

Above her head, Ghost had gone into a stalking crouch on the armoire, neck stretched forward and down, legs bent and quivering, tail swishing side to side. I had seen cats go into that pose just before sinking their fangs into a snake's body and flinging it side to side until it died. Olga Winnick and her alcohol fumes had become an enemy, prey to be pounced upon and crushed.

The shrill *beep-beep-beep* of my cell phone sounded from the kitchen, and all three of us went rigid. Distracted, Ghost's head twisted nervously toward the sound.

I said, "I really should answer that."

She grimaced. "You underestimate my intelligence, Miss Hemingway."

"Not true, Mrs. Winnick. I think you've been brilliant. I'm really impressed. But you left out the part about dressing the man and taping his head to the cat's water bowl."

She sighed again and gave me an irritated glare. "That wasn't until later. Carl was home when I got back. He had driven the man's car to the Landings and parked it there, then he took a taxi to the Sea Breeze and walked home. He was shaken and humble. We had a long talk. He begged me for forgiveness and I forgave him for what he'd done. It was one of the best talks we've ever had."

"How nice for you."

"Yes. Then he told me he thought there were photographs the police might find, and I came back to look for them. While I was looking, the man made a sound. He wasn't dead after all, you see. I knew he could identify Carl, so I dressed him and dragged him into the kitchen and taped his head to the water bowl. I would have put him in the tub, but he was too heavy and I didn't want to ask Carl to help. He was far too upset by then to be of much use anyway."

"It was a little after four o'clock when you left here, wasn't it?"

Her eyes narrowed into suspicious slits. "How did you know that?"

"Because Phillip saw you. I guess he's more like you than I realized, because he made up a big lie to save you."

"That's not true! Phillip was asleep."

"Phillip had been playing piano at the Crab House, Mrs. Winnick. He had just climbed back in his window when he saw you leave Marilee's lanai."

A tremor played over her face, as if her nerve endings were readjusting themselves, and the hand with the knife raised an inch.

Okay, if I was dead anyway, I might as well say what would hurt her the most.

"Phillip knew what you did. He loved you so much that he didn't tell, but he knew. He killed himself keeping your terrible secret."

"I don't want to hear any more!"

She charged toward me with the knife held high, enveloped in a miasma of alcohol and revenge. I lunged for the lamp and jerked it forward, pulling the cord out of the wall and plunging the room into darkness. But the thing was incredibly heavy and too thick to wrap my hand around. In the darkness, I could see her silhouette flying toward me.

I did the only thing that seemed halfway logical. I dived for her legs, hoping to knock her down before her knife plunged into my back.

As I hit her, she screamed and flailed the air. I scrabbled behind her and straightened up, ready to grab her knife hand. Something soft brushed across my face, and she screamed again. I realized it was a scream of pain and that it was Ghost's tail I had felt. Ghost was on her head, raking his claws across her face and shoulders.

I sprinted to the kitchen and grabbed my gun. I was halfway down the hall with it when I doubled back to get my cell phone. As I left the kitchen, I heard the thud of footsteps running down the hall toward the bedroom. I knew who it was. I also knew Ghost would be killed if I didn't get to him in time.

With my gun held in both hands, I rounded the bedroom door. The overhead light was on, and Olga was on her knees, thrashing her head and howling in agony. Ghost was still on her head with his claws embedded in her skull. Her face was shredded, with so much blood spilling from it that her features had disappeared. Carl Winnick stood beside her with a gun trained on Ghost, probably the same gun Phillip had used to shoot himself.

"Be still!" he shouted to Olga. "Stop moving!"

I yelled, "Drop the gun, Winnick!"

He turned his head toward me, wide-eyed and ashen, then swung the gun in my direction.

A shot rang out and his throat burst in a flare of red blood. Ghost screamed and jumped from Olga's head and streaked from the room. Winnick crumpled to the floor beside Olga, and a geyser of blood shot toward the ceiling. Covered with her own blood and his, Olga leaned over him and shrieked a sound so full of grief and rage that it will live in my head forever.

Suddenly, the room was filled with people running past me. In a daze, I turned toward the doorway where Guidry was holstering his Sig Sauer.

"Your brother called us," he said. "When you didn't answer your cell, he knew you were in trouble."

His gray eyes were calm, watching me closely.

"I had it under control," I said, but my voice warbled.

"You had it under superb control, Dixie."

The next thing I knew, my face was buried in his chest, and his arms were holding me close. Except for Michael and Paco, I hadn't felt a man's arms around me since Todd died. I hadn't thought I wanted a man's arms around me, but this felt very familiar and comforting.

34

S unlight glittered on the sailboats rocking at anchor in Sarasota Bay. A few seagulls strolled along the sidewalk, hoping for hand- outs. Phillip and I sat quietly, the way people do when there's too much to say to trust yourself to speak. Phillip's forehead still bore an ugly channel from the bullet he fired with the intention of killing him- self. If he hadn't jerked his head back just before he pulled the trigger, he would have hit the frontal lobe of his brain. If he'd jerked it forward instead of backward, he would have hit the cortex. As it was, he was physically and neurologically intact. Psychologically, he had a lot of healing to do.

A bold seagull stepped forward and pecked at Phillip's shoelace. Phillip waggled his foot and the gull fluttered its wings in a show of sassiness and then took flight, sailing out over the boats in a graceful swoop.

I said, "How do you like living with Ghost?"

The corners of his mouth twitched in something close to a smile. "He's funny. He curls up in Greg's violin case while he practices. I never was around a cat before, but I think I'll actually miss him when I leave."

"Did you get things squared away with Juilliard?"

"They said I could enroll next year."

"That's good. You'll be completely healed by then."

"Yeah."

We both heard the lie in our voices and fell silent. Plastic surgeons were going to try to smooth the deep groove in his forehead, but he would always bear the emotional scars of his parents' actions.

Do any of us ever escape those scars?